Me & My Brothers

Volume 2

Hari Tokeino

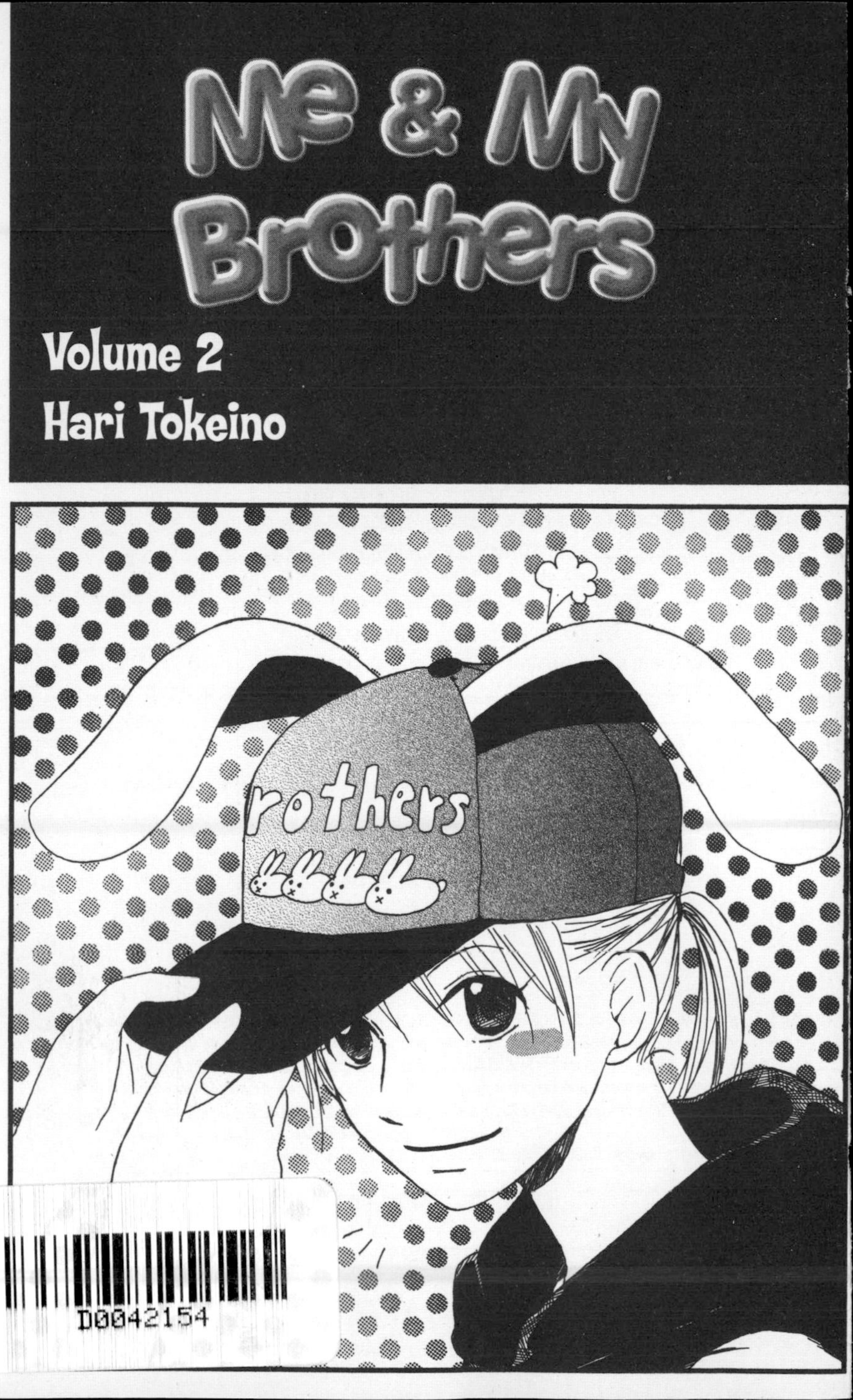
rothers

Me & My Brothers Volume 2
Created by Hari Tokeino

Translation - Haruko Furukawa
English Adaptation - Jeffrey Reeves
Copy Editor - Stephanie Duchin
Retouch and Lettering - Star Print Brokers
Production Artist - Gavin Hignight
Graphic Designer - Monalisa De Asis

Editor - Hyun Joo Kim
Digital Imaging Manager - Chris Buford
Pre-Production Supervisor - Erika Terriquez
Production Manager - Elisabeth Brizzi
Managing Editor - Vy Nguyen
Creative Director - Anne Marie Horne
Editor-in-Chief - Rob Tokar
Publisher - Mike Kiley
President and C.O.O. - John Parker
C.E.O. and Chief Creative Officer - Stuart Levy

A 🔘 **TOKYOPOP** Manga

TOKYOPOP and 🔘 are trademarks or registered trademarks of TOKYOPOP Inc.

TOKYOPOP Inc.
5900 Wilshire Blvd. Suite 2000
Los Angeles, CA 90036

E-mail: info@TOKYOPOP.com
Come visit us online at www.TOKYOPOP.com

ISBN: 978-1-4278-0072-5

First TOKYOPOP printing: November 2007
10 9 8 7 6 5 4 3 2 1
Printed in the USA or Canada

Me & My Brothers

Volume 2

Hari Tokeino

TOKYOPOP®

HAMBURG // LONDON // LOS ANGELES // TOKYO

Contents

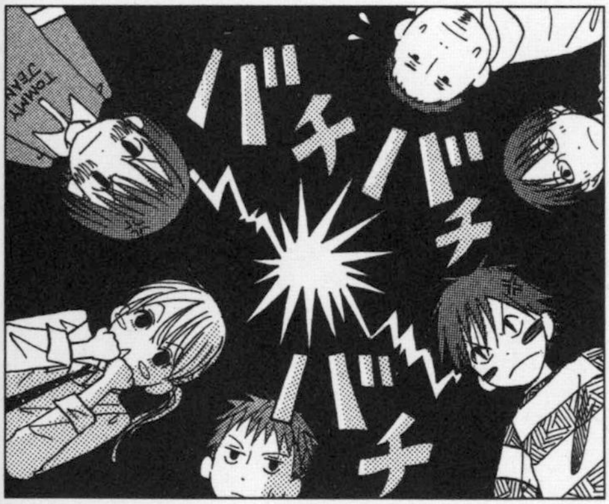
バチバチバチ

CHARACTERS PROFILE

ME & MY BROTHERS

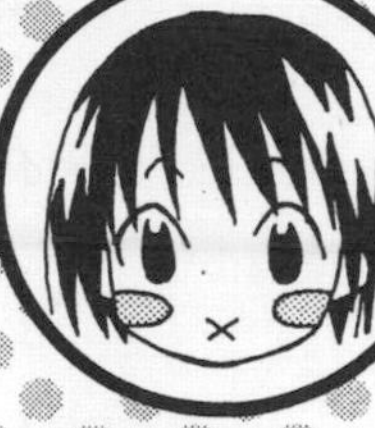

SAKURA MIYASHITA: THE YOUNGEST. IN 8TH GRADE. THE ONLY GIRL IN THE MIYASHITA FAMILY. SHE IS NOT BLOOD RELATED TO HER FOUR BROTHERS.

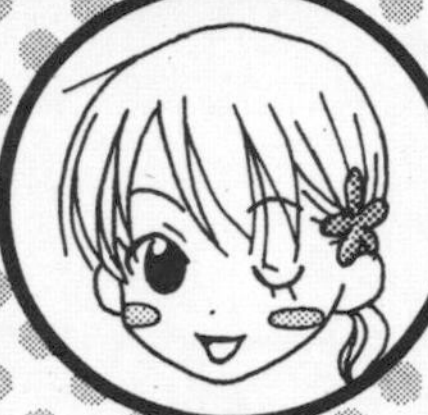

MASASHI MIYASHITA: THE ELDEST. ROMANCE NOVELIST. ACCORDING TO HIM, HE SOUNDS LIKE A WOMAN BECAUSE OF HIS JOB. HE'S THE LEADER OF THE FOUR SAKURA-SPOILERS.

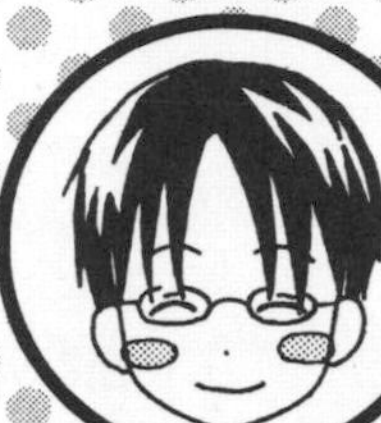

TAKASHI MIYASHITA: THE 2ND BROTHER. TEACHER. HE TEACHES JAPANESE AT SAKURA'S SCHOOL. HE'S A GENTLEMAN.

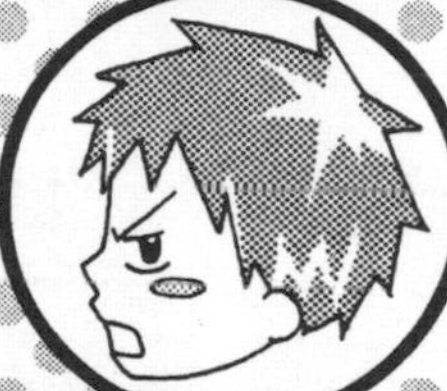

TSUYOSHI MIYASHITA: THE 3RD BROTHER. FULL-TIME PART-TIMER. HE HAS A DIRTY MOUTH, BUT IS ACTUALLY SHY.

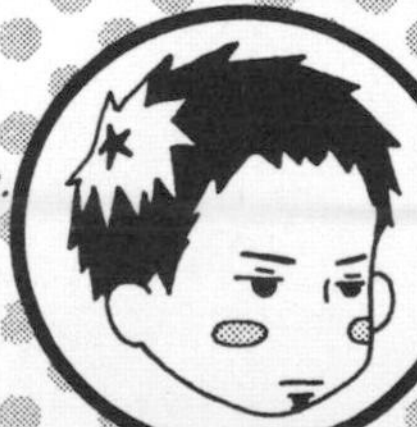

TAKESHI MIYASHITA: THE 4TH BROTHER. IN 11TH GRADE. HE LOOKS OLD, BUT HE'S THE YOUNGEST OF FOUR BROTHERS. HE'S QUIET AND LOVES PLANTS.

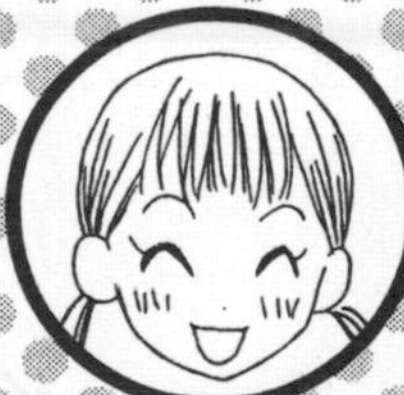

NAKA-CHAN
SAKURA'S BEST FRIEND. HER FAMILY NAME IS TANAKA. A CHEERFUL GIRL.

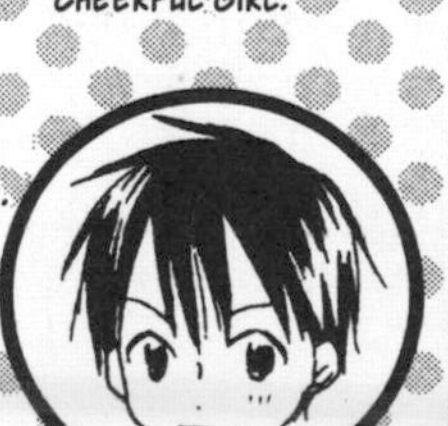

SUZUKI-KUN
SAKURA'S CLASSMATE. DOES HE HAVE A CRUSH ON SAKURA?

PLEASE READ *ME & MY BROTHERS* VOLUME 1 FOR MORE DETAILS!

STORY

SAKURA LOST HER PARENTS WHEN SHE WAS THREE AND WAS RAISED BY HER GRANDMOTHER. THEN, WHEN SAKURA WAS 14 HER GRANDMOTHER PASSED AWAY... AND SHE WAS ALONE... UNTIL FOUR STEPBROTHERS SHOWED UP! THE STEPBROTHERS ARE FROM SAKURA'S FATHER'S FIRST MARRIAGE. WHILE HER STEPBROTHER'S FATHER HAD RAISED SAKURA AS HIS OWN, SAKURA'S BIRTH FATHER IS ACTUALLY HER MOTHER'S EX-BOYFRIEND. EVEN THOUGH THE BROTHERS HAVE NO BLOOD CONNECTION TO SAKURA, AFTER 11 YEARS OF SEPARATION, NOW THEIR HOUSE IS LIVELY EVERYDAY...THEY ARE NOW LIVING TOGETHER AGAIN! ★

I think I'll write their profiles.

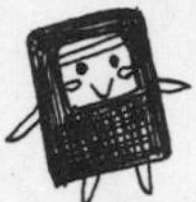

MEANINGLESS DRAWING

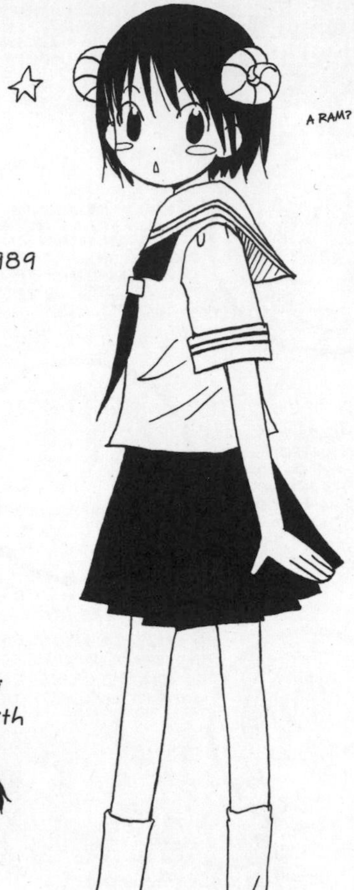

A RAM?

Sakura Miyashita

Date of Birth: April 7, 1989
Aries

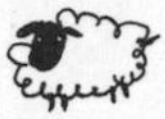

147cm tall
Blood type: A

Hobby: cooking & cleaning
↑
But not good at them

Favorite food: Ohagi (rice cake wrapped with sweet bean paste)

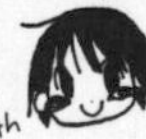

I used to make them with Grandma.

Hates: insects

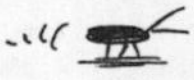

← Now let's GO!! to the main story!!

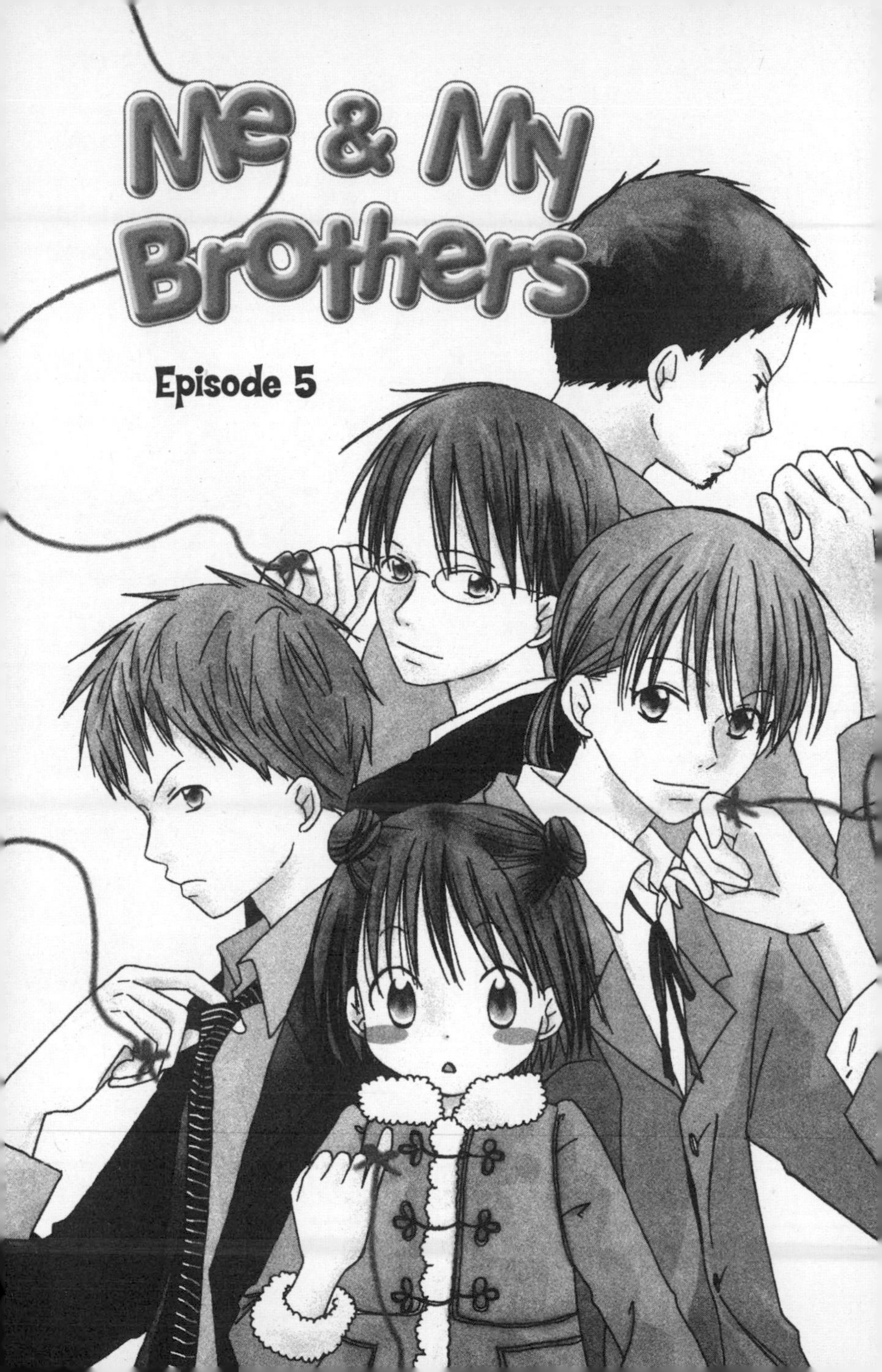
Me & My Brothers
Episode 5

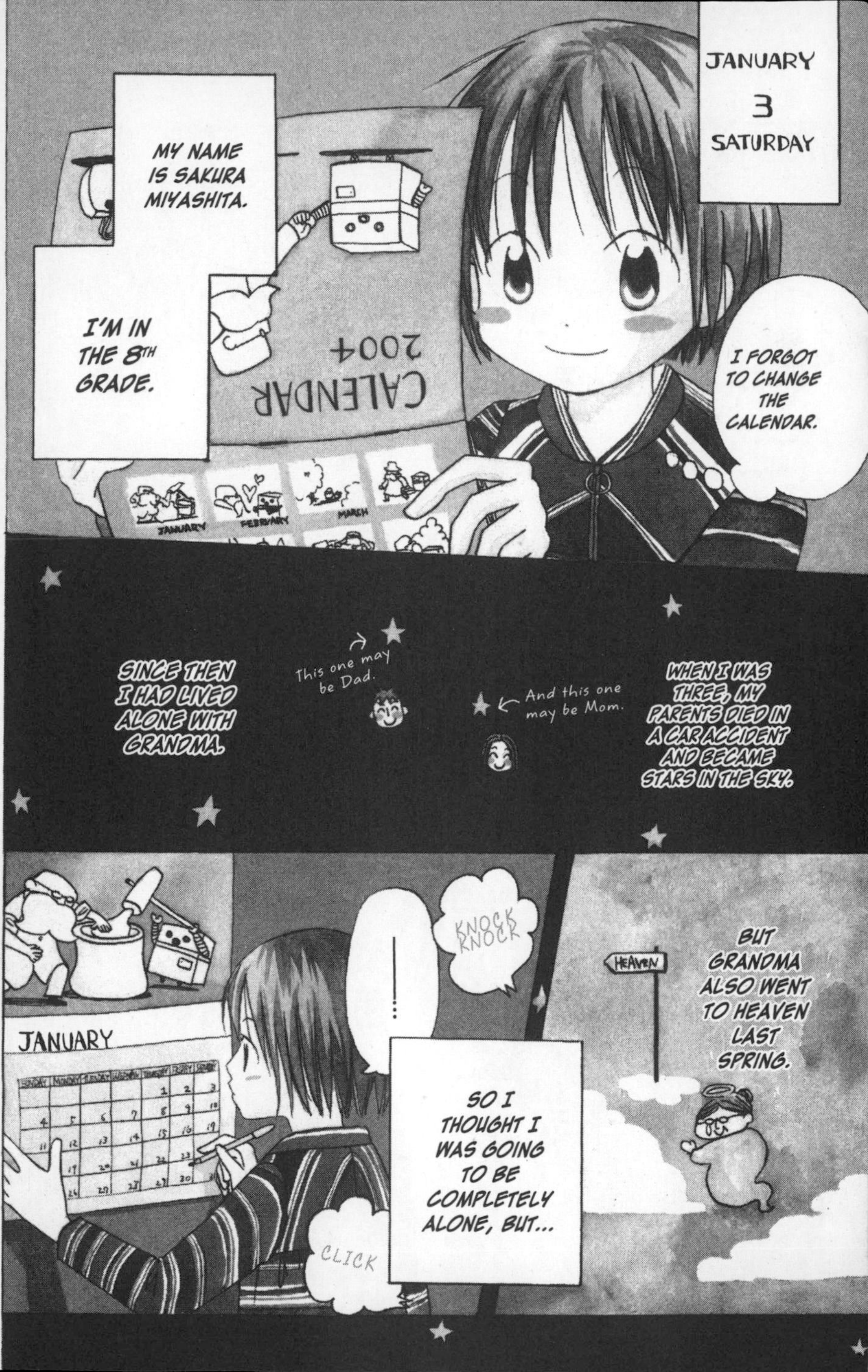
JANUARY 3 SATURDAY
I FORGOT TO CHANGE THE CALENDAR.
MY NAME IS SAKURA MIYASHITA.
I'M IN THE 8TH GRADE.
CALENDAR 2004
JANUARY
FEBRUARY
MARCH
WHEN I WAS THREE, MY PARENTS DIED IN A CAR ACCIDENT AND BECAME STARS IN THE SKY.
And this one may be Mom.
This one may be Dad.
SINCE THEN I HAD LIVED ALONE WITH GRANDMA.
BUT GRANDMA ALSO WENT TO HEAVEN LAST SPRING.
HEAVEN
SO I THOUGHT I WAS GOING TO BE COMPLETELY ALONE, BUT...
KNOCK KNOCK
—......
JANUARY
CLICK

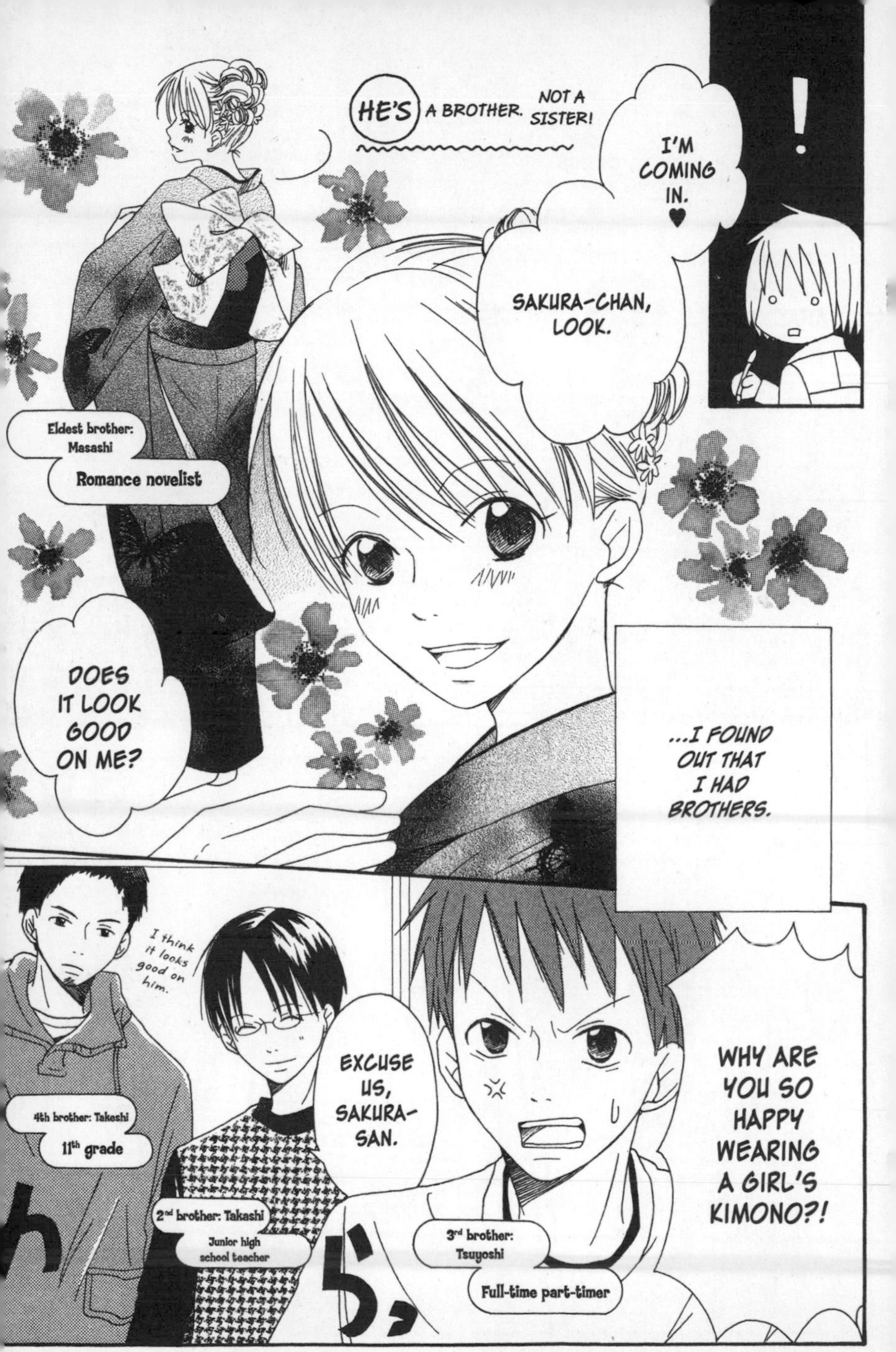
!
I'M COMING IN. ♥
SAKURA-CHAN, LOOK.
...I FOUND OUT THAT I HAD BROTHERS.
HE'S A BROTHER. NOT A SISTER!
DOES IT LOOK GOOD ON ME?
Eldest brother: Masashi
Romance novelist
WHY ARE YOU SO HAPPY WEARING A GIRL'S KIMONO?!
3rd brother: Tsuyoshi
Full-time part-timer
EXCUSE US, SAKURA-SAN.
I think it looks good on him.
2nd brother: Takashi
Junior high school teacher
4th brother: Takeshi
11th grade

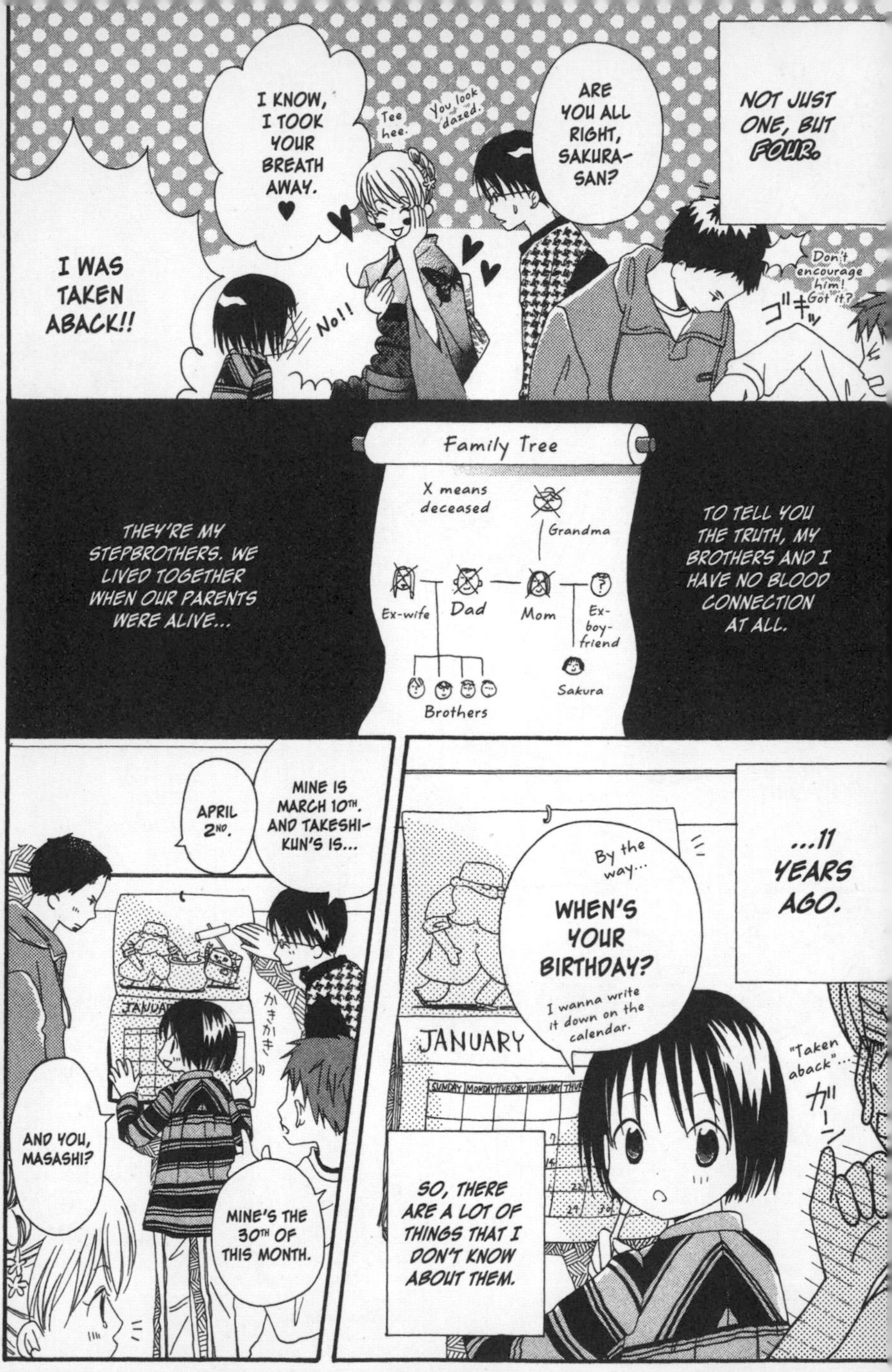
NOT JUST ONE, BUT FOUR.
Don't encourage him! Got it?
ゴキッ
ARE YOU ALL RIGHT, SAKURA-SAN?
You look dazed.
Tee hee.
I KNOW, I TOOK YOUR BREATH AWAY. ♥
No!!
I WAS TAKEN ABACK!!
TO TELL YOU THE TRUTH, MY BROTHERS AND I HAVE NO BLOOD CONNECTION AT ALL.
Family Tree
X means deceased
Grandma
Ex-wife
Dad
Mom
Ex-boy-friend
Brothers
Sakura
THEY'RE MY STEPBROTHERS. WE LIVED TOGETHER WHEN OUR PARENTS WERE ALIVE...
...11 YEARS AGO.
"Taken aback"...
ガー
By the way...
WHEN'S YOUR BIRTHDAY?
I wanna write it down on the calendar.
JANUARY
SUNDAY MONDAY TUESDAY WEDNESDAY THUR
SO, THERE ARE A LOT OF THINGS THAT I DON'T KNOW ABOUT THEM.
MINE IS MARCH 10TH. AND TAKESHI-KUN'S IS...
APRIL 2ND.
かきかき
AND YOU, MASASHI?
MINE'S THE 30TH OF THIS MONTH.

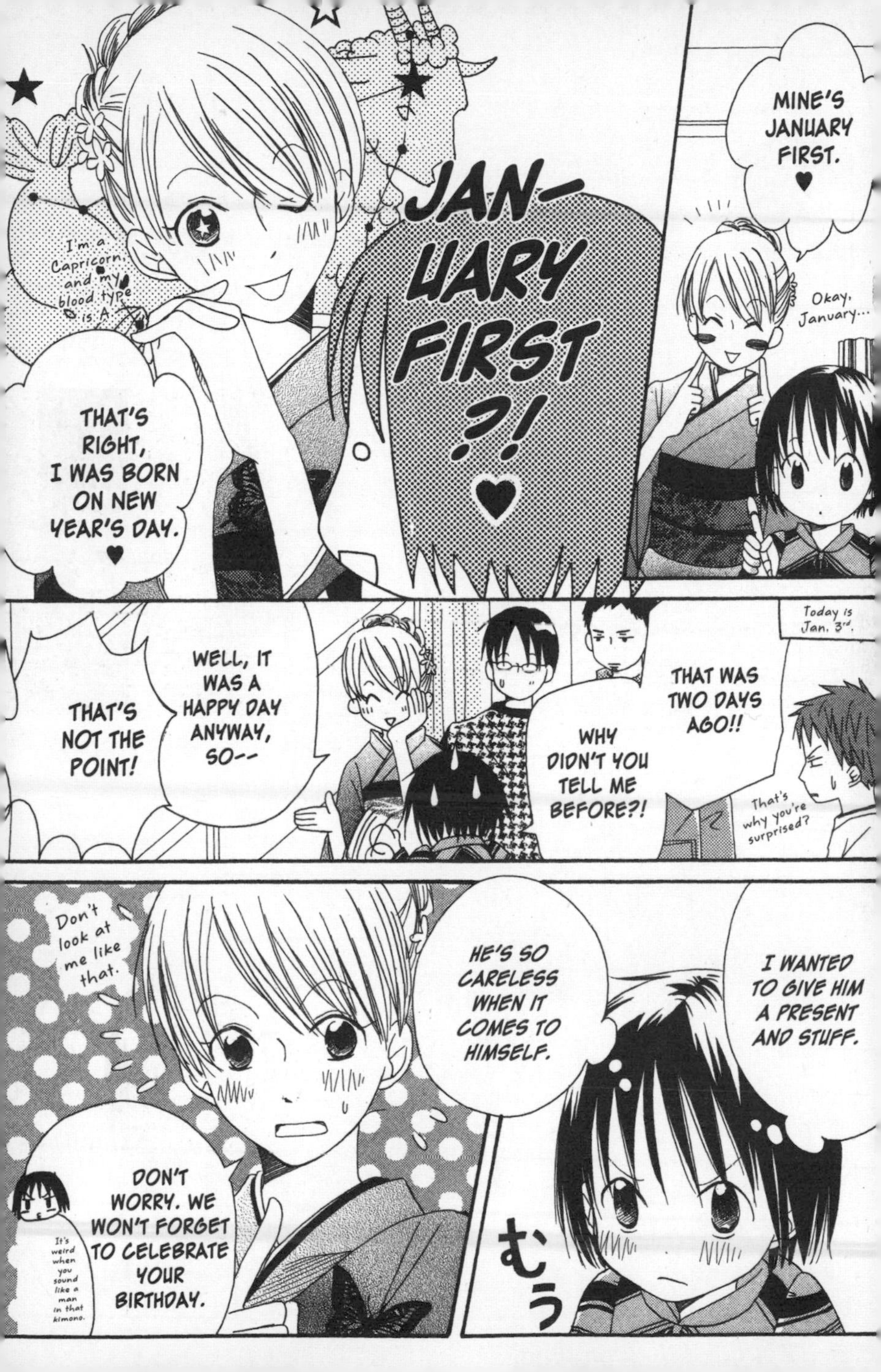
MINE'S JANUARY FIRST. ♥
Okay, January...
JAN-UARY FIRST ?!
I'm a Capricorn, and my blood type is A.
THAT'S RIGHT, I WAS BORN ON NEW YEAR'S DAY. ♥
Today is Jan. 3rd.
THAT WAS TWO DAYS AGO!!
That's why you're surprised?
WHY DIDN'T YOU TELL ME BEFORE?!
WELL, IT WAS A HAPPY DAY ANYWAY, SO--
THAT'S NOT THE POINT!
I WANTED TO GIVE HIM A PRESENT AND STUFF.
HE'S SO CARELESS WHEN IT COMES TO HIMSELF.
むう
Don't look at me like that.
DON'T WORRY. WE WON'T FORGET TO CELEBRATE YOUR BIRTHDAY.
It's weird when you sound like a man in that kimono.

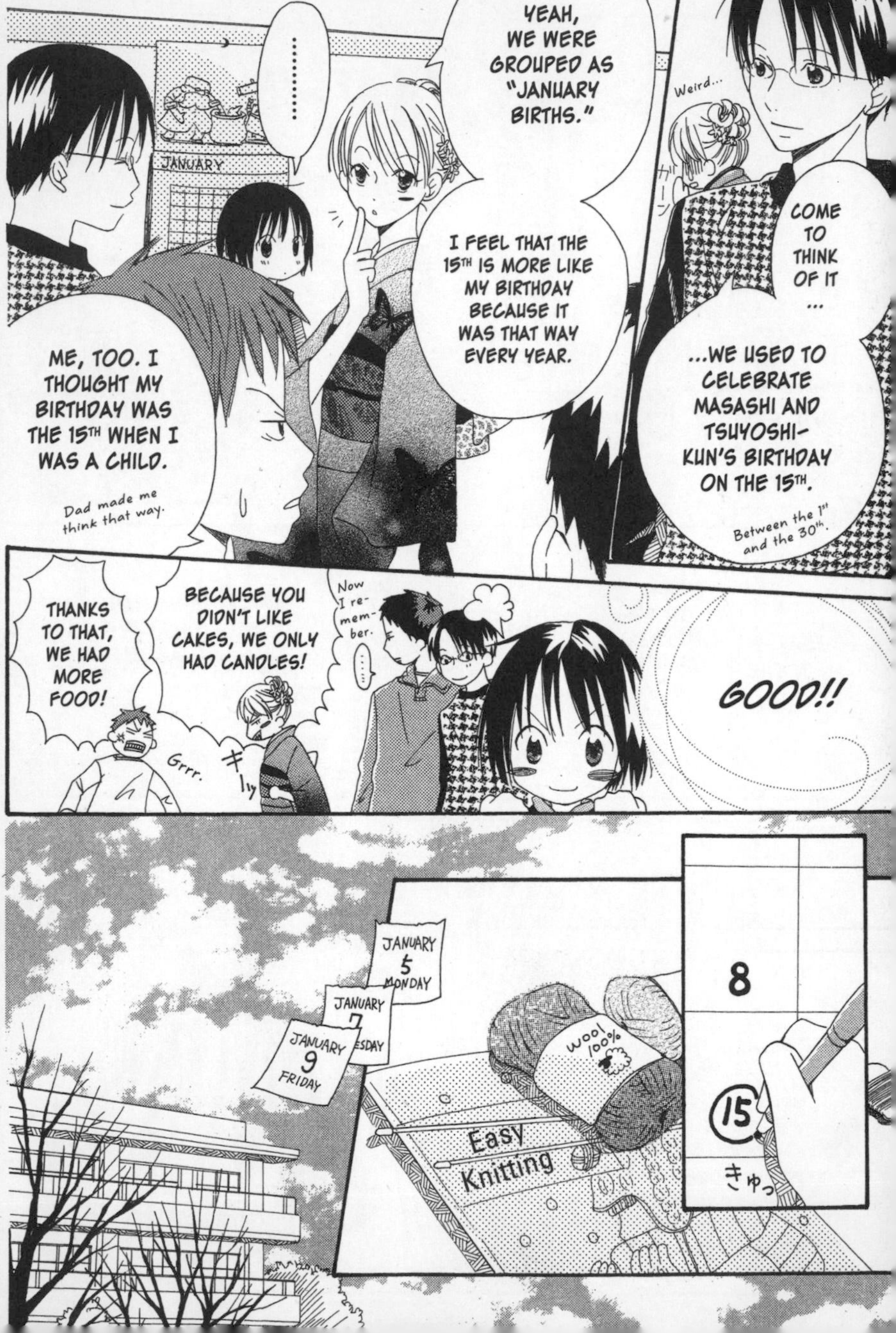
Weird...
COME TO THINK OF IT ...
...WE USED TO CELEBRATE MASASHI AND TSUYOSHI-KUN'S BIRTHDAY ON THE 15TH.
Between the 1st and the 30th.
YEAH, WE WERE GROUPED AS "JANUARY BIRTHS."
....
JANUARY
I FEEL THAT THE 15TH IS MORE LIKE MY BIRTHDAY BECAUSE IT WAS THAT WAY EVERY YEAR.
ME, TOO. I THOUGHT MY BIRTHDAY WAS THE 15TH WHEN I WAS A CHILD.
Dad made me think that way.
GOOD!!
Now I re-mem-ber.
...
BECAUSE YOU DIDN'T LIKE CAKES, WE ONLY HAD CANDLES!
THANKS TO THAT, WE HAD MORE FOOD!
Grrr.
8
15
きゅっ
wool 100%
Easy Knitting
JANUARY 5 MONDAY
JANUARY 7 ESDAY
JANUARY 9 FRIDAY

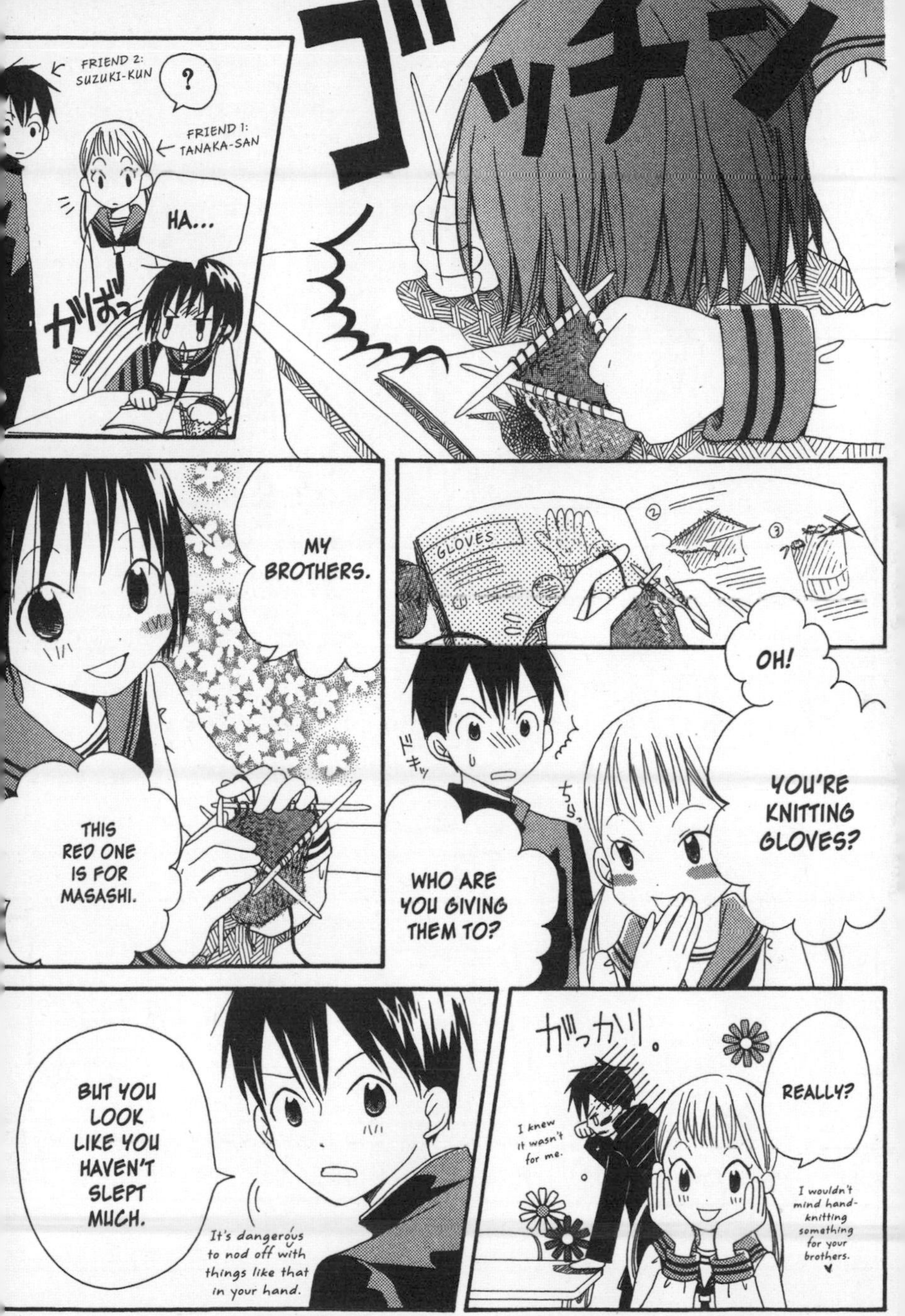
ゴッチン
FRIEND 2: SUZUKI-KUN
?
FRIEND 1: TANAKA-SAN
HA...
がばっ
GLOVES
OH!
YOU'RE KNITTING GLOVES?
ちらっ
ドキッ
WHO ARE YOU GIVING THEM TO?
MY BROTHERS.
THIS RED ONE IS FOR MASASHI.
がっかり。
REALLY?
I wouldn't mind hand-knitting something for your brothers.
I knew it wasn't for me.
BUT YOU LOOK LIKE YOU HAVEN'T SLEPT MUCH.
It's dangerous to nod off with things like that in your hand.

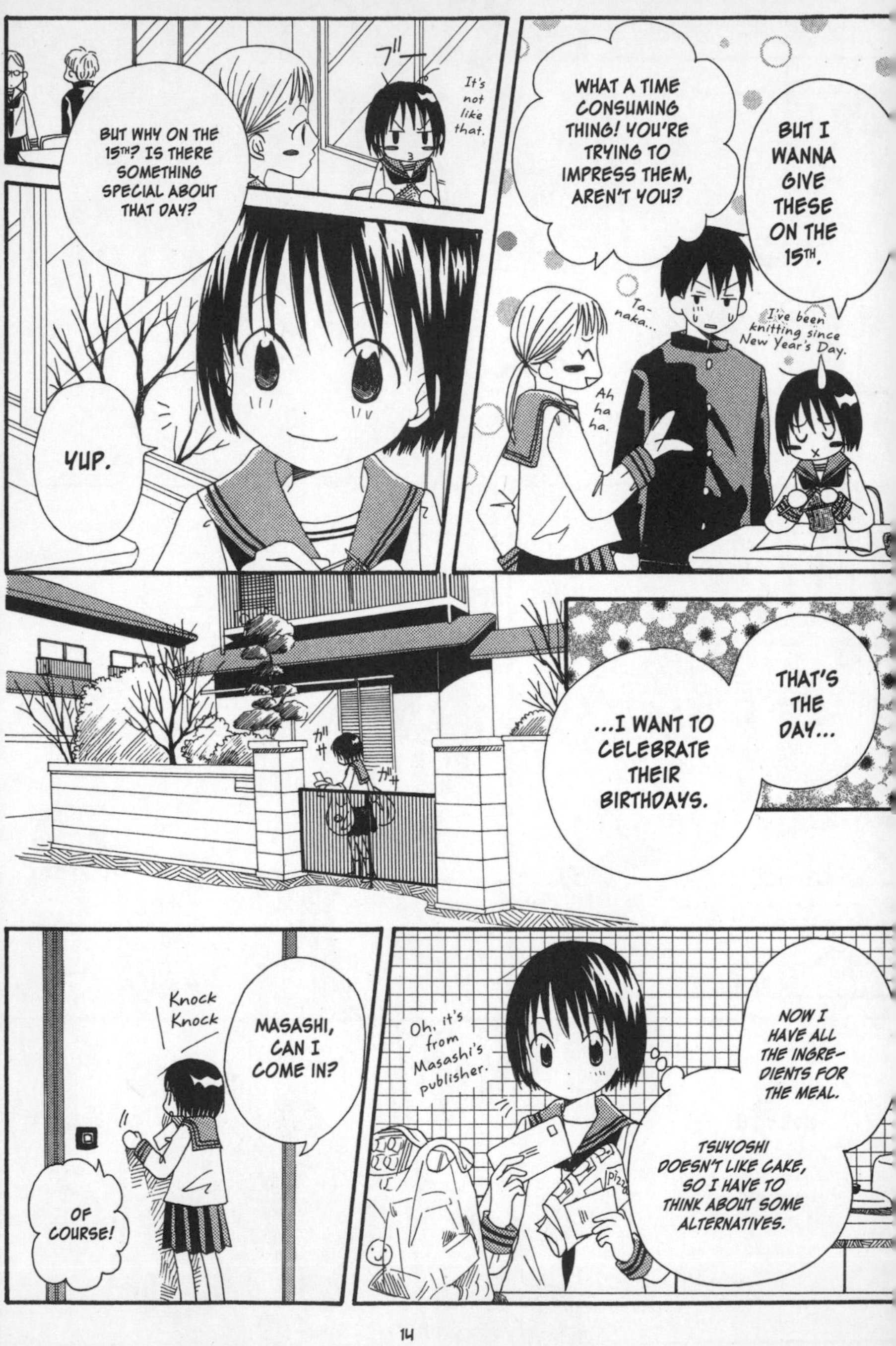
WHAT A TIME CONSUMING THING! YOU'RE TRYING TO IMPRESS THEM, AREN'T YOU?
BUT I WANNA GIVE THESE ON THE 15TH.
I've been knitting since New Year's Day.
Ta-naka...
Ah ha ha.
ブー
It's not like that.
BUT WHY ON THE 15TH? IS THERE SOMETHING SPECIAL ABOUT THAT DAY?
YUP.
THAT'S THE DAY...
...I WANT TO CELEBRATE THEIR BIRTHDAYS.
ガサ
ガサ
NOW I HAVE ALL THE INGREDIENTS FOR THE MEAL.
TSUYOSHI DOESN'T LIKE CAKE, SO I HAVE TO THINK ABOUT SOME ALTERNATIVES.
Oh, it's from Masashi's publisher.
Knock Knock
MASASHI, CAN I COME IN?
OF COURSE!

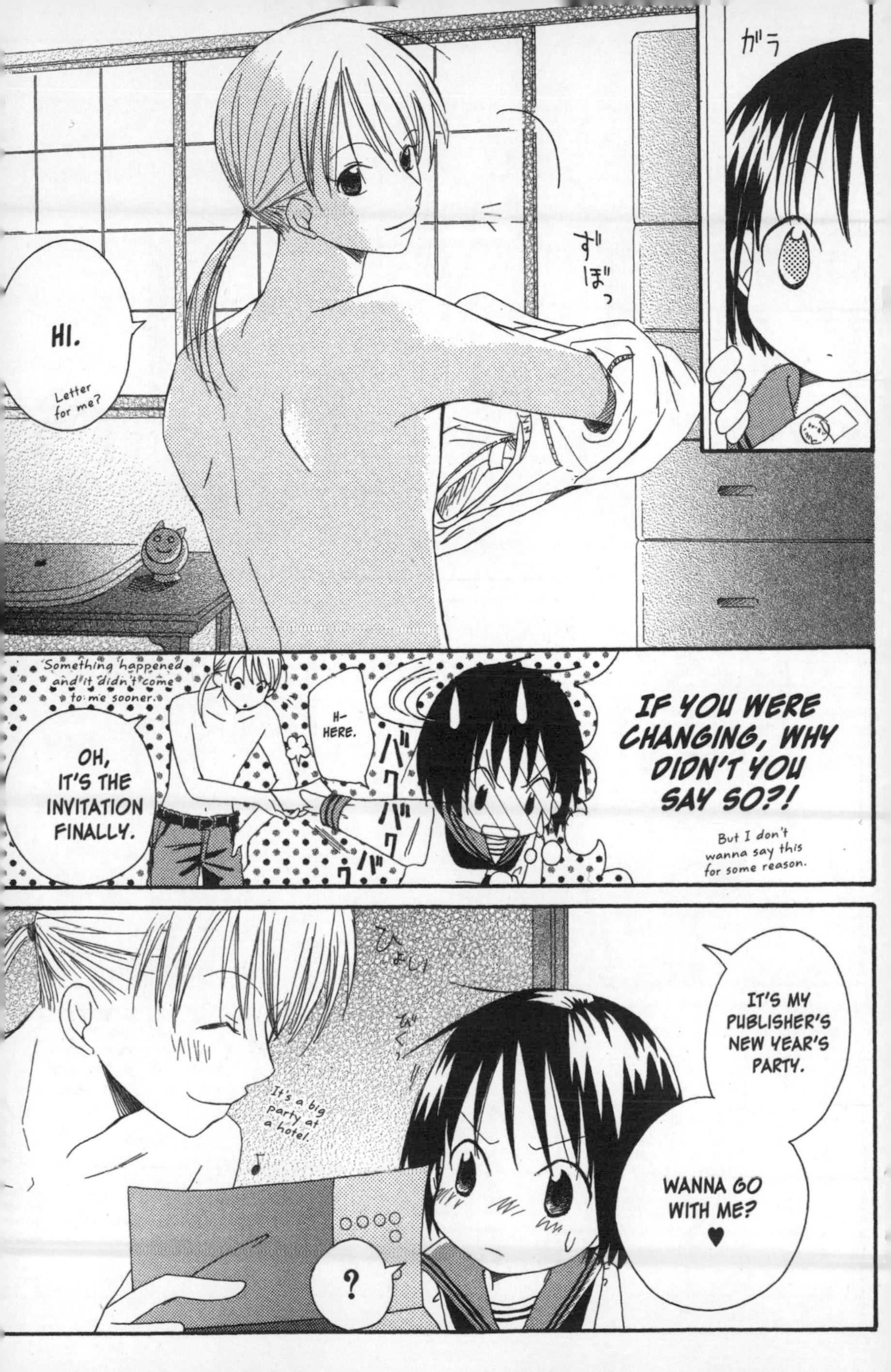
ガラ
ずぼっ
HI.
Letter for me?
IF YOU WERE CHANGING, WHY DIDN'T YOU SAY SO?!
But I don't wanna say this for some reason.
H-HERE.
バクバク
Something happened and it didn't come to me sooner.
OH, IT'S THE INVITATION FINALLY.
IT'S MY PUBLISHER'S NEW YEAR'S PARTY.
WANNA GO WITH ME? ♥
ひょい
It's a big party at a hotel.
?

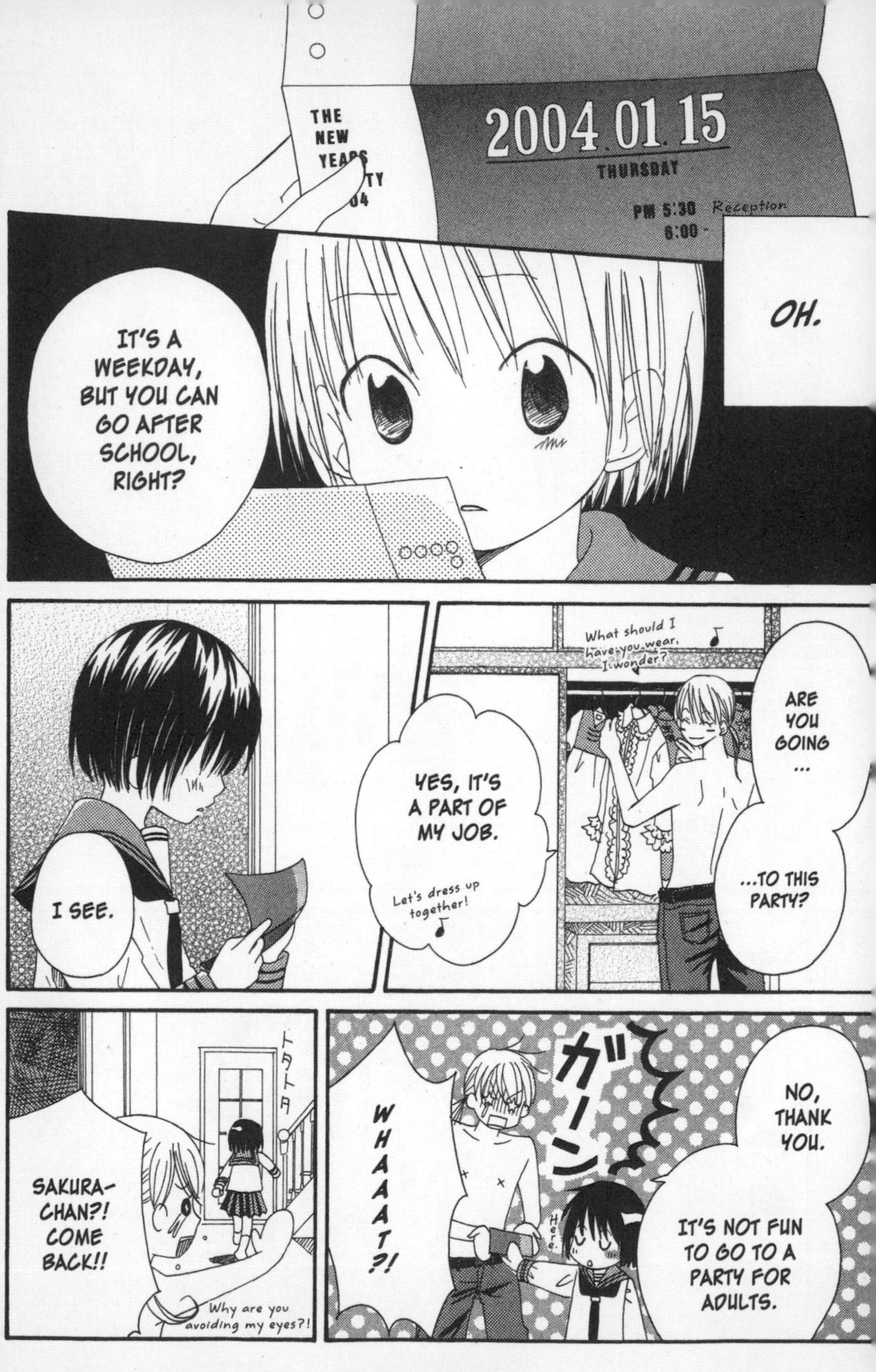
THE NEW
2004.01.15
THURSDAY
PM 5:30 Reception
6:00 -
OH.
IT'S A WEEKDAY, BUT YOU CAN GO AFTER SCHOOL, RIGHT?
ARE YOU GOING ...
...TO THIS PARTY?
What should I have you wear, I wonder?
YES, IT'S A PART OF MY JOB.
Let's dress up together!
I SEE.
NO, THANK YOU.
IT'S NOT FUN TO GO TO A PARTY FOR ADULTS.
ガーン
WHAAAAT?!
Here.
トタトタ
SAKURA-CHAN?! COME BACK!!
Why are you avoiding my eyes?!

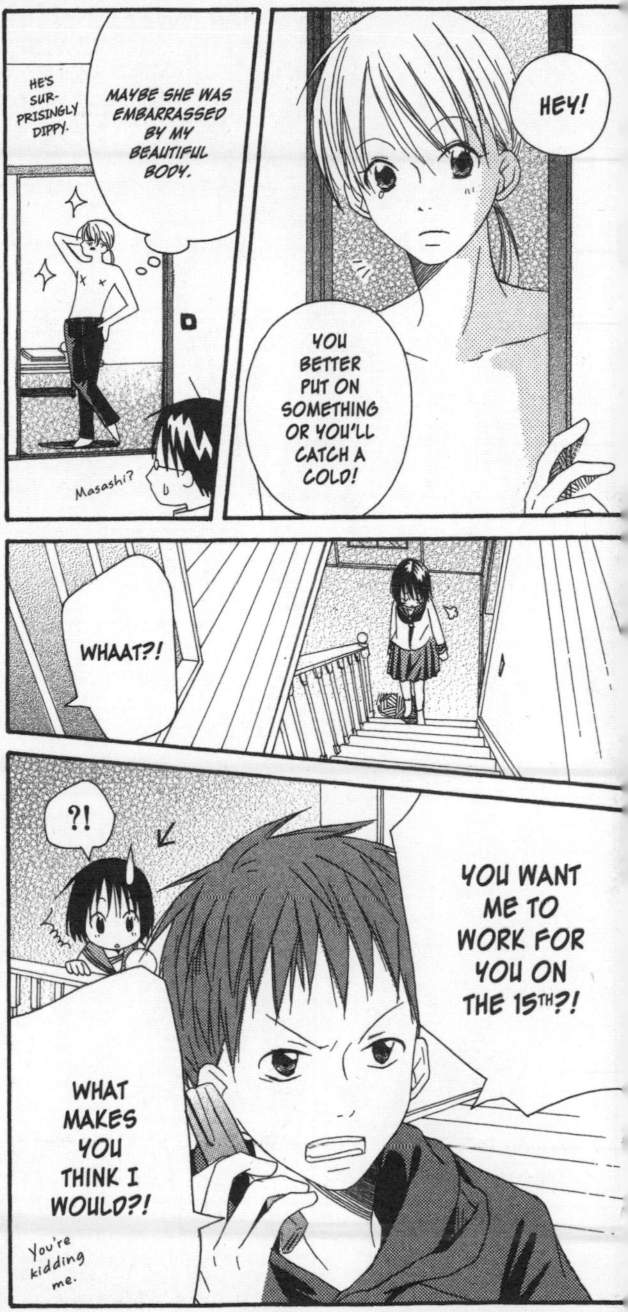
HEY!
YOU BETTER PUT ON SOMETHING OR YOU'LL CATCH A COLD!
MAYBE SHE WAS EMBARRASSED BY MY BEAUTIFUL BODY.
HE'S SUR-PRISINGLY DIPPY.
Masashi?
WHAAT?!
YOU WANT ME TO WORK FOR YOU ON THE 15TH?!
?!
WHAT MAKES YOU THINK I WOULD?!
You're kidding me.

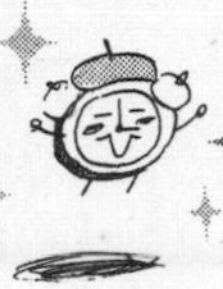

A happy jump.

☆ 1 ☆

This is volume 2!!

Volume 2!!

Yes, volume 2!!

Wow!!

Holy cow!!

Volume 2 came out!

...Sorry, I know I'm annoying you.

Anyway, this is *Me & My Brothers* volume 2.

Thanks.

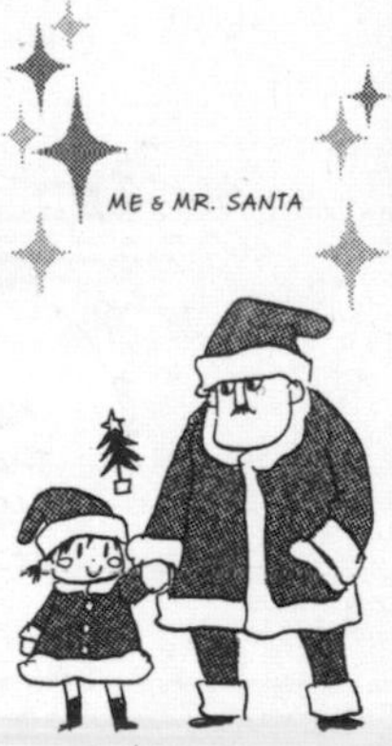
ME & MR. SANTA

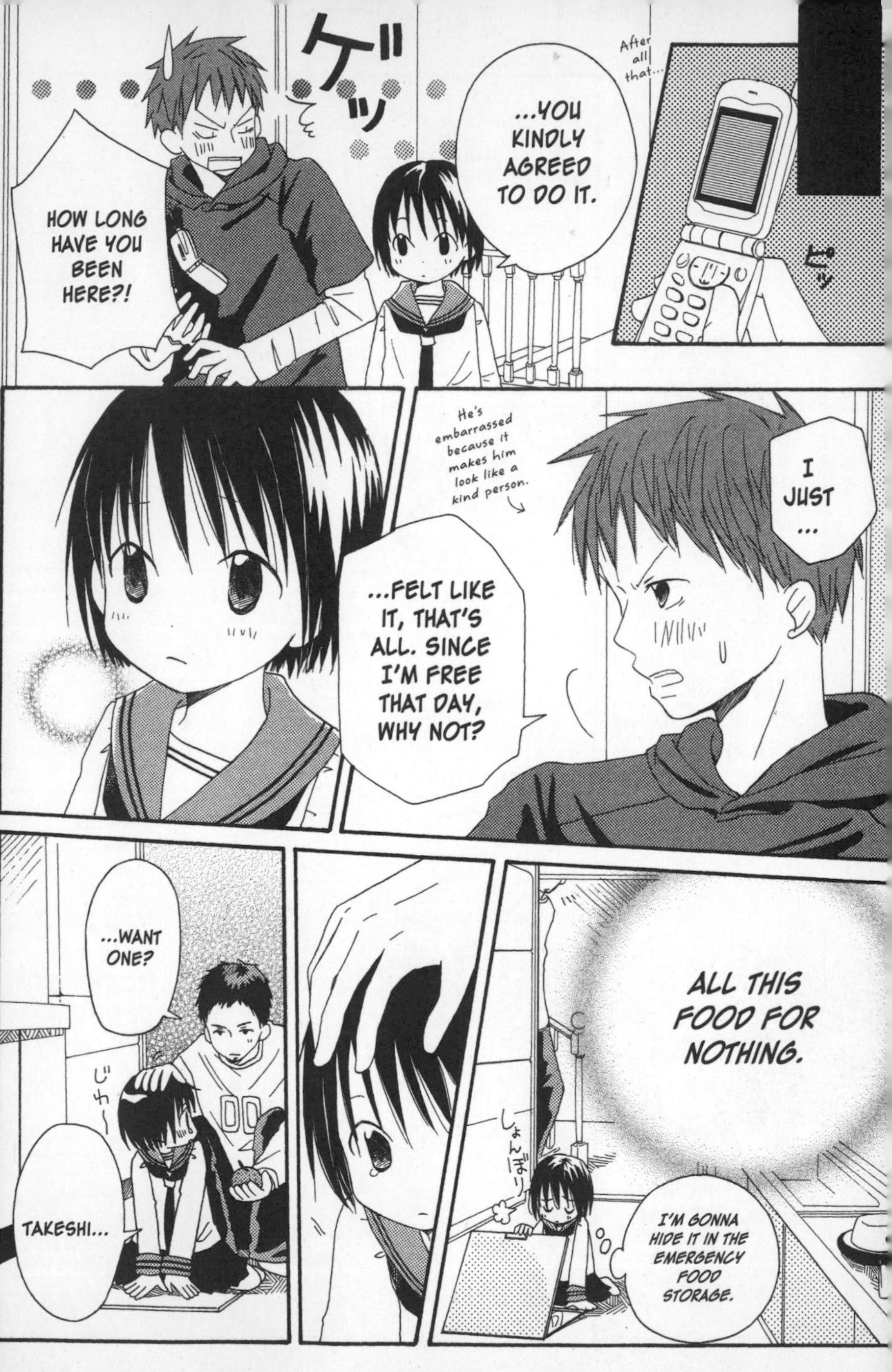
After all that...
ピッ
...YOU KINDLY AGREED TO DO IT.
ゲッ
HOW LONG HAVE YOU BEEN HERE?!
I JUST ...
He's embarrassed because it makes him look like a kind person.
...FELT LIKE IT, THAT'S ALL. SINCE I'M FREE THAT DAY, WHY NOT?
ALL THIS FOOD FOR NOTHING.
しょんぼり
I'M GONNA HIDE IT IN THE EMERGENCY FOOD STORAGE.
...WANT ONE?
TAKESHI...

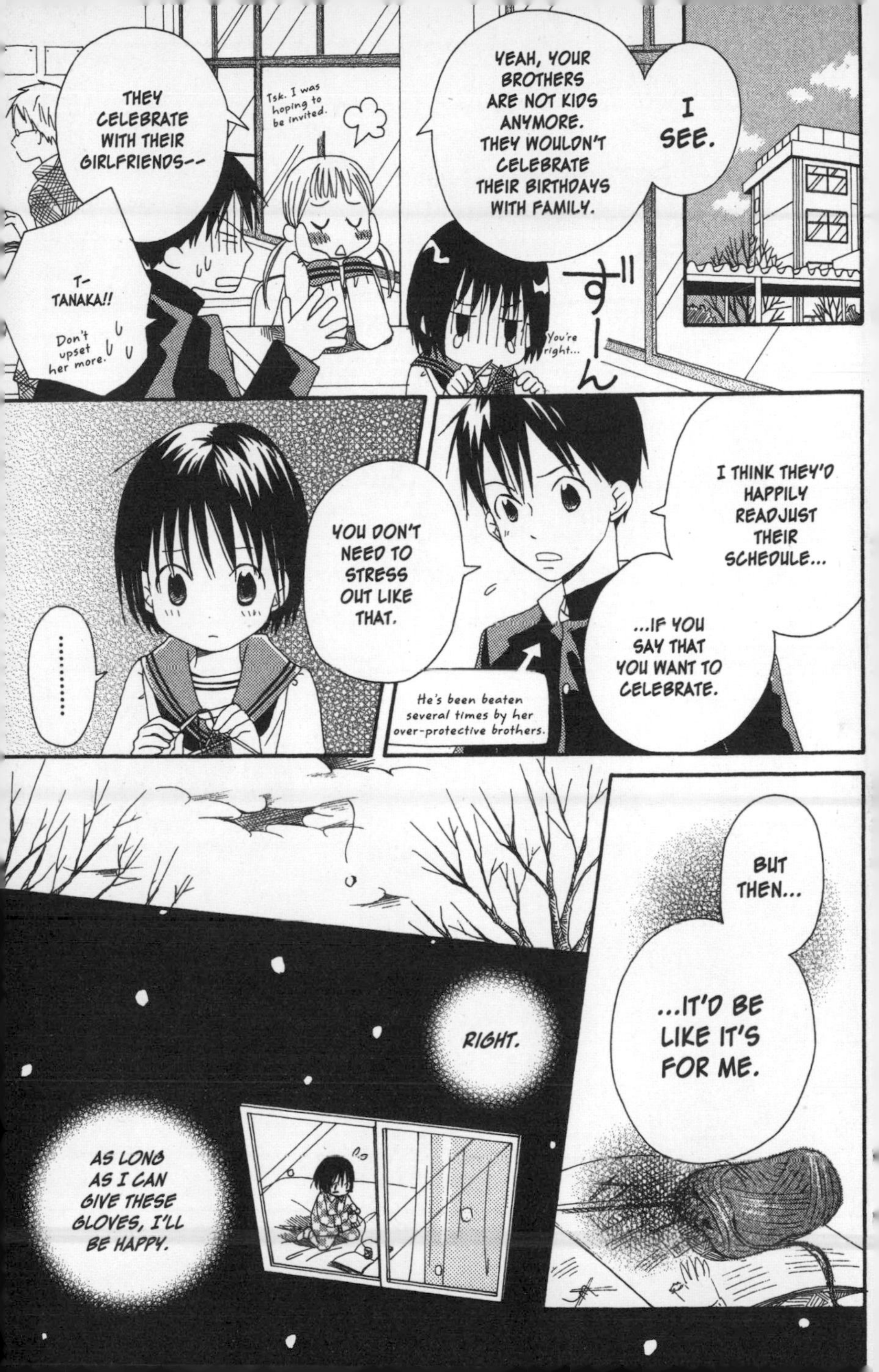
I SEE.
YEAH, YOUR BROTHERS ARE NOT KIDS ANYMORE. THEY WOULDN'T CELEBRATE THEIR BIRTHDAYS WITH FAMILY.
Tsk. I was hoping to be invited.
THEY CELEBRATE WITH THEIR GIRLFRIENDS--
すーん
You're right...
T-TANAKA!!
Don't upset her more.
I THINK THEY'D HAPPILY READJUST THEIR SCHEDULE...
...IF YOU SAY THAT YOU WANT TO CELEBRATE.
He's been beaten several times by her over-protective brothers.
YOU DON'T NEED TO STRESS OUT LIKE THAT.
......
BUT THEN...
...IT'D BE LIKE IT'S FOR ME.
RIGHT.
AS LONG AS I CAN GIVE THESE GLOVES, I'LL BE HAPPY.

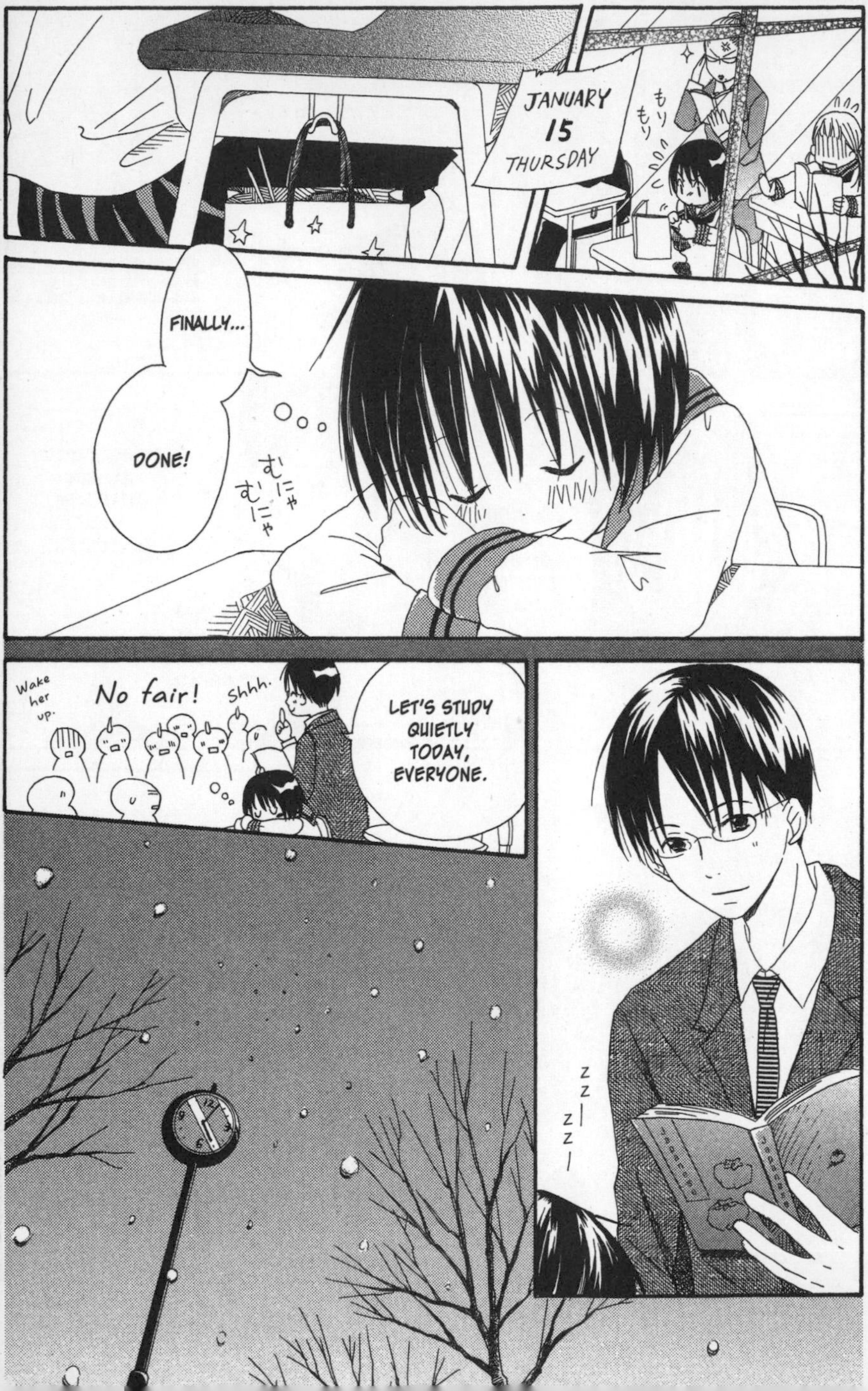
JANUARY
15
THURSDAY
もり もり
FINALLY...
DONE!
むにゃ むにゃ
Z Z Z Z
LET'S STUDY QUIETLY TODAY, EVERYONE.
Shhh.
No fair!
Wake her up.

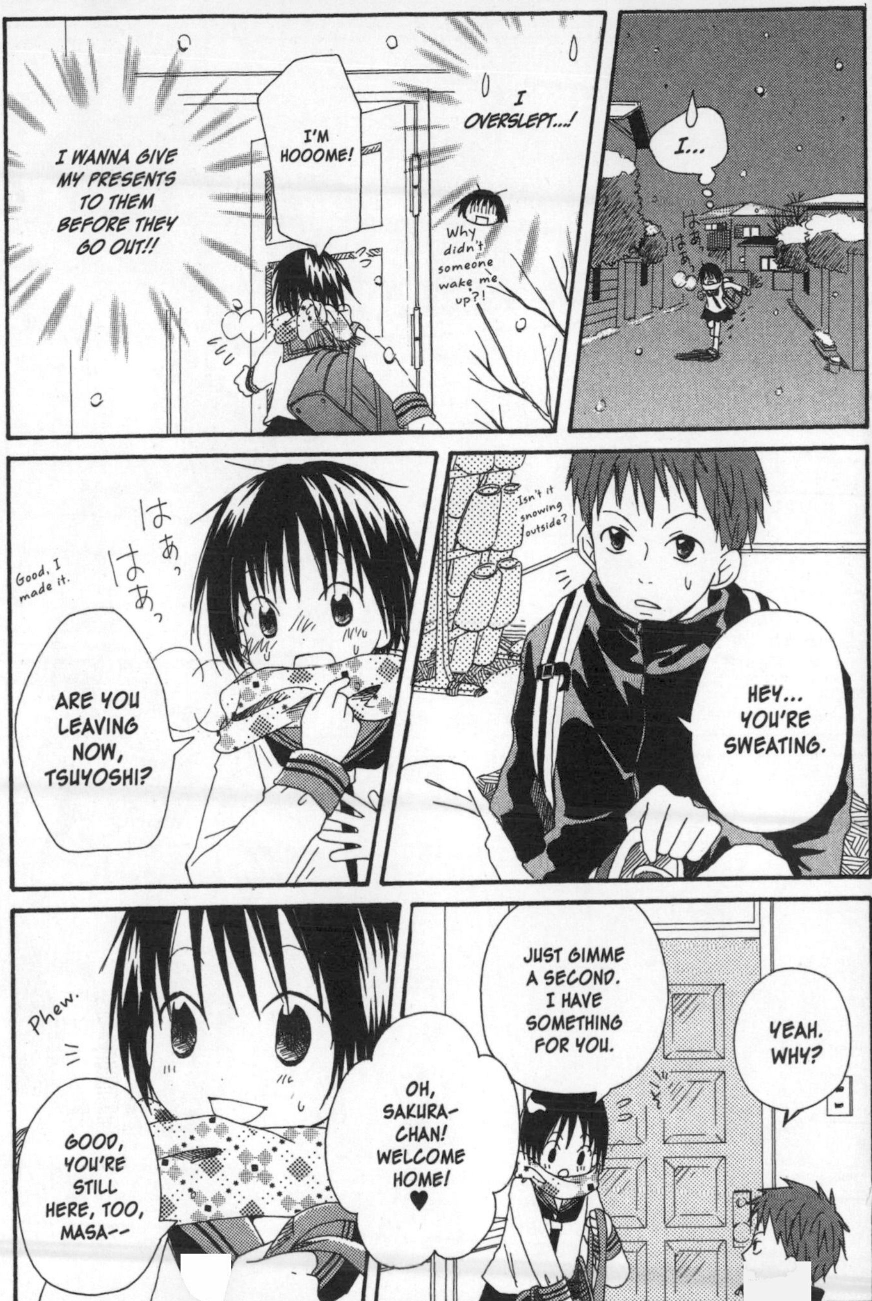
I...
I OVERSLEPT...!
Why didn't someone wake me up?!
I'M HOOOME!
I WANNA GIVE MY PRESENTS TO THEM BEFORE THEY GO OUT!!
Isn't it snowing outside?
HEY... YOU'RE SWEATING.
はぁっ はぁっ
Good, I made it.
ARE YOU LEAVING NOW, TSUYOSHI?
YEAH. WHY?
JUST GIMME A SECOND. I HAVE SOMETHING FOR YOU.
Phew.
GOOD, YOU'RE STILL HERE, TOO, MASA--
OH, SAKURA-CHAN! WELCOME HOME! ♥

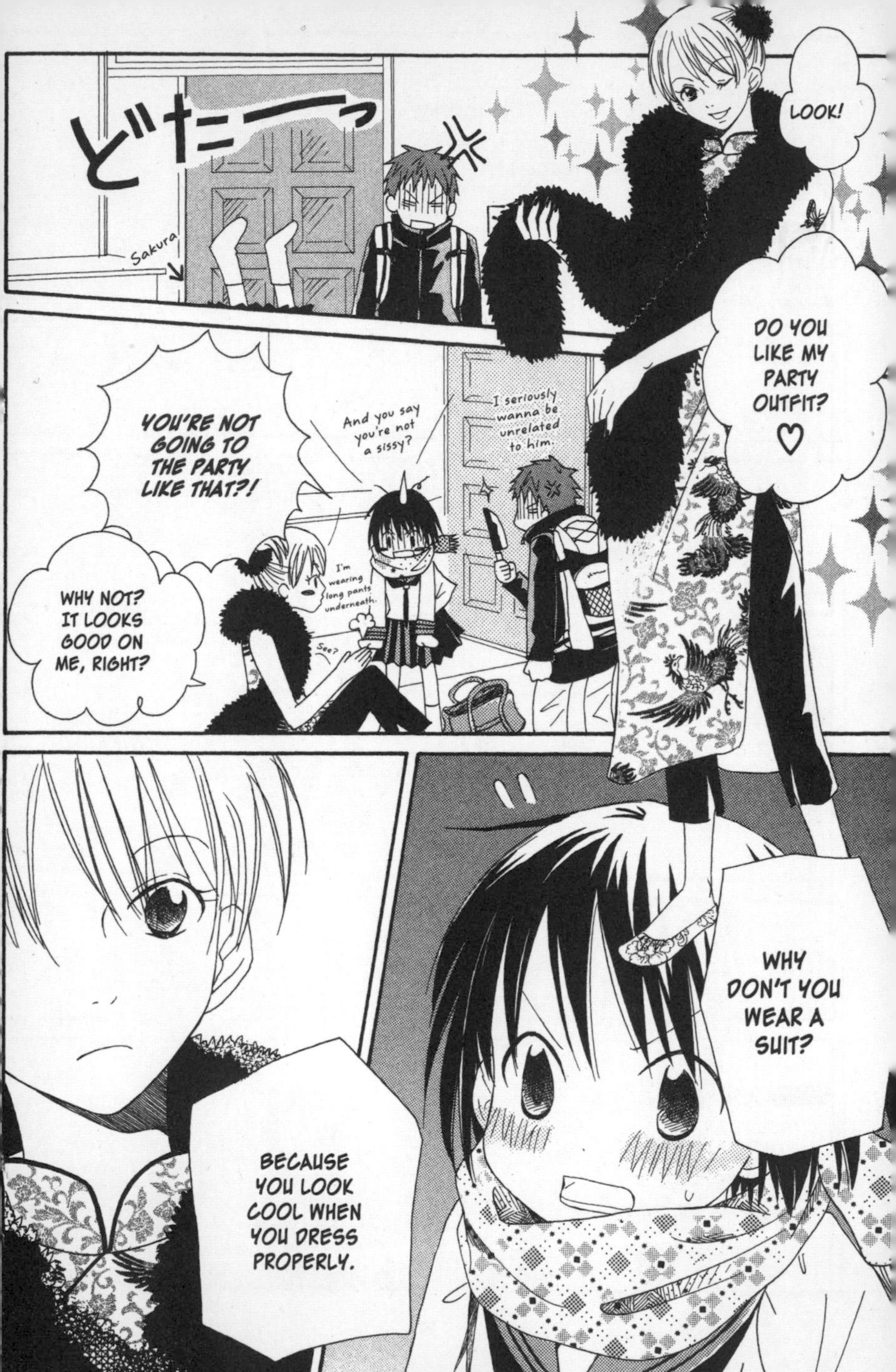

LOOK!
どたーっ
Sakura
DO YOU LIKE MY PARTY OUTFIT? ♡
YOU'RE NOT GOING TO THE PARTY LIKE THAT?!
WHY NOT? IT LOOKS GOOD ON ME, RIGHT?
I'm wearing long pants underneath.
See?
And you say you're not a sissy?
I seriously wanna be unrelated to him.
WHY DON'T YOU WEAR A SUIT?
BECAUSE YOU LOOK COOL WHEN YOU DRESS PROPERLY.

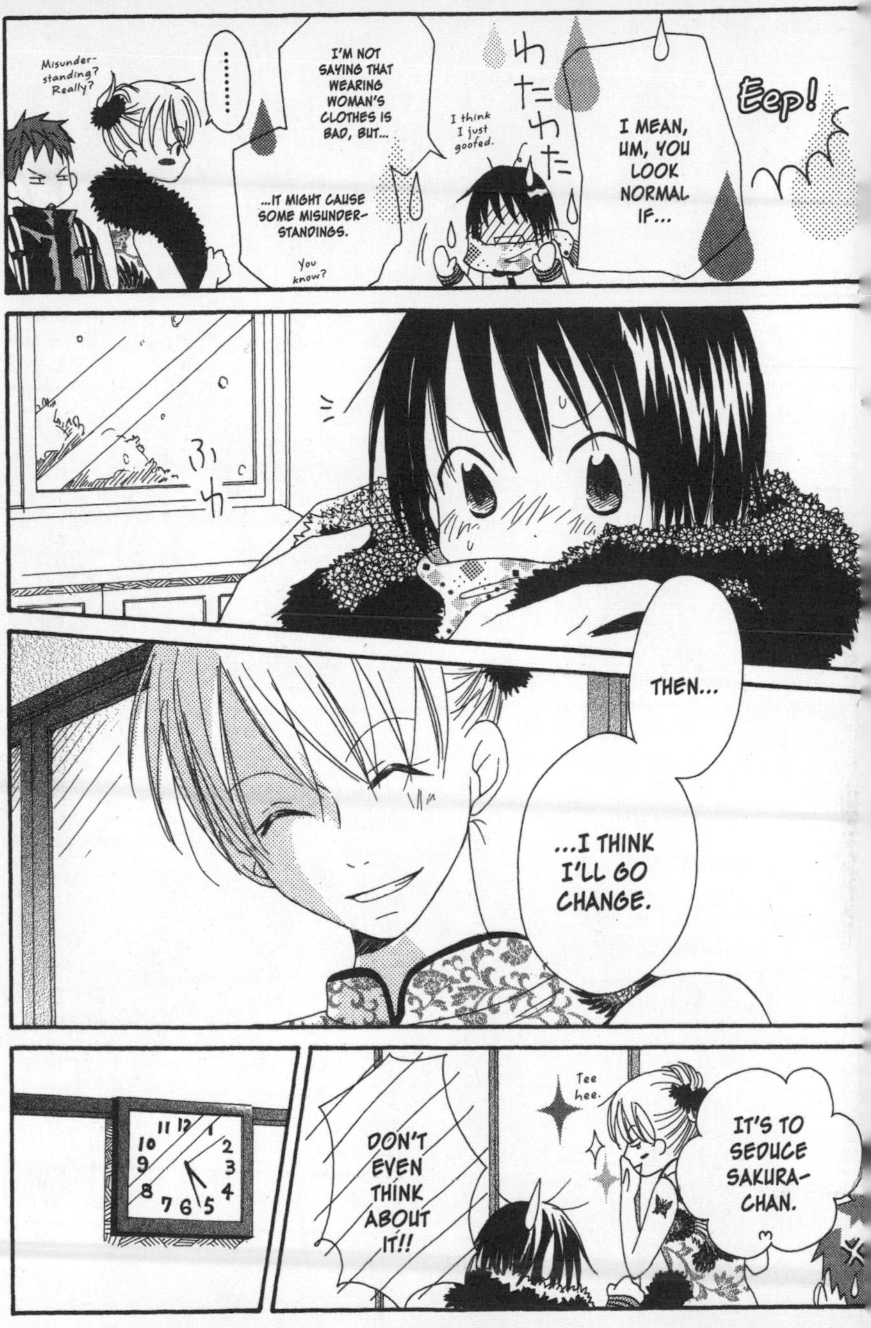
Eep!
I MEAN, UM, YOU LOOK NORMAL IF...
わたわた
I think I just goofed.
I'M NOT SAYING THAT WEARING WOMAN'S CLOTHES IS BAD, BUT...
...IT MIGHT CAUSE SOME MISUNDER-STANDINGS.
You know?
......
Misunder-standing? Really?
ふわ
THEN...
...I THINK I'LL GO CHANGE.
IT'S TO SEDUCE SAKURA-CHAN.
Tee hee.
DON'T EVEN THINK ABOUT IT!!

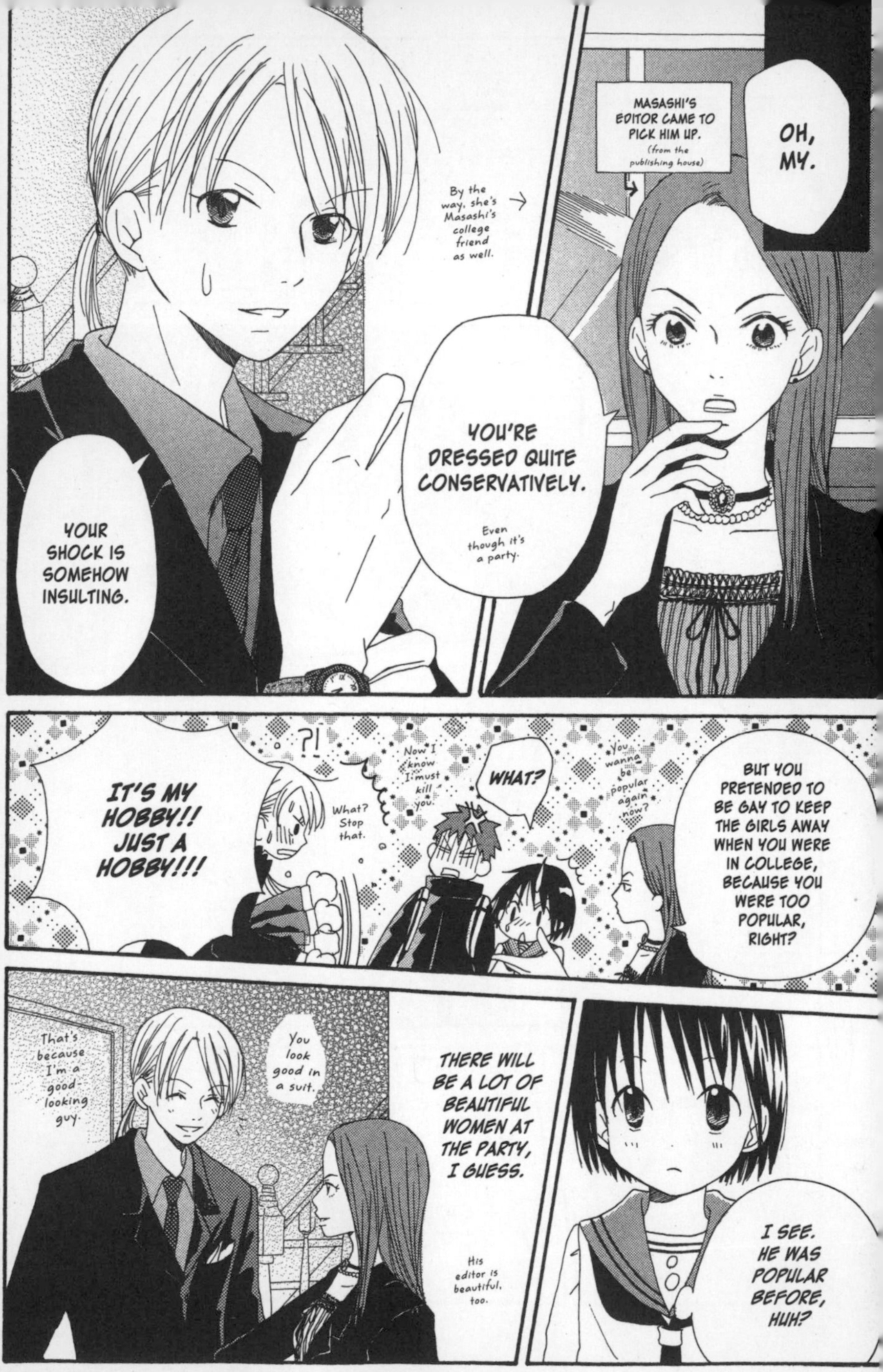
OH, MY.
MASASHI'S EDITOR CAME TO PICK HIM UP.
(from the publishing house)
By the way, she's Masashi's college friend as well.
YOU'RE DRESSED QUITE CONSERVATIVELY.
Even though it's a party.
YOUR SHOCK IS SOMEHOW INSULTING.
BUT YOU PRETENDED TO BE GAY TO KEEP THE GIRLS AWAY WHEN YOU WERE IN COLLEGE, BECAUSE YOU WERE TOO POPULAR, RIGHT?
You wanna be popular again now?
WHAT?
Now I know I must kill you.
What? Stop that.
?!
IT'S MY HOBBY!! JUST A HOBBY!!!
I SEE. HE WAS POPULAR BEFORE, HUH?
THERE WILL BE A LOT OF BEAUTIFUL WOMEN AT THE PARTY, I GUESS.
His editor is beautiful, too.
You look good in a suit.
That's because I'm a good-looking guy.

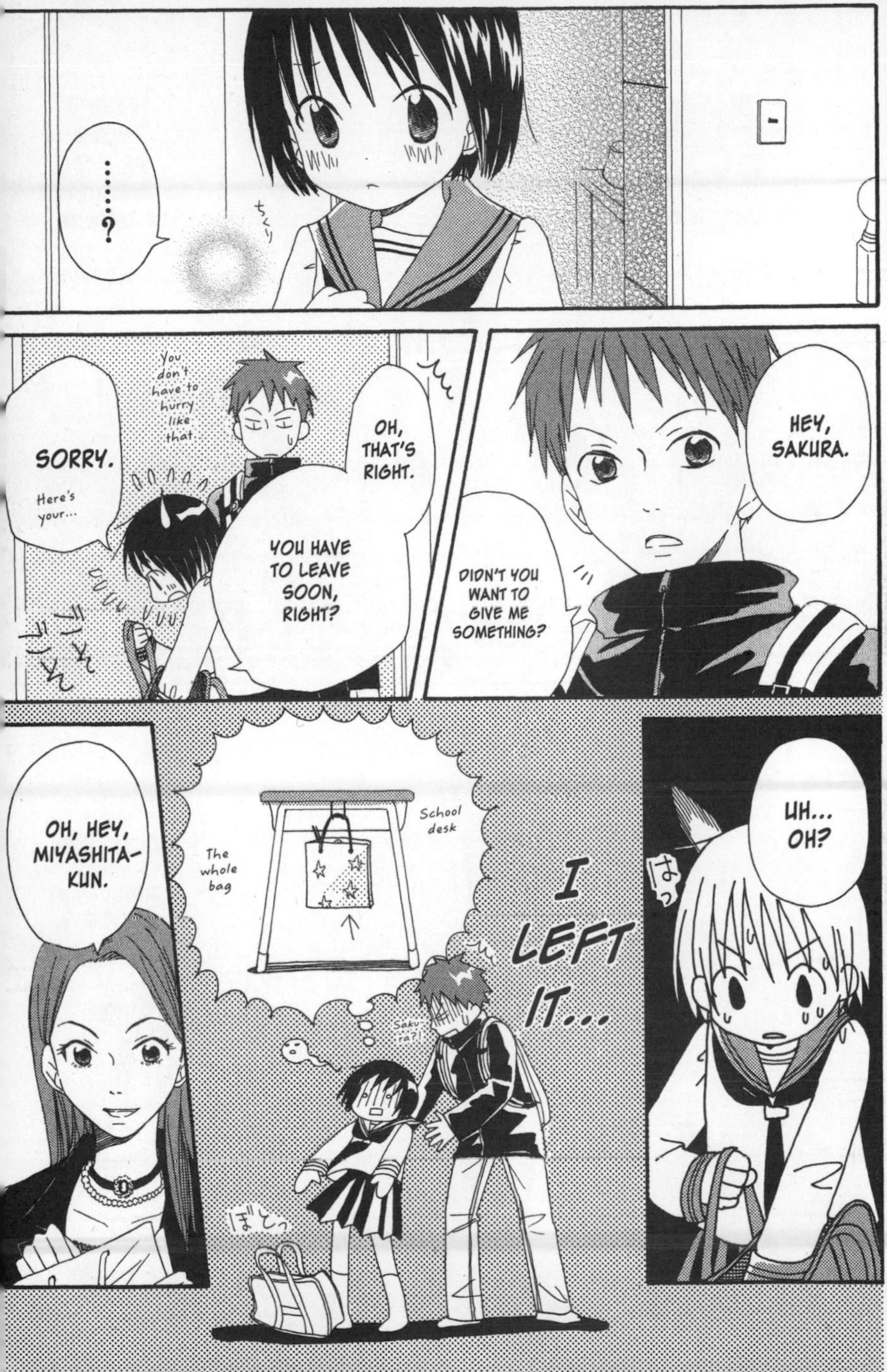
……?
ちくり
HEY, SAKURA.
DIDN'T YOU WANT TO GIVE ME SOMETHING?
OH, THAT'S RIGHT.
YOU HAVE TO LEAVE SOON, RIGHT?
You don't have to hurry like that.
SORRY.
Here's your...
UH... OH?
はっ
I LEFT IT...
School desk
The whole bag
Saku-ra?!
ぼとっ
OH, HEY, MIYASHITA-KUN.

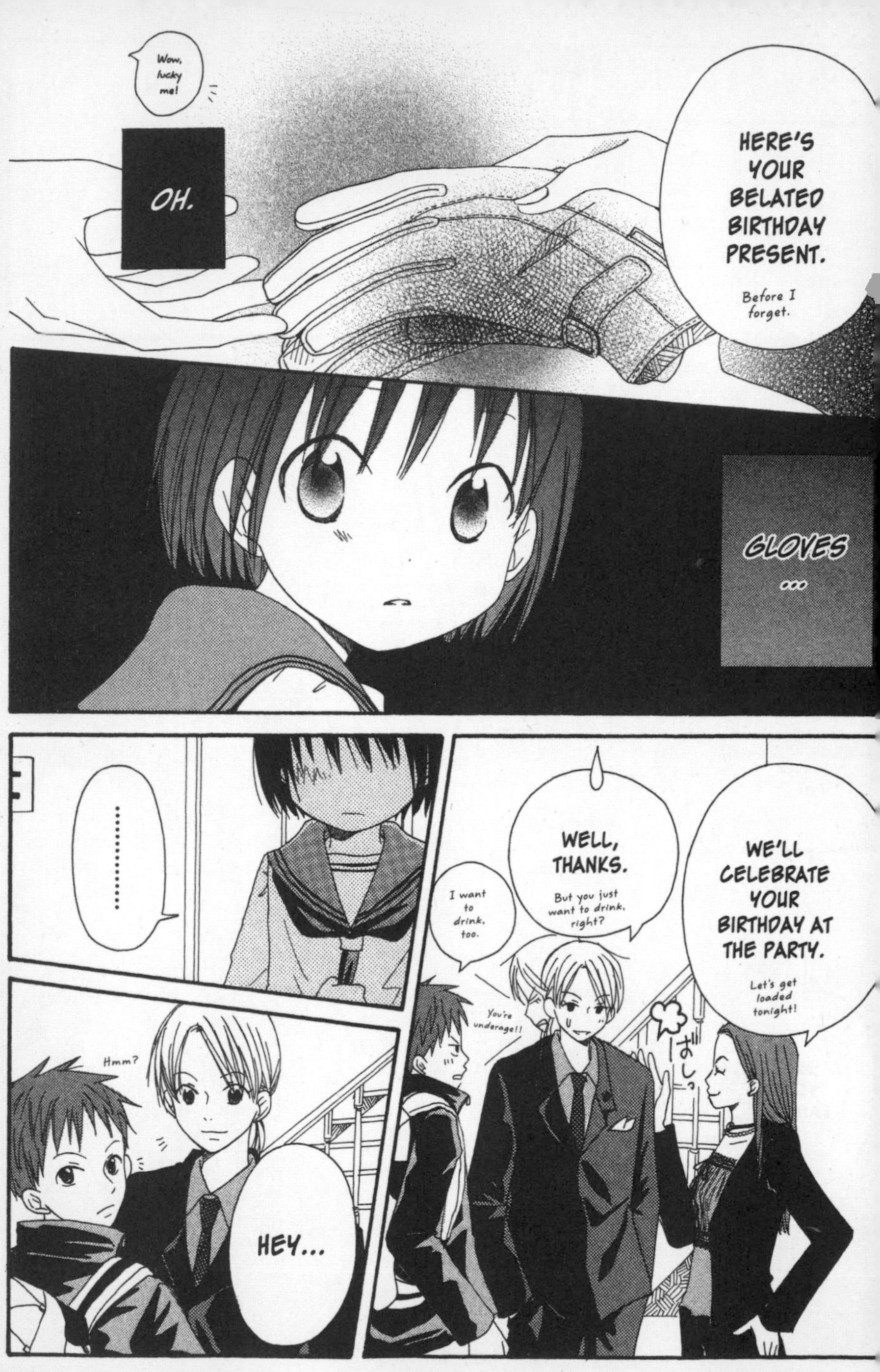
HERE'S YOUR BELATED BIRTHDAY PRESENT.
Before I forget.
Wow, lucky me!
OH.
GLOVES ...
WE'LL CELEBRATE YOUR BIRTHDAY AT THE PARTY.
Let's get loaded tonight!
ばしっ
WELL, THANKS.
But you just want to drink, right?
I want to drink, too.
You're underage!!
....
Hmm?
HEY...

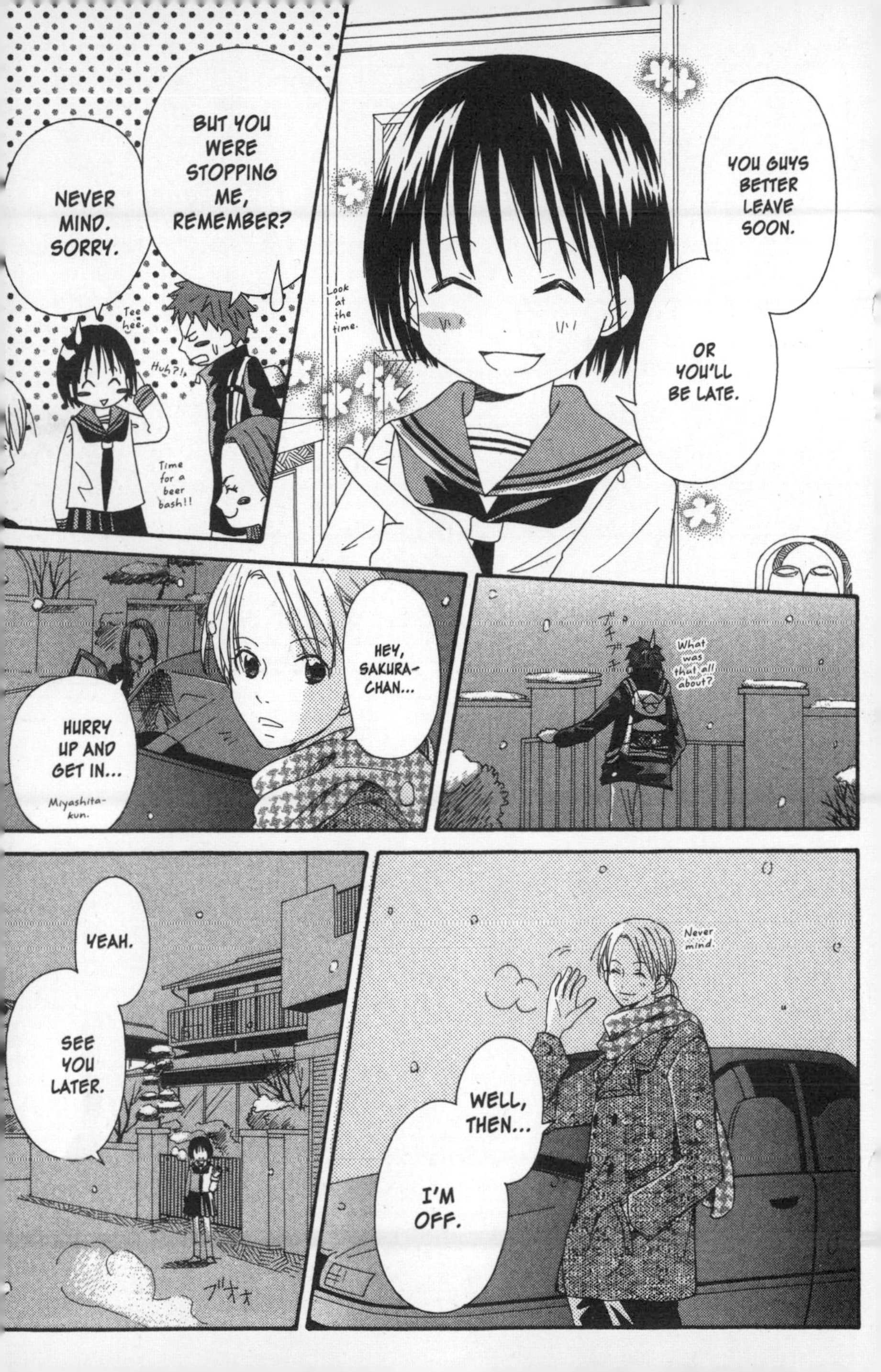
YOU GUYS BETTER LEAVE SOON.
OR YOU'LL BE LATE.
Look at the time.
BUT YOU WERE STOPPING ME, REMEMBER?
NEVER MIND. SORRY.
Tee hee.
Huh?!
Time for a beer bash!!
What was that all about?
HEY, SAKURA-CHAN...
HURRY UP AND GET IN...
Miyashita-kun.
Never mind.
WELL, THEN...
I'M OFF.
YEAH.
SEE YOU LATER.

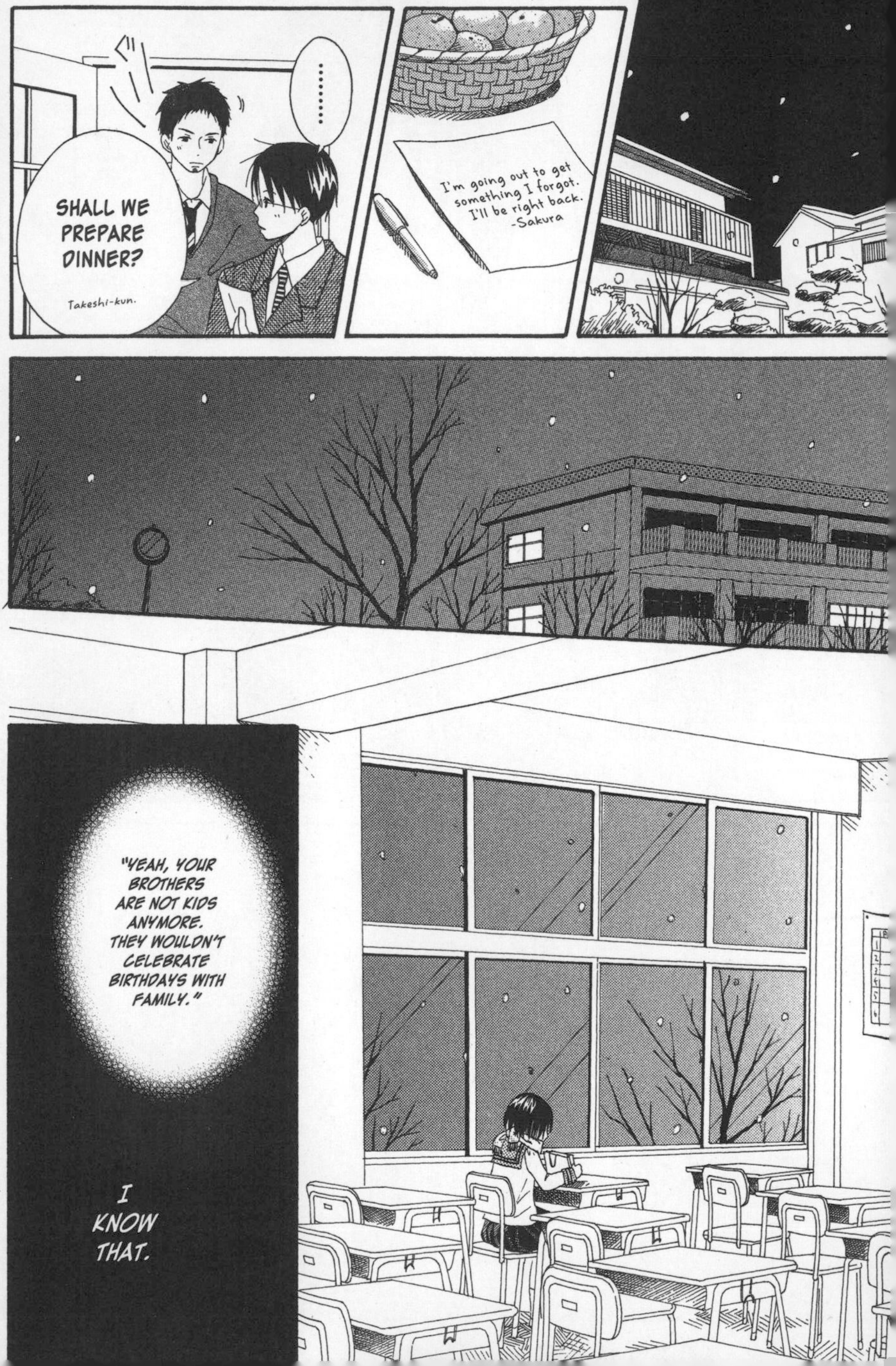
I'm going out to get something I forgot. I'll be right back. -Sakura
......
SHALL WE PREPARE DINNER? Takeshi-kun.
"YEAH, YOUR BROTHERS ARE NOT KIDS ANYMORE. THEY WOULDN'T CELEBRATE BIRTHDAYS WITH FAMILY."
I KNOW THAT.

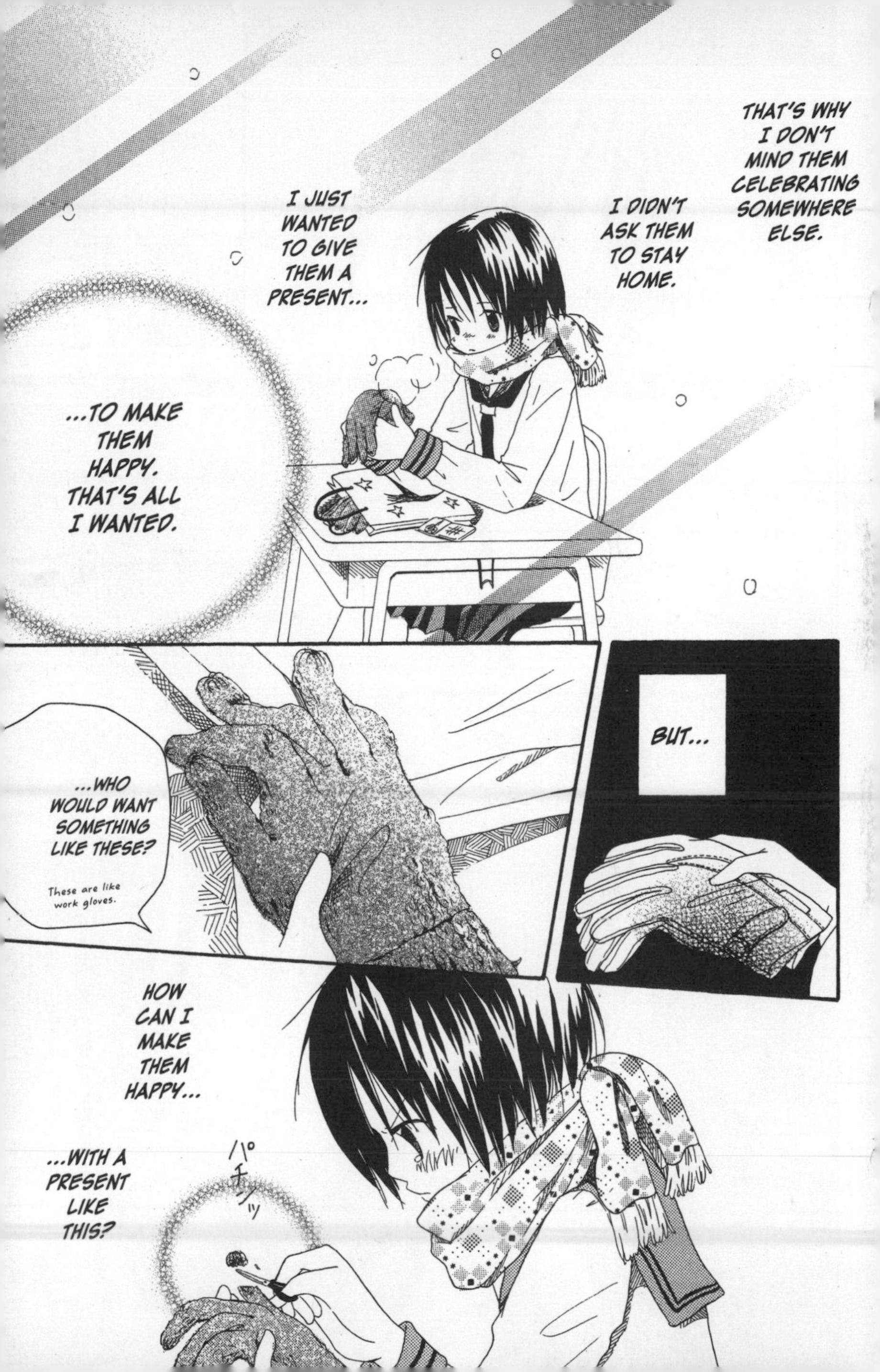
THAT'S WHY I DON'T MIND THEM CELEBRATING SOMEWHERE ELSE.
I DIDN'T ASK THEM TO STAY HOME.
I JUST WANTED TO GIVE THEM A PRESENT...
...TO MAKE THEM HAPPY. THAT'S ALL I WANTED.
BUT...
...WHO WOULD WANT SOMETHING LIKE THESE?
These are like work gloves.
HOW CAN I MAKE THEM HAPPY...
パチッ
...WITH A PRESENT LIKE THIS?

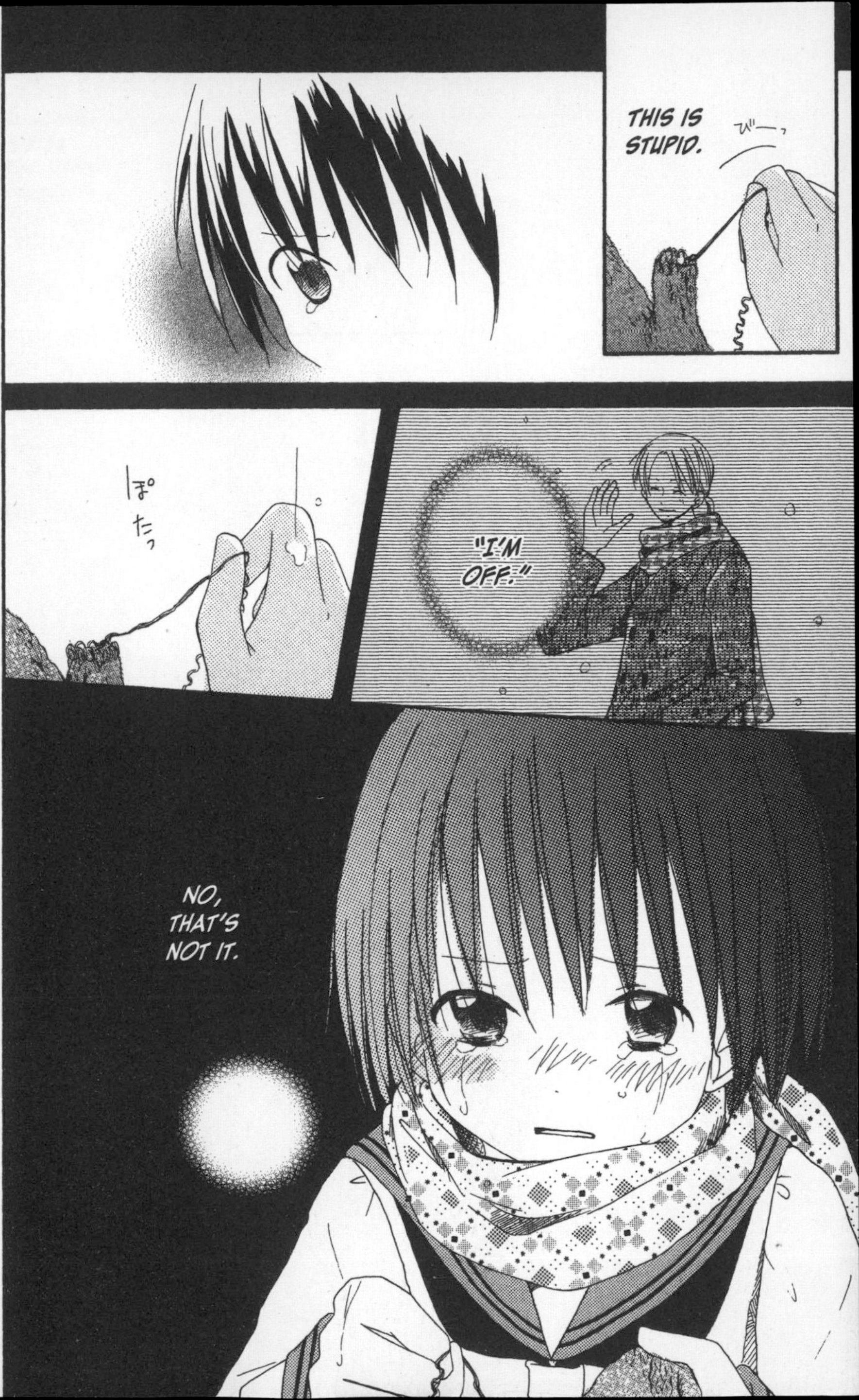
THIS IS STUPID.
びーっ
"I'M OFF."
ぽたっ
NO, THAT'S NOT IT.

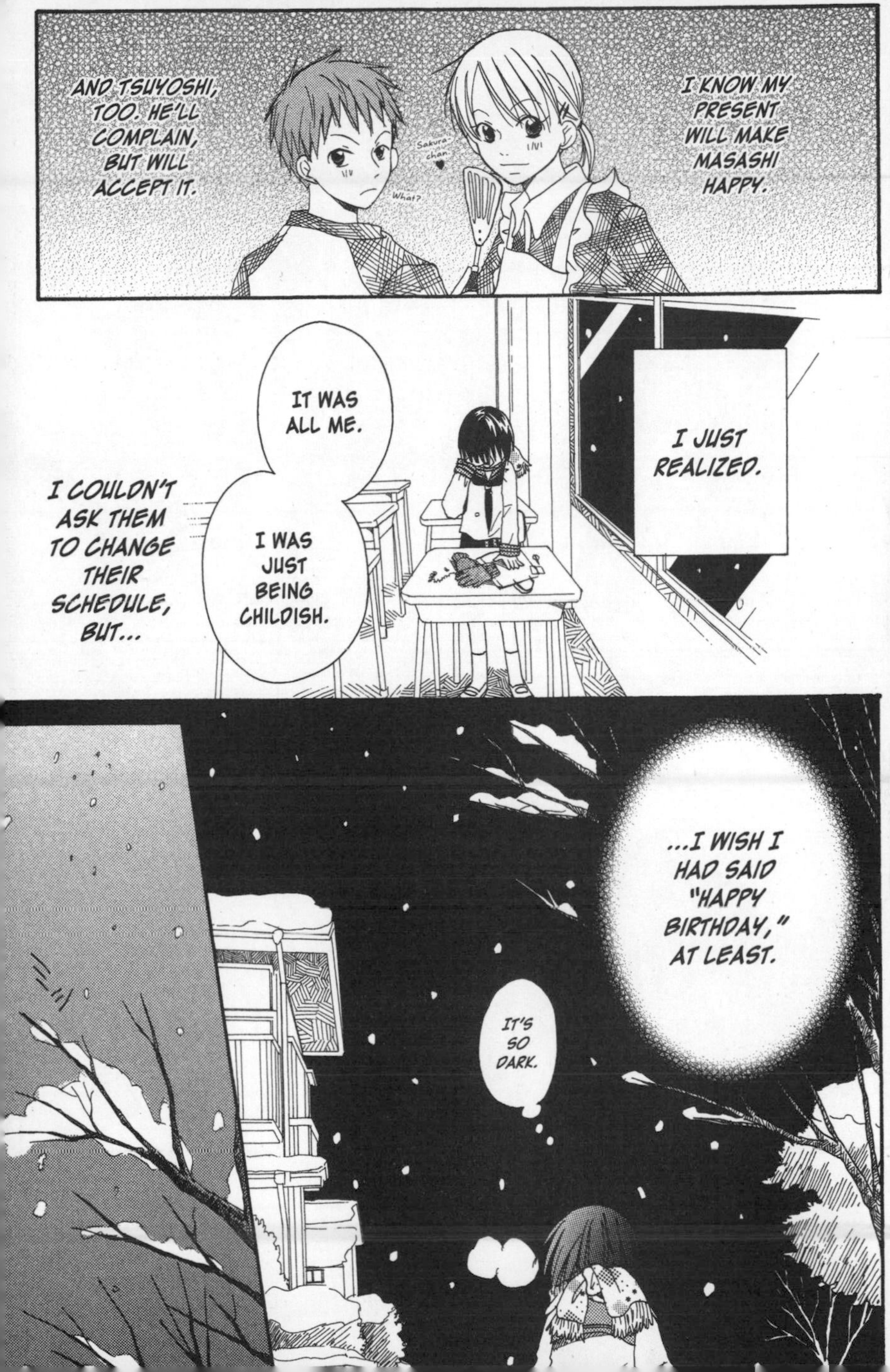
I KNOW MY PRESENT WILL MAKE MASASHI HAPPY.
Sakura-chan.
What?
AND TSUYOSHI, TOO. HE'LL COMPLAIN, BUT WILL ACCEPT IT.
I JUST REALIZED.
IT WAS ALL ME.
I WAS JUST BEING CHILDISH.
I COULDN'T ASK THEM TO CHANGE THEIR SCHEDULE, BUT...
...I WISH I HAD SAID "HAPPY BIRTHDAY," AT LEAST.
IT'S SO DARK.

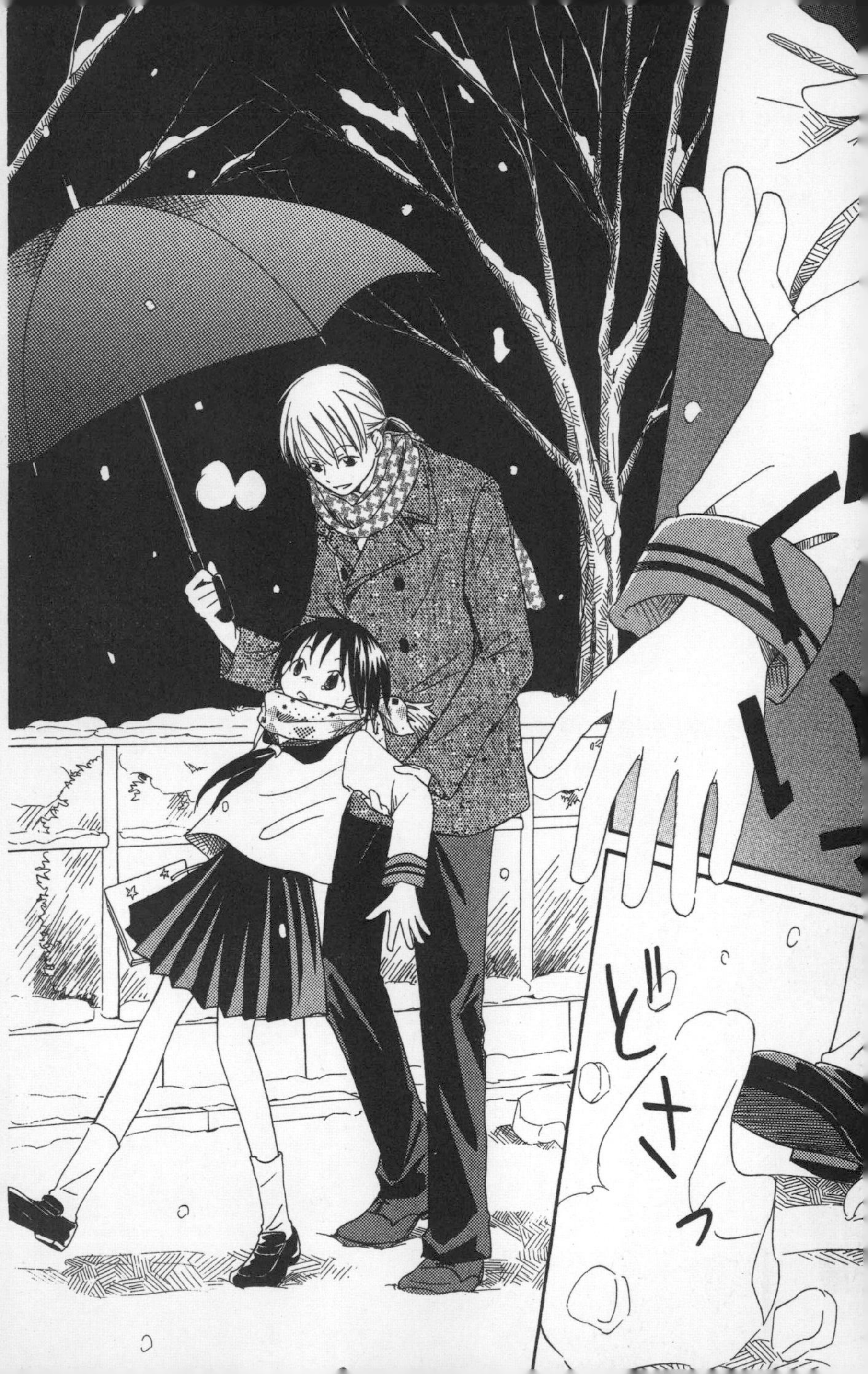
どさっ

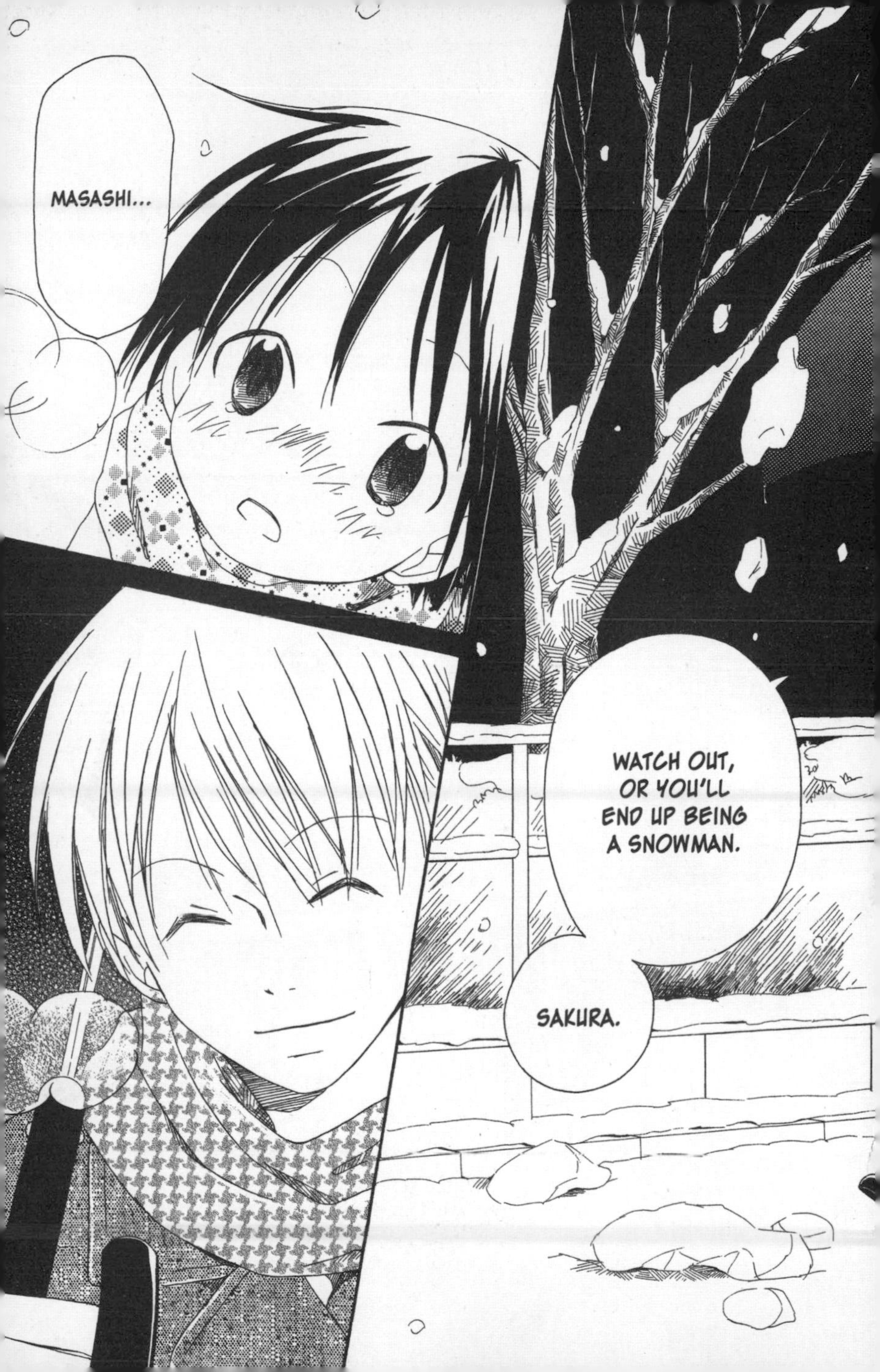
MASASHI...
WATCH OUT, OR YOU'LL END UP BEING A SNOWMAN.
SAKURA.

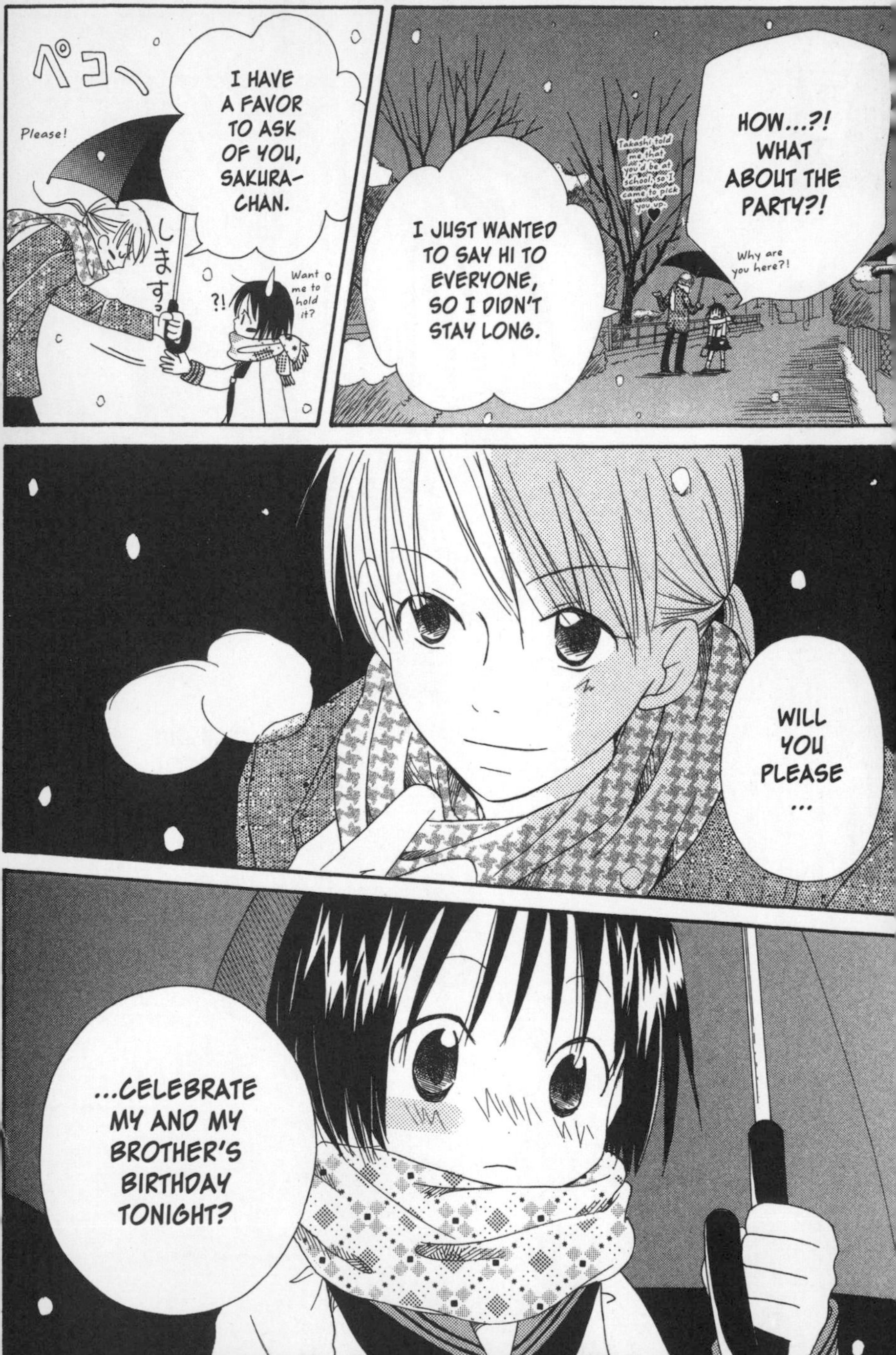
HOW...?! WHAT ABOUT THE PARTY?!
Why are you here?!
Takashi told me that you'd be at school, so I came to pick you up. ♥
I JUST WANTED TO SAY HI TO EVERYONE, SO I DIDN'T STAY LONG.
ペコ
I HAVE A FAVOR TO ASK OF YOU, SAKURA-CHAN.
Please!
します
?!
Want me to hold it?
WILL YOU PLEASE ...
...CELEBRATE MY AND MY BROTHER'S BIRTHDAY TONIGHT?

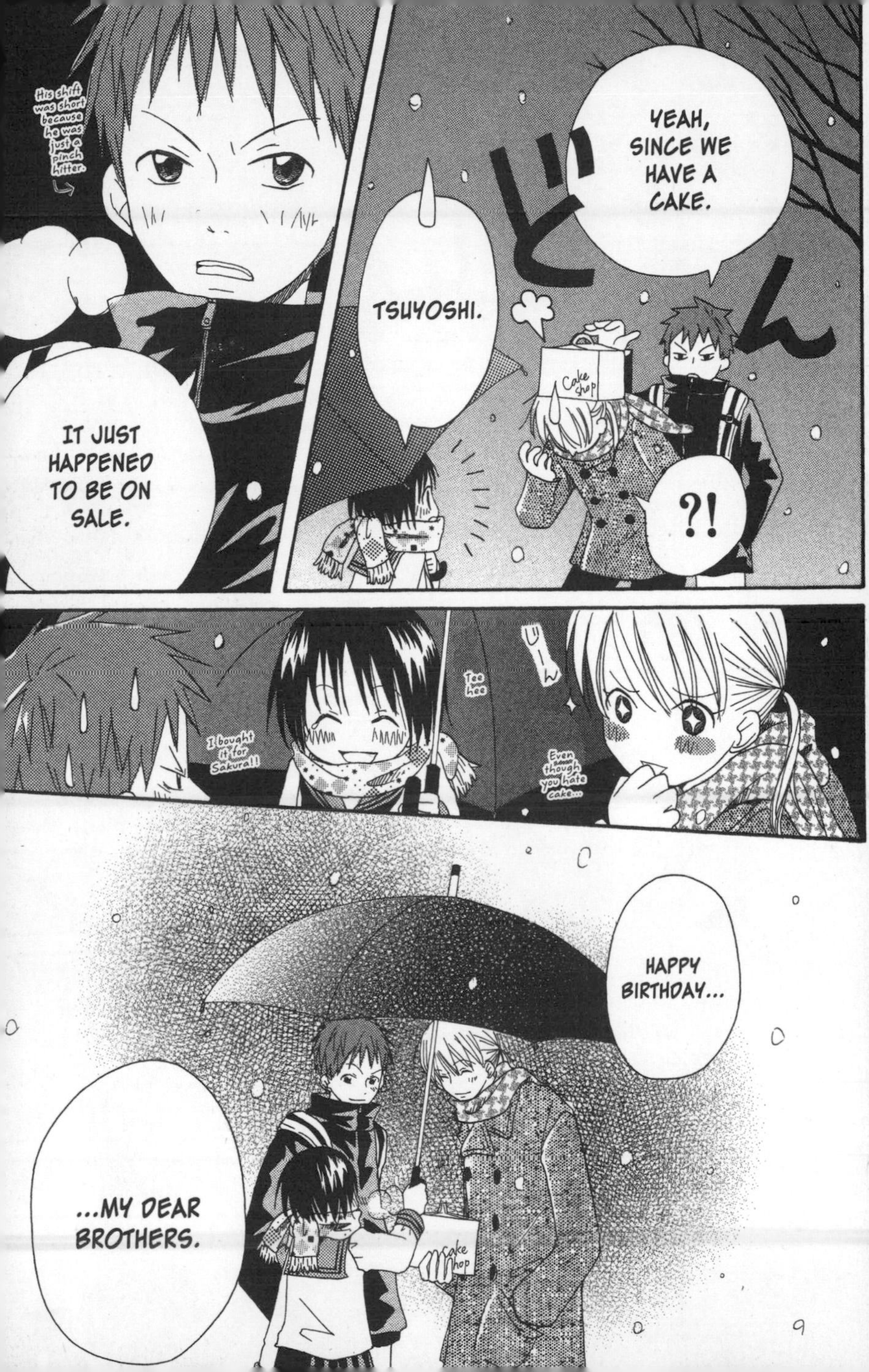
YEAH, SINCE WE HAVE A CAKE.
どん
TSUYOSHI.
?!
His shift was short because he was just a pinch hitter.
IT JUST HAPPENED TO BE ON SALE.
Even though you hate cake...
Tee hee
I bought it for Sakura!!
HAPPY BIRTHDAY...
...MY DEAR BROTHERS.

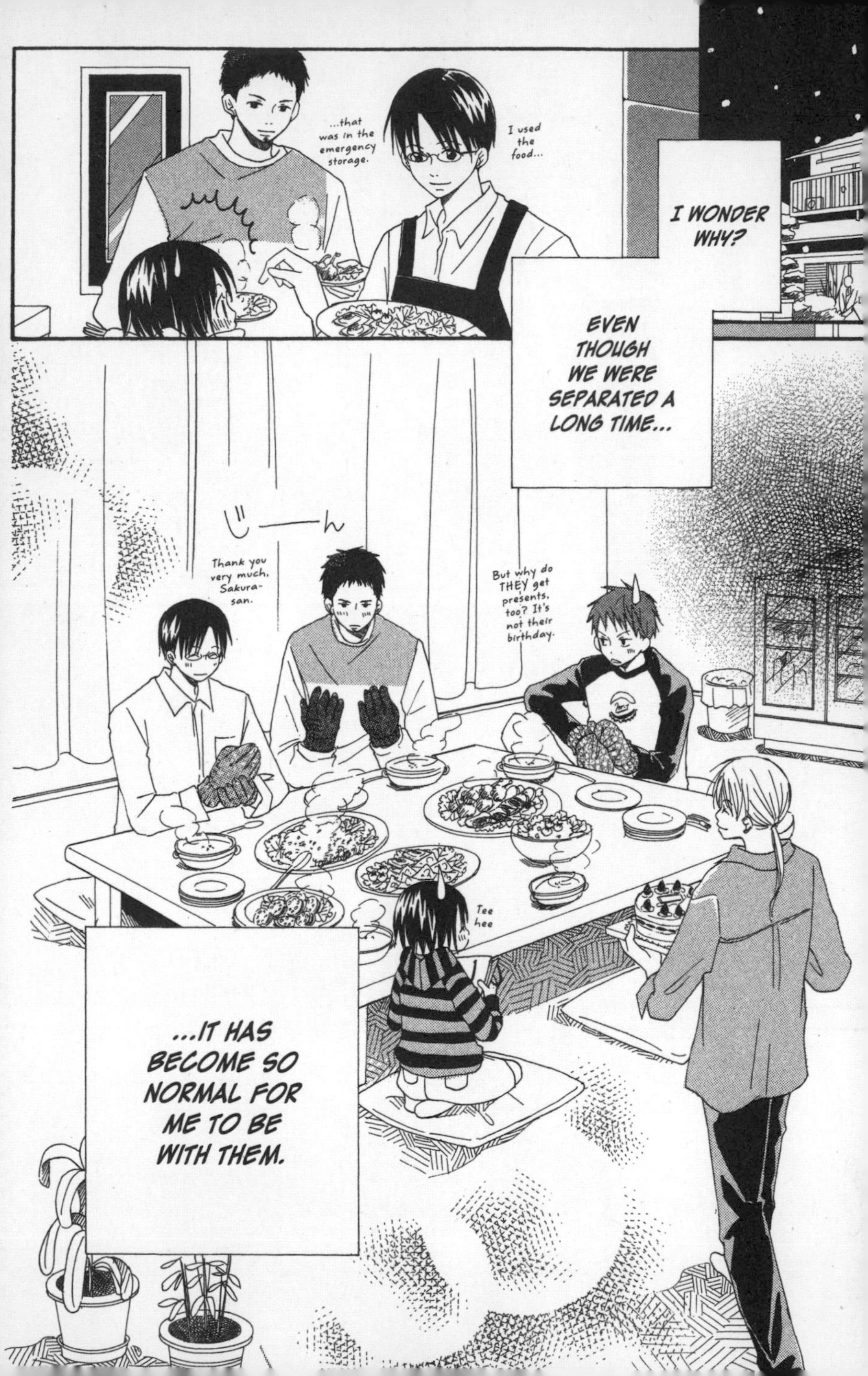
I WONDER WHY?
I used the food...
...that was in the emergency storage.
EVEN THOUGH WE WERE SEPARATED A LONG TIME...
じーーん
But why do THEY get presents, too? It's not their birthday.
Thank you very much, Sakura-san.
Tee hee
...IT HAS BECOME SO NORMAL FOR ME TO BE WITH THEM.

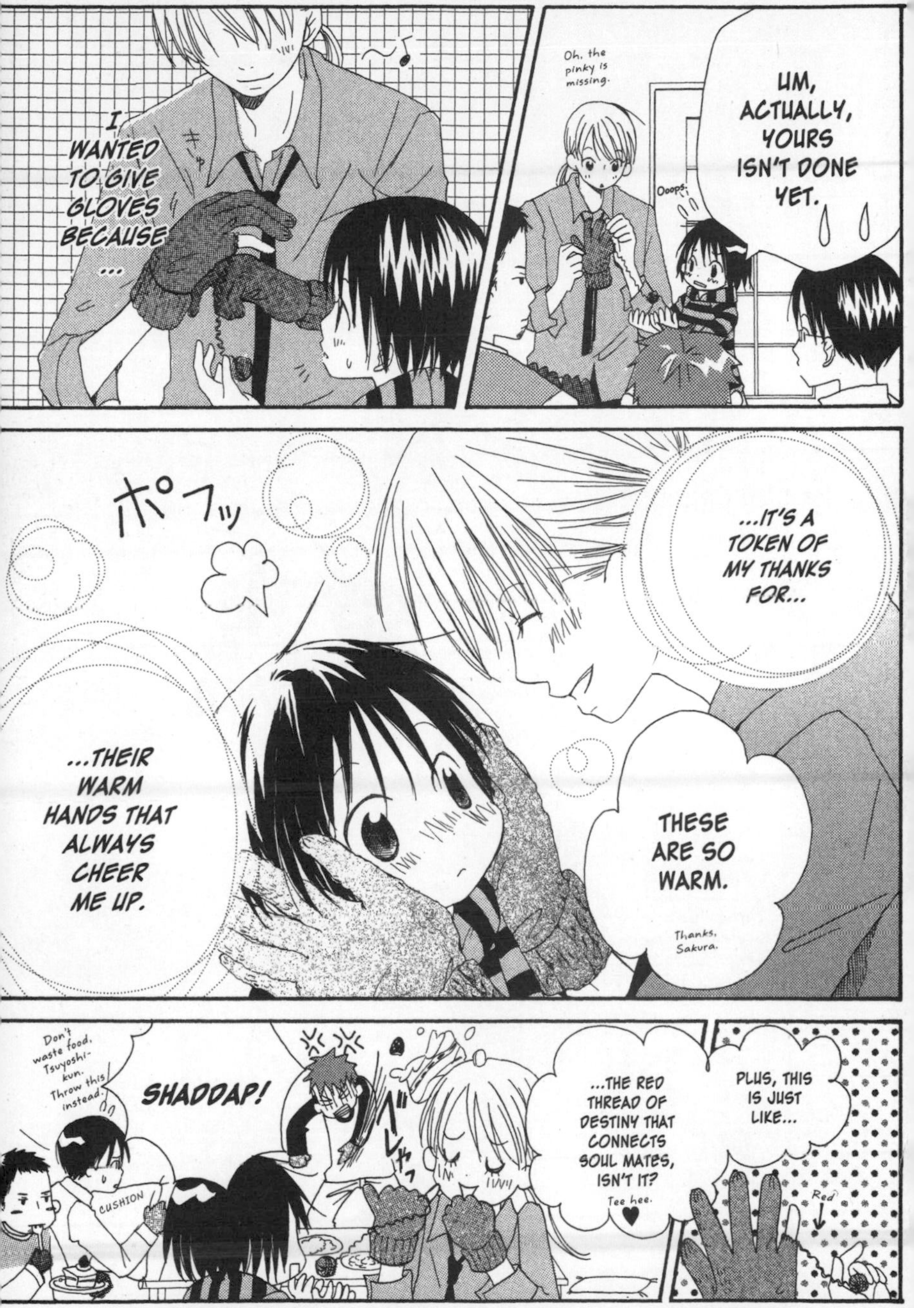
UM, ACTUALLY, YOURS ISN'T DONE YET.
Oh, the pinky is missing.
Ooops.
I WANTED TO GIVE GLOVES BECAUSE ...
...IT'S A TOKEN OF MY THANKS FOR...
ポフッ
...THEIR WARM HANDS THAT ALWAYS CHEER ME UP.
THESE ARE SO WARM.
Thanks, Sakura.
PLUS, THIS IS JUST LIKE...
Red
...THE RED THREAD OF DESTINY THAT CONNECTS SOUL MATES, ISN'T IT?
Tee hee.
SHADDAP!
Don't waste food, Tsuyoshi-kun. Throw this instead.
CUSHION

Is he gay?

Masashi Miyashita

Bonus! ♥

Drop dead!

Tuna

Date of Birth:
Jan. 1ˢᵗ, 1978
Capricorn, blood type A

↑

He's actually a serious man.
But his hobby is wearing
women's clothes.
It's starting to become his job.

Height: 176cm

Likes: Sakura-chan ♥

Of course!!!

Hates: Cats
Because they scratch
his beautiful face...
How about that?

← Here's the main story.

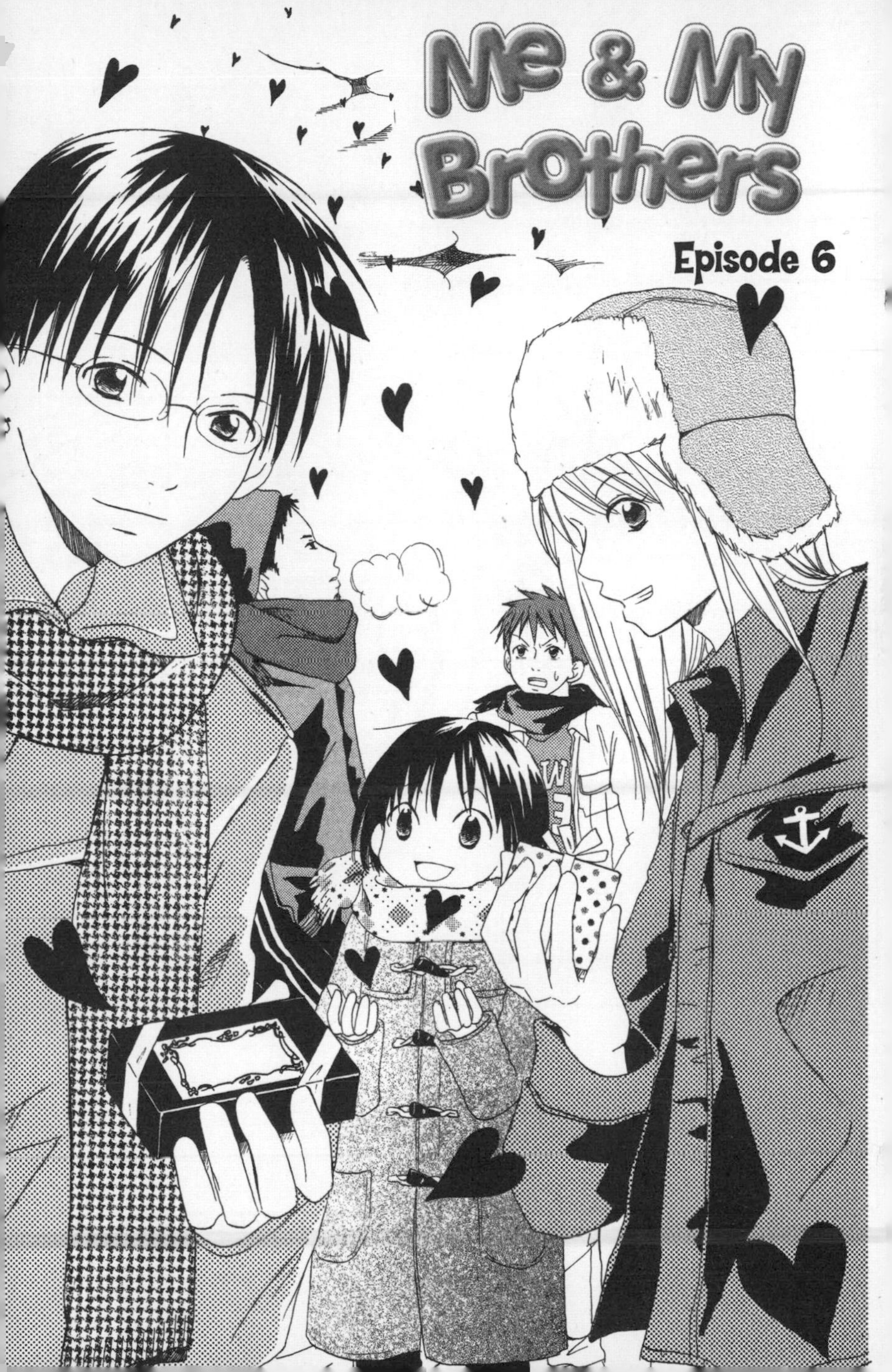
Me & My Brothers
Episode 6

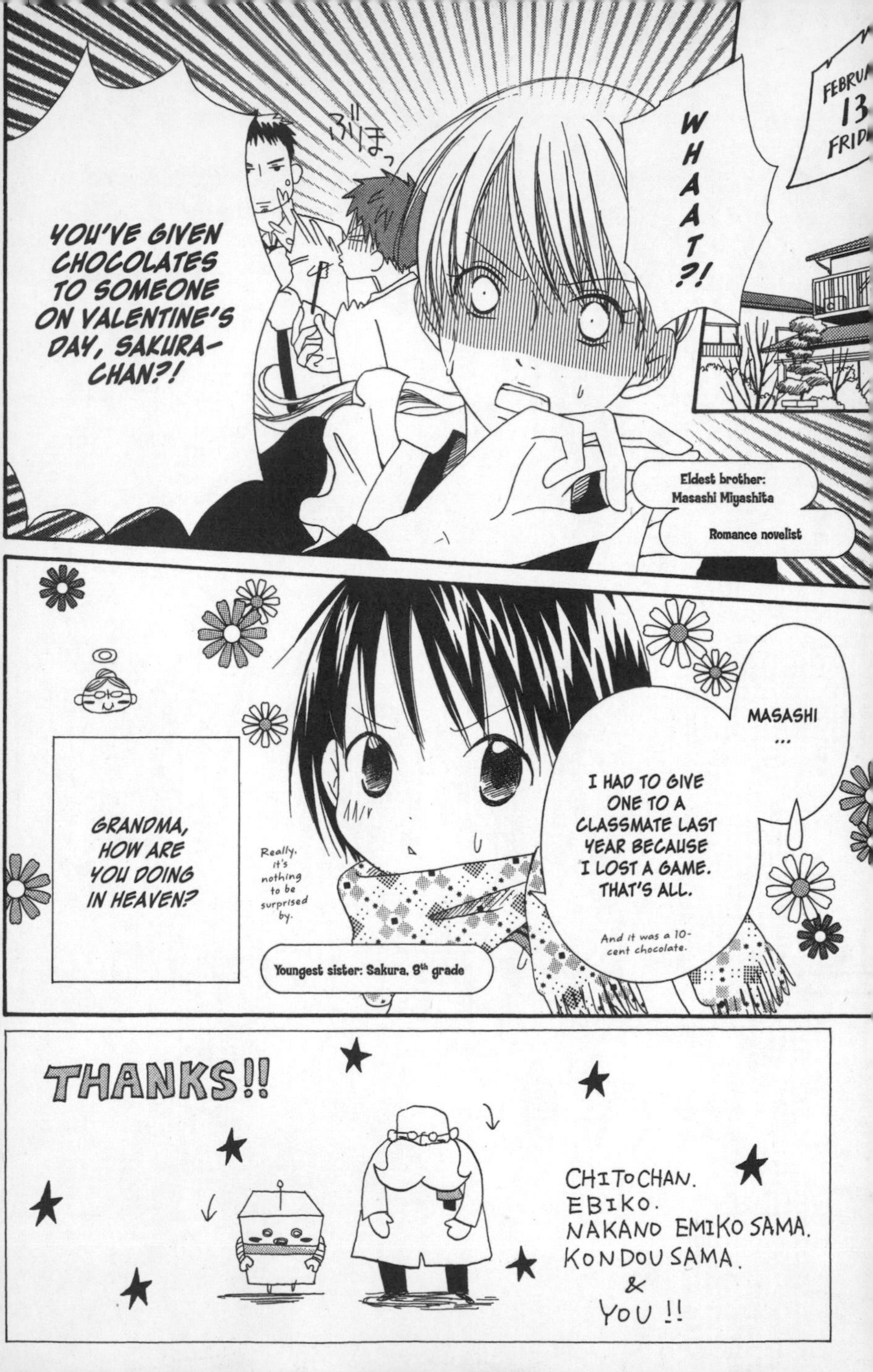
FEBRU
13
FRID
WHAAT?!
YOU'VE GIVEN CHOCOLATES TO SOMEONE ON VALENTINE'S DAY, SAKURA-CHAN?!
Eldest brother: Masashi Miyashita
Romance novelist
MASASHI ...
I HAD TO GIVE ONE TO A CLASSMATE LAST YEAR BECAUSE I LOST A GAME. THAT'S ALL.
And it was a 10-cent chocolate.
Really, it's nothing to be surprised by.
Youngest sister: Sakura, 8th grade
GRANDMA, HOW ARE YOU DOING IN HEAVEN?
THANKS!!
CHITOCHAN.
EBIKO.
NAKANO EMIKO SAMA.
KONDOU SAMA.
&
YOU !!

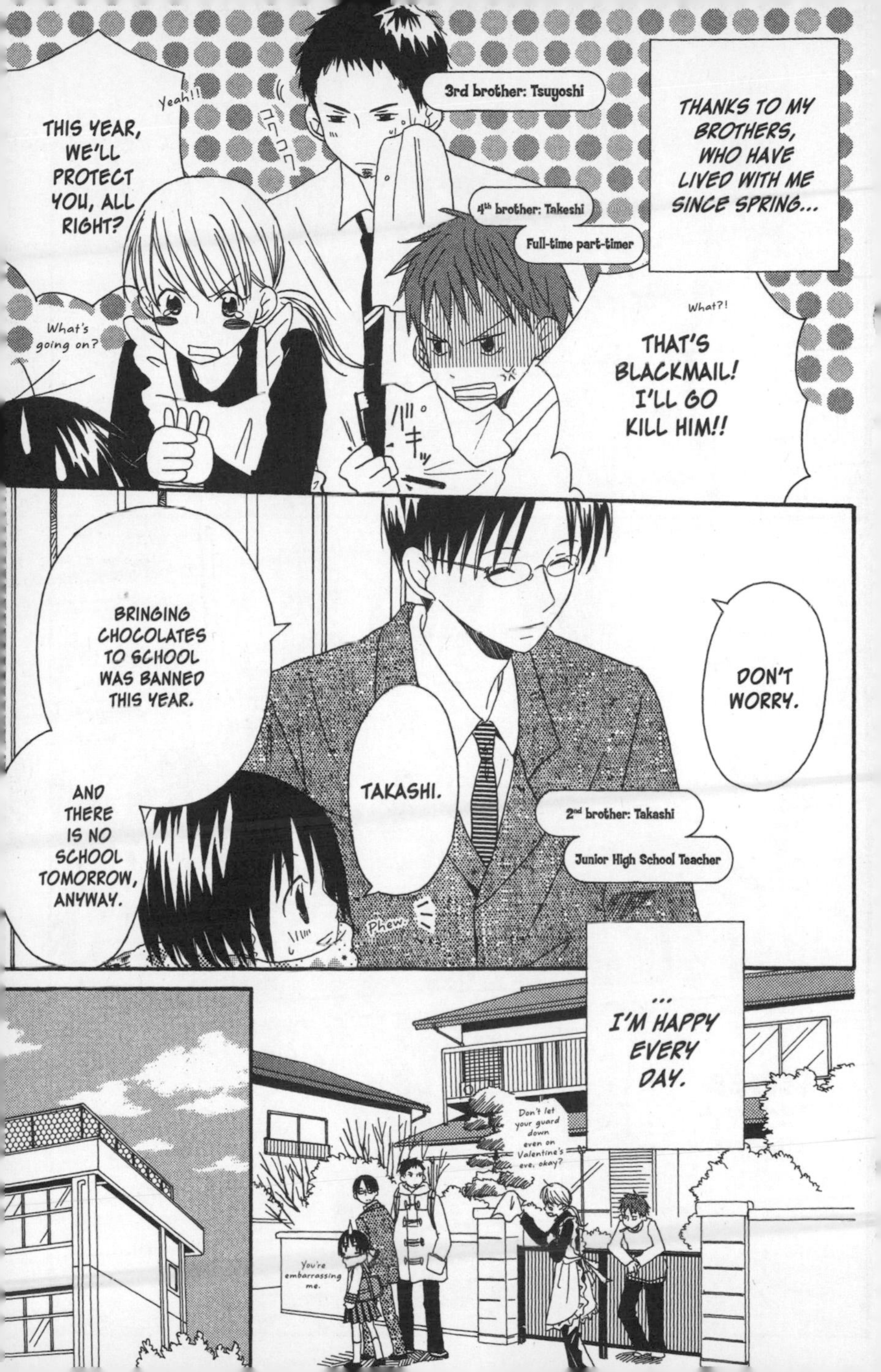
THANKS TO MY BROTHERS, WHO HAVE LIVED WITH ME SINCE SPRING...
3rd brother: Tsuyoshi
4th brother: Takeshi
Full-time part-timer
Yeah!!
THIS YEAR, WE'LL PROTECT YOU, ALL RIGHT?
What?!
THAT'S BLACKMAIL! I'LL GO KILL HIM!!
What's going on?
DON'T WORRY.
2nd brother: Takashi
Junior High School Teacher
TAKASHI.
BRINGING CHOCOLATES TO SCHOOL WAS BANNED THIS YEAR.
AND THERE IS NO SCHOOL TOMORROW, ANYWAY.
Phew.
... I'M HAPPY EVERY DAY.
Don't let your guard down even on Valentine's eve, okay?
You're embarrassing me.

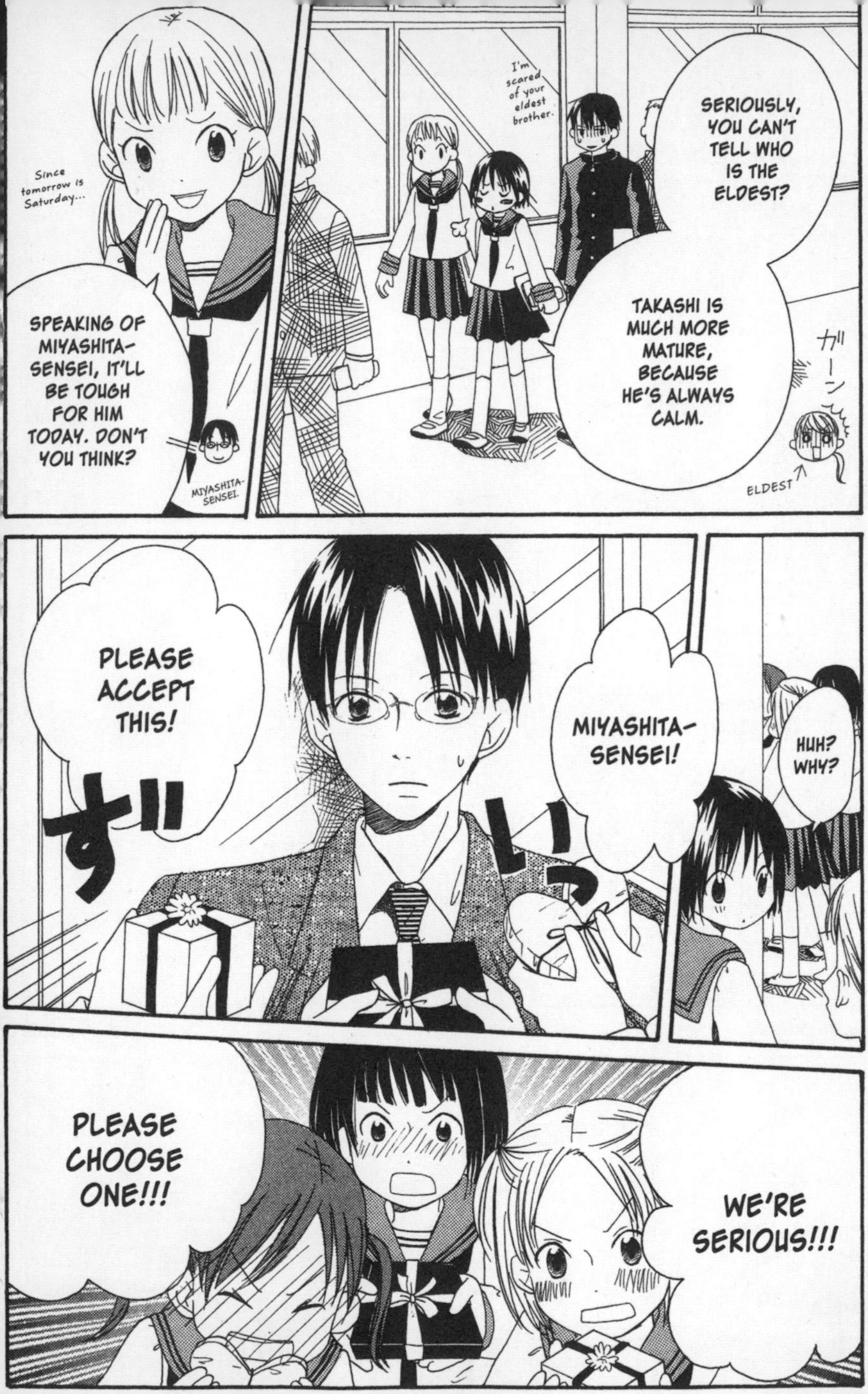
SERIOUSLY, YOU CAN'T TELL WHO IS THE ELDEST?
I'm scared of your eldest brother.
TAKASHI IS MUCH MORE MATURE, BECAUSE HE'S ALWAYS CALM.
ガーン
ELDEST
Since tomorrow is Saturday...
SPEAKING OF MIYASHITA-SENSEI, IT'LL BE TOUGH FOR HIM TODAY. DON'T YOU THINK?
MIYASHITA-SENSEI.
HUH? WHY?
MIYASHITA-SENSEI!
PLEASE ACCEPT THIS!
すッ
WE'RE SERIOUS!!!
PLEASE CHOOSE ONE!!!

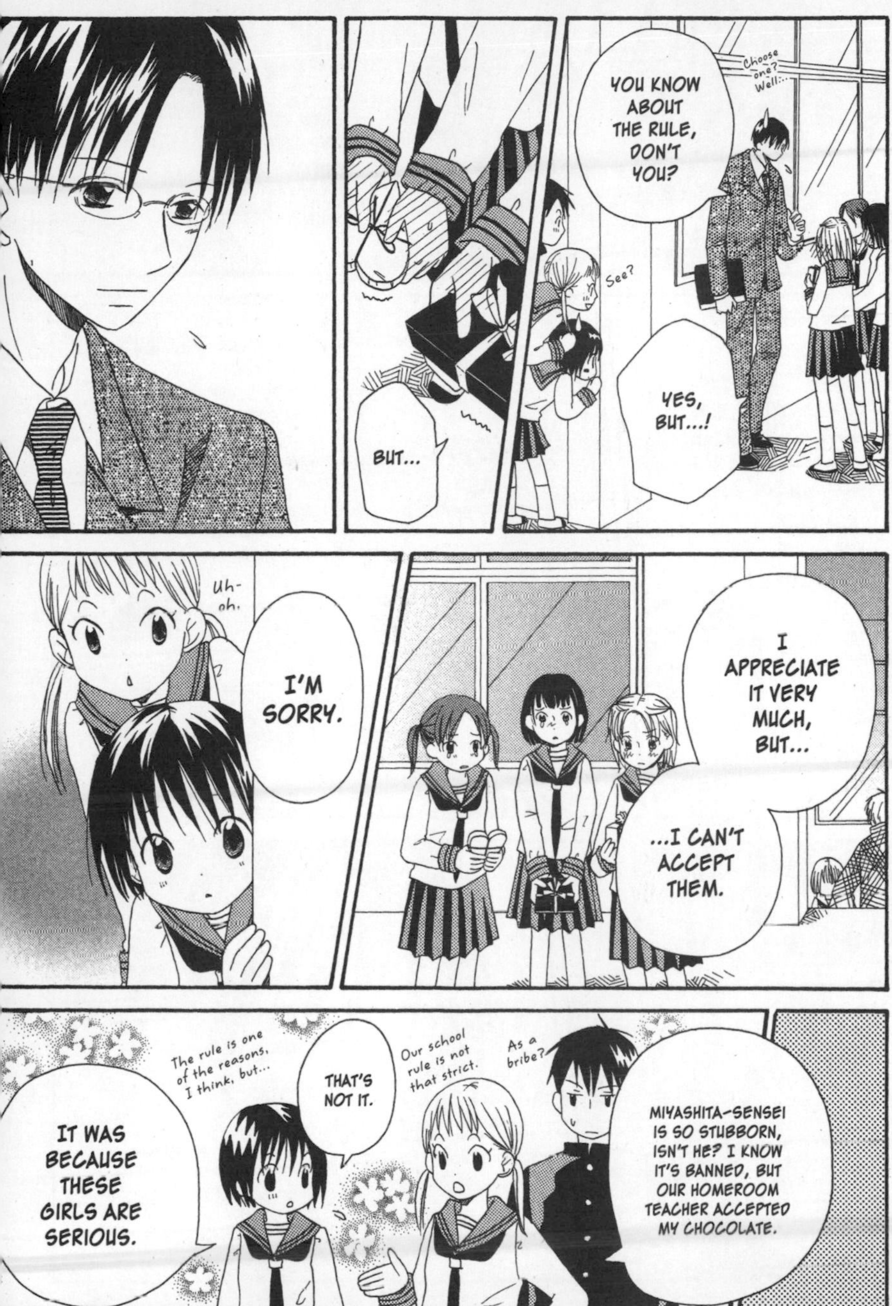
Choose one? Well...
YOU KNOW ABOUT THE RULE, DON'T YOU?
See?
YES, BUT...!
BUT...
I APPRECIATE IT VERY MUCH, BUT...
...I CAN'T ACCEPT THEM.
Uh-oh.
I'M SORRY.
MIYASHITA-SENSEI IS SO STUBBORN, ISN'T HE? I KNOW IT'S BANNED, BUT OUR HOMEROOM TEACHER ACCEPTED MY CHOCOLATE.
As a bribe?
Our school rule is not that strict.
THAT'S NOT IT.
The rule is one of the reasons, I think, but...
IT WAS BECAUSE THESE GIRLS ARE SERIOUS.

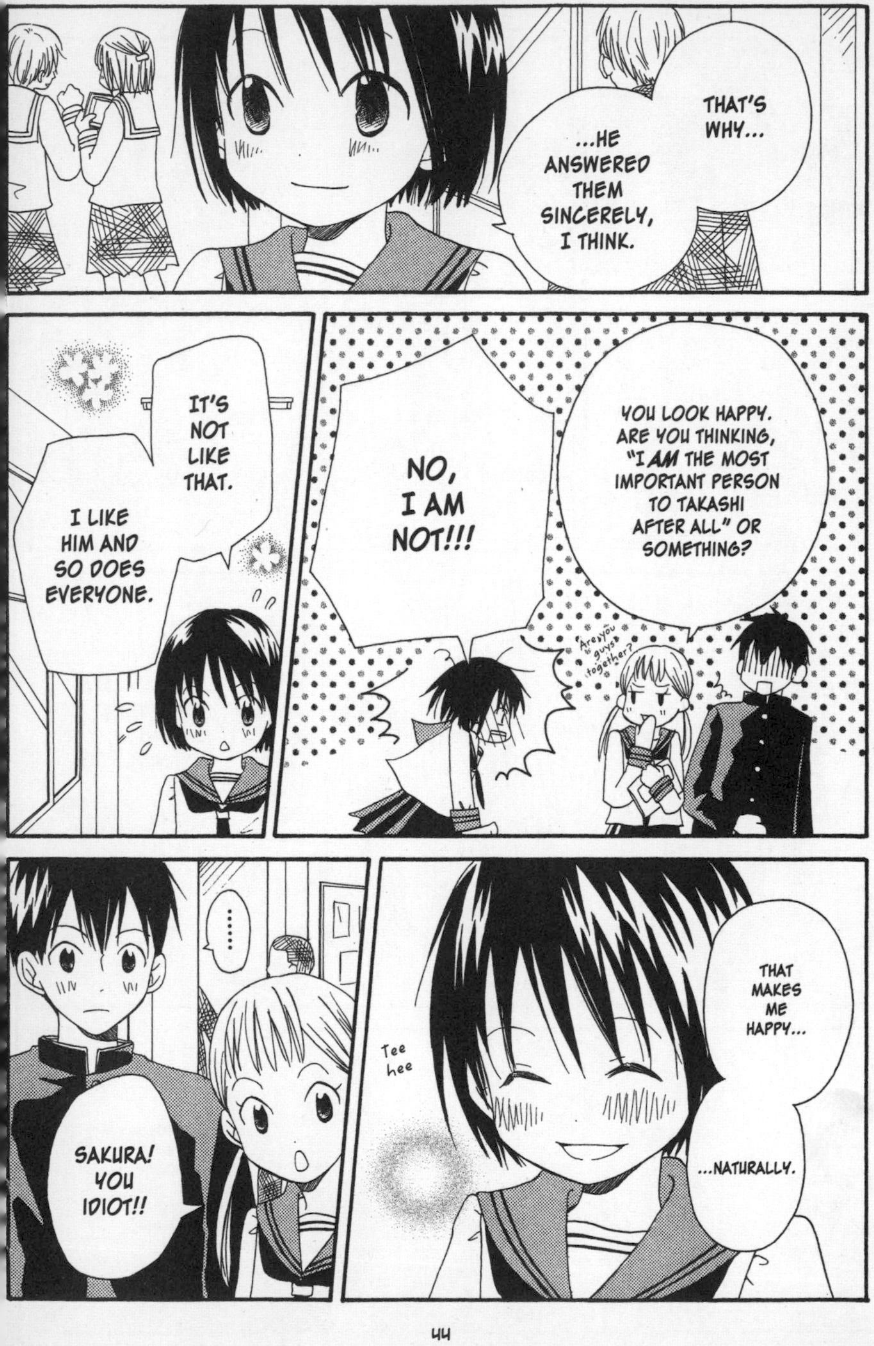
THAT'S WHY...
...HE ANSWERED THEM SINCERELY, I THINK.
YOU LOOK HAPPY. ARE YOU THINKING, "I AM THE MOST IMPORTANT PERSON TO TAKASHI AFTER ALL" OR SOMETHING?
Are you guys together?
NO, I AM NOT!!!
IT'S NOT LIKE THAT.
I LIKE HIM AND SO DOES EVERYONE.
THAT MAKES ME HAPPY...
...NATURALLY.
Tee hee
......
SAKURA! YOU IDIOT!!

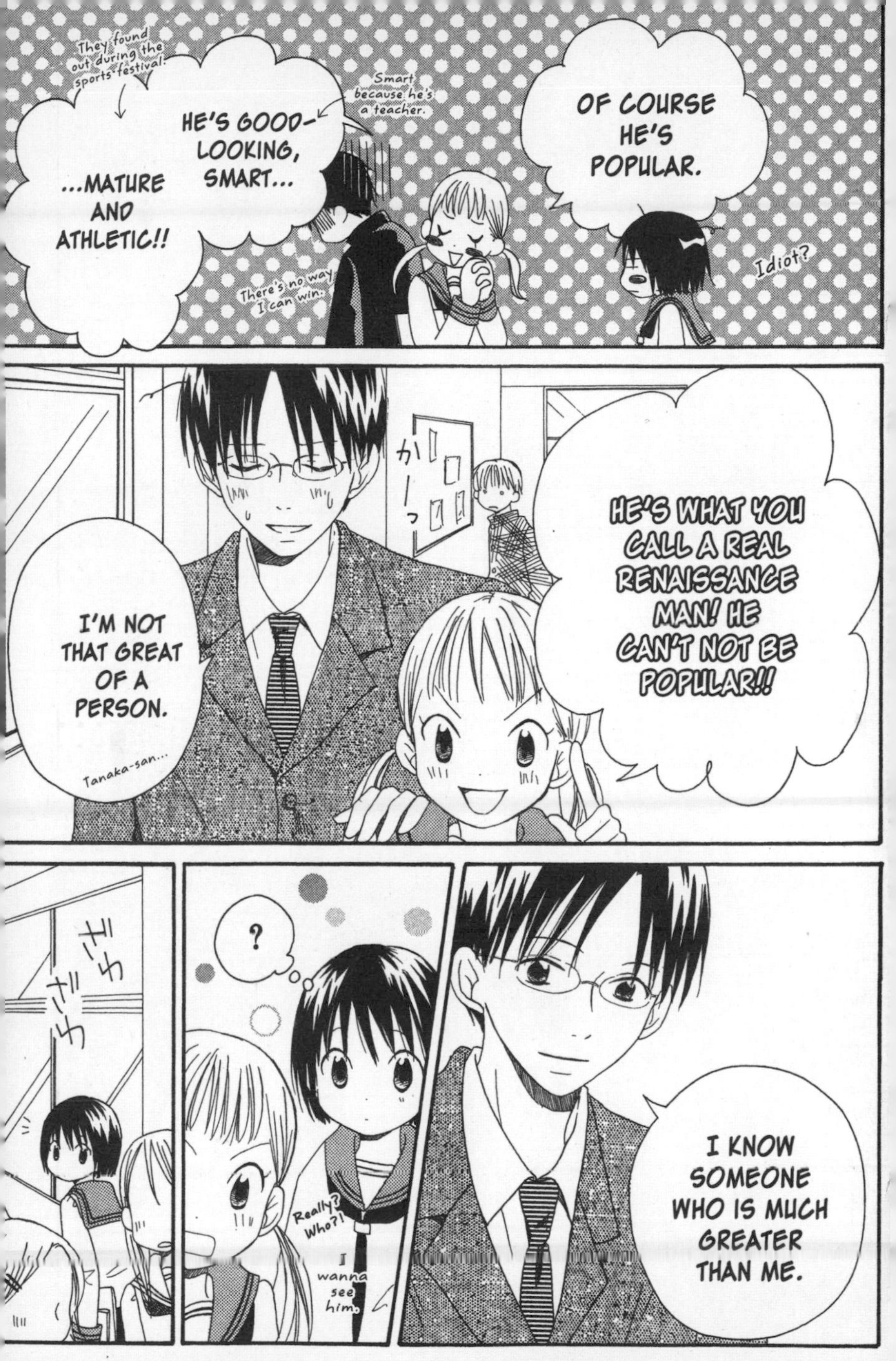
OF COURSE HE'S POPULAR.
Idiot?
Smart, because he's a teacher.
HE'S GOOD-LOOKING, SMART...
They found out during the sports festival.
...MATURE AND ATHLETIC!!
There's no way I can win.
HE'S WHAT YOU CALL A REAL RENAISSANCE MAN! HE CAN'T NOT BE POPULAR!!
I'M NOT THAT GREAT OF A PERSON.
Tanaka-san...
I KNOW SOMEONE WHO IS MUCH GREATER THAN ME.
?
Really? Who?!
I wanna see him.

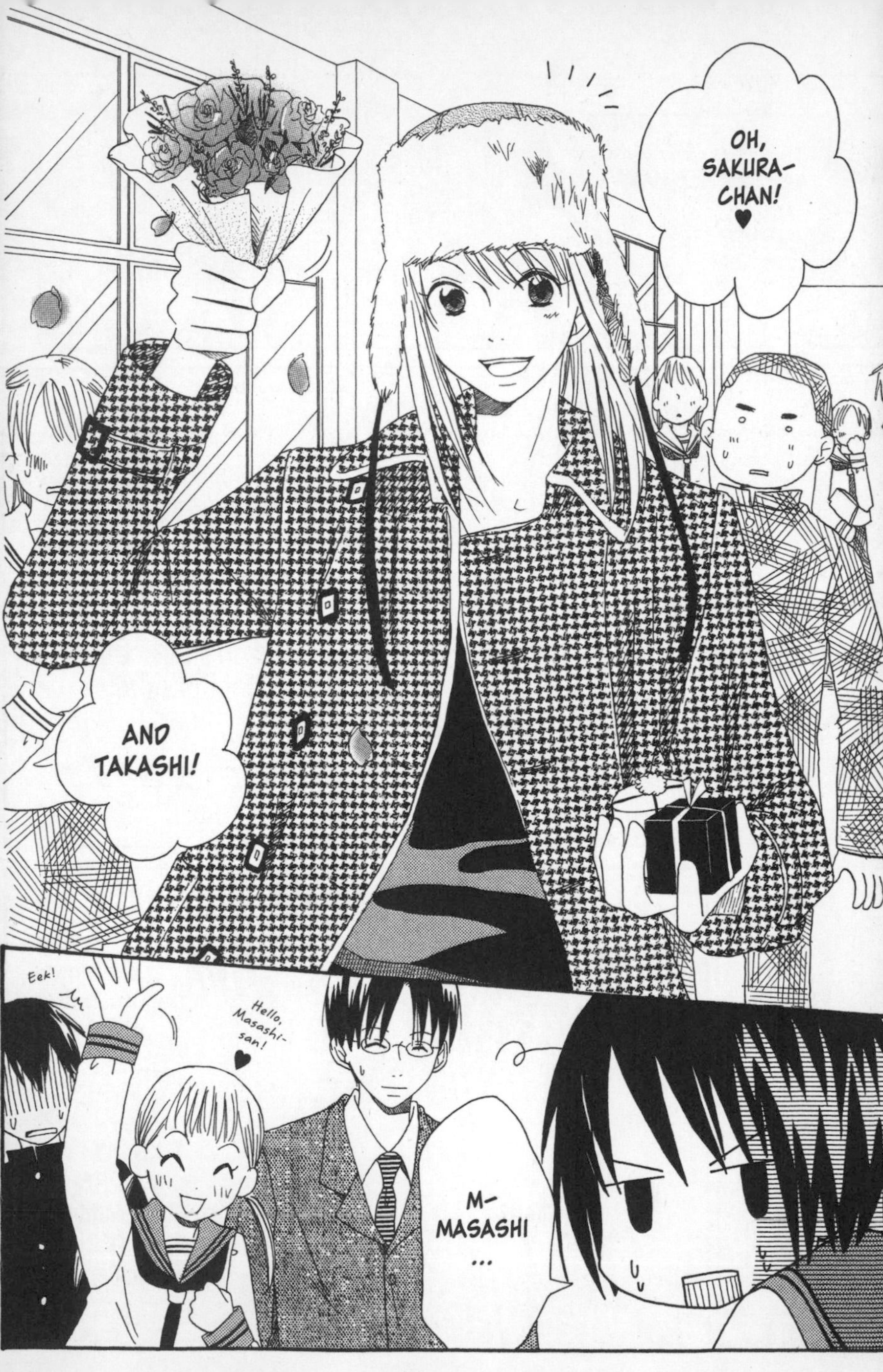
OH, SAKURA-CHAN! ♥
AND TAKASHI!
M-MASASHI...
Hello, Masashi-san! ♥
Eek!

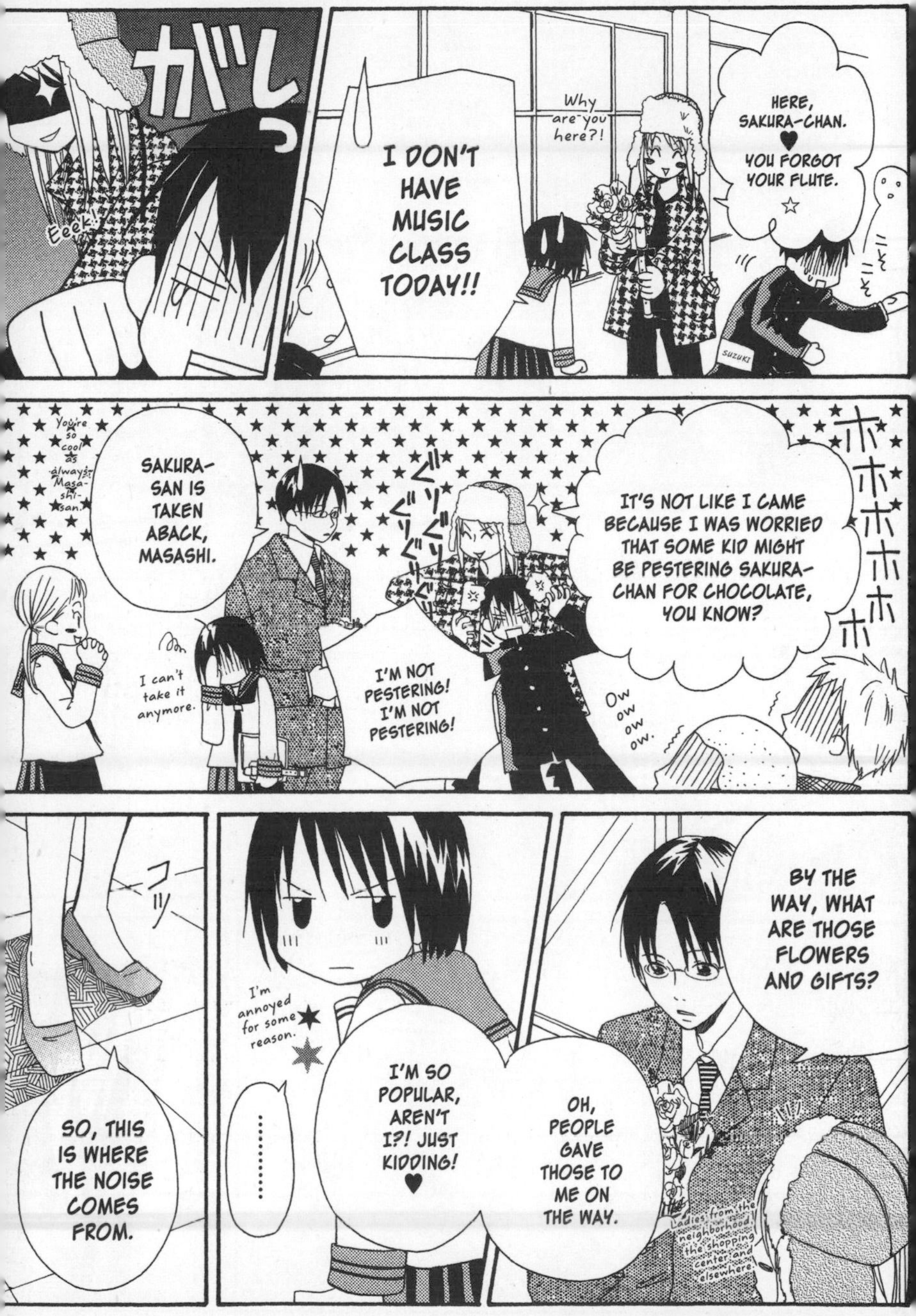
HERE, SAKURA-CHAN. ♥ YOU FORGOT YOUR FLUTE. ☆
こそこそ
SUZUKI
Why are you here?!
I DON'T HAVE MUSIC CLASS TODAY!!
がしっ
Eeek!
IT'S NOT LIKE I CAME BECAUSE I WAS WORRIED THAT SOME KID MIGHT BE PESTERING SAKURA-CHAN FOR CHOCOLATE, YOU KNOW?
ホホホホホホ
Ow ow ow ow.
I'M NOT PESTERING! I'M NOT PESTERING!
ぐりぐりぐりぐり
SAKURA-SAN IS TAKEN ABACK, MASASHI.
You're so cool as always, Masashi-san.
I can't take it anymore.
BY THE WAY, WHAT ARE THOSE FLOWERS AND GIFTS?
OH, PEOPLE GAVE THOSE TO ME ON THE WAY.
Ladies from the neighborhood, the shopping center and elsewhere.
I'M SO POPULAR, AREN'T I?! JUST KIDDING! ♥
I'm annoyed for some reason.
....
コツ
SO, THIS IS WHERE THE NOISE COMES FROM.

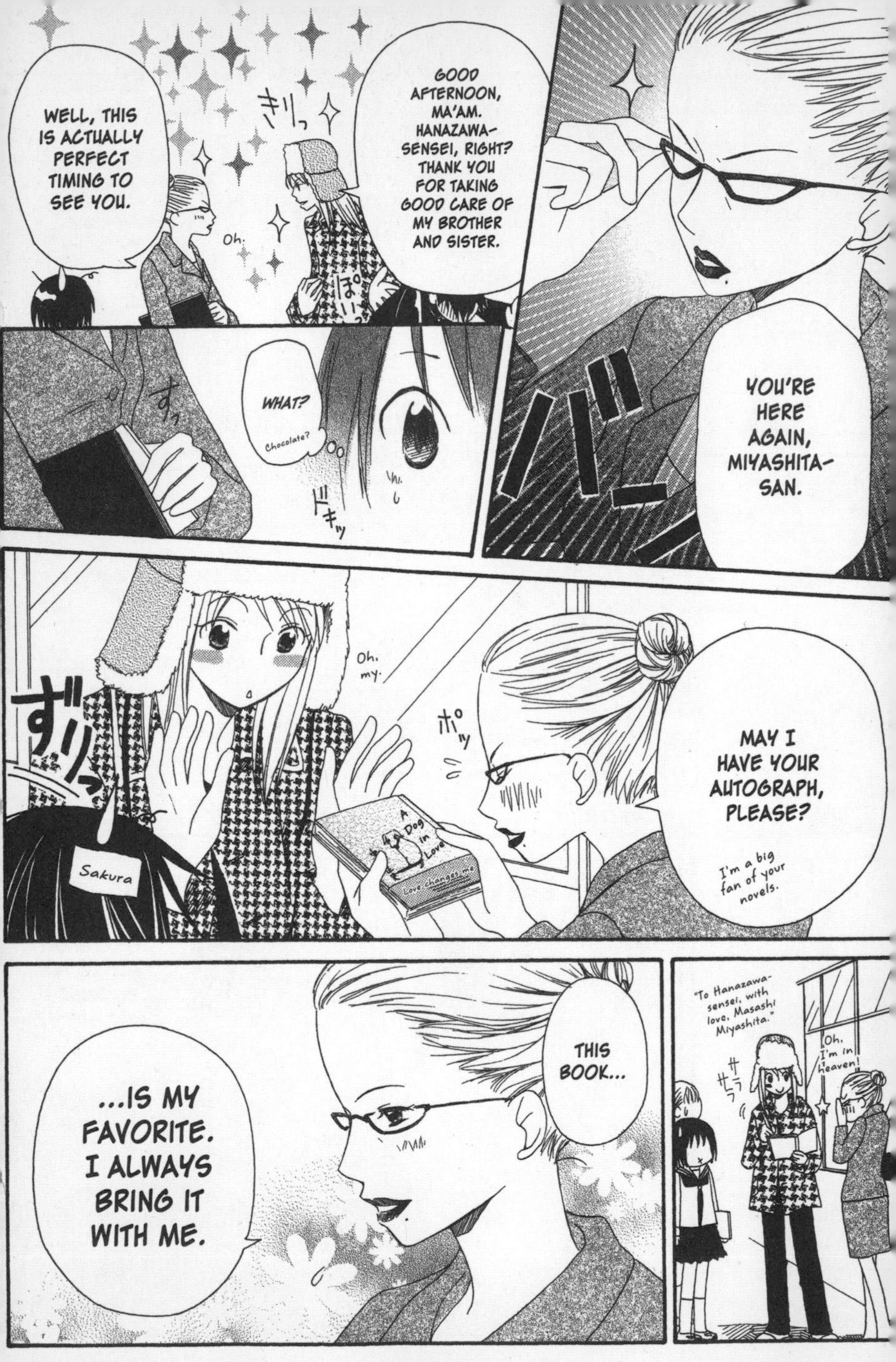
YOU'RE HERE AGAIN, MIYASHITA-SAN.
GOOD AFTERNOON, MA'AM. HANAZAWA-SENSEI, RIGHT? THANK YOU FOR TAKING GOOD CARE OF MY BROTHER AND SISTER.
きりっ
Oh.
WELL, THIS IS ACTUALLY PERFECT TIMING TO SEE YOU.
WHAT?
Chocolate?
ドキッ
MAY I HAVE YOUR AUTOGRAPH, PLEASE?
I'm a big fan of your novels.
ポッ
A Dog in Love
Love changes me
Oh, my.
ずりっ
Sakura
"To Hanazawa-sensei, with love, Masashi Miyashita."
Oh, I'm in heaven!
THIS BOOK...
...IS MY FAVORITE. I ALWAYS BRING IT WITH ME.

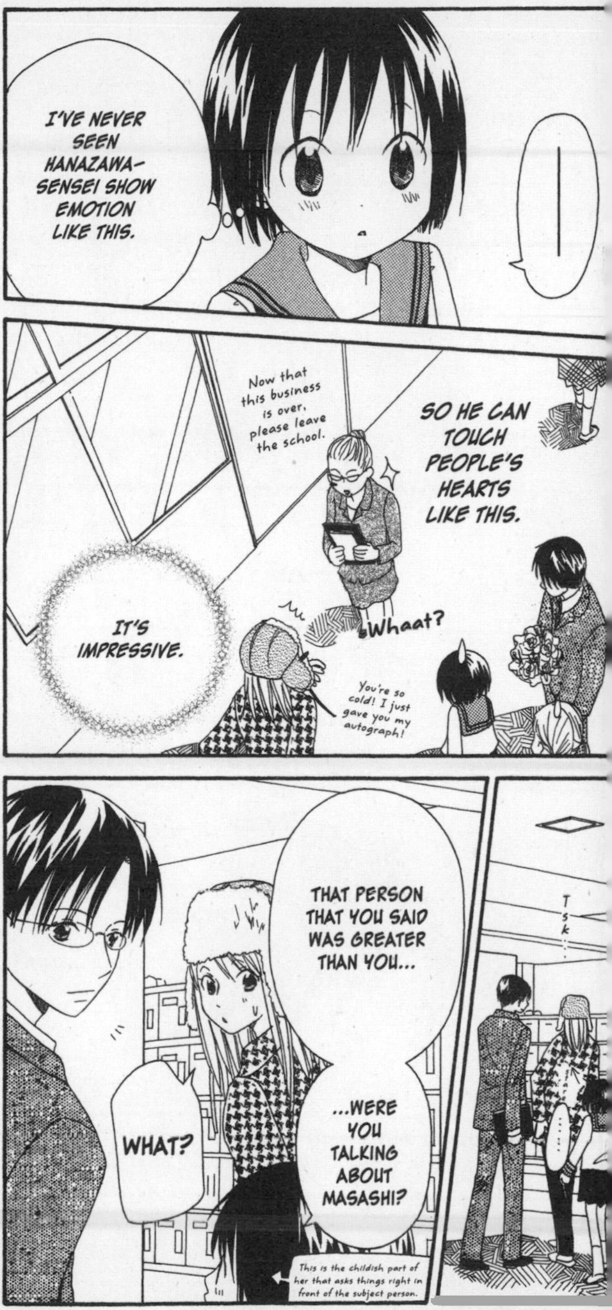
—
I'VE NEVER SEEN HANAZAWA-SENSEI SHOW EMOTION LIKE THIS.
SO HE CAN TOUCH PEOPLE'S HEARTS LIKE THIS.
Now that this business is over, please leave the school.
Whaat?
You're so cold! I just gave you my autograph!
IT'S IMPRESSIVE.
Tsk...
......
THAT PERSON THAT YOU SAID WAS GREATER THAN YOU...
...WERE YOU TALKING ABOUT MASASHI?
WHAT?
This is the childish part of her that asks things right in front of the subject person.

☆ 2 ☆

I wrote the characters' profiles between the episodes. There are two people missing, though. You can find out their birthdays in the story, but everyone was born in winter or spring. Well, that can happen.

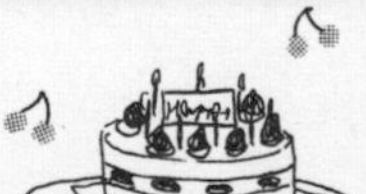

The years the brothers were born had already been decided (because I happened to add it to their date of birth before). I felt close to them because they are about my age.

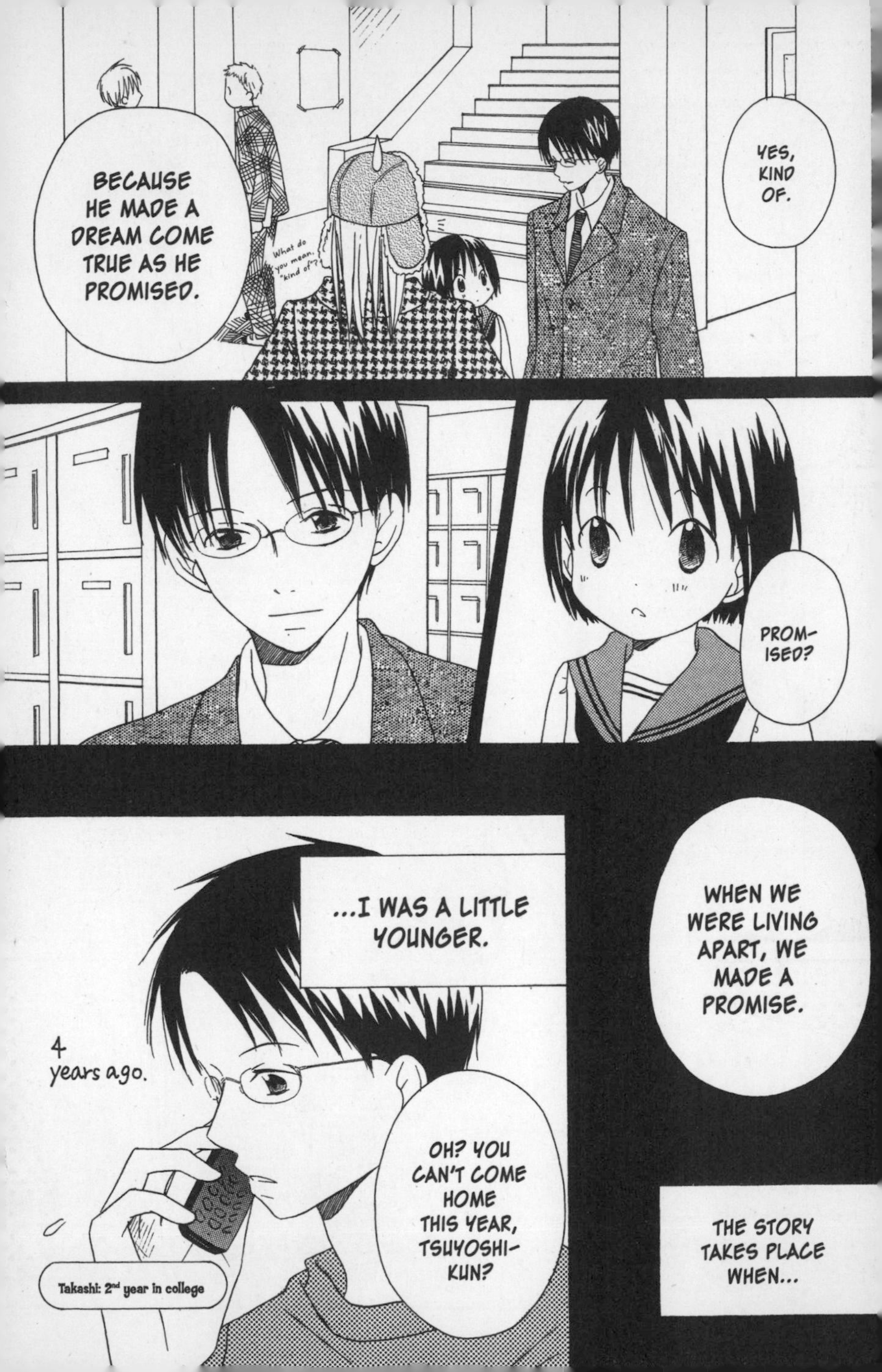
YES, KIND OF.
What do you mean, "kind of"?
BECAUSE HE MADE A DREAM COME TRUE AS HE PROMISED.
PROM-ISED?
WHEN WE WERE LIVING APART, WE MADE A PROMISE.
THE STORY TAKES PLACE WHEN...
...I WAS A LITTLE YOUNGER.
4 years ago.
OH? YOU CAN'T COME HOME THIS YEAR, TSUYOSHI-KUN?
Takashi: 2nd year in college

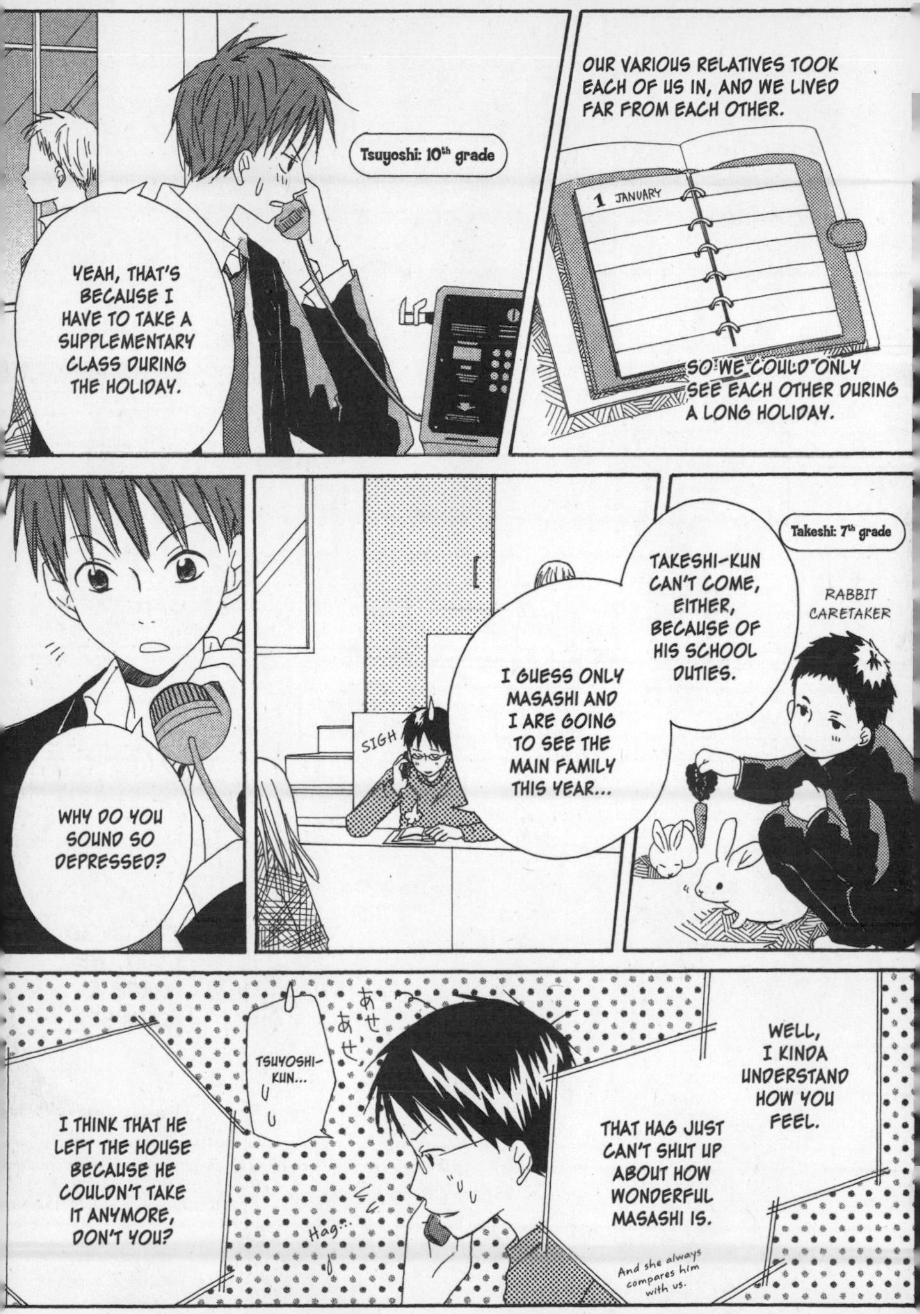
OUR VARIOUS RELATIVES TOOK EACH OF US IN, AND WE LIVED FAR FROM EACH OTHER.
1 JANUARY
SO WE COULD ONLY SEE EACH OTHER DURING A LONG HOLIDAY.
Tsuyoshi: 10th grade
YEAH, THAT'S BECAUSE I HAVE TO TAKE A SUPPLEMENTARY CLASS DURING THE HOLIDAY.
Takeshi: 7th grade
TAKESHI-KUN CAN'T COME, EITHER, BECAUSE OF HIS SCHOOL DUTIES.
RABBIT CARETAKER
I GUESS ONLY MASASHI AND I ARE GOING TO SEE THE MAIN FAMILY THIS YEAR...
SIGH
WHY DO YOU SOUND SO DEPRESSED?
WELL, I KINDA UNDERSTAND HOW YOU FEEL.
THAT HAG JUST CAN'T SHUT UP ABOUT HOW WONDERFUL MASASHI IS.
And she always compares him with us.
Hag...
あせ あせ
TSUYOSHI-KUN...
I THINK THAT HE LEFT THE HOUSE BECAUSE HE COULDN'T TAKE IT ANYMORE, DON'T YOU?

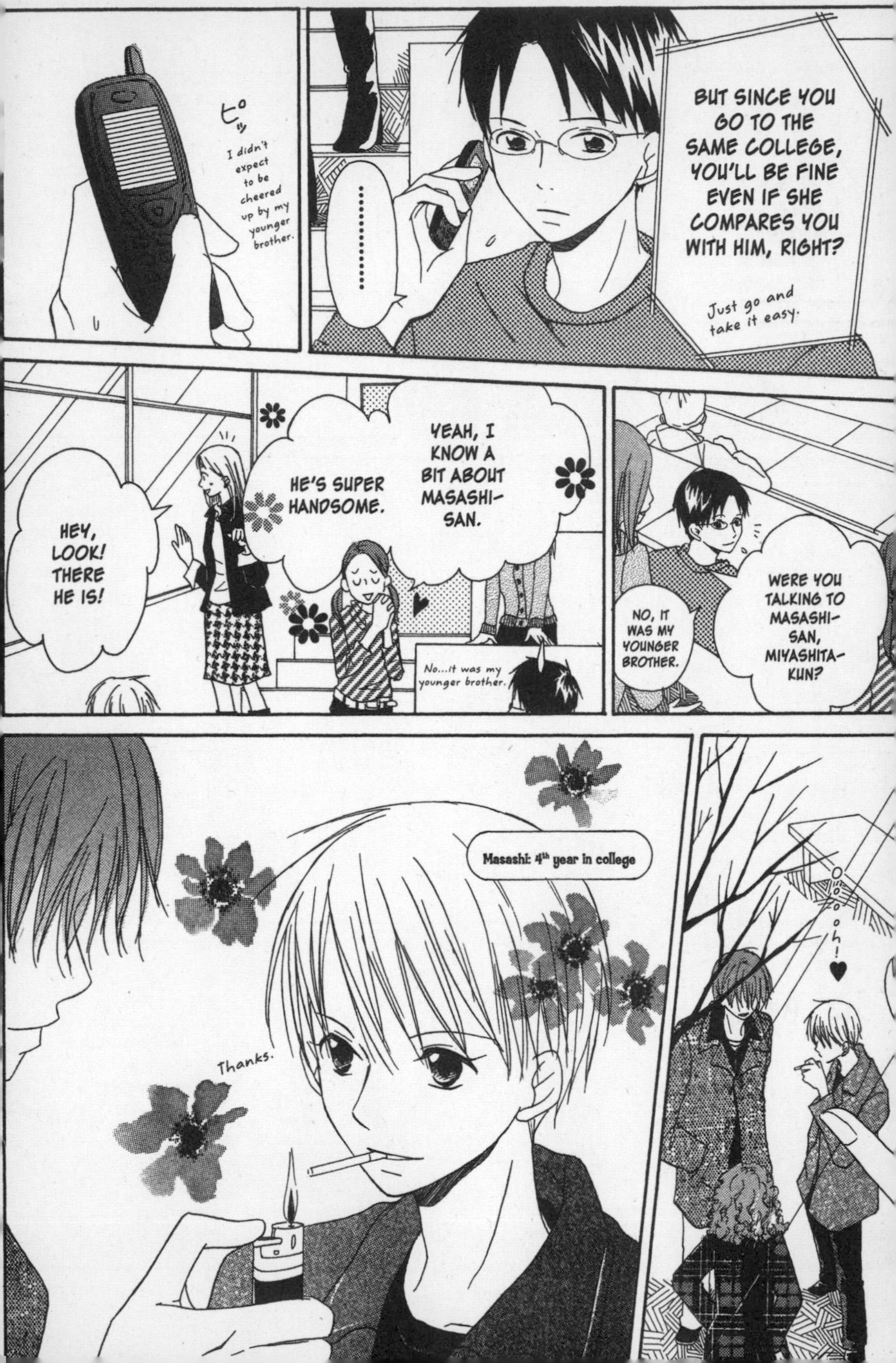
BUT SINCE YOU GO TO THE SAME COLLEGE, YOU'LL BE FINE EVEN IF SHE COMPARES YOU WITH HIM, RIGHT?
Just go and take it easy.
……
ピッ
I didn't expect to be cheered up by my younger brother.
WERE YOU TALKING TO MASASHI-SAN, MIYASHITA-KUN?
NO, IT WAS MY YOUNGER BROTHER.
YEAH, I KNOW A BIT ABOUT MASASHI-SAN.
HE'S SUPER HANDSOME.
No...it was my younger brother.
HEY, LOOK! THERE HE IS!
Ooooh!
Masashi: 4th year in college
Thanks.

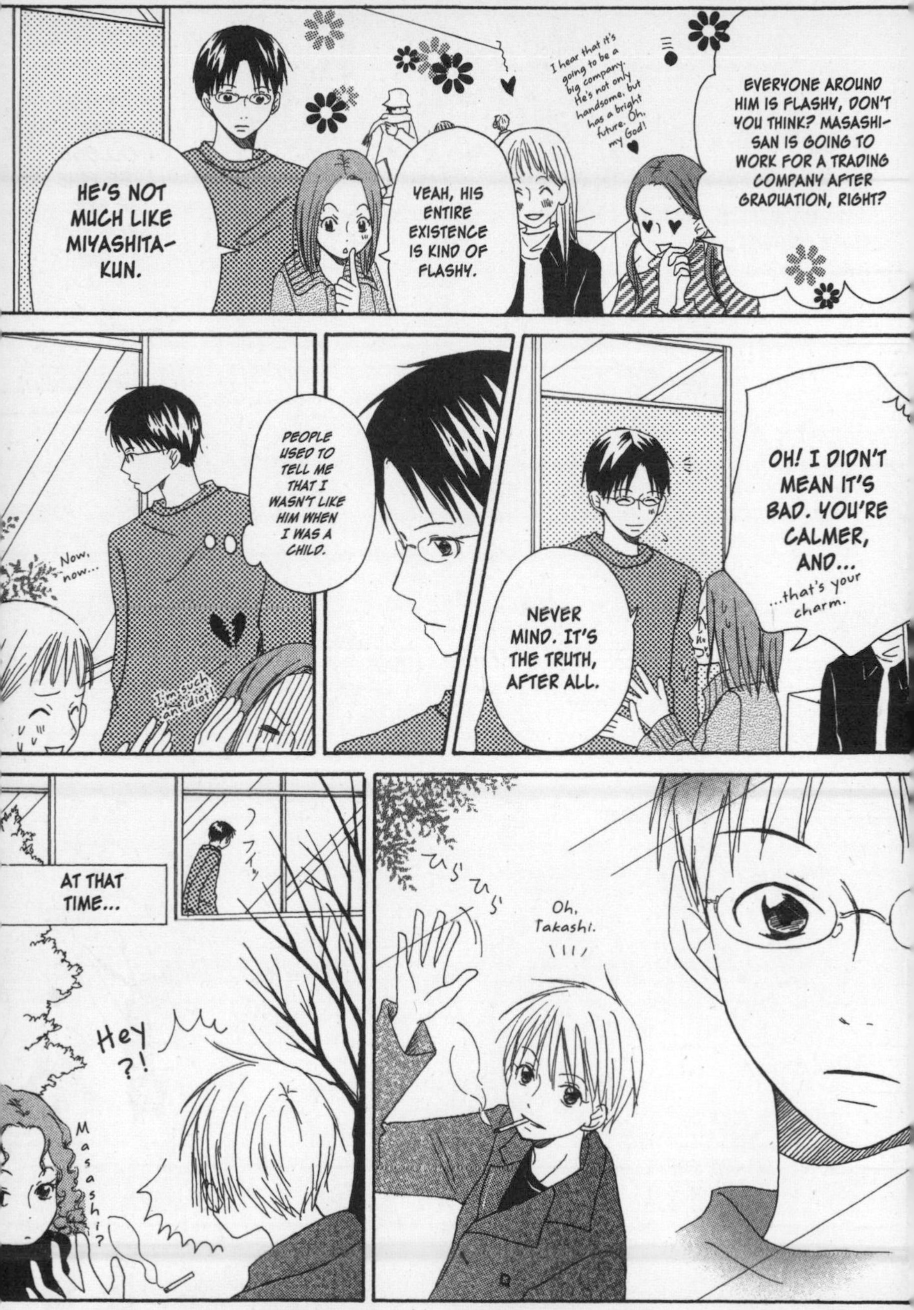
EVERYONE AROUND HIM IS FLASHY, DON'T YOU THINK? MASASHI-SAN IS GOING TO WORK FOR A TRADING COMPANY AFTER GRADUATION, RIGHT?
I hear that it's going to be a big company. He's not only handsome, but has a bright future. Oh, my God!
YEAH, HIS ENTIRE EXISTENCE IS KIND OF FLASHY.
HE'S NOT MUCH LIKE MIYASHITA-KUN.
OH! I DIDN'T MEAN IT'S BAD. YOU'RE CALMER, AND...
...that's your charm.
NEVER MIND. IT'S THE TRUTH, AFTER ALL.
PEOPLE USED TO TELL ME THAT I WASN'T LIKE HIM WHEN I WAS A CHILD.
Now, now...
I'm such an idiot!
ひらひら
Oh, Takashi.
AT THAT TIME...
フイッ
Hey?!
Masashi?

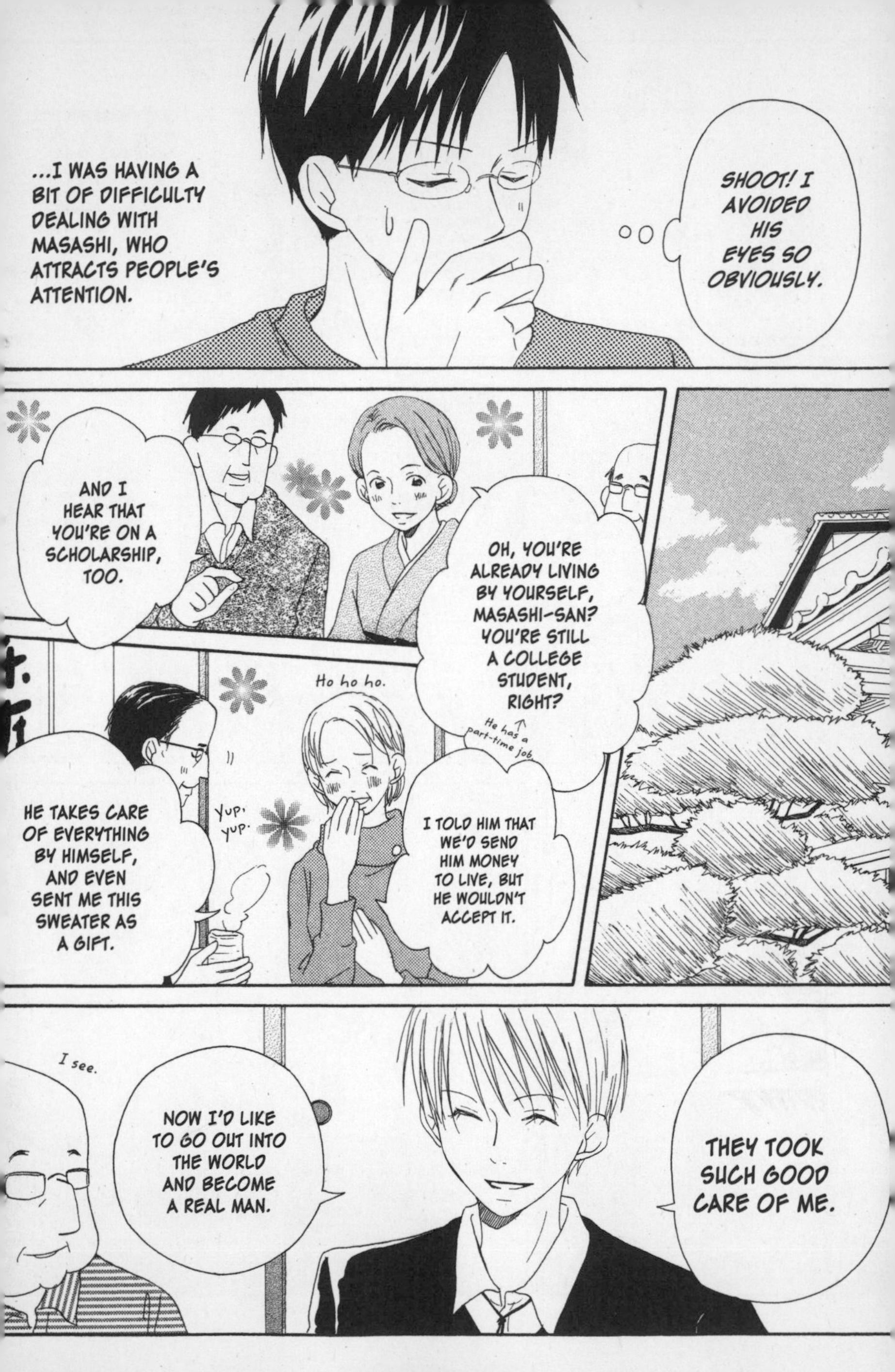
SHOOT! I AVOIDED HIS EYES SO OBVIOUSLY.
...I WAS HAVING A BIT OF DIFFICULTY DEALING WITH MASASHI, WHO ATTRACTS PEOPLE'S ATTENTION.
OH, YOU'RE ALREADY LIVING BY YOURSELF, MASASHI-SAN? YOU'RE STILL A COLLEGE STUDENT, RIGHT?
AND I HEAR THAT YOU'RE ON A SCHOLARSHIP, TOO.
He has a part-time job.
I TOLD HIM THAT WE'D SEND HIM MONEY TO LIVE, BUT HE WOULDN'T ACCEPT IT.
Ho ho ho.
Yup, yup.
HE TAKES CARE OF EVERYTHING BY HIMSELF, AND EVEN SENT ME THIS SWEATER AS A GIFT.
THEY TOOK SUCH GOOD CARE OF ME.
NOW I'D LIKE TO GO OUT INTO THE WORLD AND BECOME A REAL MAN.
I see.

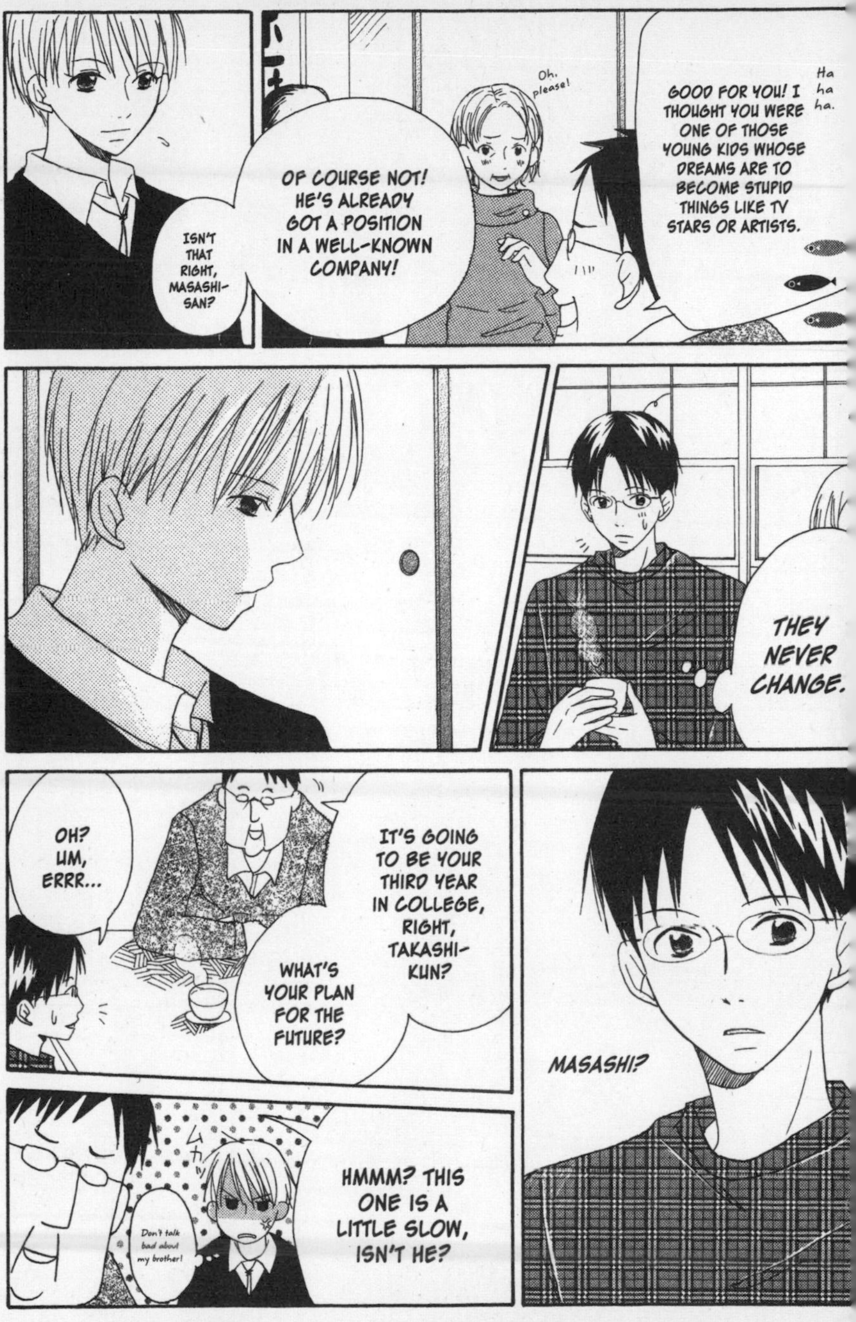
GOOD FOR YOU! I THOUGHT YOU WERE ONE OF THOSE YOUNG KIDS WHOSE DREAMS ARE TO BECOME STUPID THINGS LIKE TV STARS OR ARTISTS.
Ha ha ha.
Oh, please!
OF COURSE NOT! HE'S ALREADY GOT A POSITION IN A WELL-KNOWN COMPANY!
ISN'T THAT RIGHT, MASASHI-SAN?
THEY NEVER CHANGE.
MASASHI?
IT'S GOING TO BE YOUR THIRD YEAR IN COLLEGE, RIGHT, TAKASHI-KUN?
WHAT'S YOUR PLAN FOR THE FUTURE?
OH? UM, ERRR...
HMMM? THIS ONE IS A LITTLE SLOW, ISN'T HE?
Don't talk bad about my brother!

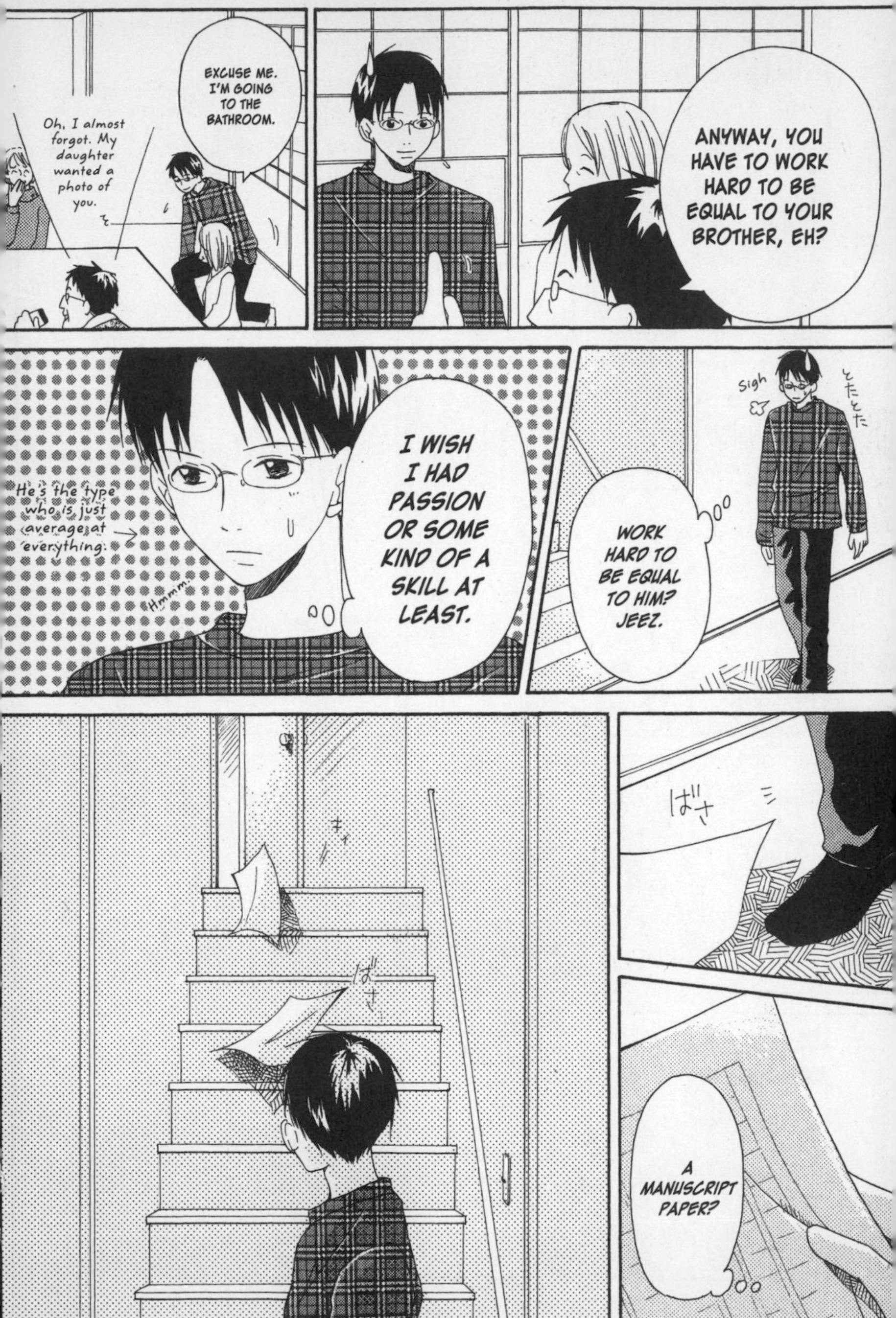
ANYWAY, YOU HAVE TO WORK HARD TO BE EQUAL TO YOUR BROTHER, EH?
EXCUSE ME. I'M GOING TO THE BATHROOM.
Oh, I almost forgot. My daughter wanted a photo of you.
Sigh
とたとた
WORK HARD TO BE EQUAL TO HIM? JEEZ.
I WISH I HAD PASSION OR SOME KIND OF A SKILL AT LEAST.
He's the type who is just average at everything.
Hmmm.
ばさ
A MANUSCRIPT PAPER?
ばさ

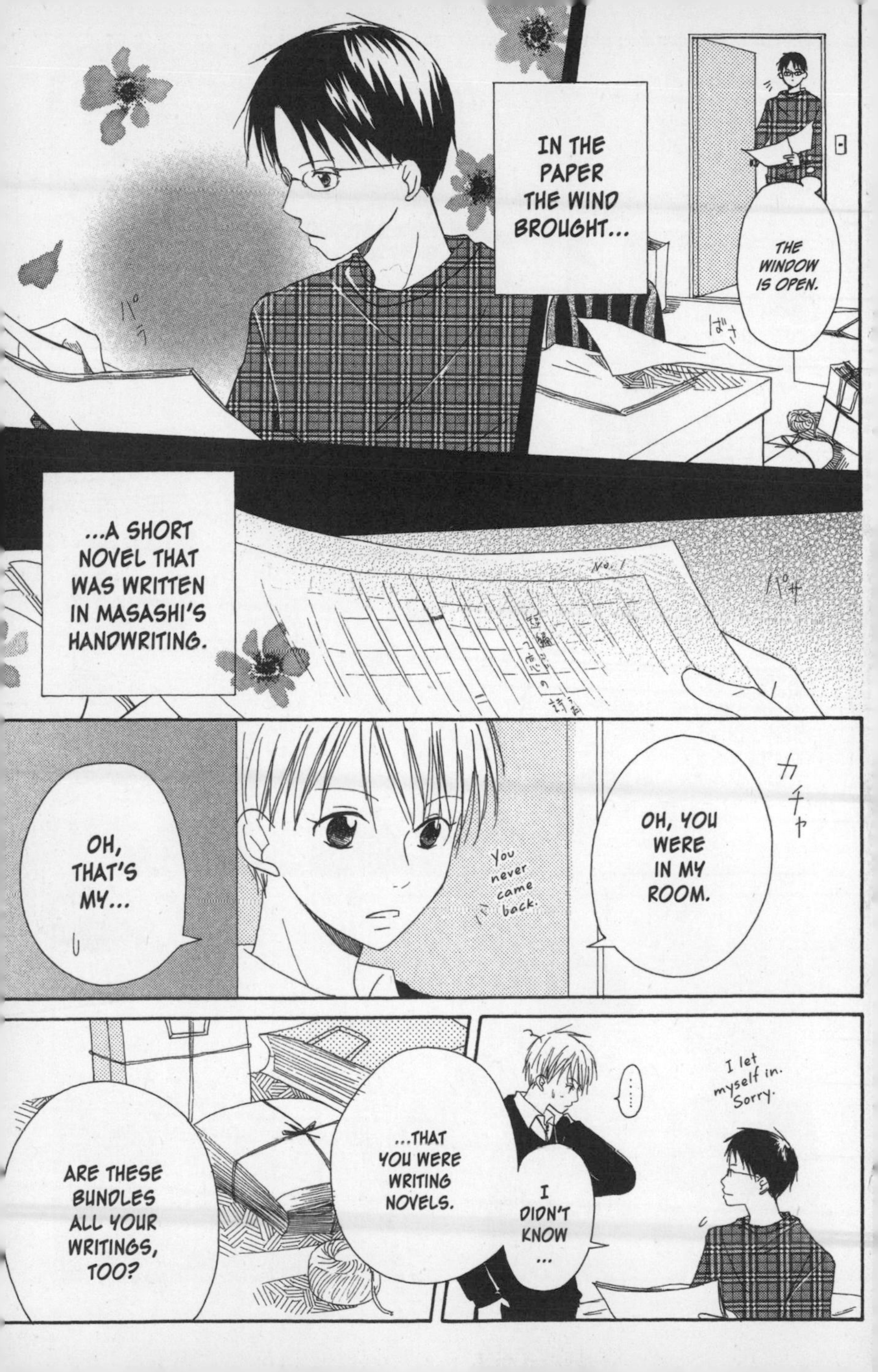
THE WINDOW IS OPEN.
ばさ
IN THE PAPER THE WIND BROUGHT...
パラ
パサ
No. 1
...A SHORT NOVEL THAT WAS WRITTEN IN MASASHI'S HANDWRITING.
カチャ
OH, YOU WERE IN MY ROOM.
You never came back.
OH, THAT'S MY...
I let myself in. Sorry.
......
I DIDN'T KNOW...
...THAT YOU WERE WRITING NOVELS.
ARE THESE BUNDLES ALL YOUR WRITINGS, TOO?

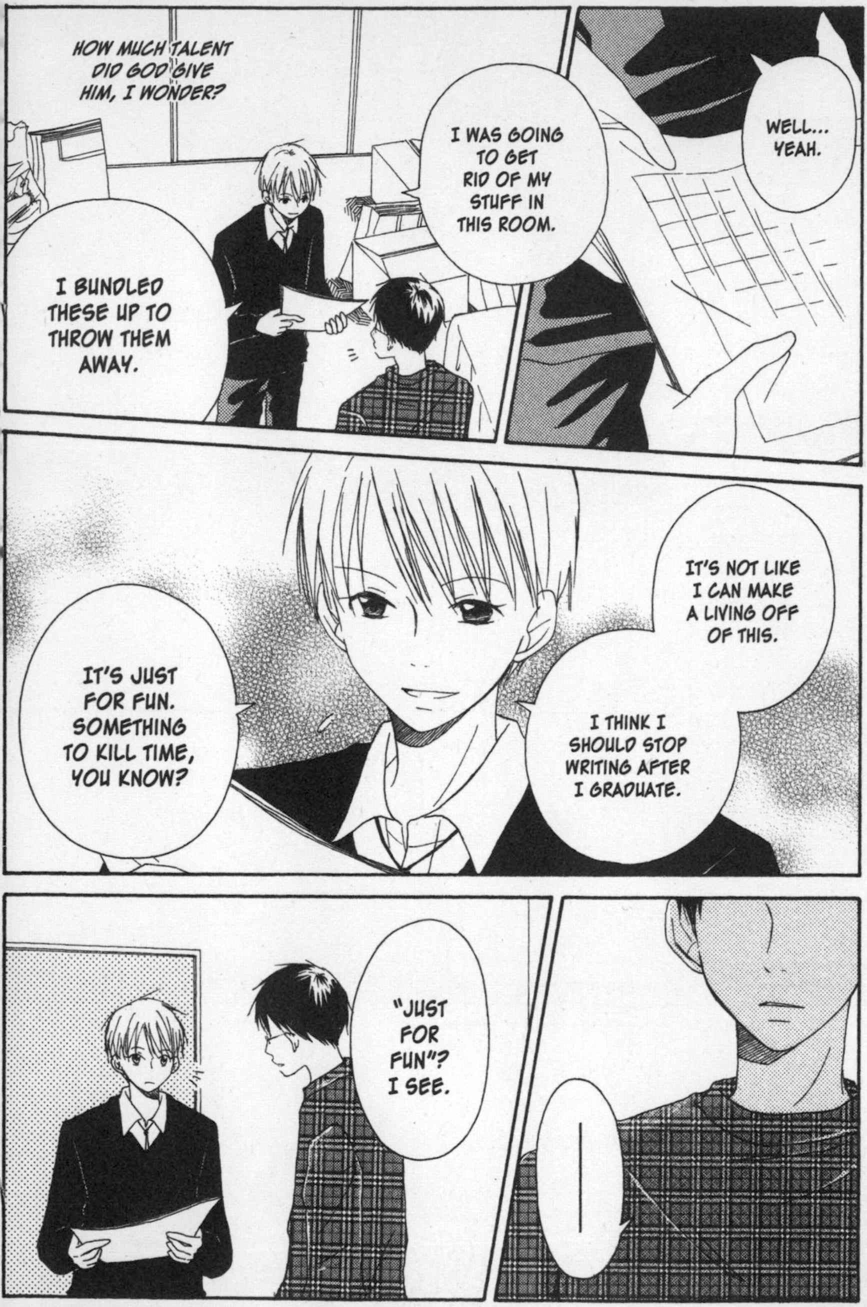
WELL... YEAH.
HOW MUCH TALENT DID GOD GIVE HIM, I WONDER?
I WAS GOING TO GET RID OF MY STUFF IN THIS ROOM.
I BUNDLED THESE UP TO THROW THEM AWAY.
IT'S NOT LIKE I CAN MAKE A LIVING OFF OF THIS.
I THINK I SHOULD STOP WRITING AFTER I GRADUATE.
IT'S JUST FOR FUN. SOMETHING TO KILL TIME, YOU KNOW?
—
"JUST FOR FUN"? I SEE.

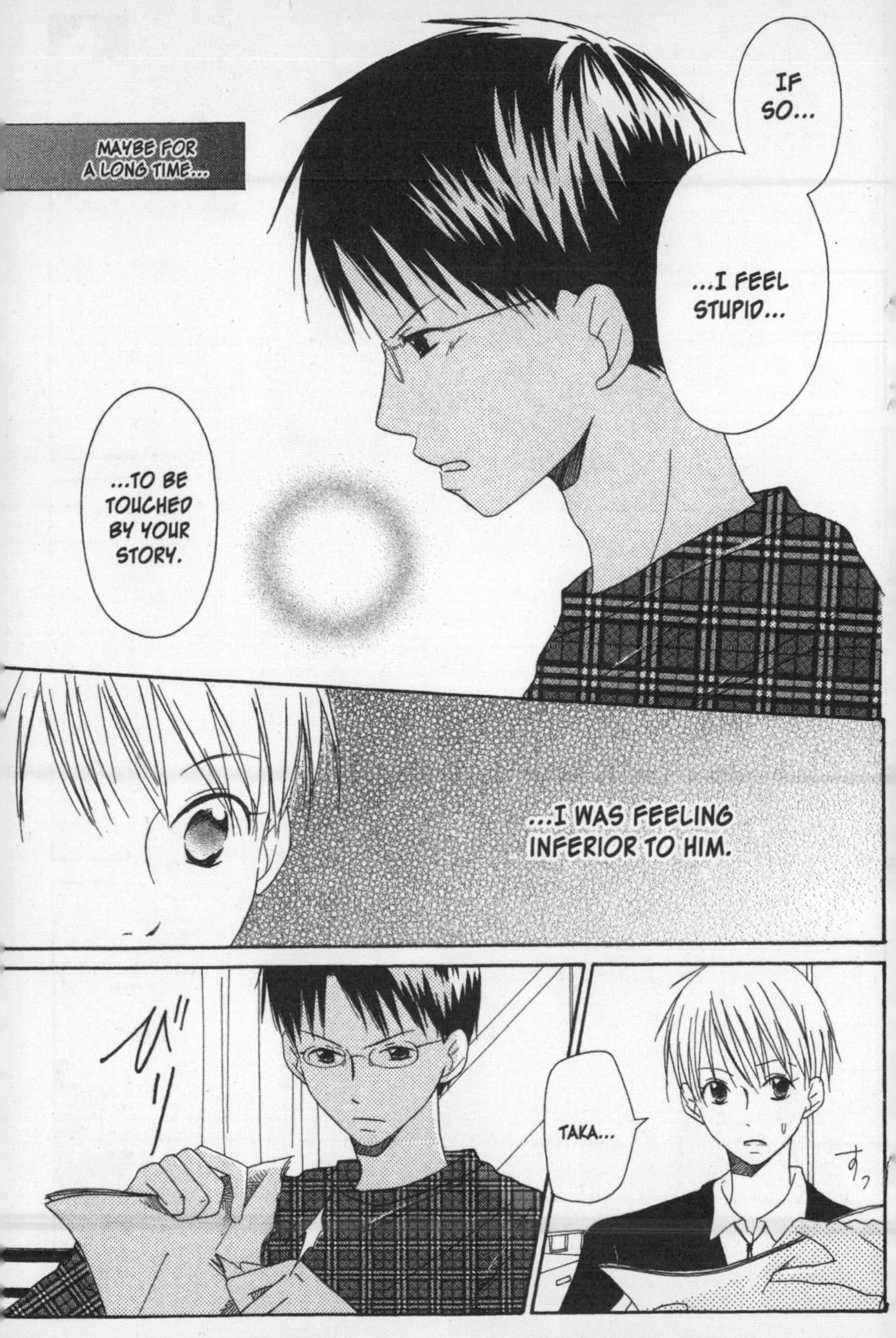
IF SO...
...I FEEL STUPID...
...TO BE TOUCHED BY YOUR STORY.
MAYBE FOR A LONG TIME...
...I WAS FEELING INFERIOR TO HIM.
TAKA...
すっ

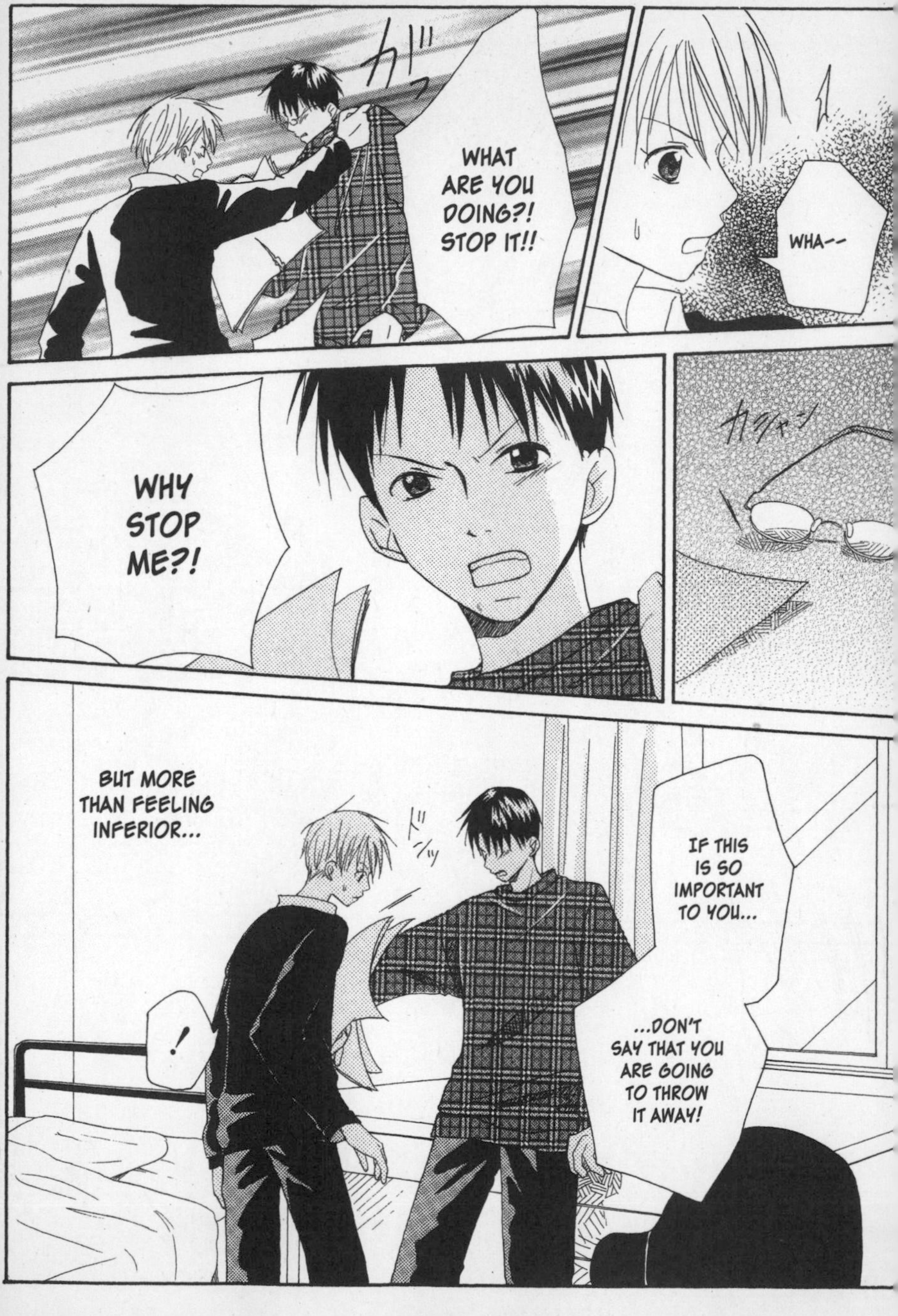
WHA--
ガッ
WHAT ARE YOU DOING?! STOP IT!!
カシャン
WHY STOP ME?!
IF THIS IS SO IMPORTANT TO YOU...
...DON'T SAY THAT YOU ARE GOING TO THROW IT AWAY!
BUT MORE THAN FEELING INFERIOR...
ドシッ
!

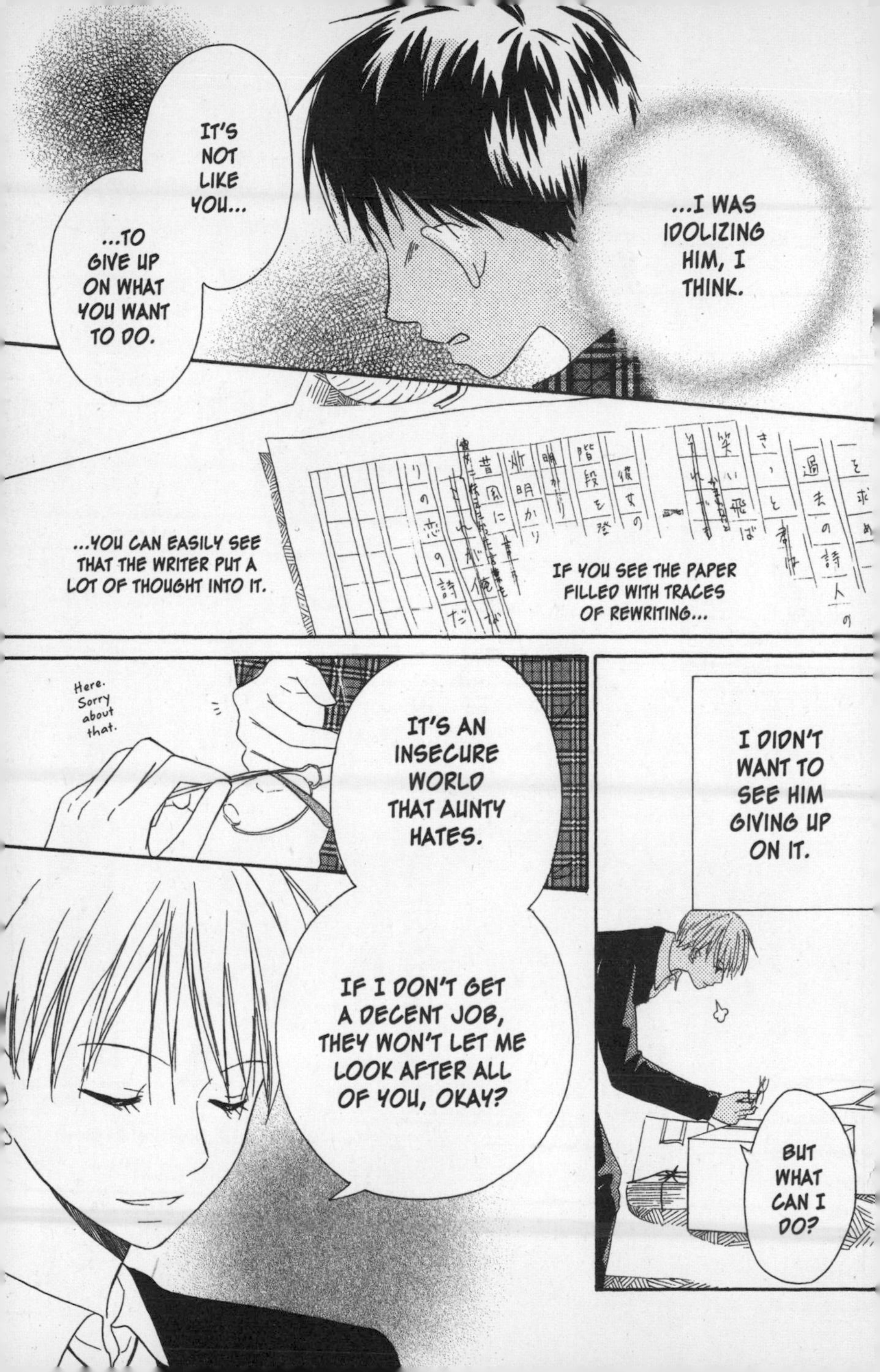
...I WAS IDOLIZING HIM, I THINK.
IT'S NOT LIKE YOU...
...TO GIVE UP ON WHAT YOU WANT TO DO.
IF YOU SEE THE PAPER FILLED WITH TRACES OF REWRITING...
...YOU CAN EASILY SEE THAT THE WRITER PUT A LOT OF THOUGHT INTO IT.
I DIDN'T WANT TO SEE HIM GIVING UP ON IT.
BUT WHAT CAN I DO?
IT'S AN INSECURE WORLD THAT AUNTY HATES.
Here. Sorry about that.
IF I DON'T GET A DECENT JOB, THEY WON'T LET ME LOOK AFTER ALL OF YOU, OKAY?

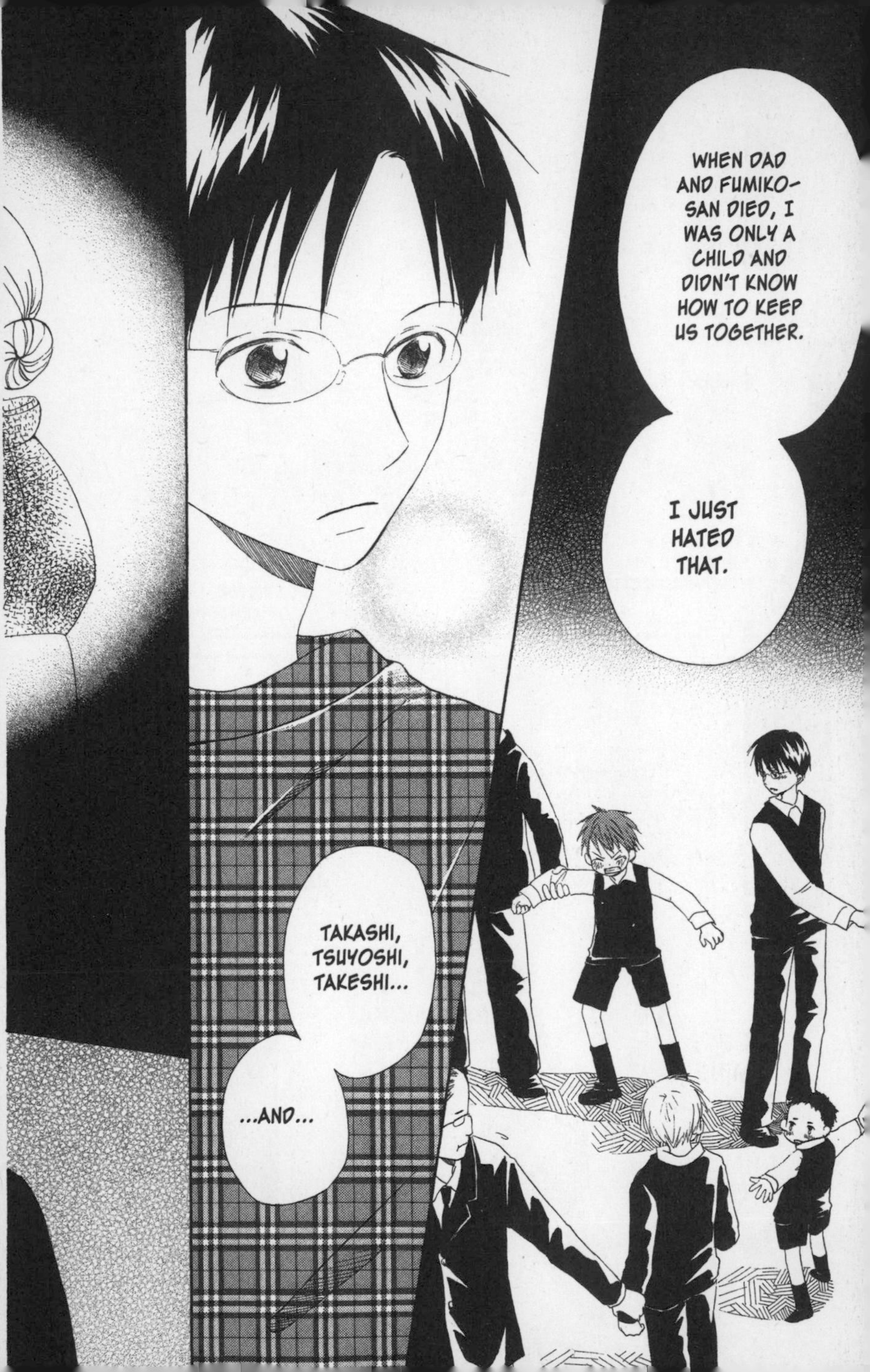
WHEN DAD AND FUMIKO-SAN DIED, I WAS ONLY A CHILD AND DIDN'T KNOW HOW TO KEEP US TOGETHER.
I JUST HATED THAT.
TAKASHI, TSUYOSHI, TAKESHI...
...AND...

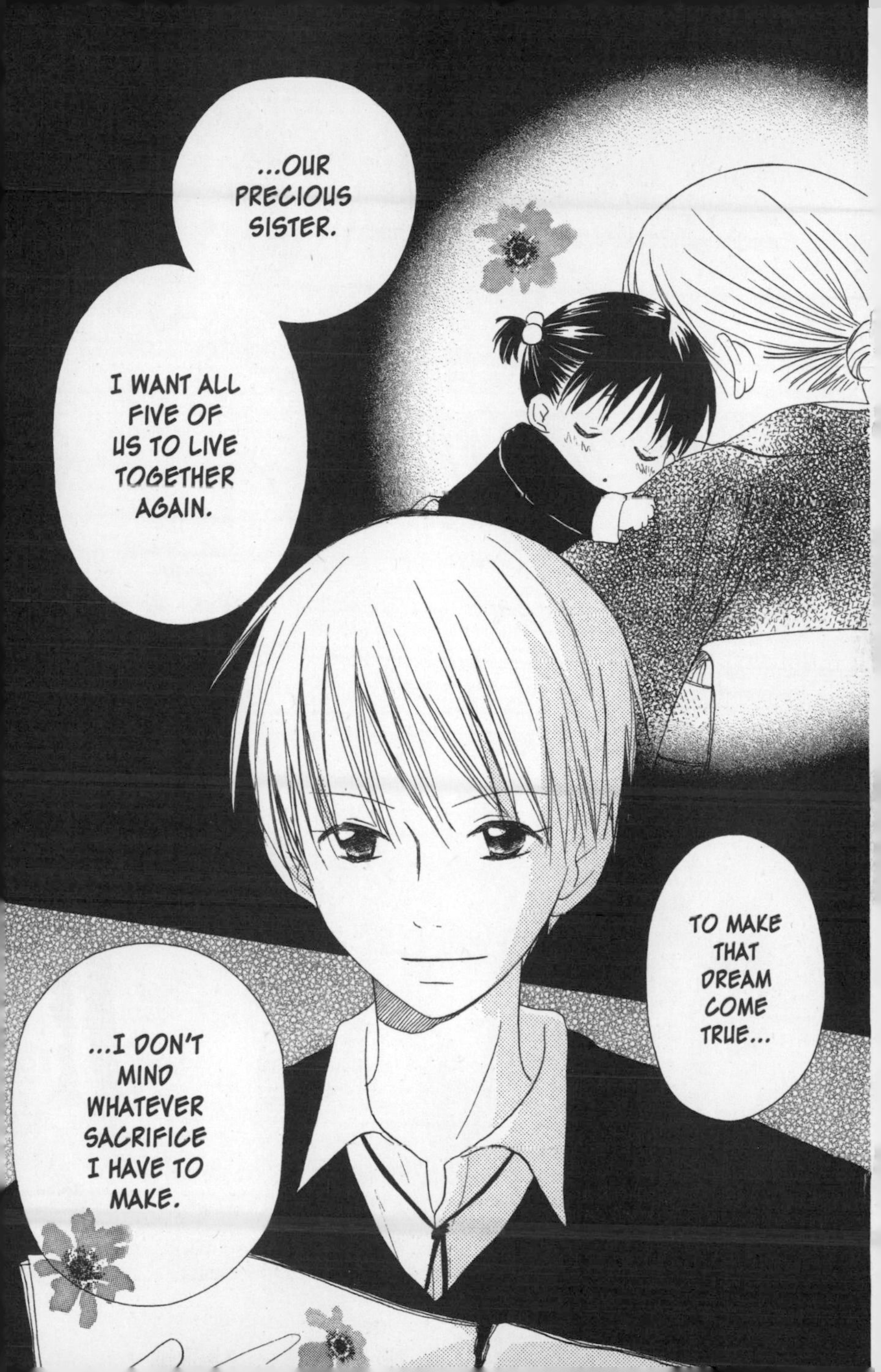
...OUR PRECIOUS SISTER.
I WANT ALL FIVE OF US TO LIVE TOGETHER AGAIN.
TO MAKE THAT DREAM COME TRUE...
...I DON'T MIND WHATEVER SACRIFICE I HAVE TO MAKE.

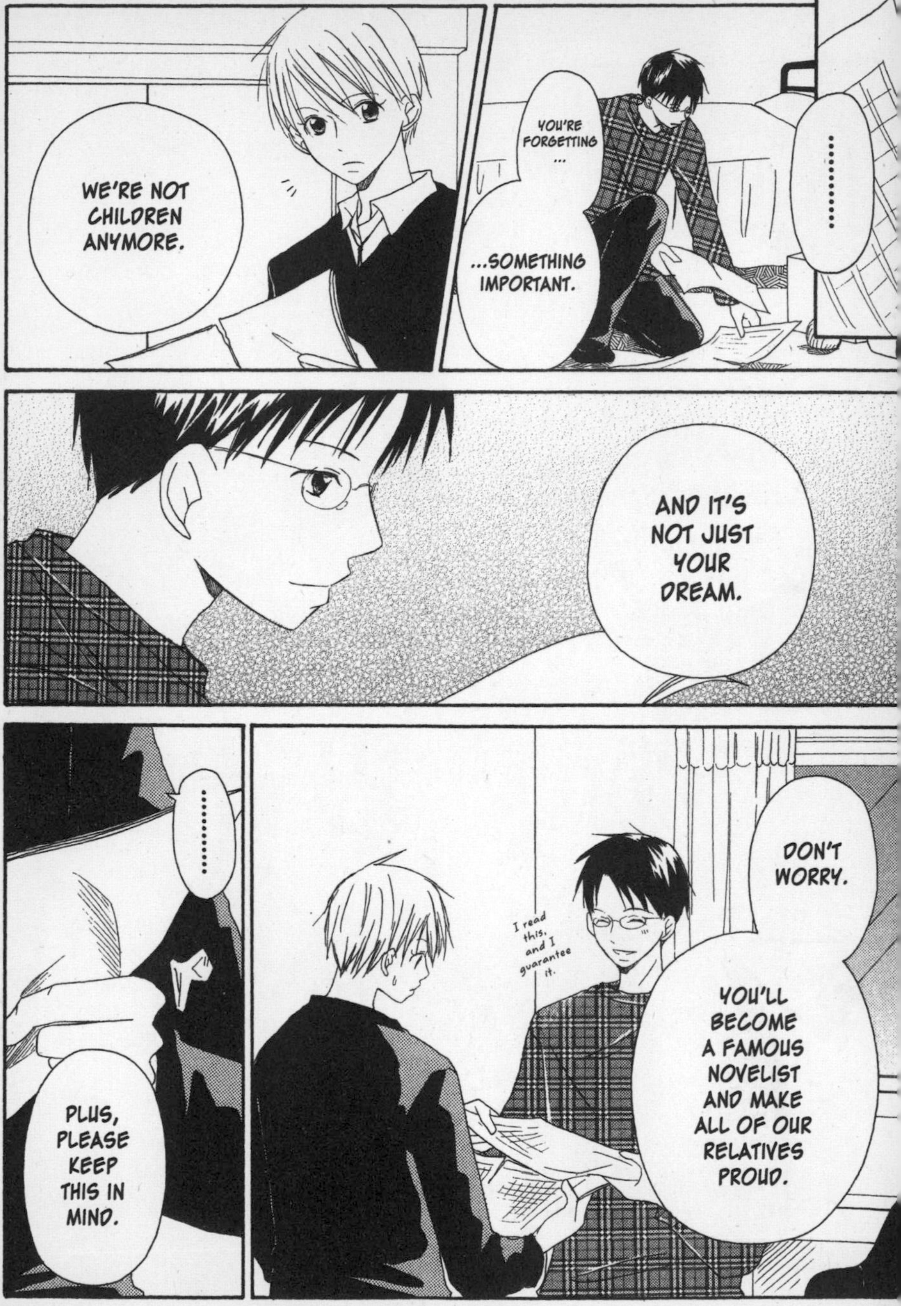
......
YOU'RE FORGETTING ...
...SOMETHING IMPORTANT.
WE'RE NOT CHILDREN ANYMORE.
AND IT'S NOT JUST YOUR DREAM.
DON'T WORRY.
YOU'LL BECOME A FAMOUS NOVELIST AND MAKE ALL OF OUR RELATIVES PROUD.
I read this, and I guarantee it.
......
PLUS, PLEASE KEEP THIS IN MIND.

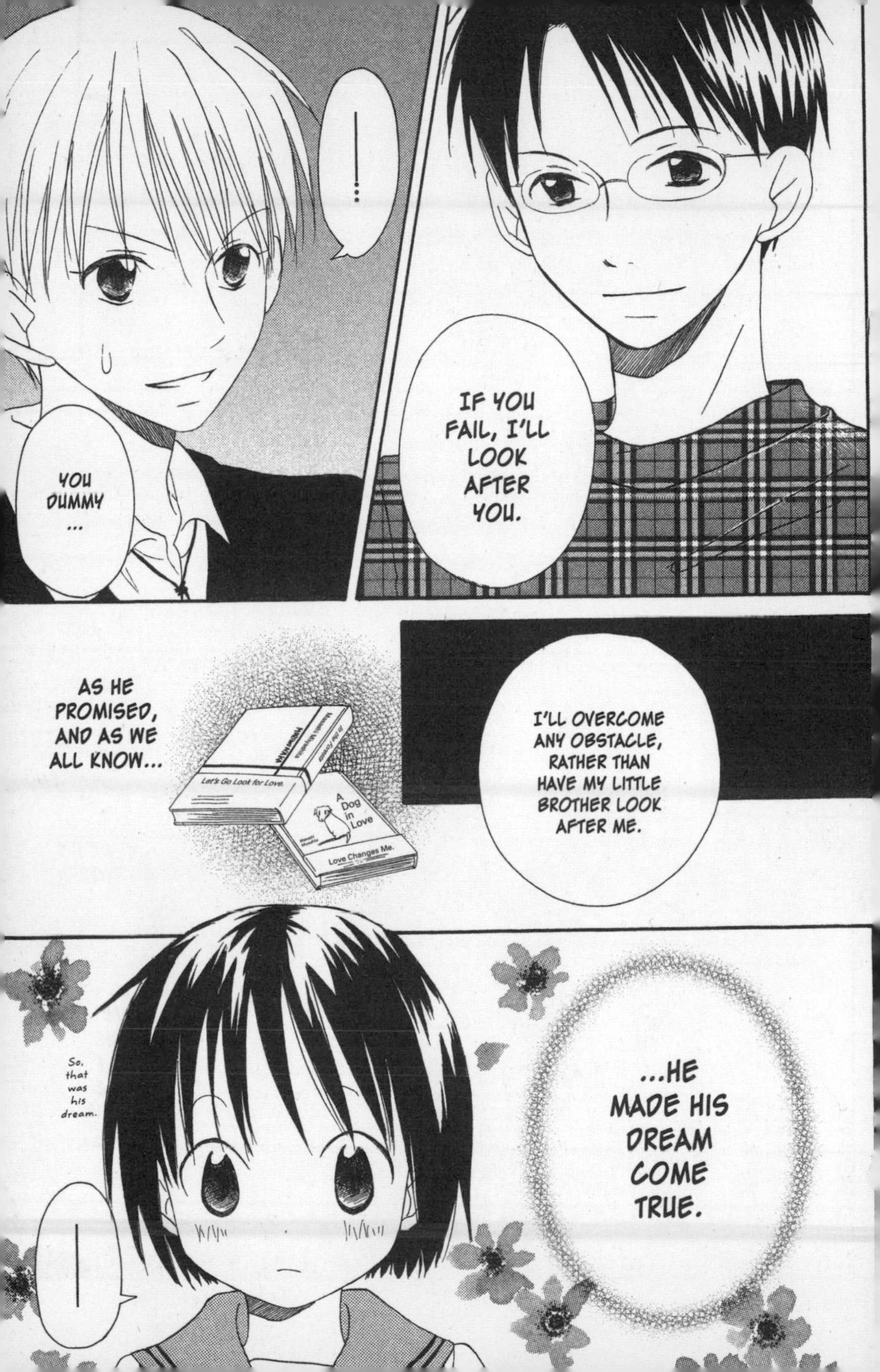
IF YOU FAIL, I'LL LOOK AFTER YOU.
!
YOU DUMMY ...
I'LL OVERCOME ANY OBSTACLE, RATHER THAN HAVE MY LITTLE BROTHER LOOK AFTER ME.
AS HE PROMISED, AND AS WE ALL KNOW...
Let's Go Look for Love.
A Dog in Love
Love Changes Me.
...HE MADE HIS DREAM COME TRUE.
So, that was his dream.
!

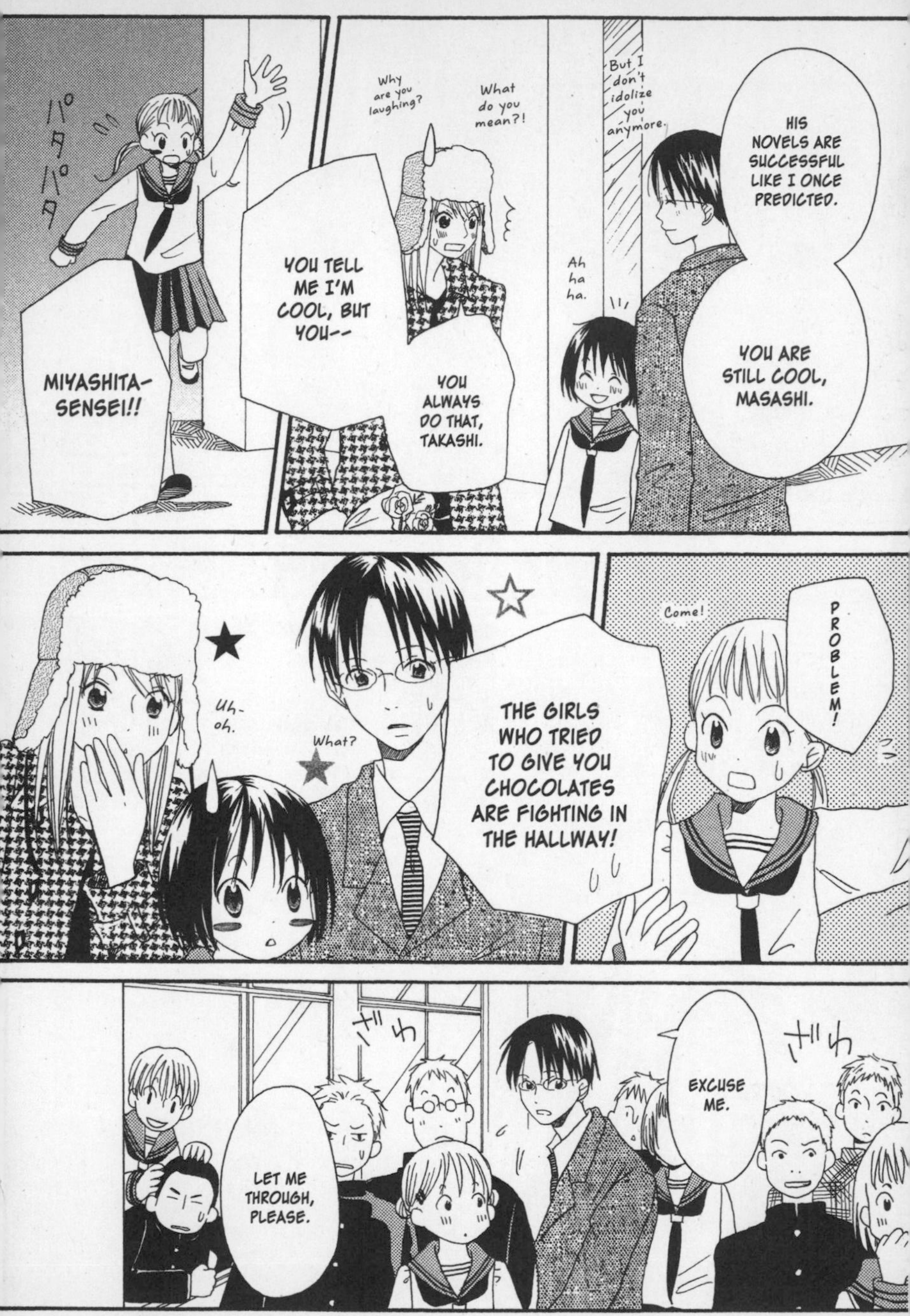

HIS NOVELS ARE SUCCESSFUL LIKE I ONCE PREDICTED.
YOU ARE STILL COOL, MASASHI.
But I don't idolize you anymore.
Ah ha ha.
What do you mean?!
Why are you laughing?
YOU TELL ME I'M COOL, BUT YOU--
YOU ALWAYS DO THAT, TAKASHI.
パタパタ
MIYASHITA-SENSEI!!
PROBLEM!
Come!
THE GIRLS WHO TRIED TO GIVE YOU CHOCOLATES ARE FIGHTING IN THE HALLWAY!
What?
Uh-oh.
ざわ
EXCUSE ME.
LET ME THROUGH, PLEASE.
ざわ

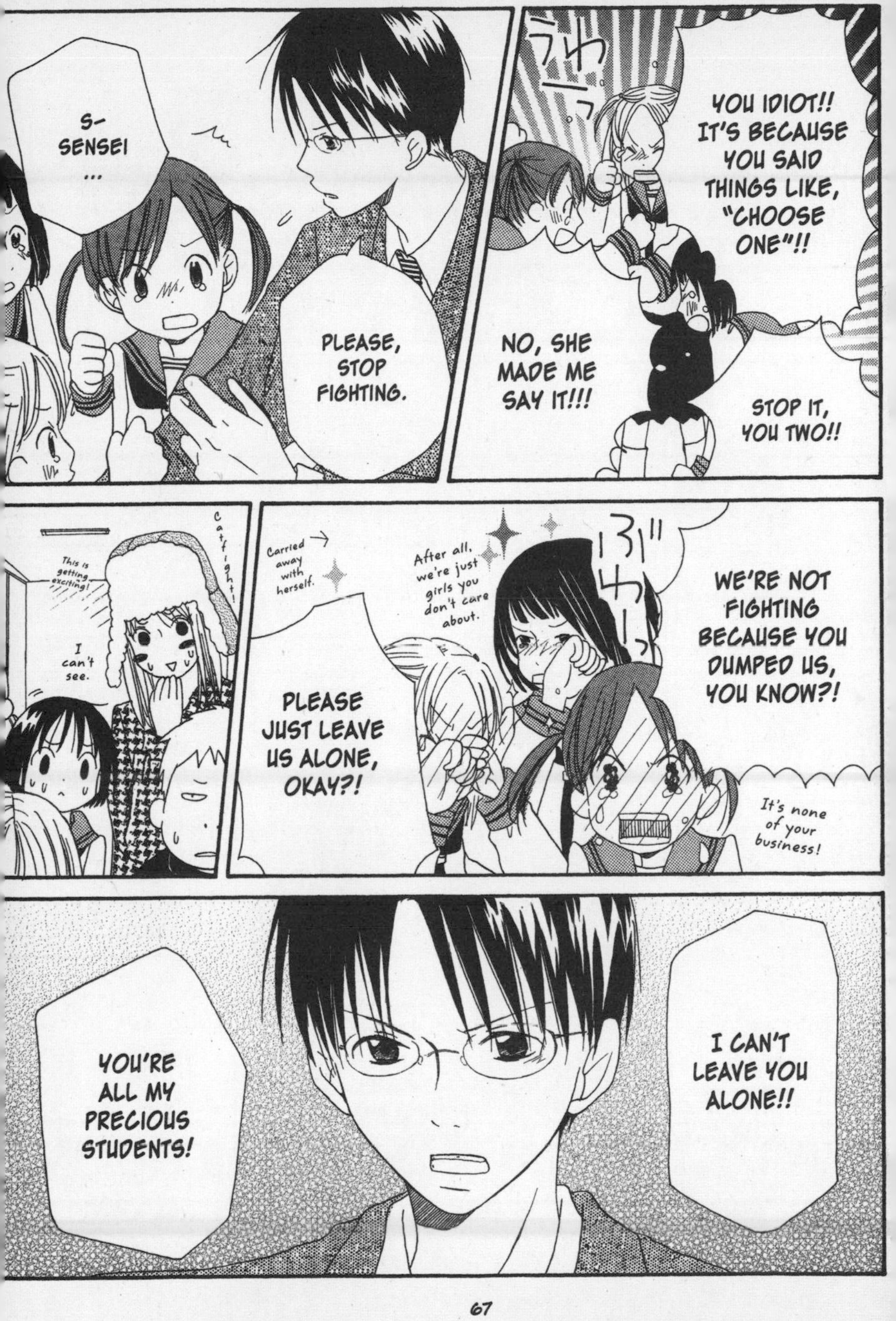
YOU IDIOT!! IT'S BECAUSE YOU SAID THINGS LIKE, "CHOOSE ONE"!!
NO, SHE MADE ME SAY IT!!!
STOP IT, YOU TWO!!
S-SENSEI ...
PLEASE, STOP FIGHTING.
WE'RE NOT FIGHTING BECAUSE YOU DUMPED US, YOU KNOW?!
After all, we're just girls you don't care about.
Carried away with herself.
PLEASE JUST LEAVE US ALONE, OKAY?!
It's none of your business!
Catfight!
This is getting exciting!
I can't see.
I CAN'T LEAVE YOU ALONE!!
YOU'RE ALL MY PRECIOUS STUDENTS!

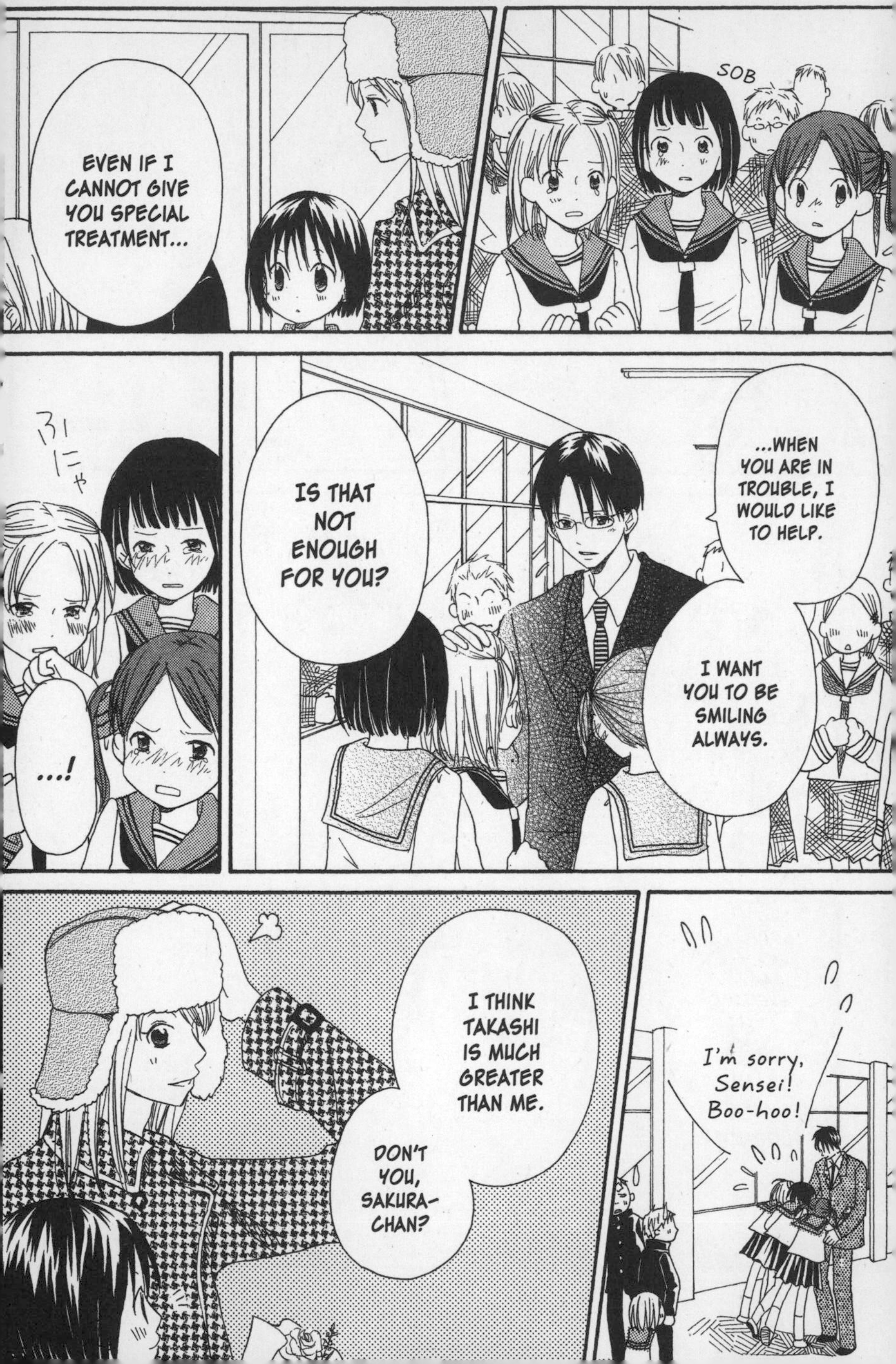
SOB
EVEN IF I CANNOT GIVE YOU SPECIAL TREATMENT...
...WHEN YOU ARE IN TROUBLE, I WOULD LIKE TO HELP.
I WANT YOU TO BE SMILING ALWAYS.
IS THAT NOT ENOUGH FOR YOU?
ふにゃ
...!
I'm sorry, Sensei! Boo-hoo!
I THINK TAKASHI IS MUCH GREATER THAN ME.
DON'T YOU, SAKURA-CHAN?

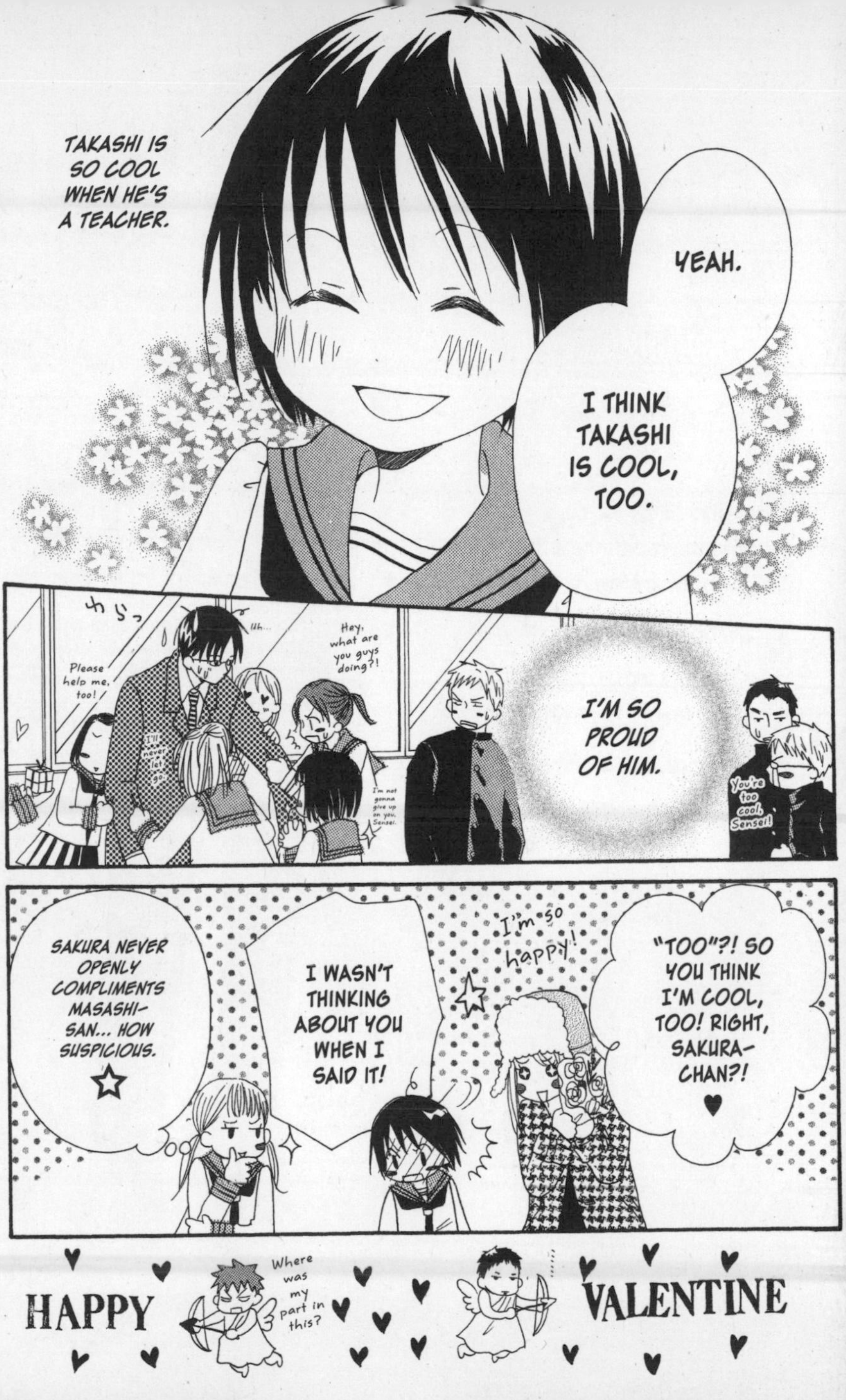
TAKASHI IS SO COOL WHEN HE'S A TEACHER.
YEAH.
I THINK TAKASHI IS COOL, TOO.
I'M SO PROUD OF HIM.
You're too cool, Sensei!
Hey, what are you guys doing?!
Uh...
ゆらっ
Please help me, too!
I'll never let go.
I'm not gonna give up on you, Sensei.
"TOO"?! SO YOU THINK I'M COOL, TOO! RIGHT, SAKURA-CHAN?!
I'm so happy!
I WASN'T THINKING ABOUT YOU WHEN I SAID IT!
SAKURA NEVER OPENLY COMPLIMENTS MASASHI-SAN... HOW SUSPICIOUS.
......
VALENTINE
Where was my part in this?
HAPPY

Takashi Miyashita

Date of Birth:
March 10th, 1980

Pisces, blood type O

↑

He seems to be type A,
but actually is an
easy-going O.

Height: 180cm

Hobby: Must be...
reading, right?

Likes: Cats

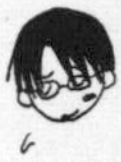
If only Masashi didn't hate them.

Hates: Nothing
(for now)

★ I got tired after drawing the whole figure, so I'll write about the other two on another occasion.

What?!
Sorry.

← The main story continues.

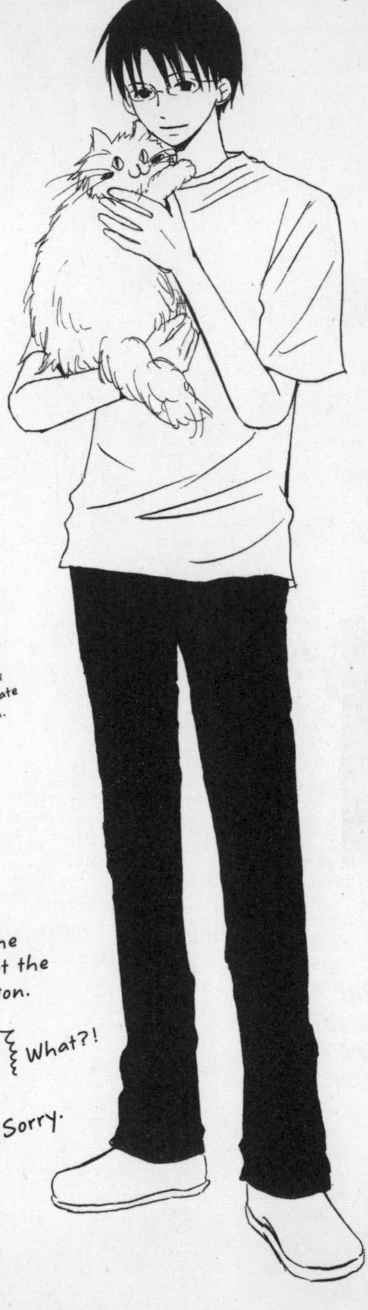

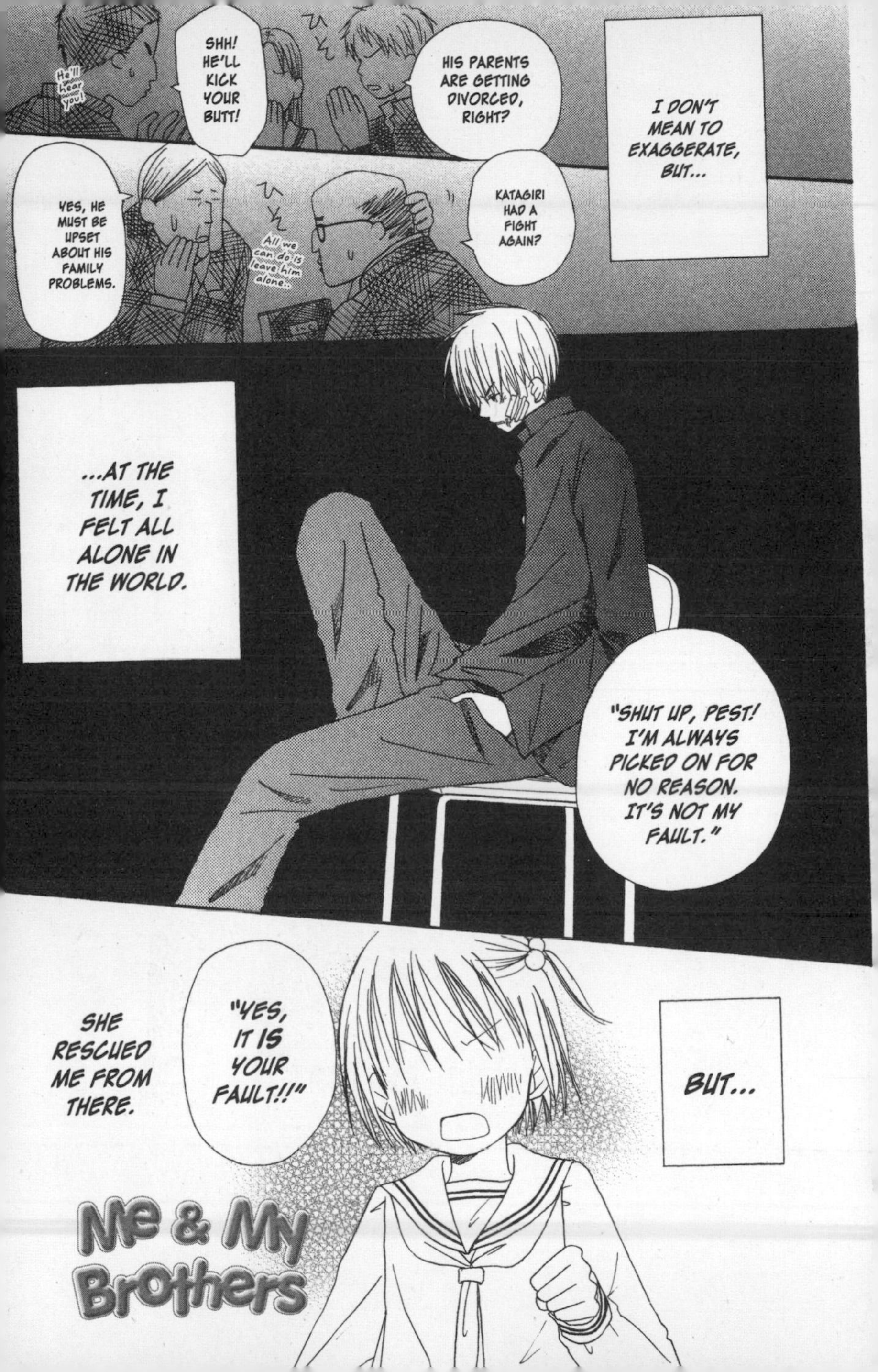
I DON'T MEAN TO EXAGGERATE, BUT...
HIS PARENTS ARE GETTING DIVORCED, RIGHT?
SHH! HE'LL KICK YOUR BUTT!
He'll hear you!
KATAGIRI HAD A FIGHT AGAIN?
All we can do is leave him alone..
YES, HE MUST BE UPSET ABOUT HIS FAMILY PROBLEMS.
...AT THE TIME, I FELT ALL ALONE IN THE WORLD.
"SHUT UP, PEST! I'M ALWAYS PICKED ON FOR NO REASON. IT'S NOT MY FAULT."
BUT...
"YES, IT IS YOUR FAULT!!"
SHE RESCUED ME FROM THERE.
Me & My Brothers

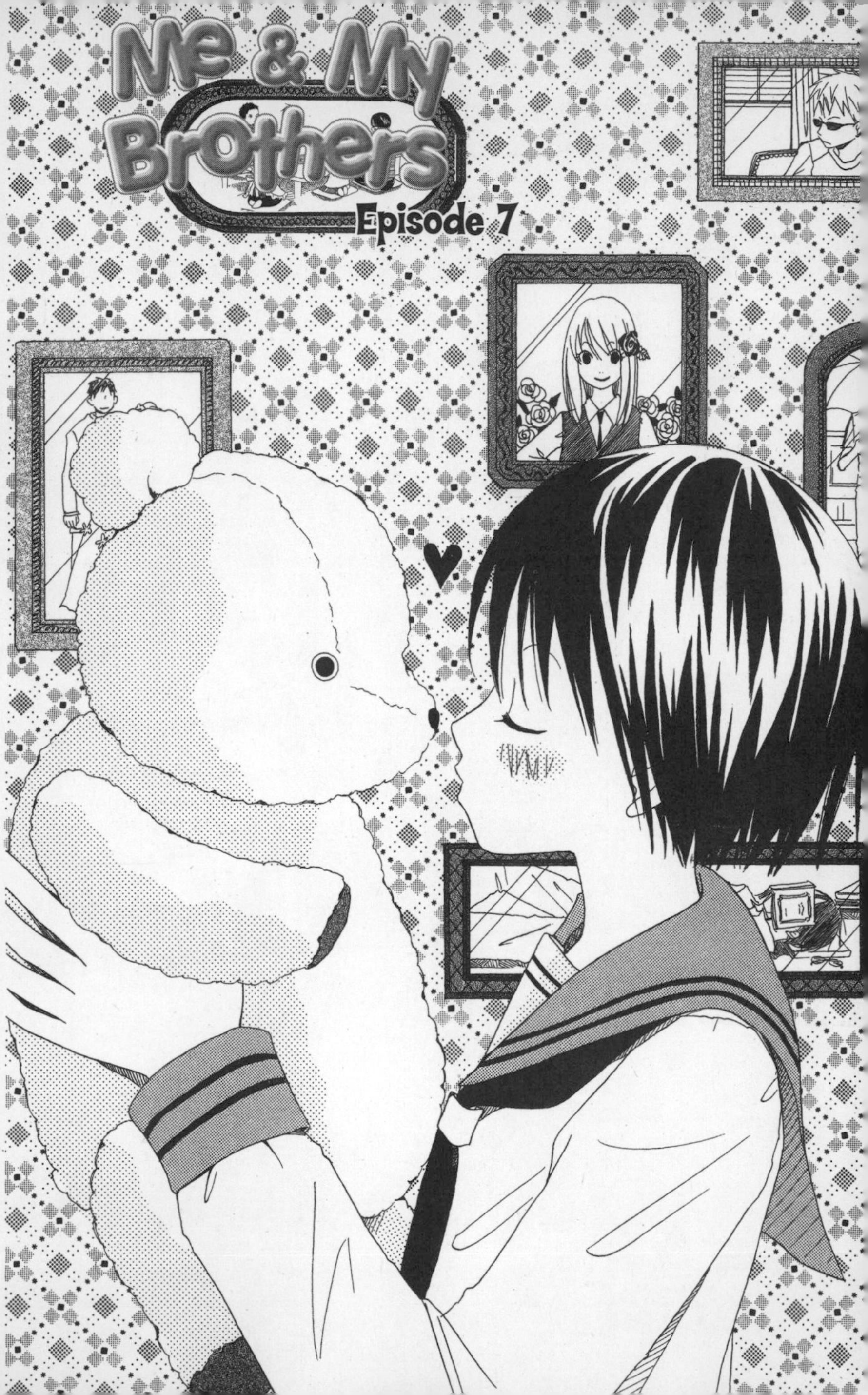

Me & My Brothers
Episode 7

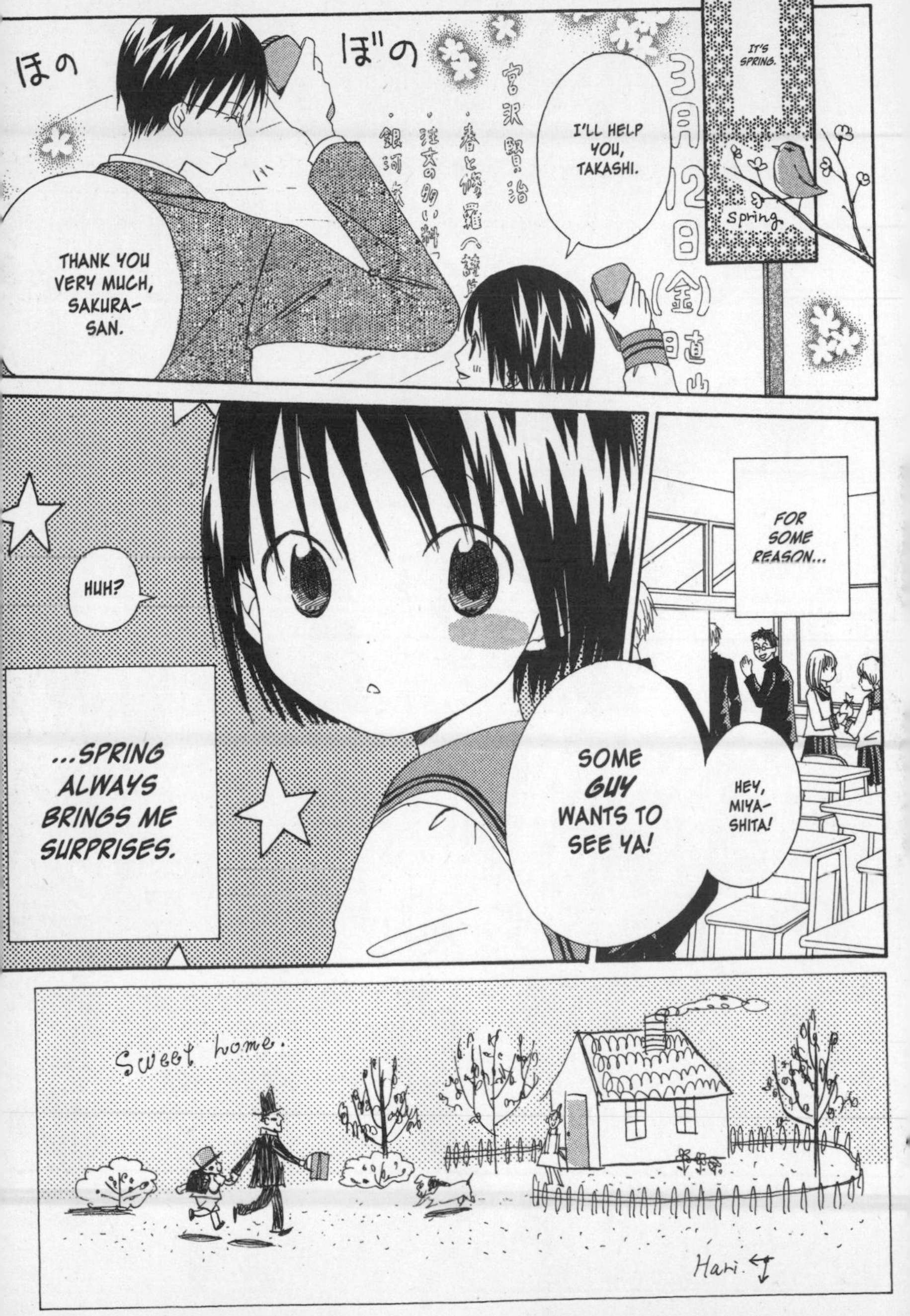
IT'S SPRING.
Spring.
3月12日(金)
I'LL HELP YOU, TAKASHI.
宮沢賢治
ほの ぼの
THANK YOU VERY MUCH, SAKURA-SAN.
FOR SOME REASON...
HEY, MIYA-SHITA!
SOME GUY WANTS TO SEE YA!
HUH?
...SPRING ALWAYS BRINGS ME SURPRISES.
Sweet home.
Hari.

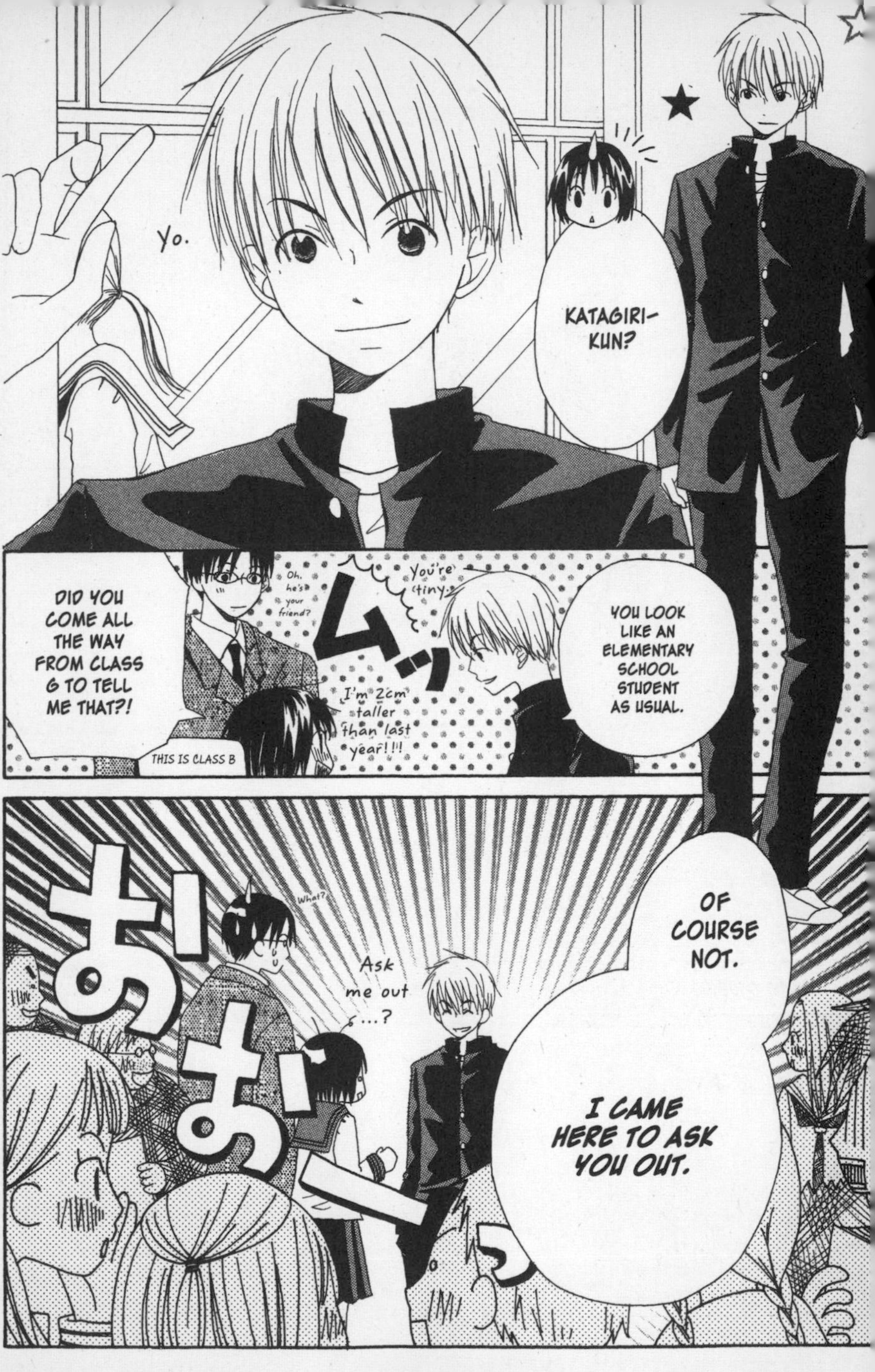
KATAGIRI-KUN?
Yo.
YOU LOOK LIKE AN ELEMENTARY SCHOOL STUDENT AS USUAL.
You're tiny.
ムッ
I'm 2cm taller than last year!!!
Oh, he's your friend?
DID YOU COME ALL THE WAY FROM CLASS G TO TELL ME THAT?!
THIS IS CLASS B
OF COURSE NOT.
I CAME HERE TO ASK YOU OUT.
Ask me out...?
What?
おおおーっ

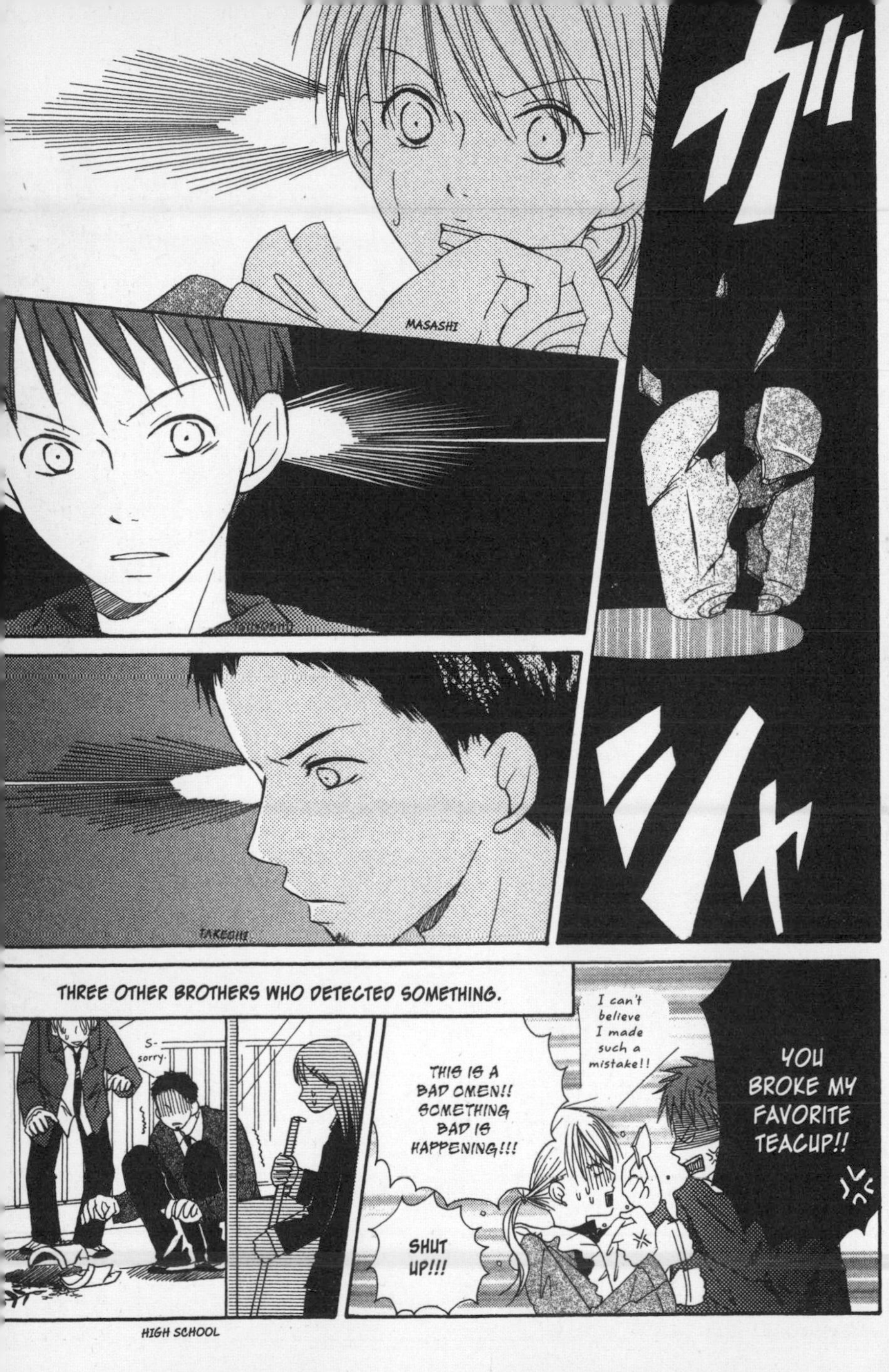
ガ
シャ
MASASHI
TAKESHI
THREE OTHER BROTHERS WHO DETECTED SOMETHING.
YOU BROKE MY FAVORITE TEACUP!!
I can't believe I made such a mistake!!
THIS IS A BAD OMEN!! SOMETHING BAD IS HAPPENING!!!
SHUT UP!!!
S-sorry.
HIGH SCHOOL

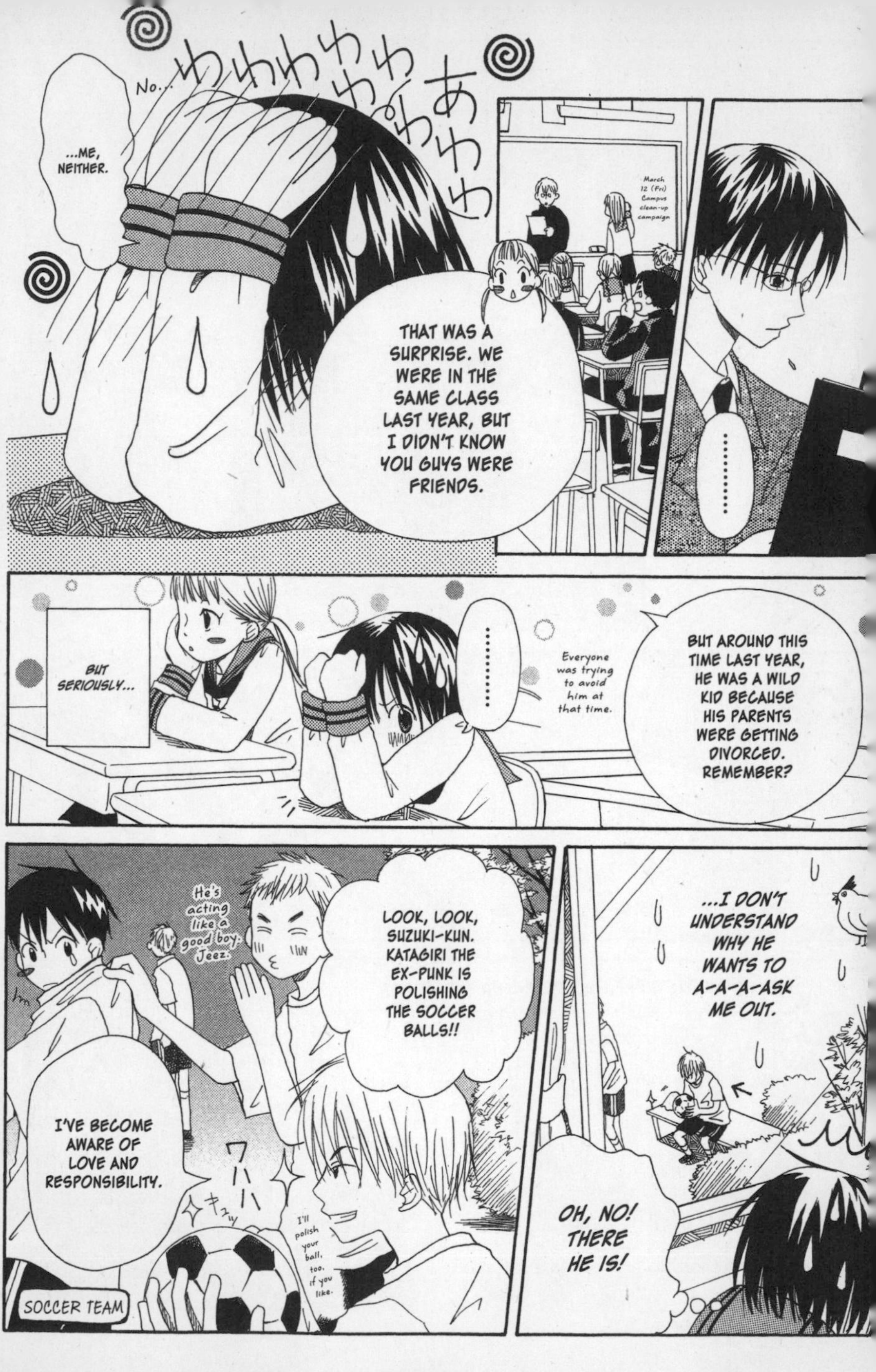
......
March 12 (Fri) Campus clean-up campaign
THAT WAS A SURPRISE. WE WERE IN THE SAME CLASS LAST YEAR, BUT I DIDN'T KNOW YOU GUYS WERE FRIENDS.
No...
...ME, NEITHER.
BUT AROUND THIS TIME LAST YEAR, HE WAS A WILD KID BECAUSE HIS PARENTS WERE GETTING DIVORCED. REMEMBER?
Everyone was trying to avoid him at that time.
......
BUT SERIOUSLY...
...I DON'T UNDERSTAND WHY HE WANTS TO A-A-A-ASK ME OUT.
OH, NO! THERE HE IS!
LOOK, LOOK, SUZUKI-KUN. KATAGIRI THE EX-PUNK IS POLISHING THE SOCCER BALLS!!
He's acting like a good boy. Jeez.
I'VE BECOME AWARE OF LOVE AND RESPONSIBILITY.
ワハハ
キュッ
I'll polish your ball, too, if you like.
SOCCER TEAM

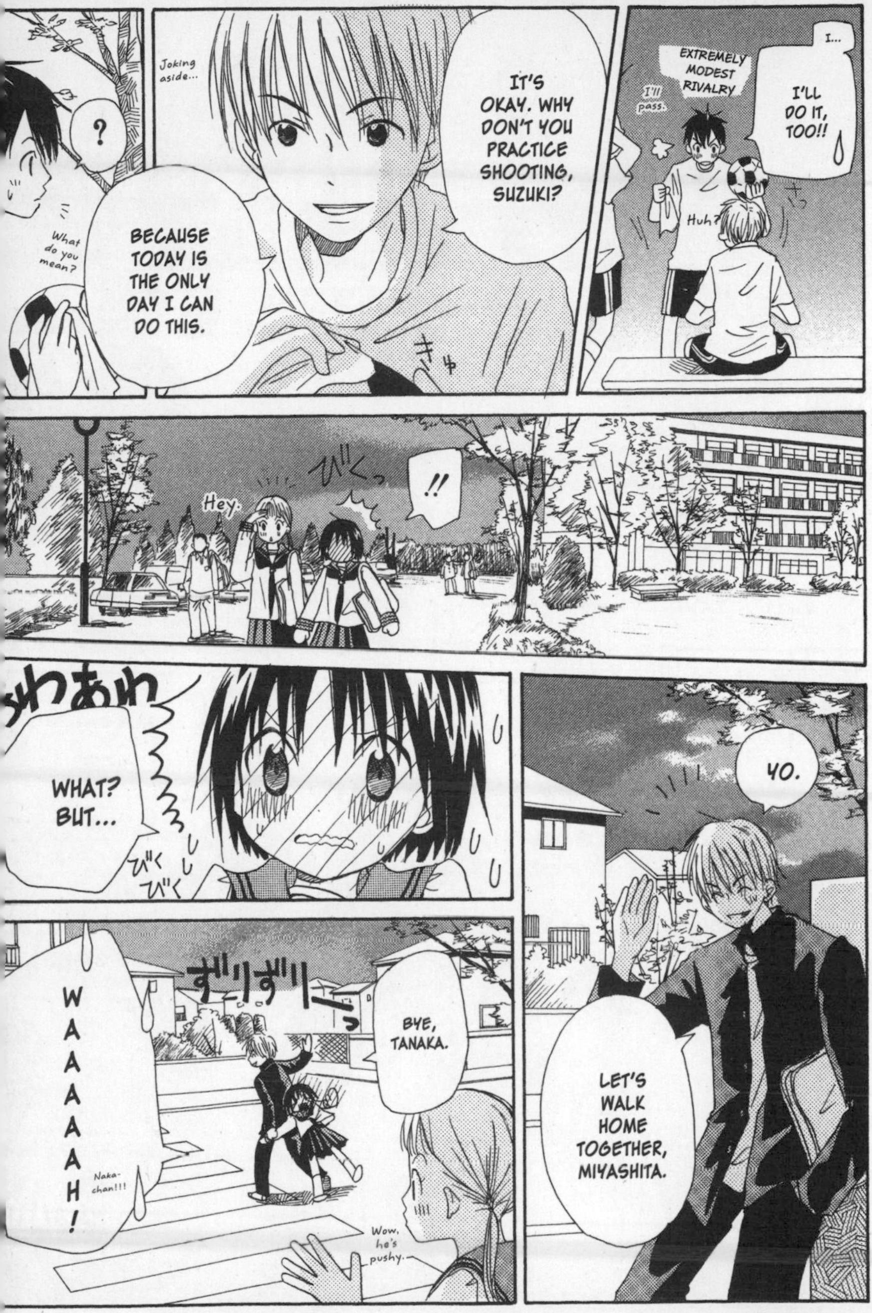
I...
I'LL DO IT, TOO!!
EXTREMELY MODEST RIVALRY
I'll pass.
Huh?
Joking aside...
IT'S OKAY. WHY DON'T YOU PRACTICE SHOOTING, SUZUKI?
?
What do you mean?
BECAUSE TODAY IS THE ONLY DAY I CAN DO THIS.
!!
Hey.
YO.
LET'S WALK HOME TOGETHER, MIYASHITA.
WHAT? BUT...
BYE, TANAKA.
Wow, he's pushy.
WAAAAAAH!
Naka-chan!!!

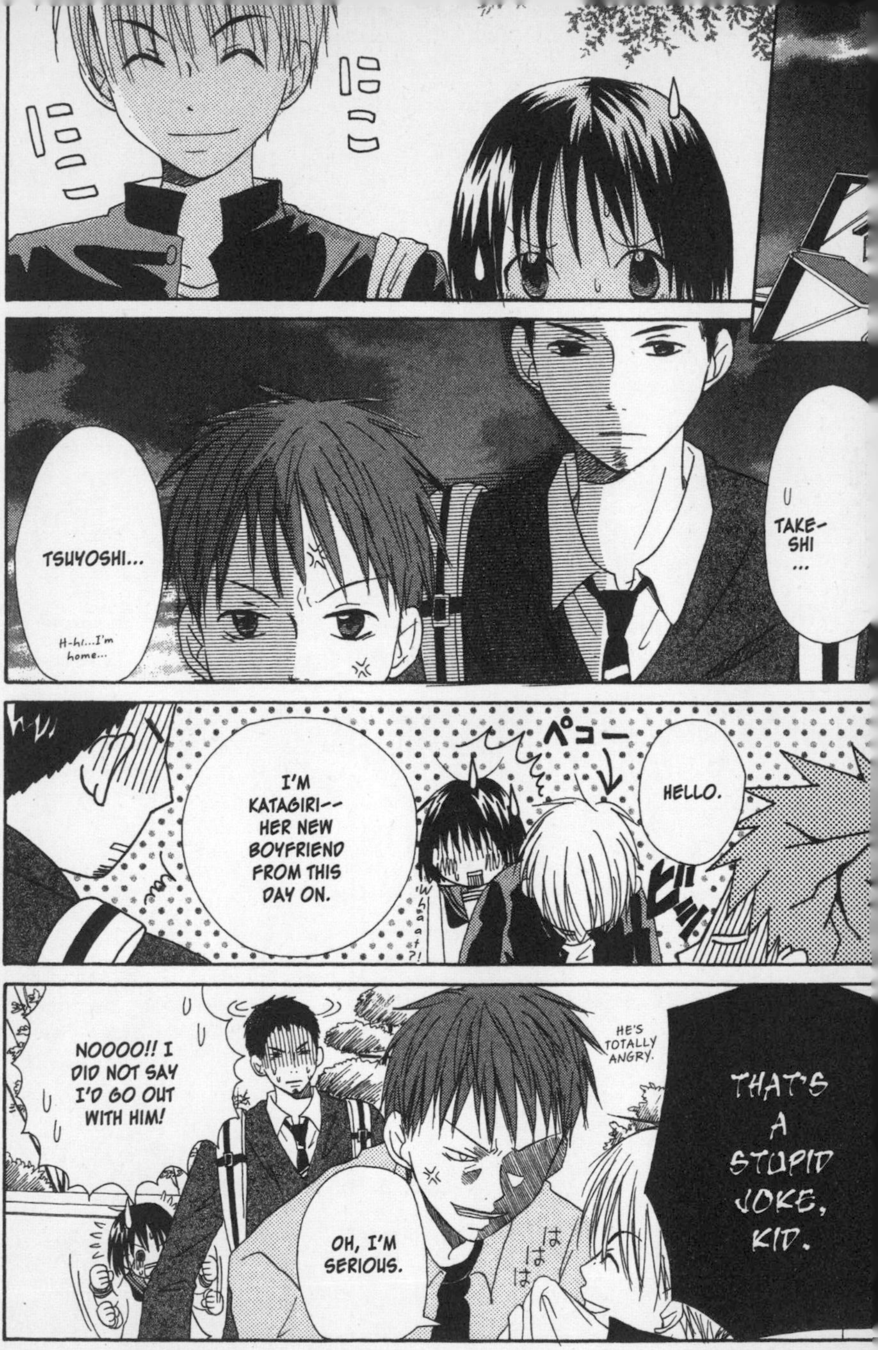
TAKE-SHI ...
TSUYOSHI...
H-hi...I'm home...
HELLO.
ペコー
Whaaat?!
I'M KATAGIRI-- HER NEW BOYFRIEND FROM THIS DAY ON.
THAT'S A STUPID JOKE, KID.
HE'S TOTALLY ANGRY.
はははは
OH, I'M SERIOUS.
NOOOO!! I DID NOT SAY I'D GO OUT WITH HIM!

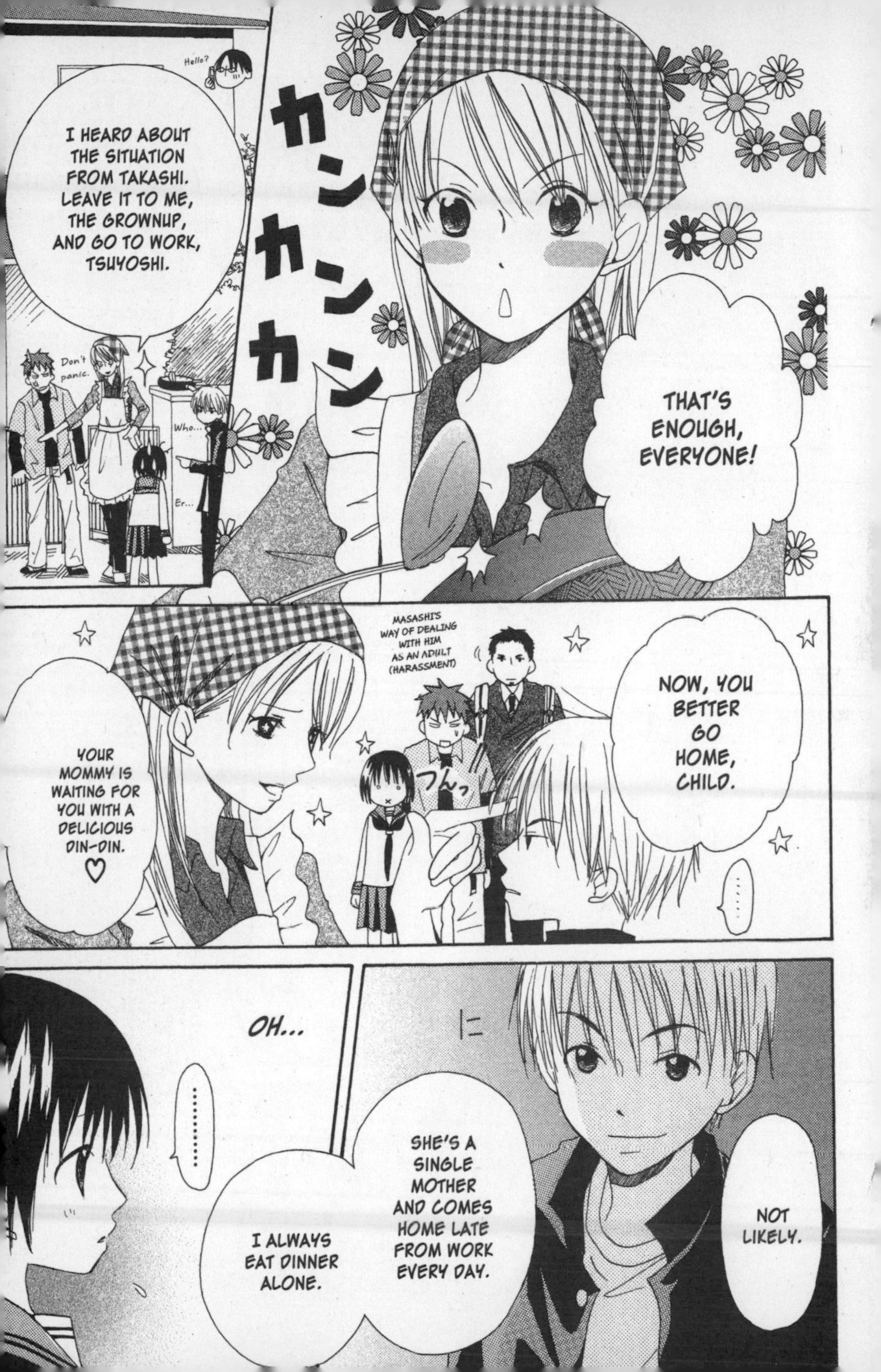
カンカンカン
THAT'S ENOUGH, EVERYONE!
Hello?
I HEARD ABOUT THE SITUATION FROM TAKASHI. LEAVE IT TO ME, THE GROWNUP, AND GO TO WORK, TSUYOSHI.
Don't panic.
Who...
Er...
NOW, YOU BETTER GO HOME, CHILD.
......
MASASHI'S WAY OF DEALING WITH HIM AS AN ADULT (HARASSMENT)
つんっ
YOUR MOMMY IS WAITING FOR YOU WITH A DELICIOUS DIN-DIN. ♡
NOT LIKELY.
SHE'S A SINGLE MOTHER AND COMES HOME LATE FROM WORK EVERY DAY.
I ALWAYS EAT DINNER ALONE.
に
OH...
....

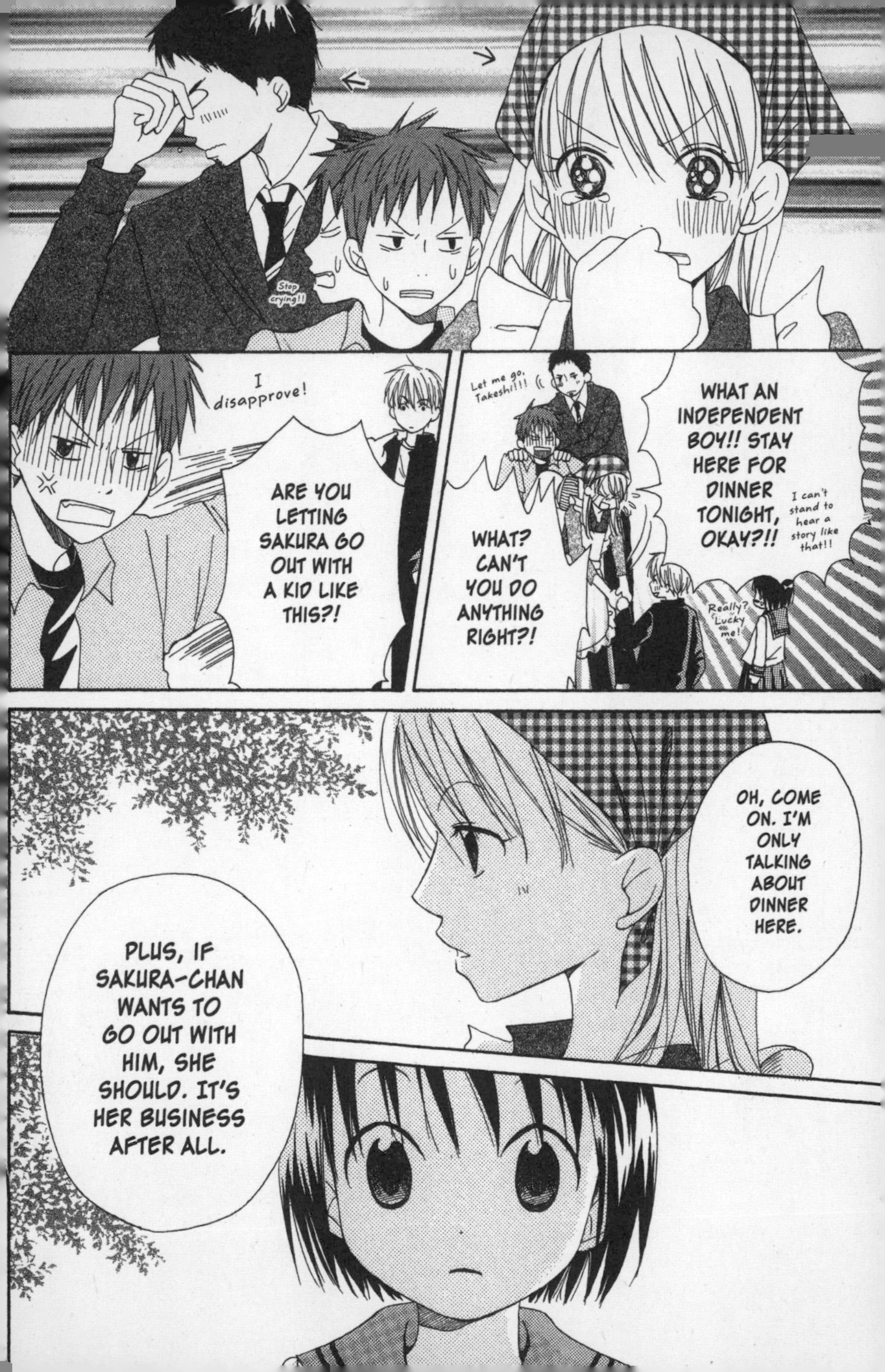
Stop crying!!
WHAT AN INDEPENDENT BOY!! STAY HERE FOR DINNER TONIGHT, OKAY?!!
I can't stand to hear a story like that!!
Let me go, Takeshi!!!
WHAT? CAN'T YOU DO ANYTHING RIGHT?!
Really? Lucky me!
I disapprove!
ARE YOU LETTING SAKURA GO OUT WITH A KID LIKE THIS?!
OH, COME ON. I'M ONLY TALKING ABOUT DINNER HERE.
PLUS, IF SAKURA-CHAN WANTS TO GO OUT WITH HIM, SHE SHOULD. IT'S HER BUSINESS AFTER ALL.

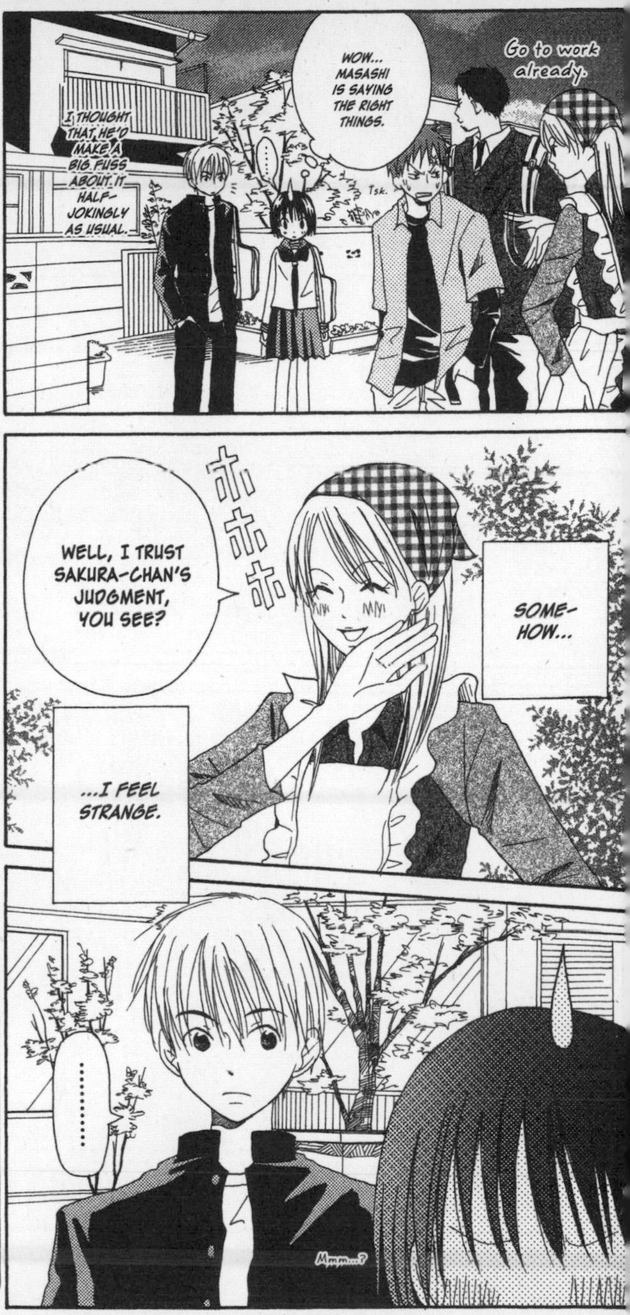
Go to work already.
WOW... MASASHI IS SAYING THE RIGHT THINGS.
Tsk.
I THOUGHT THAT HE'D MAKE A BIG FUSS ABOUT IT HALF-JOKINGLY AS USUAL.
...
SOME-HOW...
ホホホ
WELL, I TRUST SAKURA-CHAN'S JUDGMENT, YOU SEE?
...I FEEL STRANGE.
Mmm...?
....

☆3☆

It was fun to draw Katagiri-kun, because he was a new character. I love drawing students. They're so pure. Someday I'd like to show you more of Suzuki-kun. (Though many of you might be thinking, "huh? Who?") I'm secretly thinking that he'd be a good husband.

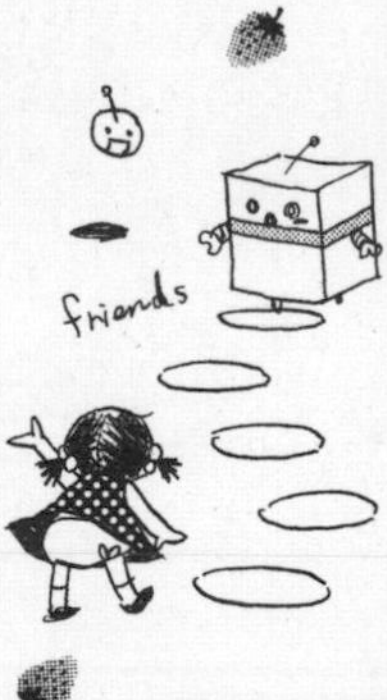
friends

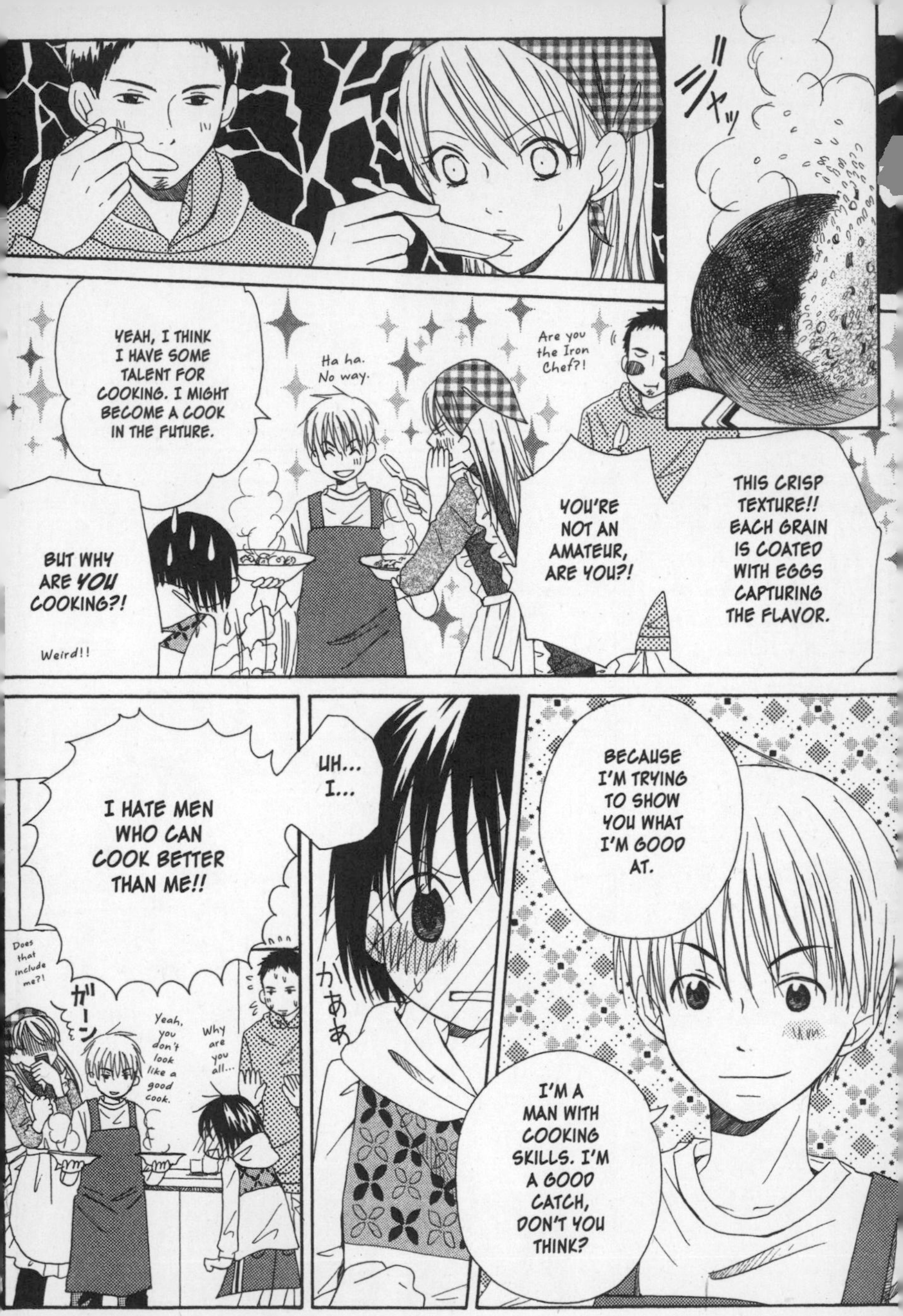
ジャッ
THIS CRISP TEXTURE!! EACH GRAIN IS COATED WITH EGGS CAPTURING THE FLAVOR.
YOU'RE NOT AN AMATEUR, ARE YOU?!
Are you the Iron Chef?!
Ha ha. No way.
YEAH, I THINK I HAVE SOME TALENT FOR COOKING. I MIGHT BECOME A COOK IN THE FUTURE.
BUT WHY ARE *YOU* COOKING?!
Weird!!
BECAUSE I'M TRYING TO SHOW YOU WHAT I'M GOOD AT.
I'M A MAN WITH COOKING SKILLS. I'M A GOOD CATCH, DON'T YOU THINK?
UH... I...
かあぁ
I HATE MEN WHO CAN COOK BETTER THAN ME!!
Does that include me?!
ガーン
Yeah, you don't look like a good cook.
Why are you all...

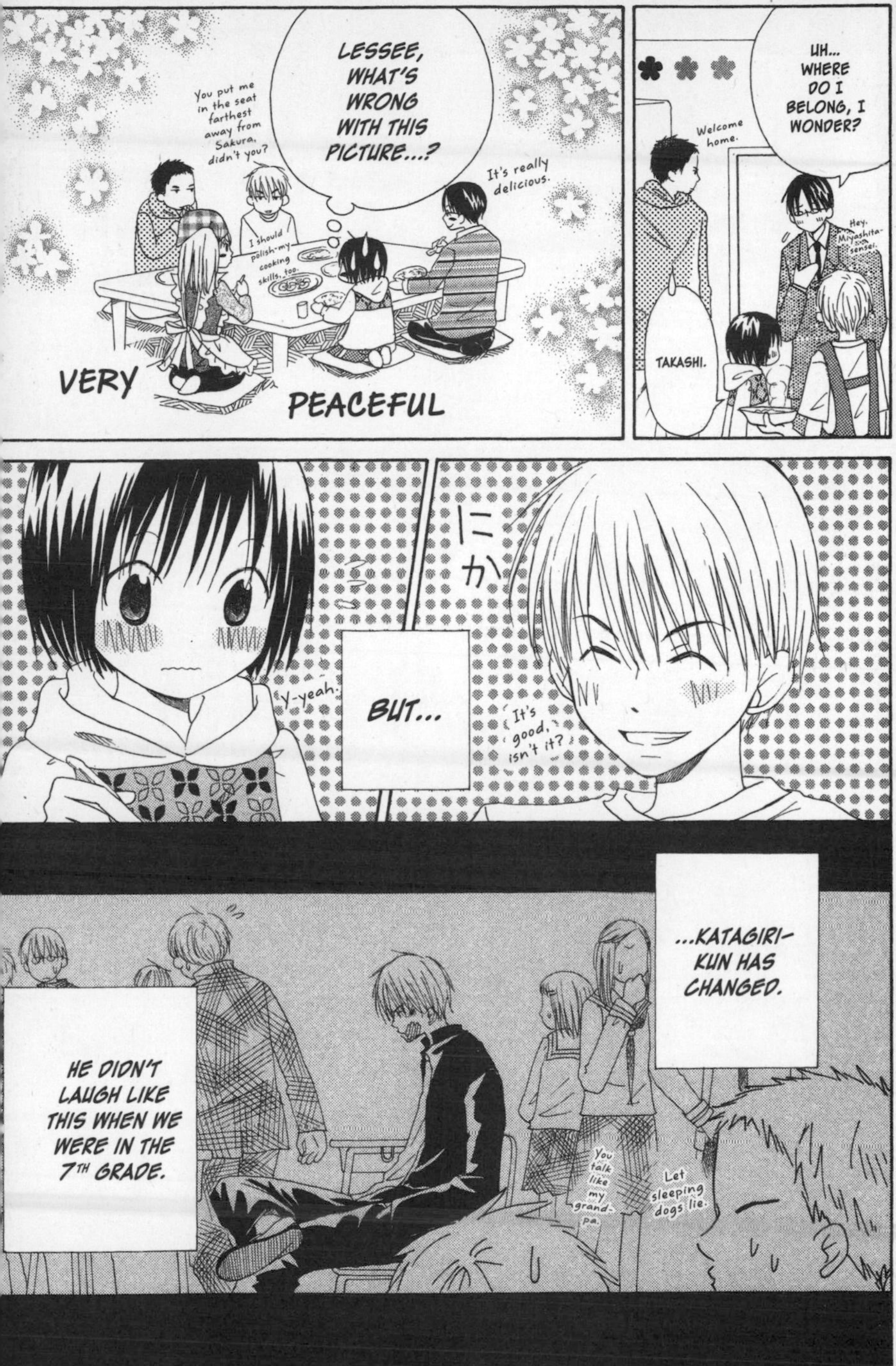
UH... WHERE DO I BELONG, I WONDER?
Welcome home.
Hey, Miyashita-sensei.
TAKASHI.
LESSEE, WHAT'S WRONG WITH THIS PICTURE...?
You put me in the seat farthest away from Sakura, didn't you?
It's really delicious.
I should polish my cooking skills, too.
VERY
PEACEFUL
にか
It's good, isn't it?
BUT...
Y-yeah.
...KATAGIRI-KUN HAS CHANGED.
Let sleeping dogs lie.
You talk like my grand-pa.
HE DIDN'T LAUGH LIKE THIS WHEN WE WERE IN THE 7TH GRADE.

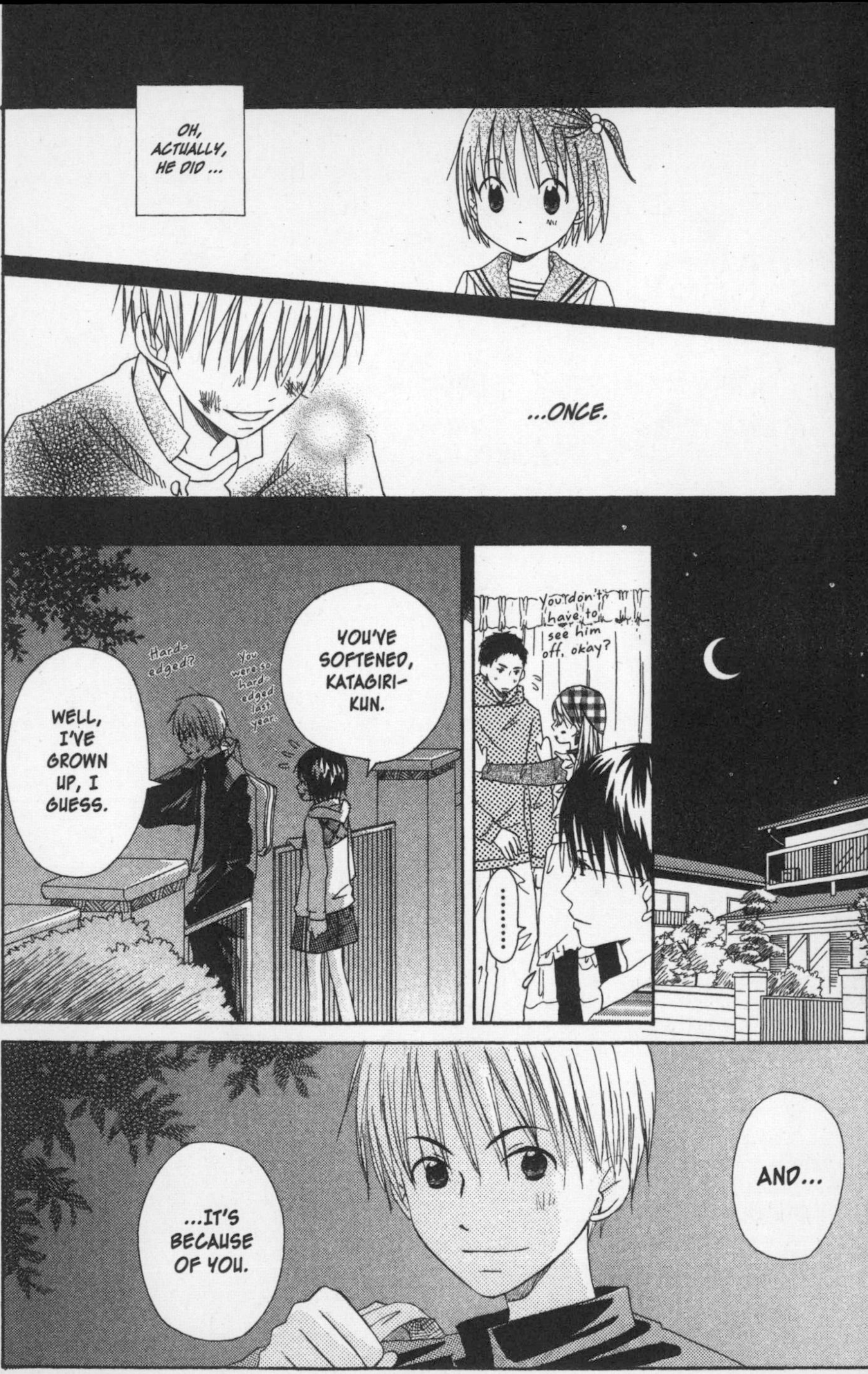
OH, ACTUALLY, HE DID ...
...ONCE.
You don't have to see him off, okay?
......
YOU'VE SOFTENED, KATAGIRI-KUN.
You were so hard-edged last year.
Hard-edged?
WELL, I'VE GROWN UP, I GUESS.
AND...
...IT'S BECAUSE OF YOU.

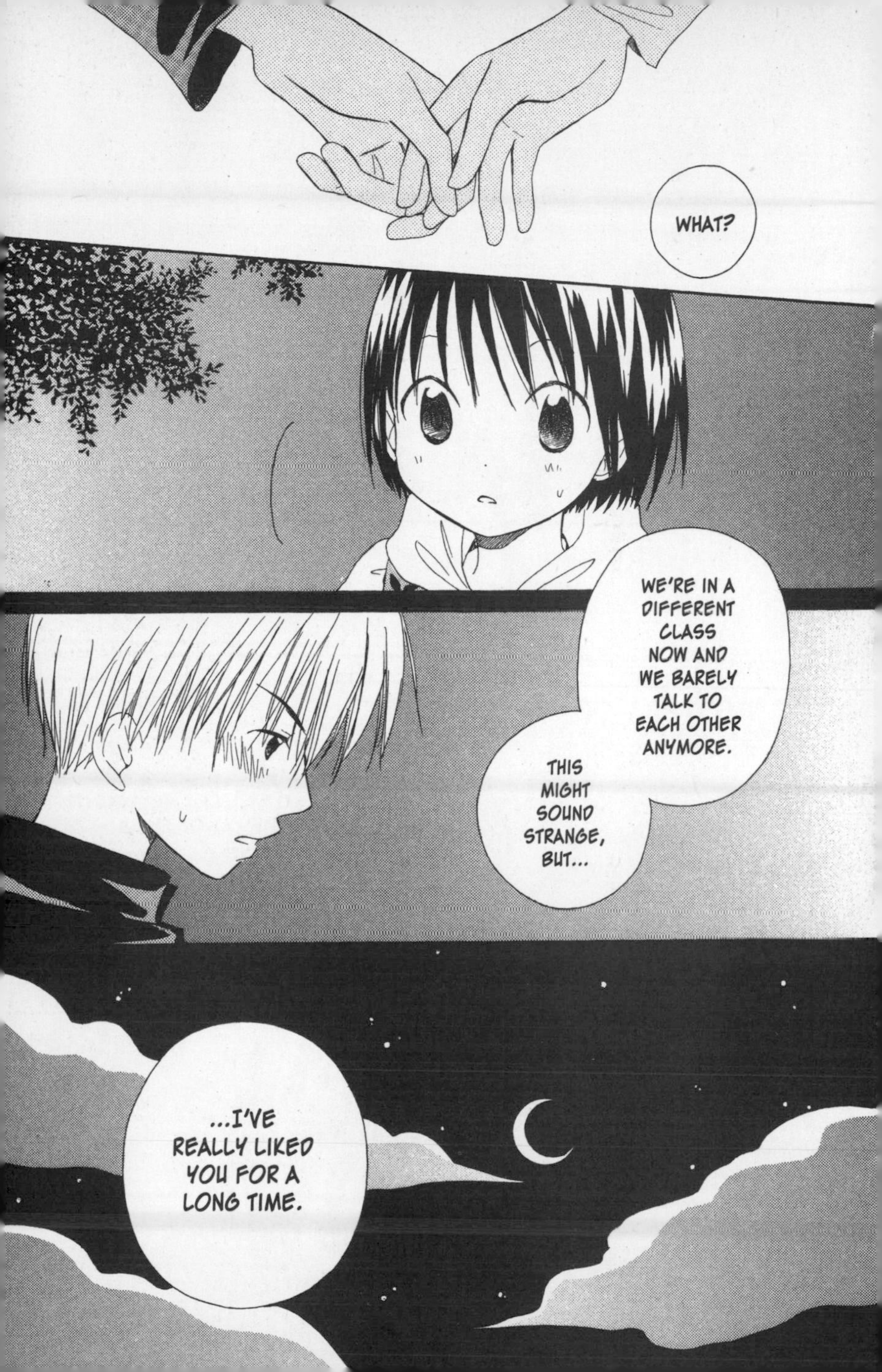
WHAT?
WE'RE IN A DIFFERENT CLASS NOW AND WE BARELY TALK TO EACH OTHER ANYMORE.
THIS MIGHT SOUND STRANGE, BUT...
...I'VE REALLY LIKED YOU FOR A LONG TIME.

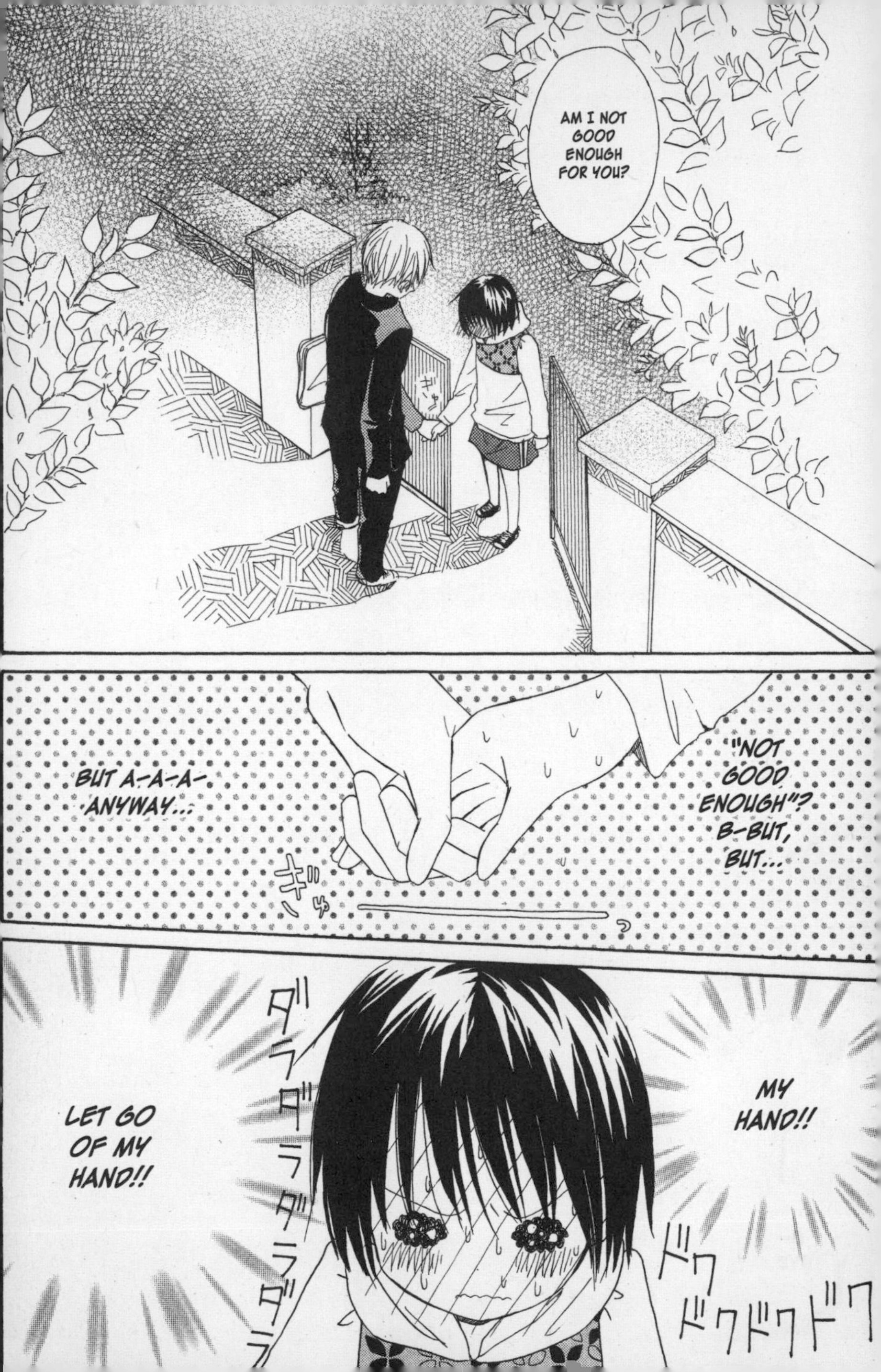
AM I NOT GOOD ENOUGH FOR YOU?
"NOT GOOD ENOUGH"? B-BUT, BUT...
BUT A-A-A-ANYWAY...
ぎゅ
MY HAND!!
ドクドクドクドク
ダラダラダラ
LET GO OF MY HAND!!

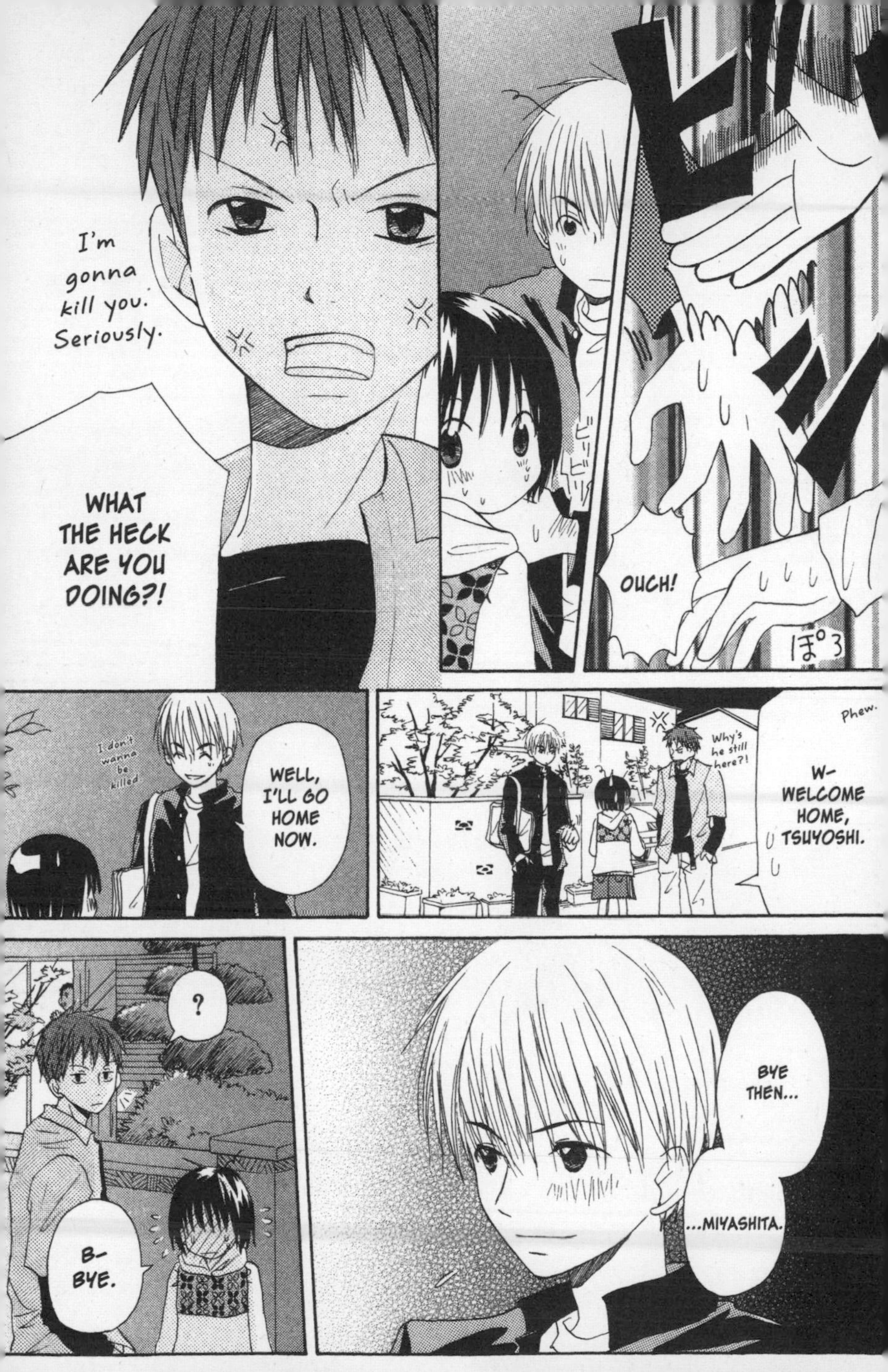
OUCH!
ぽろ
I'm gonna kill you. Seriously.
WHAT THE HECK ARE YOU DOING?!
Phew.
W- WELCOME HOME, TSUYOSHI.
Why's he still here?!
WELL, I'LL GO HOME NOW.
I don't wanna be killed.
BYE THEN...
...MIYASHITA.
?
B- BYE.

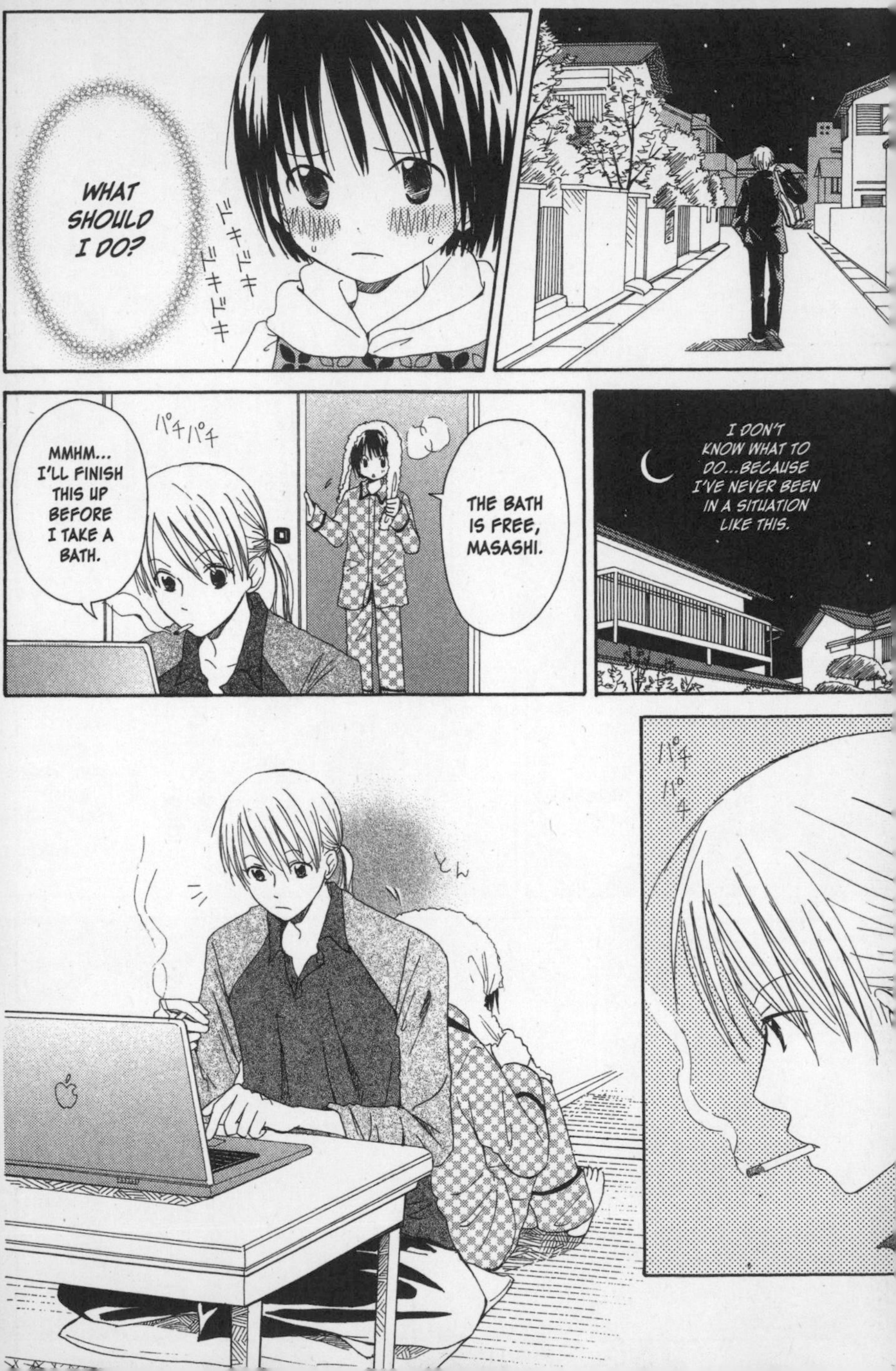
WHAT SHOULD I DO?
ドキドキ
ドキドキ
I DON'T KNOW WHAT TO DO...BECAUSE I'VE NEVER BEEN IN A SITUATION LIKE THIS.
THE BATH IS FREE, MASASHI.
パチパチ
MMHM... I'LL FINISH THIS UP BEFORE I TAKE A BATH.
パチパチ
とん

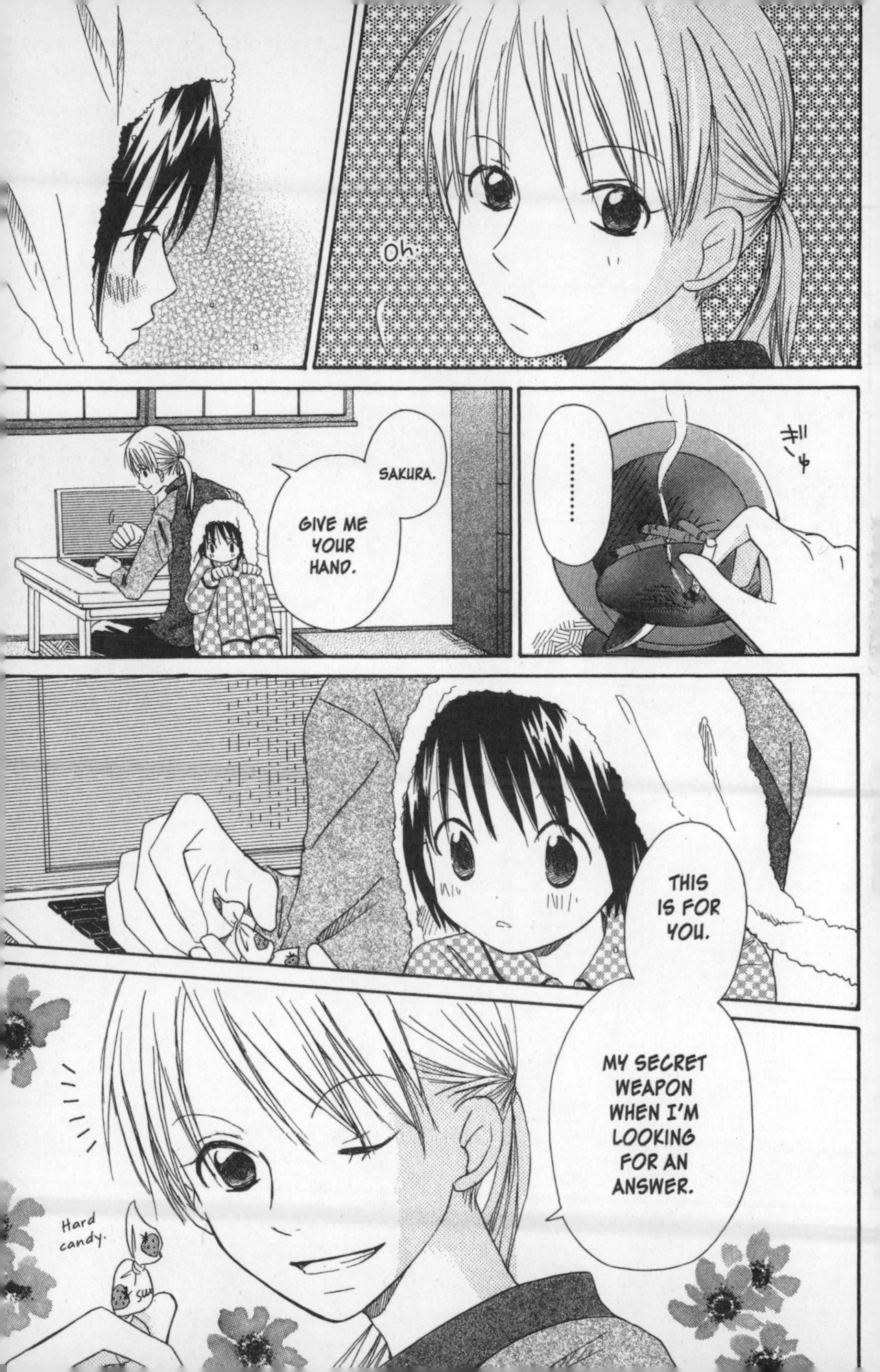
Oh.
......
SAKURA.
GIVE ME YOUR HAND.
THIS IS FOR YOU.
MY SECRET WEAPON WHEN I'M LOOKING FOR AN ANSWER.
Hard candy.

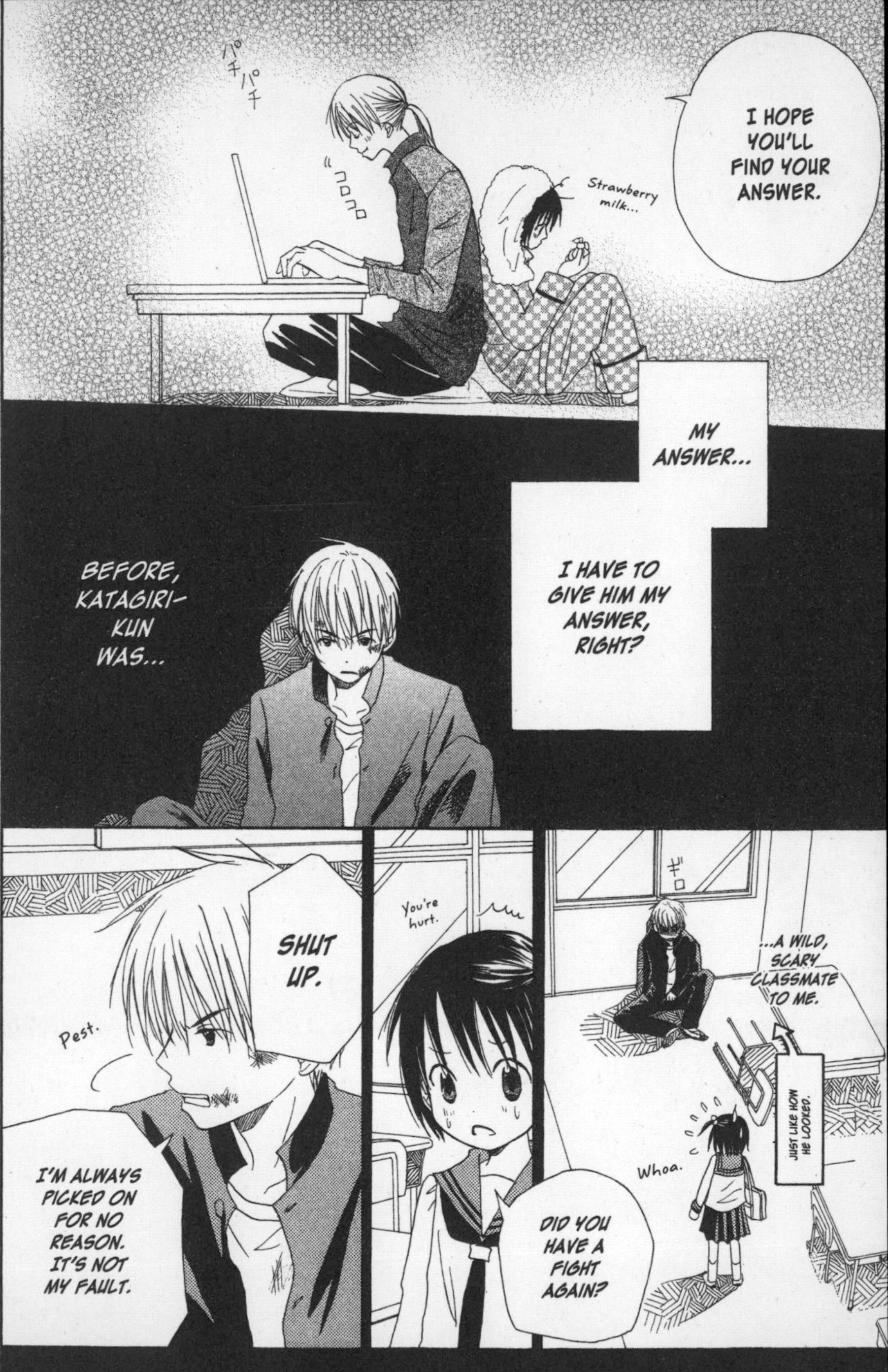
I HOPE YOU'LL FIND YOUR ANSWER.
Strawberry milk...
コロコロ
パチパチ
MY ANSWER...
I HAVE TO GIVE HIM MY ANSWER, RIGHT?
BEFORE, KATAGIRI-KUN WAS...
ギロ
...A WILD, SCARY CLASSMATE TO ME.
JUST LIKE HOW HE LOOKED.
Whoa.
You're hurt.
DID YOU HAVE A FIGHT AGAIN?
SHUT UP.
Pest.
I'M ALWAYS PICKED ON FOR NO REASON. IT'S NOT MY FAULT.

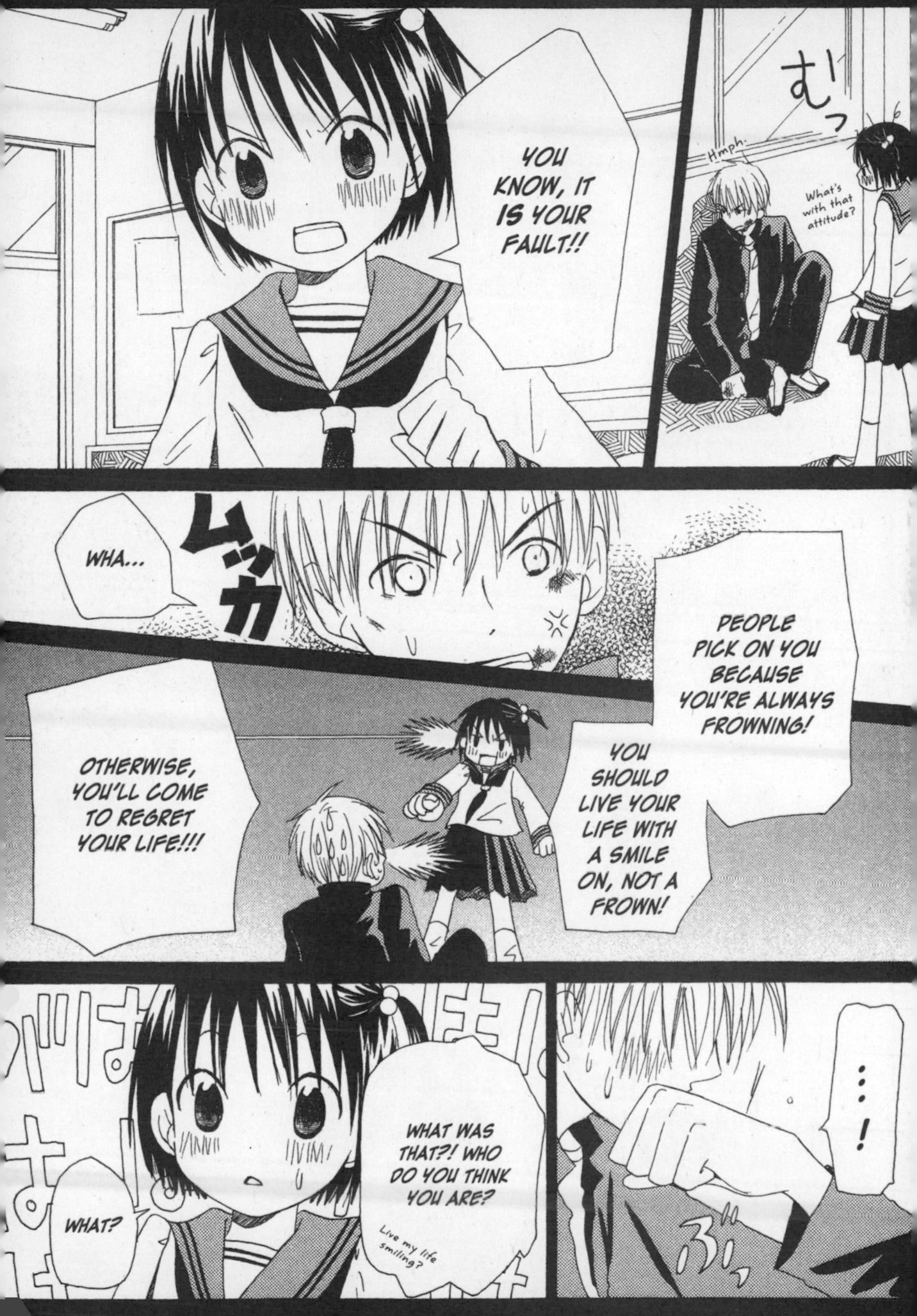
むっ
Hmph.
What's with that attitude?
YOU KNOW, IT IS YOUR FAULT!!
WHA...
ムッカ
PEOPLE PICK ON YOU BECAUSE YOU'RE ALWAYS FROWNING!
YOU SHOULD LIVE YOUR LIFE WITH A SMILE ON, NOT A FROWN!
OTHERWISE, YOU'LL COME TO REGRET YOUR LIFE!!!
...!
WHAT WAS THAT?! WHO DO YOU THINK YOU ARE?
Live my life smiling?
WHAT?

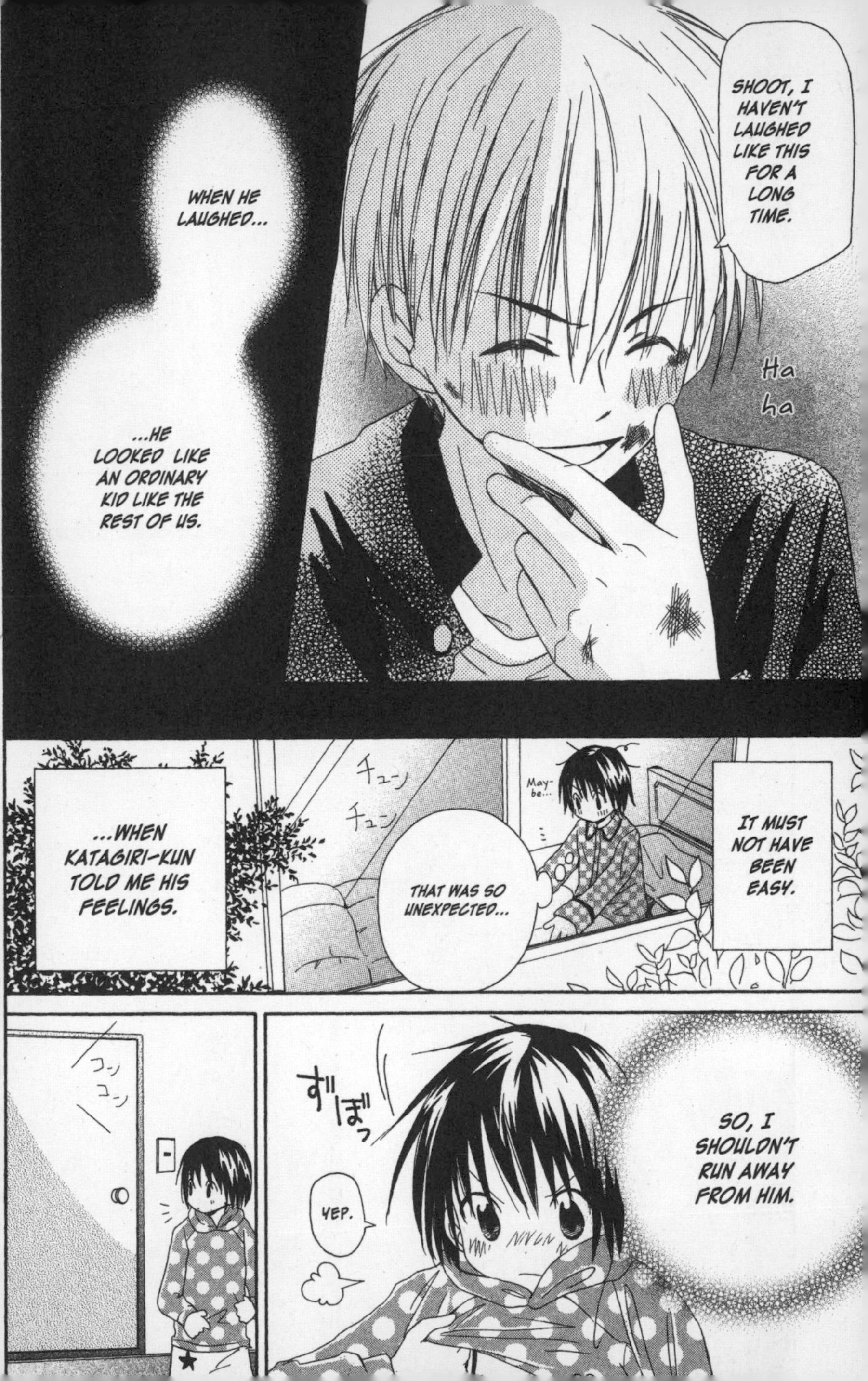
SHOOT, I HAVEN'T LAUGHED LIKE THIS FOR A LONG TIME.
Ha ha
WHEN HE LAUGHED...
...HE LOOKED LIKE AN ORDINARY KID LIKE THE REST OF US.
IT MUST NOT HAVE BEEN EASY.
May-be...
THAT WAS SO UNEXPECTED...
チュン
チュン
...WHEN KATAGIRI-KUN TOLD ME HIS FEELINGS.
SO, I SHOULDN'T RUN AWAY FROM HIM.
ずぼっ
YEP.
コン
コン

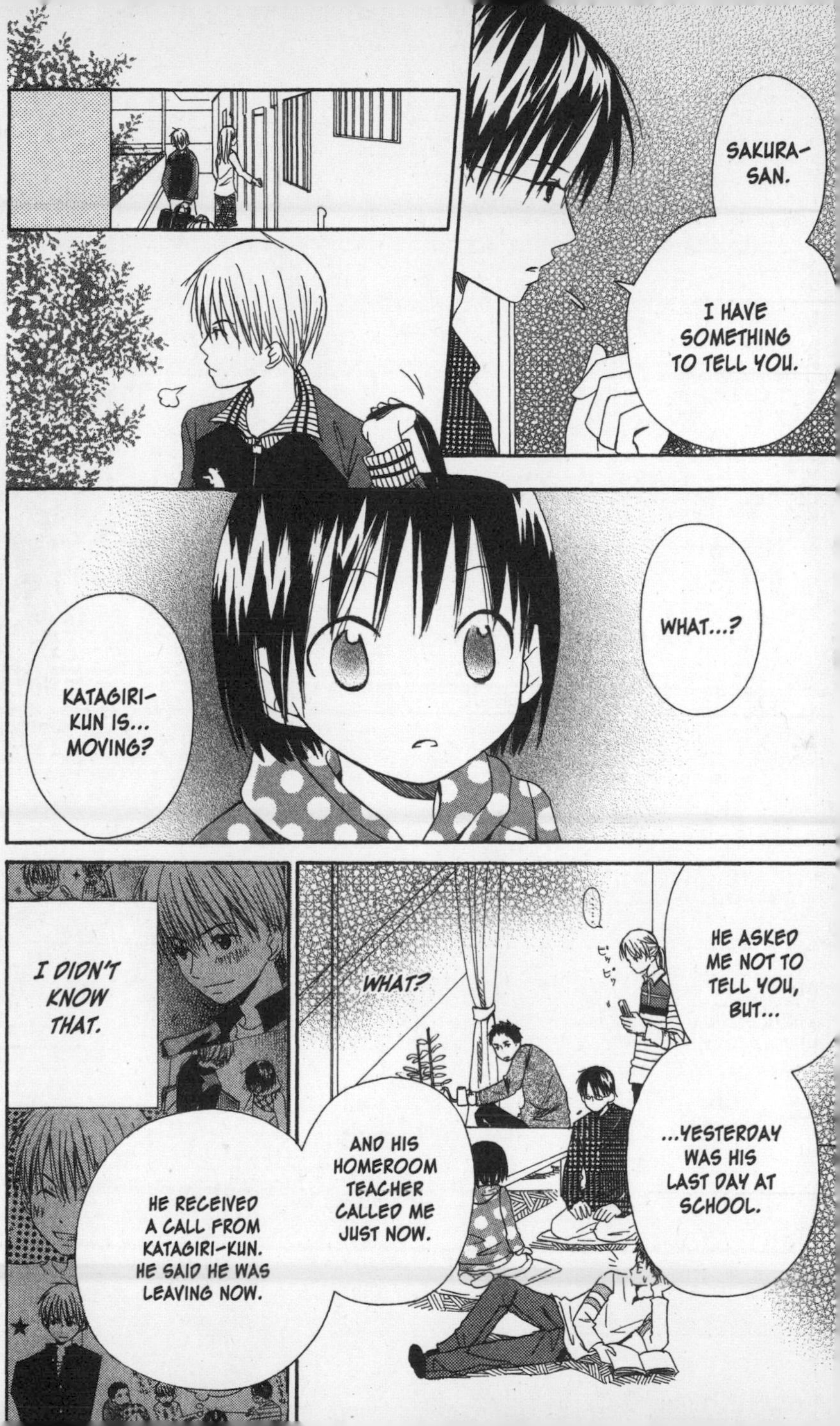
SAKURA-SAN.
I HAVE SOMETHING TO TELL YOU.
WHAT...?
KATAGIRI-KUN IS... MOVING?
HE ASKED ME NOT TO TELL YOU, BUT...
...YESTERDAY WAS HIS LAST DAY AT SCHOOL.
WHAT?
AND HIS HOMEROOM TEACHER CALLED ME JUST NOW.
HE RECEIVED A CALL FROM KATAGIRI-KUN. HE SAID HE WAS LEAVING NOW.
I DIDN'T KNOW THAT.

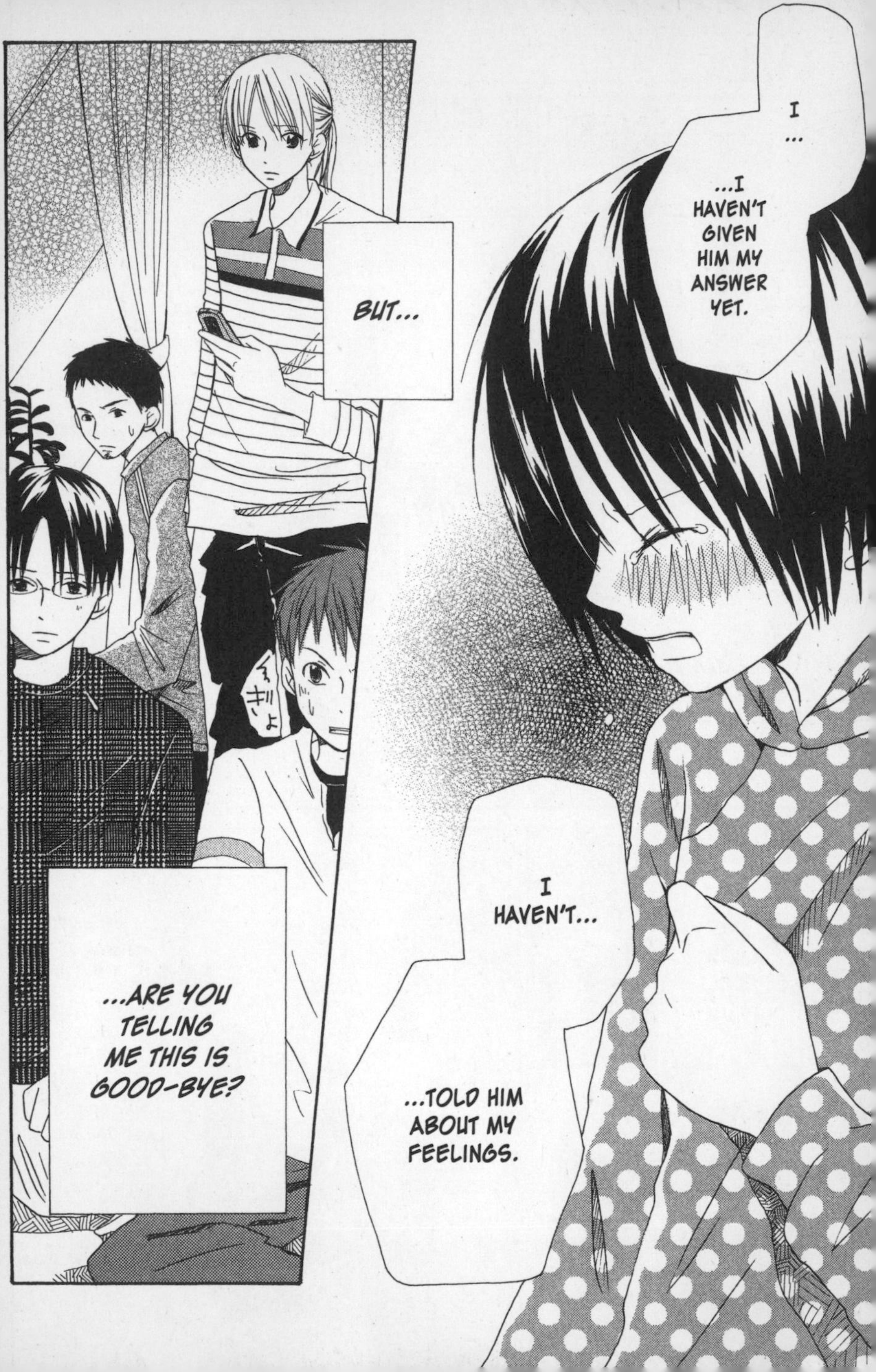
I
...
...I HAVEN'T GIVEN HIM MY ANSWER YET.
I HAVEN'T...
...TOLD HIM ABOUT MY FEELINGS.
BUT...
...ARE YOU TELLING ME THIS IS GOOD-BYE?

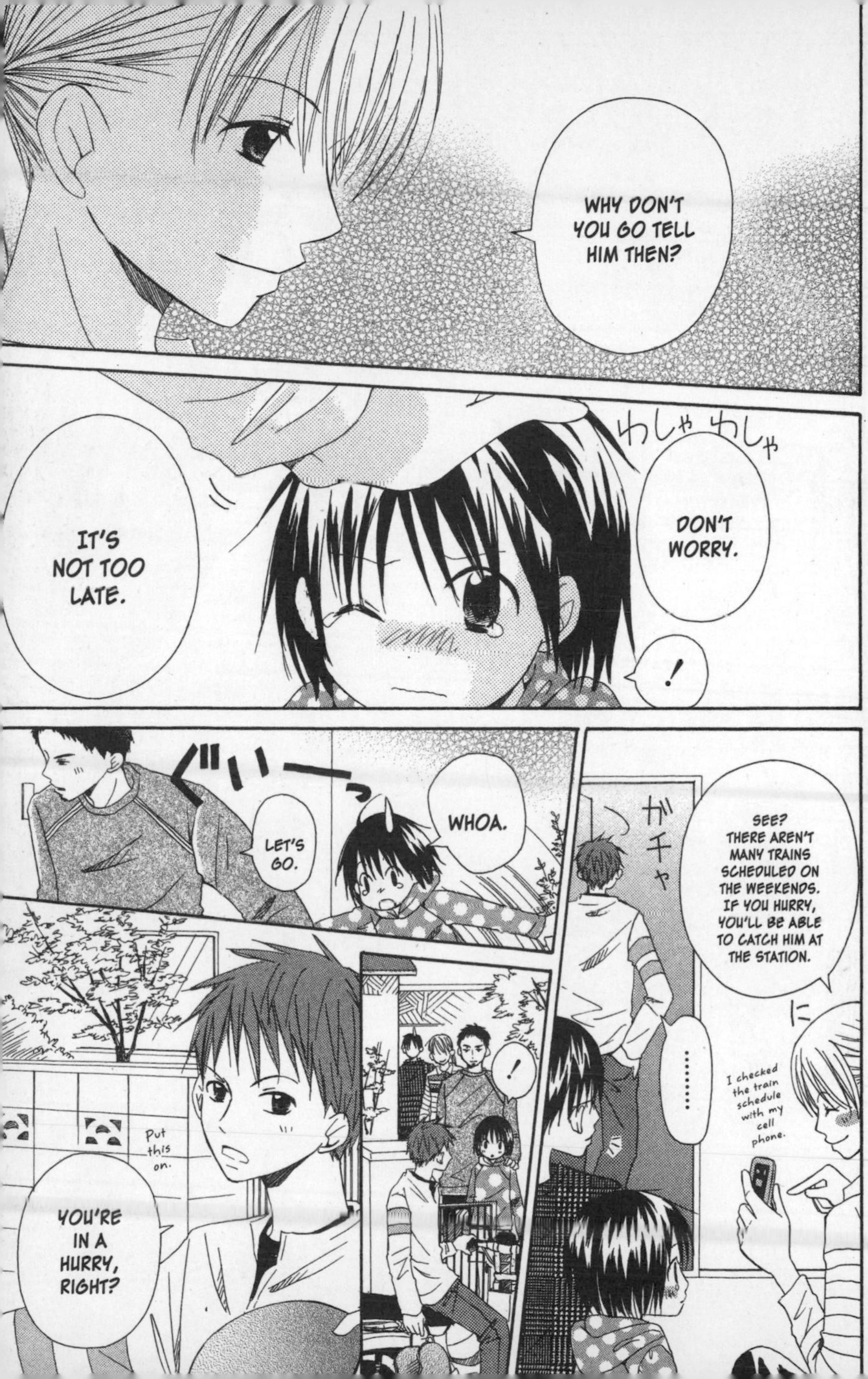
WHY DON'T YOU GO TELL HIM THEN?
わしゃ わしゃ
DON'T WORRY.
IT'S NOT TOO LATE.
!
ガチャ
SEE? THERE AREN'T MANY TRAINS SCHEDULED ON THE WEEKENDS. IF YOU HURRY, YOU'LL BE ABLE TO CATCH HIM AT THE STATION.
に
I checked the train schedule with my cell phone.
......
ぐいーっ
WHOA.
LET'S GO.
!
Put this on.
YOU'RE IN A HURRY, RIGHT?

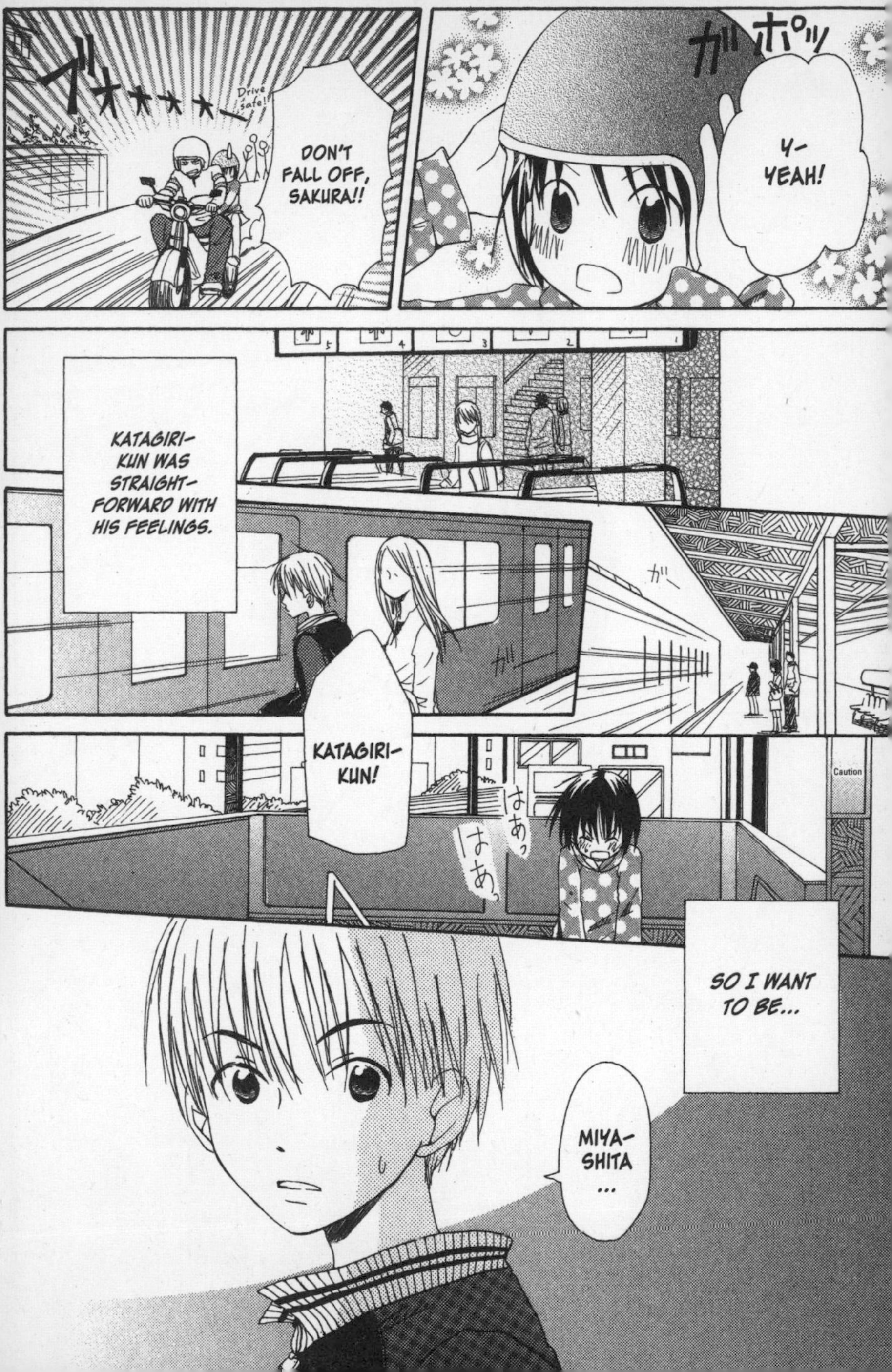
ガポッ
Y-YEAH!
ブォォォォー
Drive safe!!
DON'T FALL OFF, SAKURA!!
KATAGIRI-KUN WAS STRAIGHT-FORWARD WITH HIS FEELINGS.
ガー
ガー
KATAGIRI-KUN!
Caution
はあっ
はあ
SO I WANT TO BE...
MIYA-SHITA ...

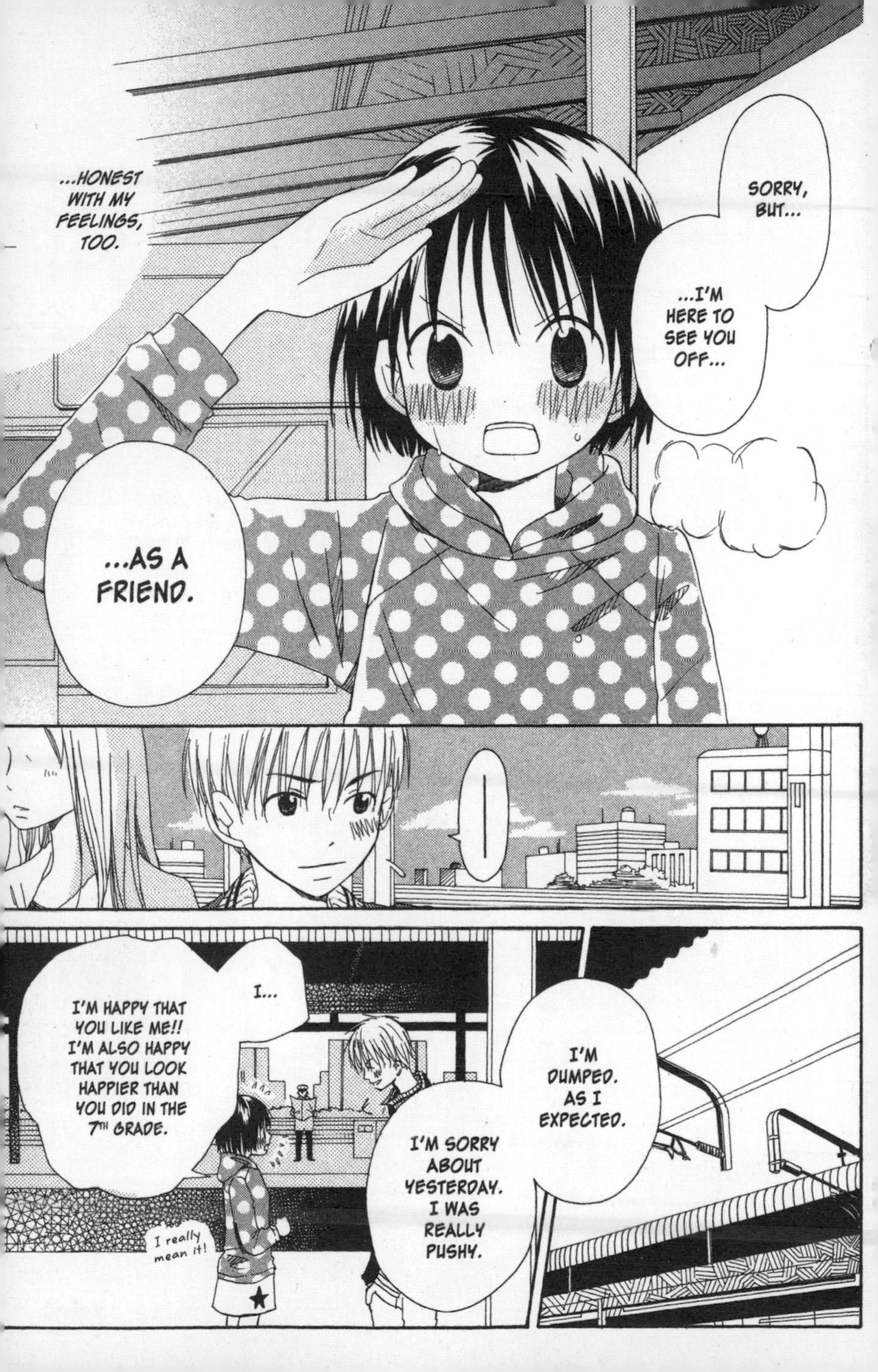
SORRY, BUT...
...I'M HERE TO SEE YOU OFF...
...HONEST WITH MY FEELINGS, TOO.
...AS A FRIEND.
!
I'M DUMPED. AS I EXPECTED.
I'M SORRY ABOUT YESTERDAY. I WAS REALLY PUSHY.
I...
I'M HAPPY THAT YOU LIKE ME!! I'M ALSO HAPPY THAT YOU LOOK HAPPIER THAN YOU DID IN THE 7TH GRADE.
I really mean it!

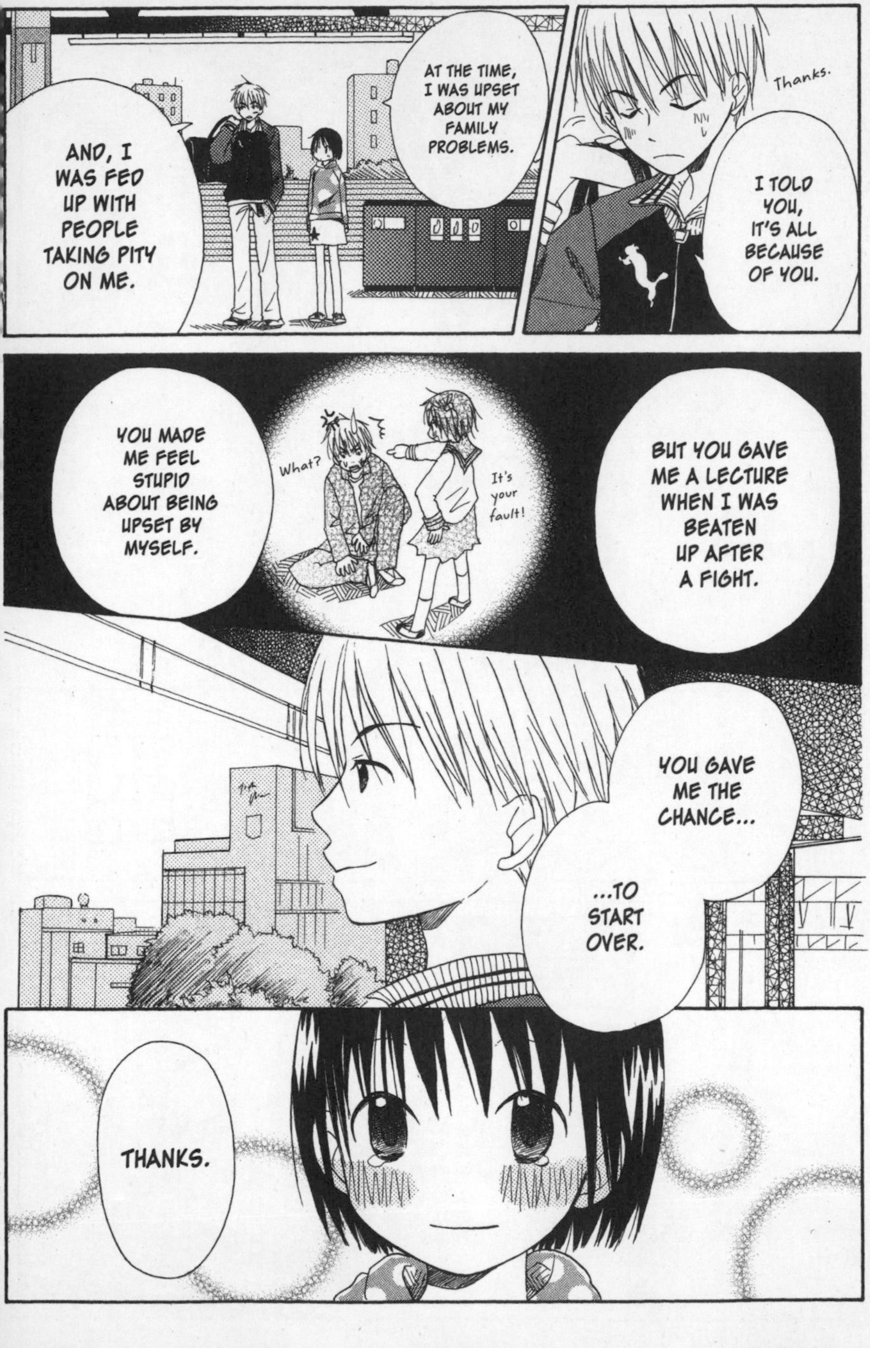
Thanks.
I TOLD YOU, IT'S ALL BECAUSE OF YOU.
AT THE TIME, I WAS UPSET ABOUT MY FAMILY PROBLEMS.
AND, I WAS FED UP WITH PEOPLE TAKING PITY ON ME.
BUT YOU GAVE ME A LECTURE WHEN I WAS BEATEN UP AFTER A FIGHT.
It's your fault!
What?
YOU MADE ME FEEL STUPID ABOUT BEING UPSET BY MYSELF.
YOU GAVE ME THE CHANCE...
...TO START OVER.
THANKS.

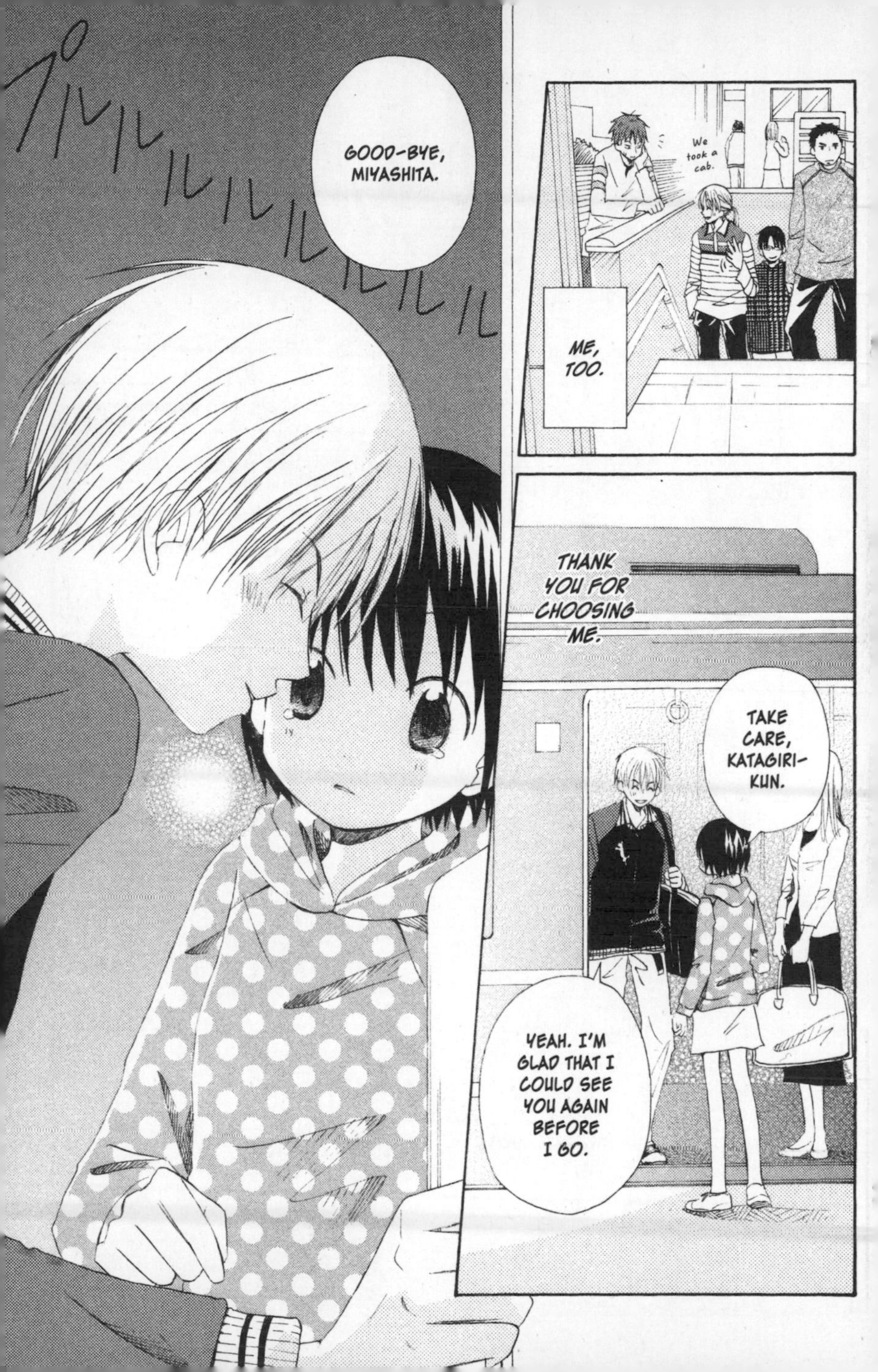
We took a cab.
ME, TOO.
THANK YOU FOR CHOOSING ME.
TAKE CARE, KATAGIRI-KUN.
YEAH. I'M GLAD THAT I COULD SEE YOU AGAIN BEFORE I GO.
GOOD-BYE, MIYASHITA.
プルルルルルルル

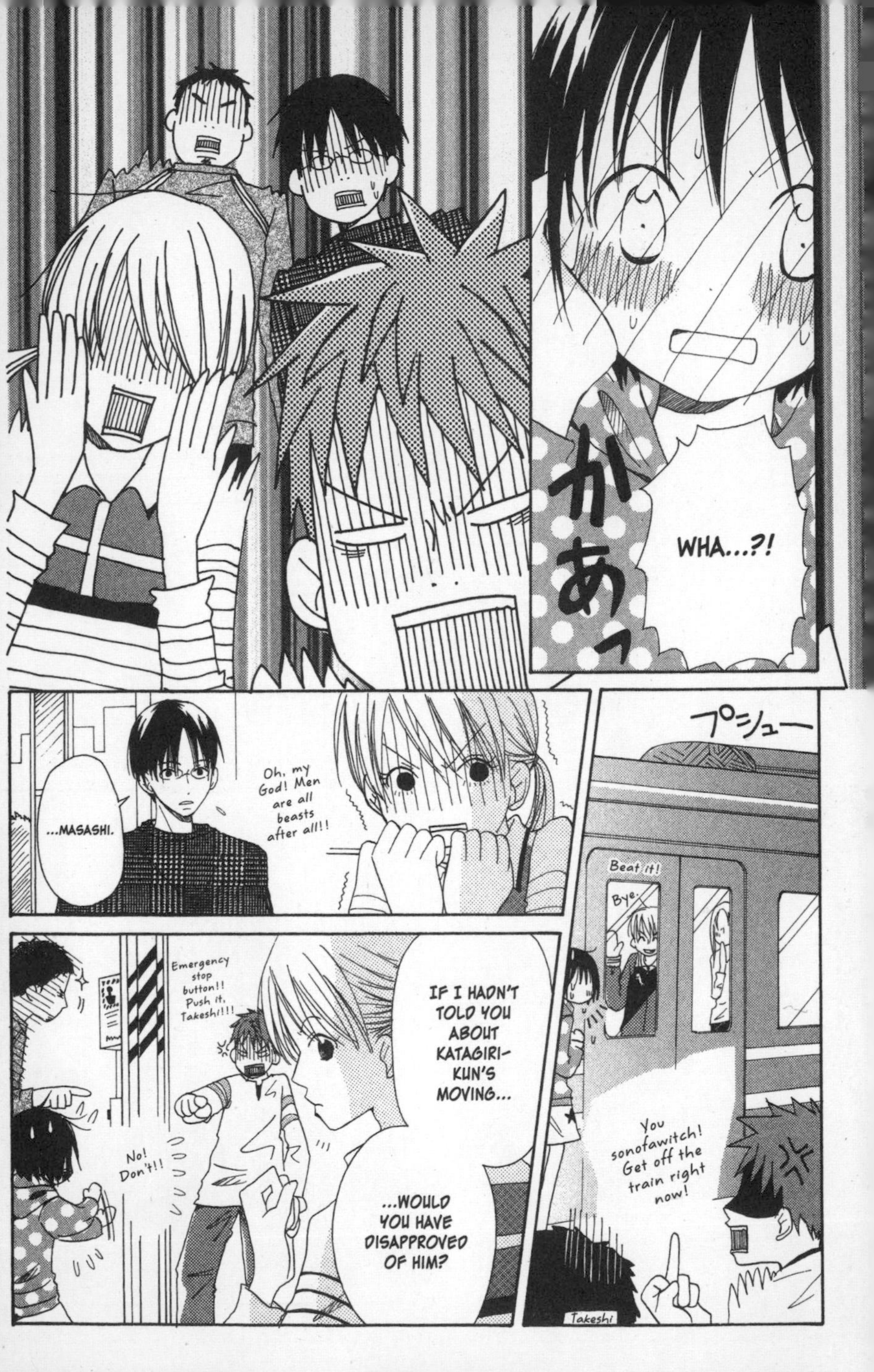
かあっ
WHA...?!
プシュー
Beat it!
Bye.
You sonofawitch! Get off the train right now!
Takeshi
Oh, my God! Men are all beasts after all!!
...MASASHI.
IF I HADN'T TOLD YOU ABOUT KATAGIRI-KUN'S MOVING...
...WOULD YOU HAVE DISAPPROVED OF HIM?
Emergency stop button!! Push it, Takeshi!!!
No! Don't!!

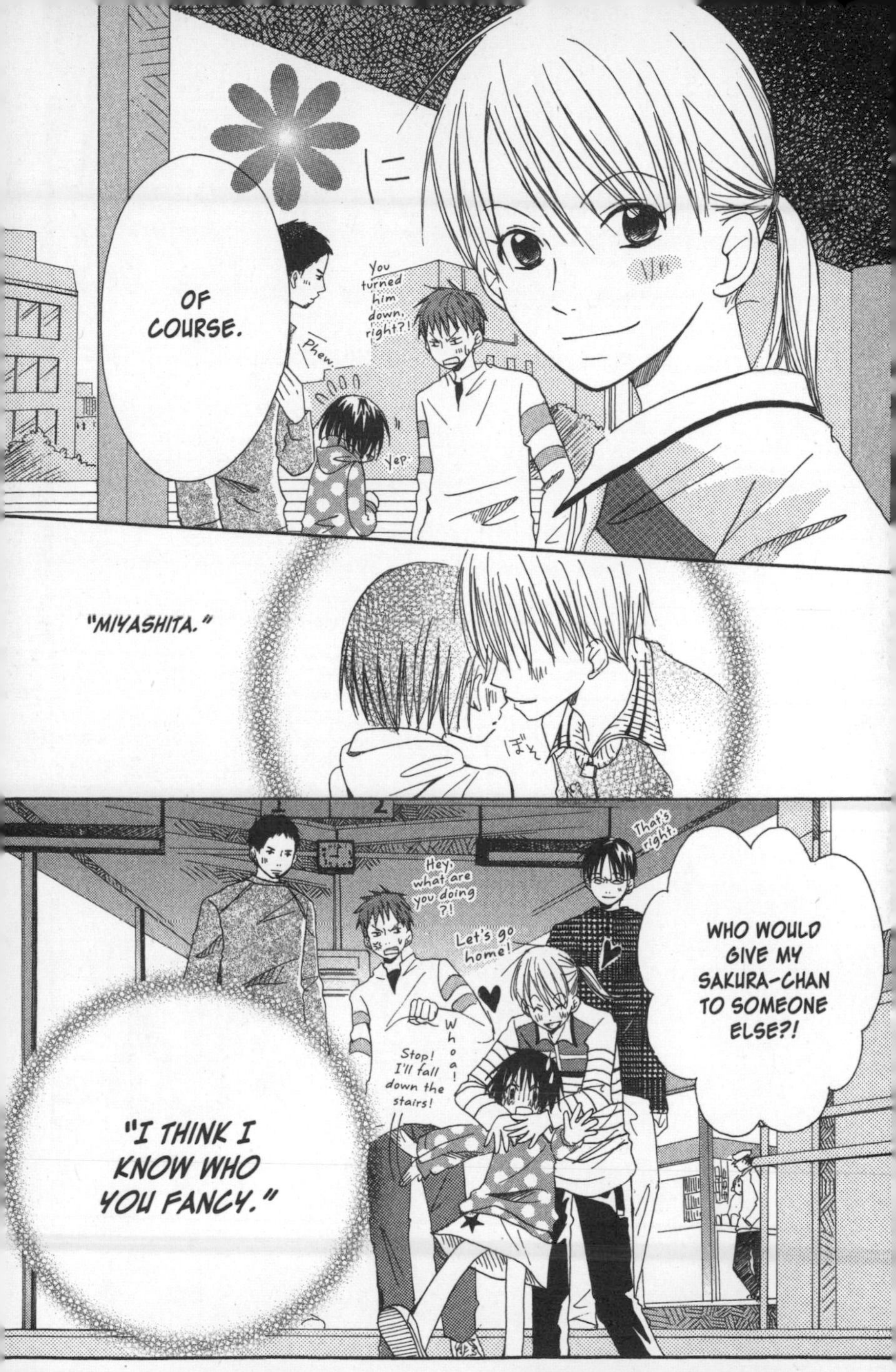
You turned him down, right?!
OF COURSE.
Phew.
Yep.
"MIYASHITA."
ぼそ
That's right.
WHO WOULD GIVE MY SAKURA-CHAN TO SOMEONE ELSE?!
Hey, what are you doing?!
Let's go home!
Whoa!
Stop! I'll fall down the stairs!
"I THINK I KNOW WHO YOU FANCY."

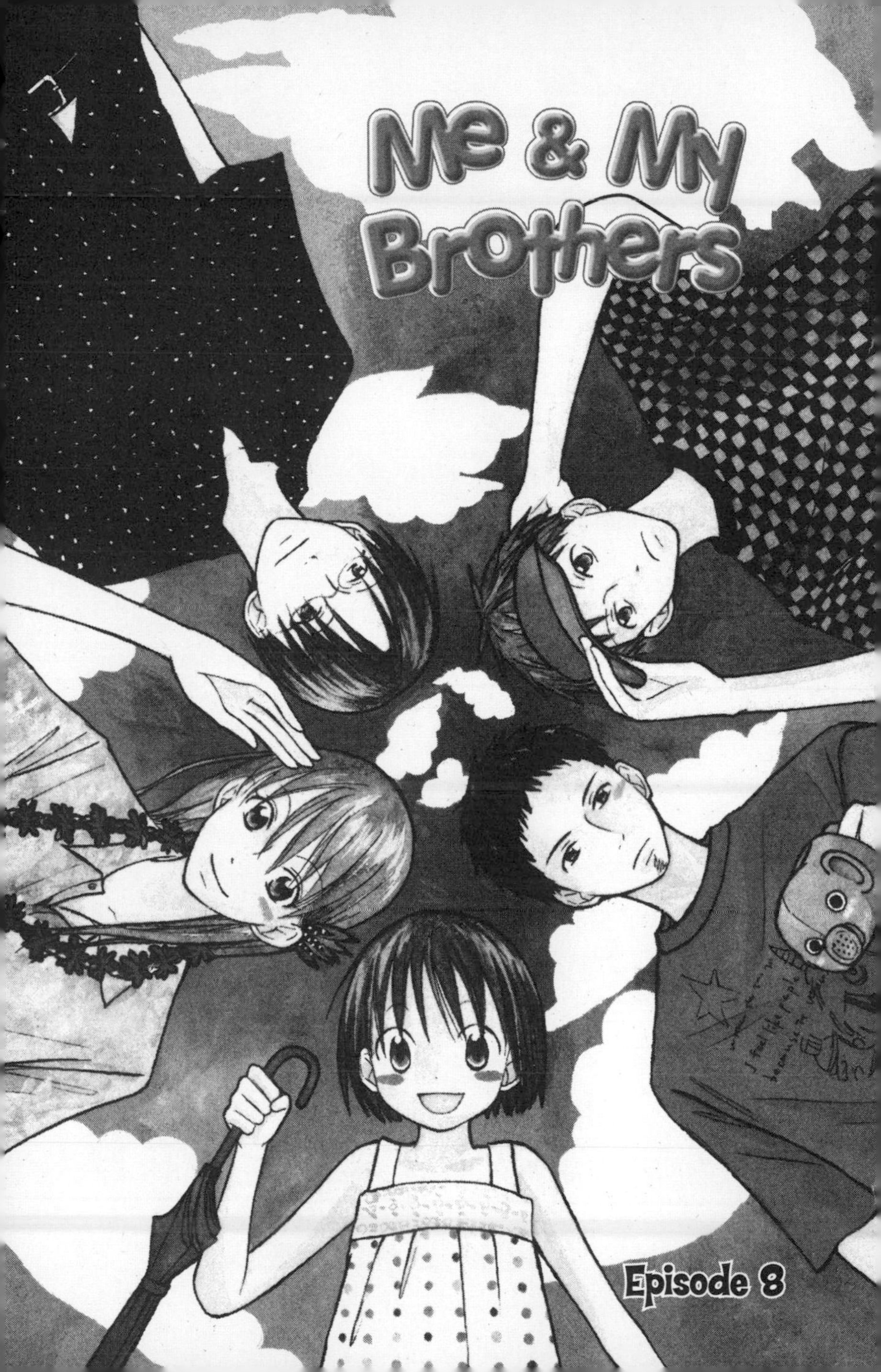
Me & My Brothers
Episode 8

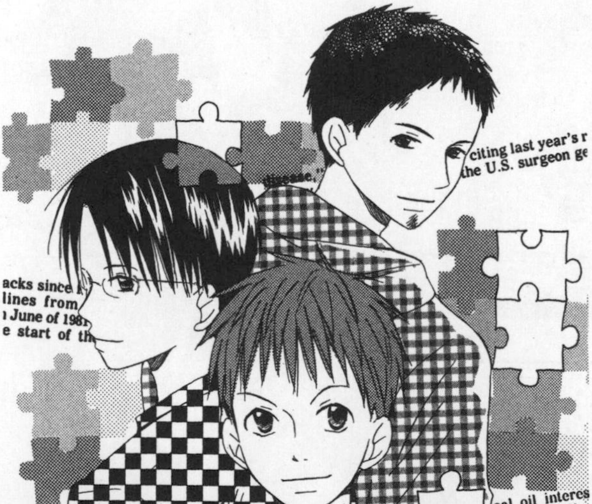

citing last year's
the U.S. surgeon
acks since
lines from
June of 198
e start of th
cal oil interes
health effe
alaysian P
Council has
tion camp
ritten me
port its ca
makers.

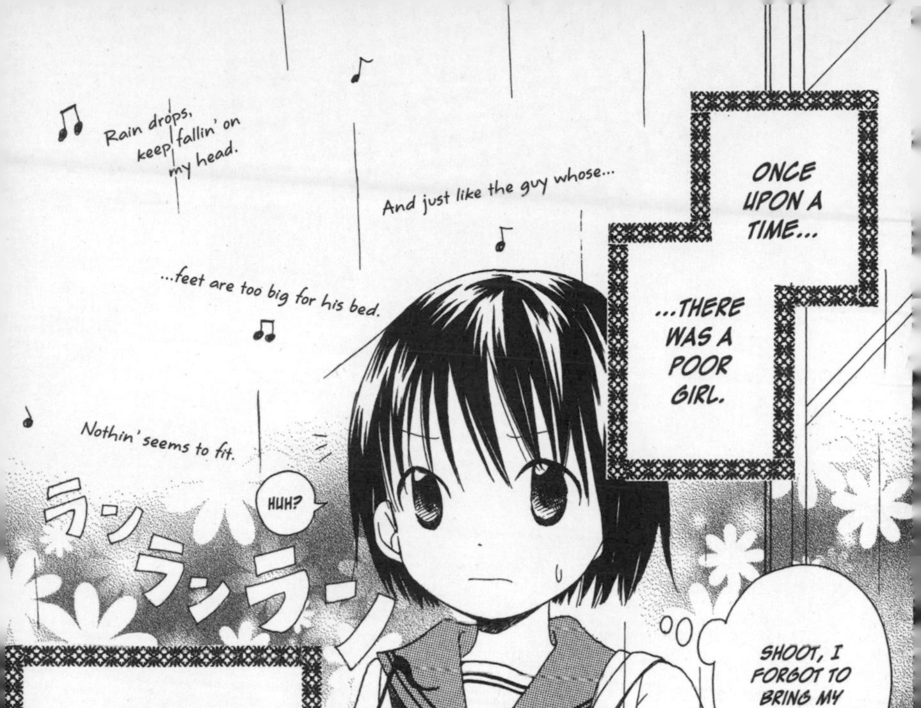
ONCE UPON A TIME...
...THERE WAS A POOR GIRL.
Rain drops, keep fallin' on my head.
And just like the guy whose...
...feet are too big for his bed.
Nothin' seems to fit.
ラン ランラン
SHOOT, I FORGOT TO BRING MY UMBRELLA.
HUH?
SHE WAS RAISED BY HER GRANDMOTHER BECAUSE HER PARENTS DIED WHEN SHE WAS VERY LITTLE, BUT THEN LAST YEAR, THE GRANDMOTHER DIED.
Sakura Miyashita: 9th grade
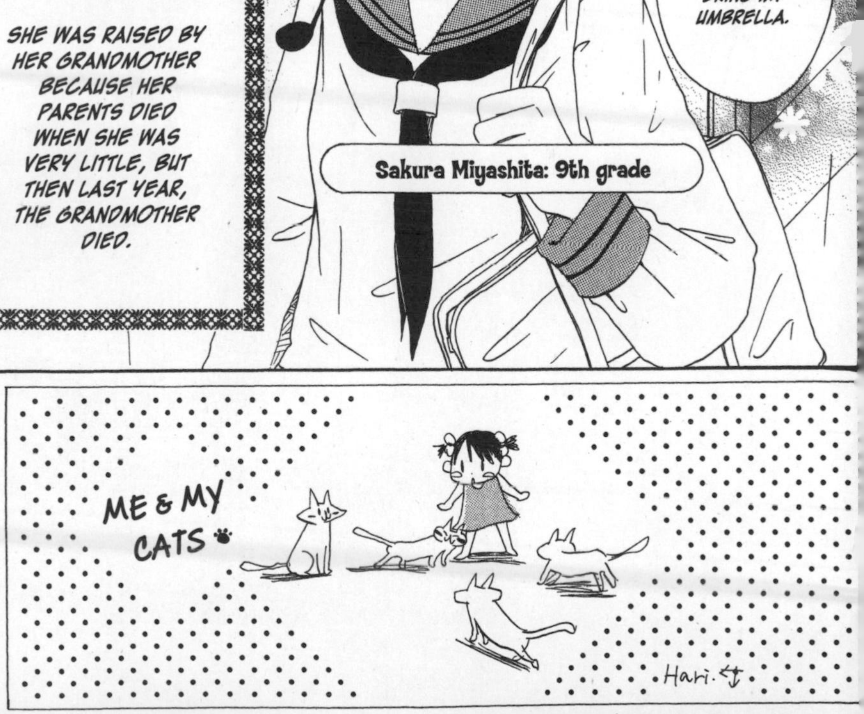
ME & MY CATS
Hari.

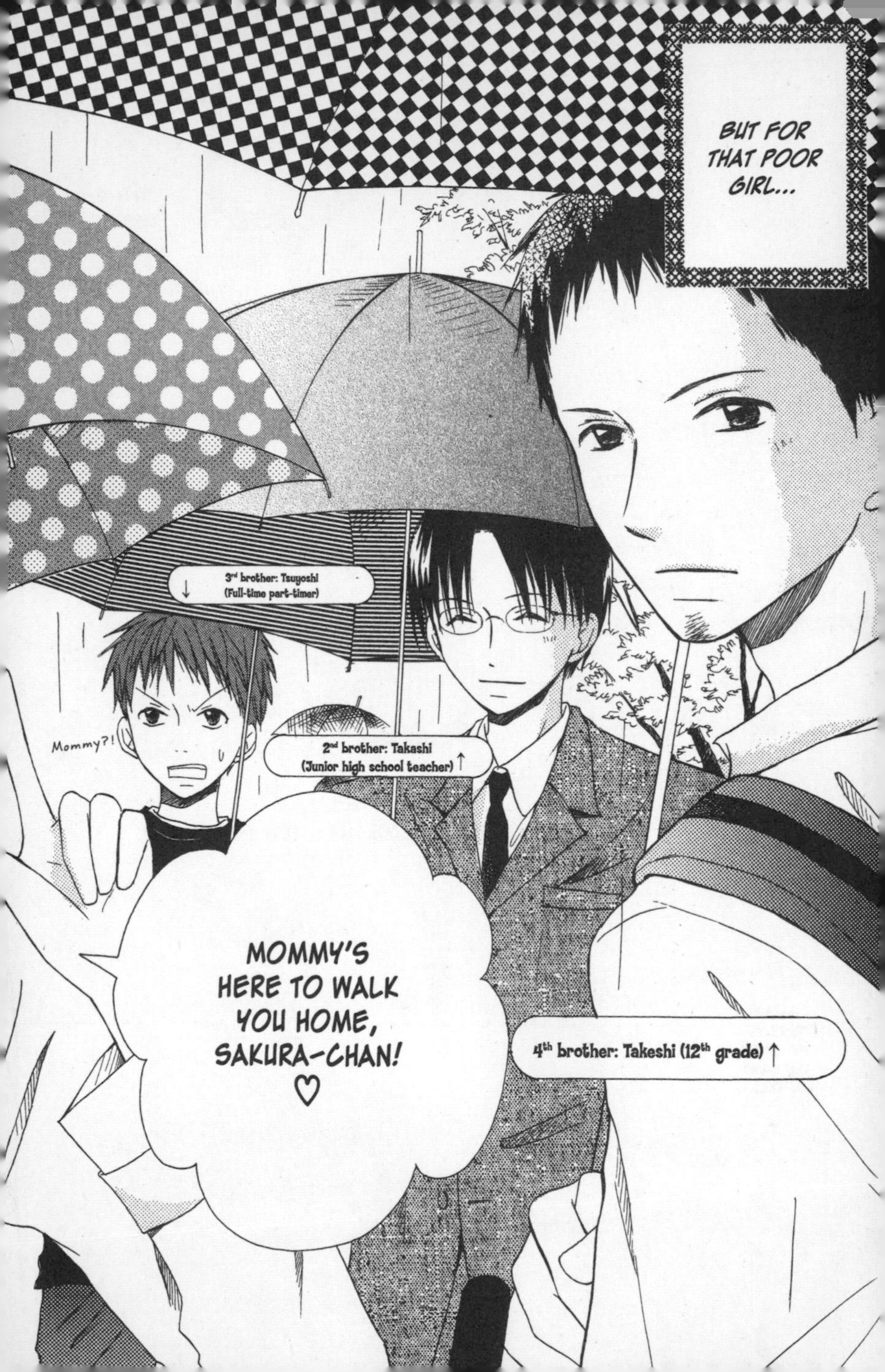
BUT FOR THAT POOR GIRL...
3rd brother: Tsuyoshi ↓ (Full-time part-timer)
2nd brother: Takashi (Junior high school teacher) ↑
Mommy?!
4th brother: Takeshi (12th grade) ↑
MOMMY'S HERE TO WALK YOU HOME, SAKURA-CHAN! ♡

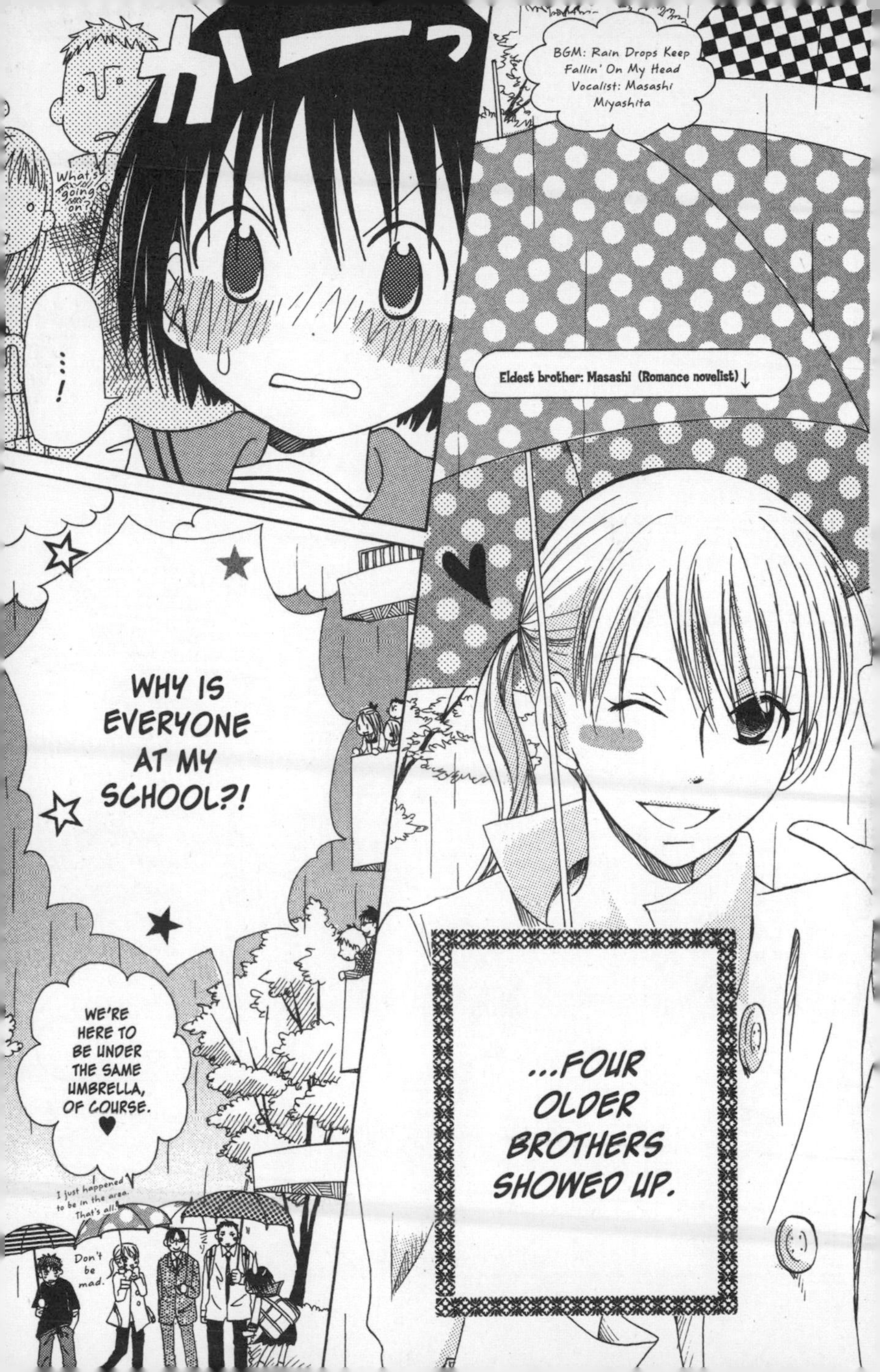
BGM: Rain Drops Keep Fallin' On My Head Vocalist: Masashi Miyashita
Eldest brother: Masashi (Romance novelist) ↓
...FOUR OLDER BROTHERS SHOWED UP.
カーっ
What's going on?
...!
WHY IS EVERYONE AT MY SCHOOL?!
WE'RE HERE TO BE UNDER THE SAME UMBRELLA, OF COURSE. ♥
I just happened to be in the area. That's all!!
Don't be mad.

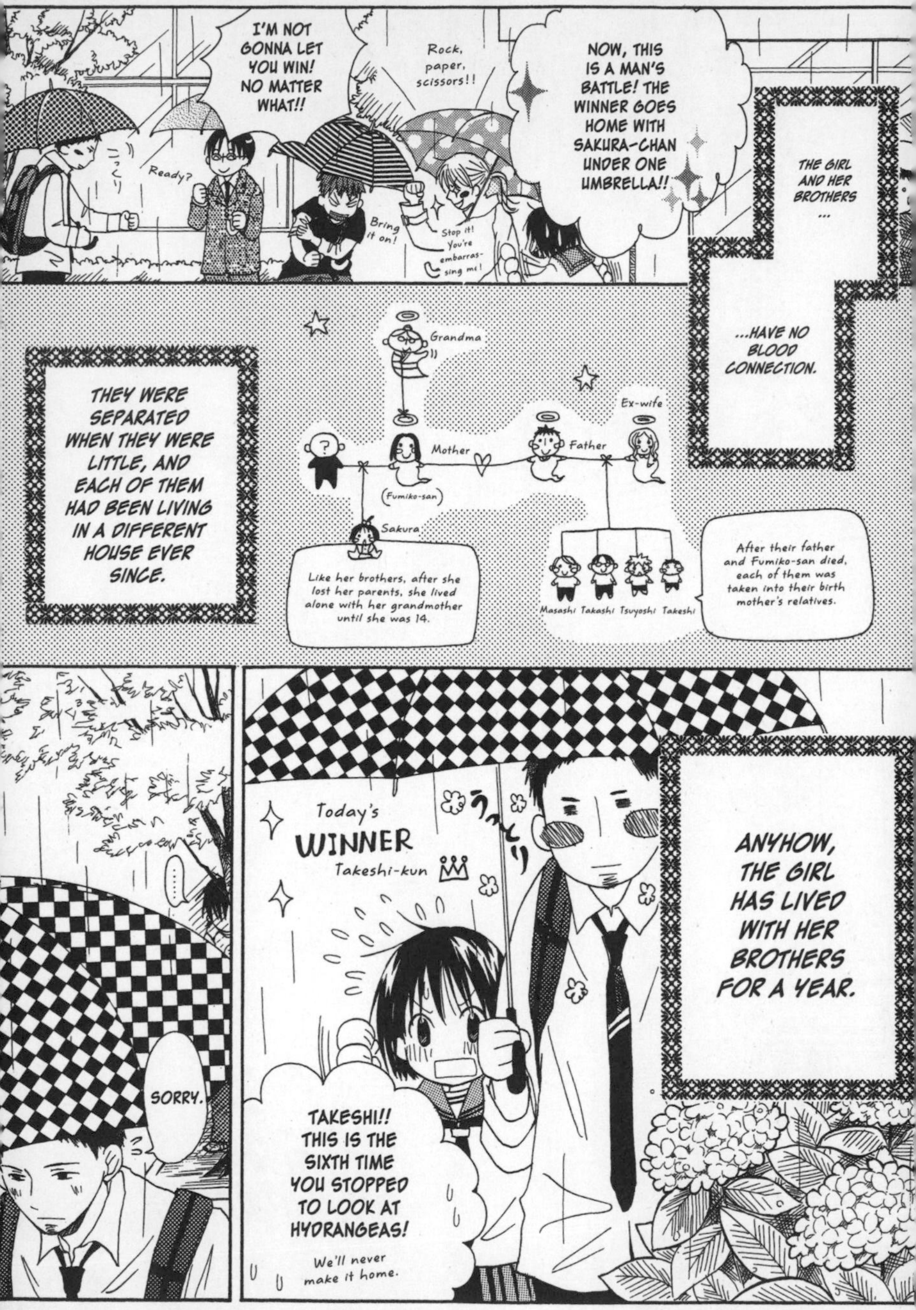
THE GIRL AND HER BROTHERS ...
NOW, THIS IS A MAN'S BATTLE! THE WINNER GOES HOME WITH SAKURA-CHAN UNDER ONE UMBRELLA!!
Rock, paper, scissors!!
I'M NOT GONNA LET YOU WIN! NO MATTER WHAT!!
Stop it! You're embarrassing me!
Bring it on!
Ready?
...HAVE NO BLOOD CONNECTION.
THEY WERE SEPARATED WHEN THEY WERE LITTLE, AND EACH OF THEM HAD BEEN LIVING IN A DIFFERENT HOUSE EVER SINCE.
Grandma
Ex-wife
Father
Mother
(Fumiko-san)
Sakura
Masashi Takashi Tsuyoshi Takeshi
After their father and Fumiko-san died, each of them was taken into their birth mother's relatives.
Like her brothers, after she lost her parents, she lived alone with her grandmother until she was 14.
ANYHOW, THE GIRL HAS LIVED WITH HER BROTHERS FOR A YEAR.
Today's WINNER Takeshi-kun
TAKESHI!! THIS IS THE SIXTH TIME YOU STOPPED TO LOOK AT HYDRANGEAS!
We'll never make it home.
......
SORRY.

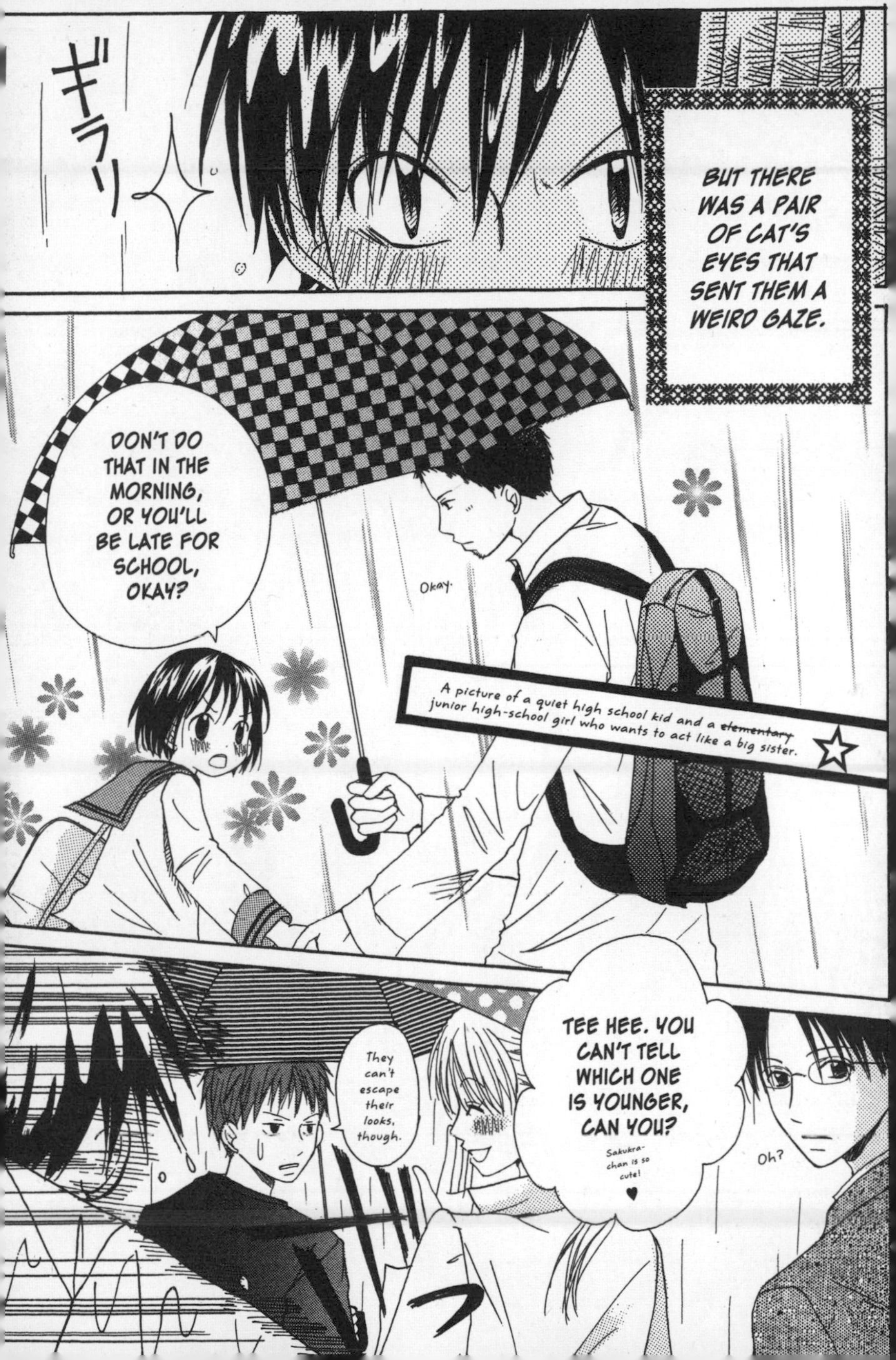
BUT THERE WAS A PAIR OF CAT'S EYES THAT SENT THEM A WEIRD GAZE.
ギラリ
DON'T DO THAT IN THE MORNING, OR YOU'LL BE LATE FOR SCHOOL, OKAY?
Okay.
A picture of a quiet high school kid and a ~~elementary~~ junior high-school girl who wants to act like a big sister.
Oh?
TEE HEE. YOU CAN'T TELL WHICH ONE IS YOUNGER, CAN YOU?
Sakukra-chan is so cute! ♥
They can't escape their looks, though.

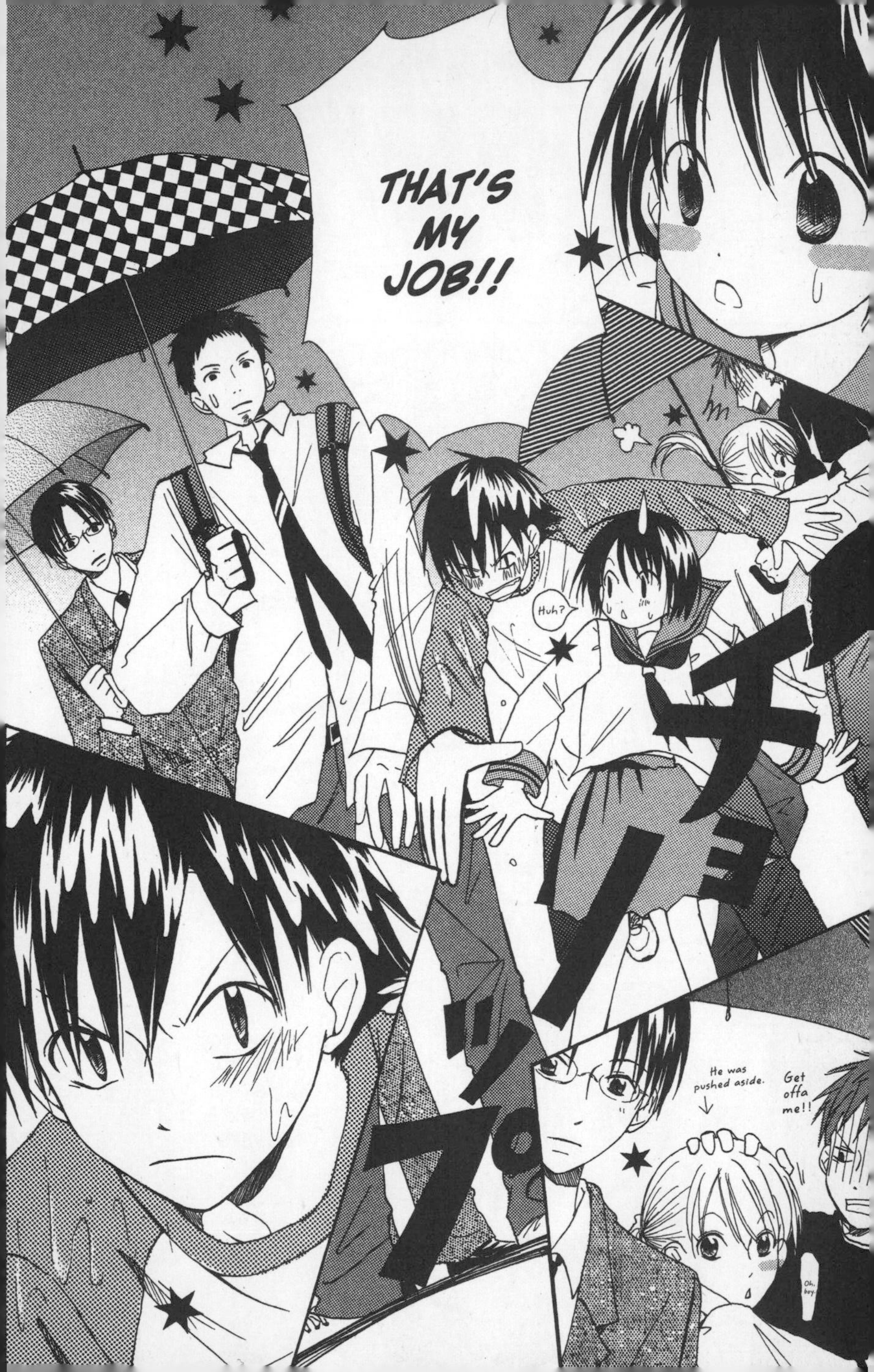
THAT'S MY JOB!!
Huh?
Get offa me!!
He was pushed aside.
Oh, boy.

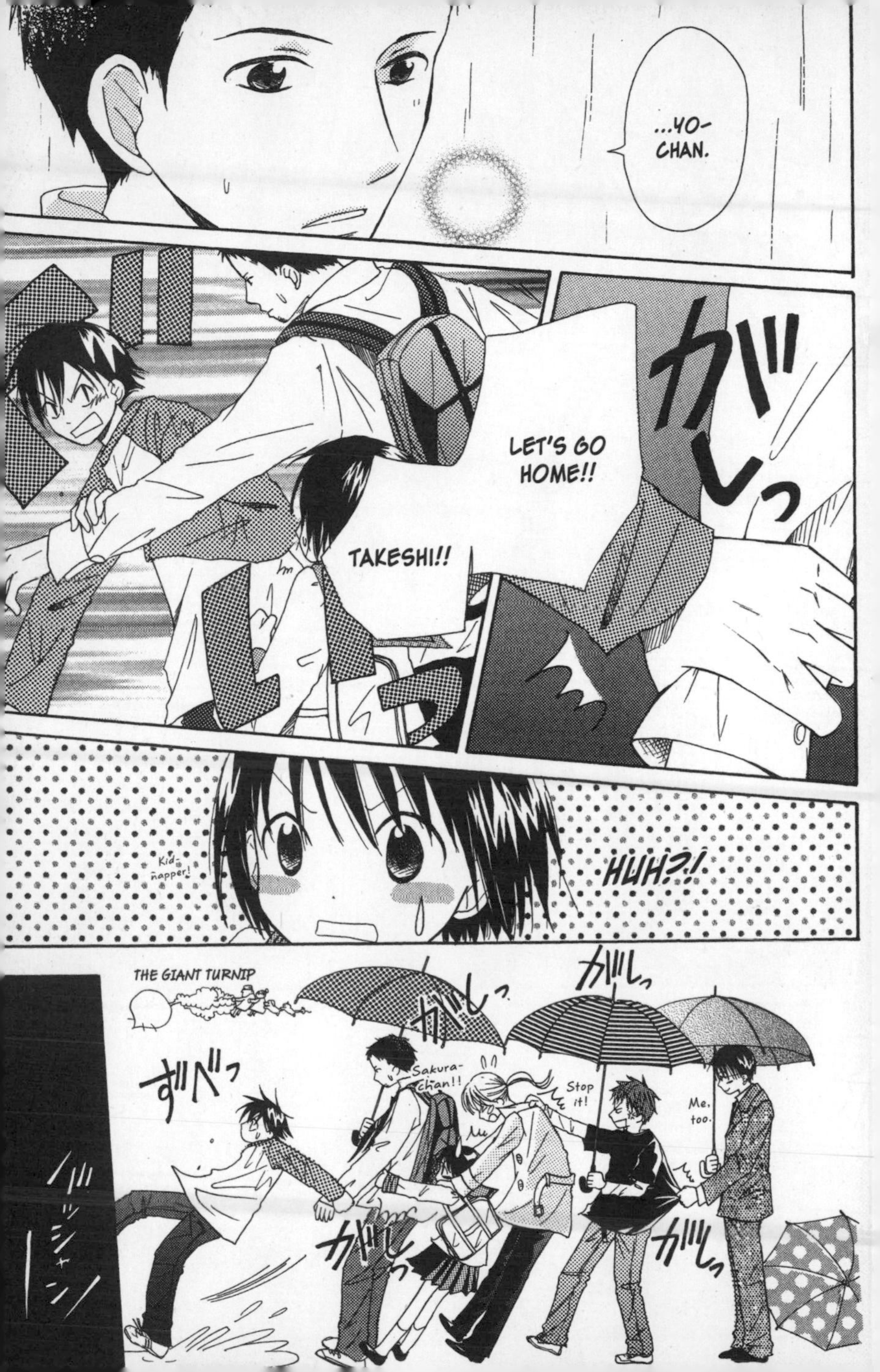
...YO-CHAN.
ガしっ
LET'S GO HOME!!
TAKESHI!!
HUH?!
Kid-napper!
THE GIANT TURNIP
ガしっ
Me, too.
ガしっ
Stop it!
ガしっ
Sakura-chan!!
ガしっ
ずべっ
バッシャン

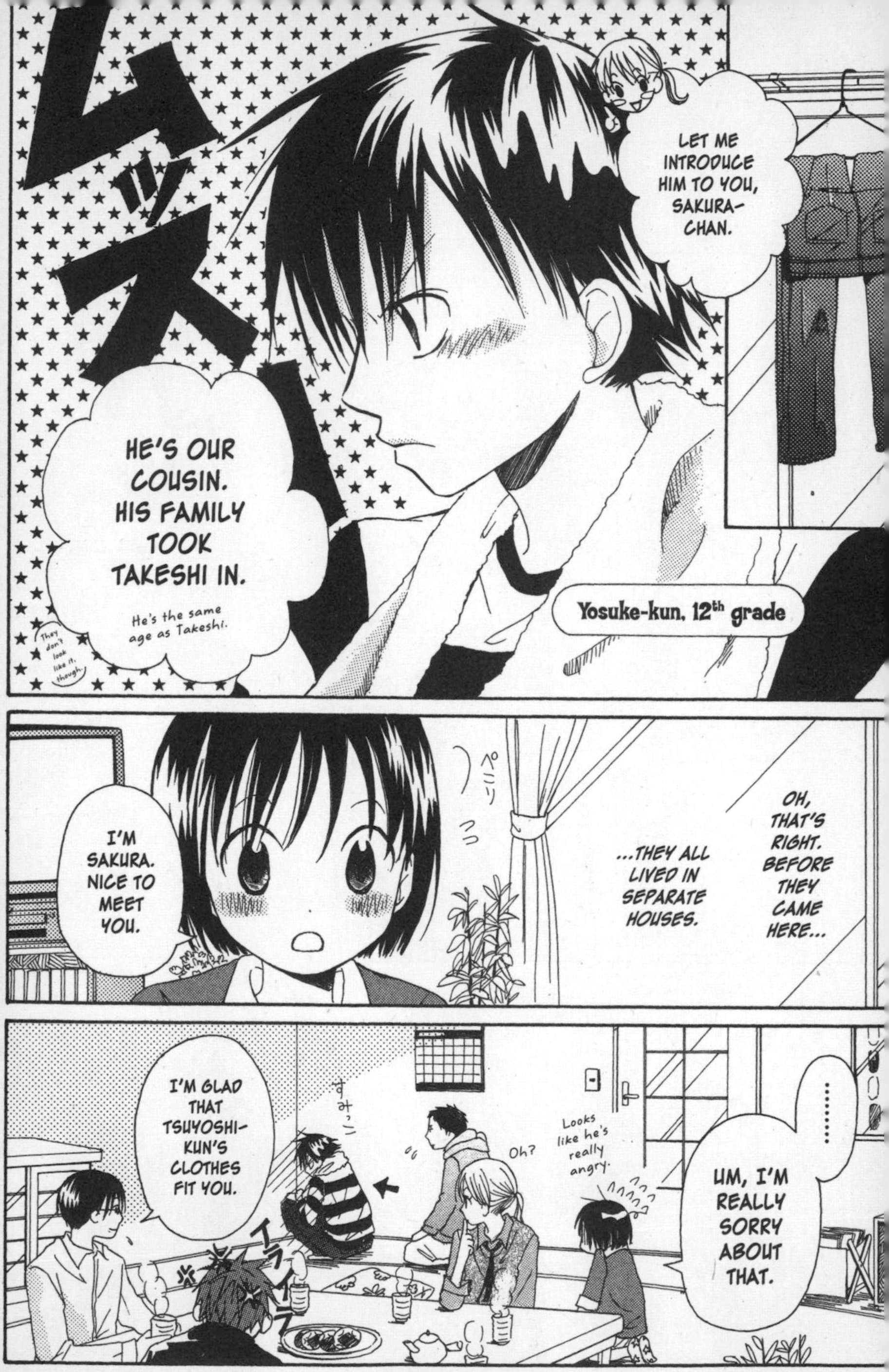
LET ME INTRODUCE HIM TO YOU, SAKURA-CHAN.
Yosuke-kun, 12th grade
HE'S OUR COUSIN. HIS FAMILY TOOK TAKESHI IN.
He's the same age as Takeshi.
They don't look like it, though.
OH, THAT'S RIGHT. BEFORE THEY CAME HERE...
...THEY ALL LIVED IN SEPARATE HOUSES.
I'M SAKURA. NICE TO MEET YOU.
......
UM, I'M REALLY SORRY ABOUT THAT.
Looks like he's really angry.
Oh?
I'M GLAD THAT TSUYOSHI-KUN'S CLOTHES FIT YOU.

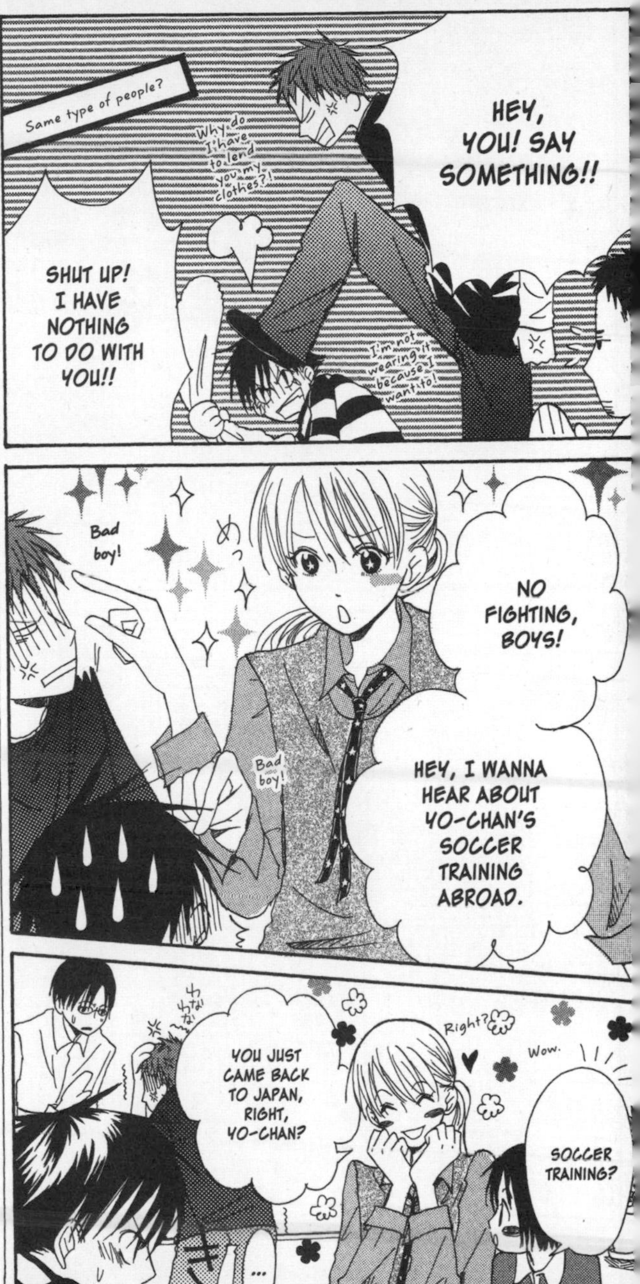
HEY, YOU! SAY SOMETHING!!
Same type of people?
Why do I have to lend you my clothes?!
I'm not wearing it because I want to!
SHUT UP! I HAVE NOTHING TO DO WITH YOU!!
NO FIGHTING, BOYS!
HEY, I WANNA HEAR ABOUT YO-CHAN'S SOCCER TRAINING ABROAD.
Bad boy!
Bad boy!
SOCCER TRAINING?
Wow.
Right?
YOU JUST CAME BACK TO JAPAN, RIGHT, YO-CHAN?
...

☆4☆

Yo-chan was a fun character to draw. I like his personality, but it's also true that I think he's too childish for a 12th grader. But my older sister said that guys can be childish, so he's fine.

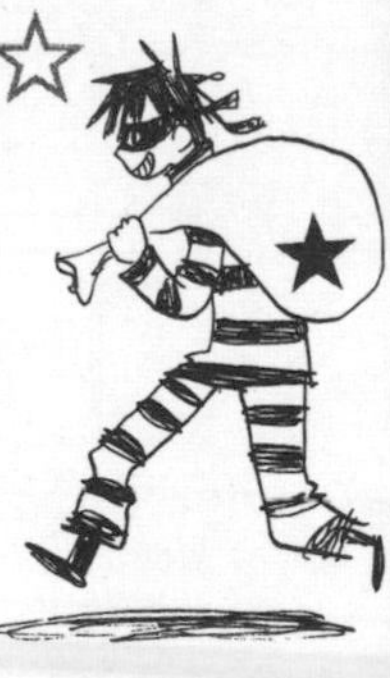

Cat eye boy, the Mysterious Thief

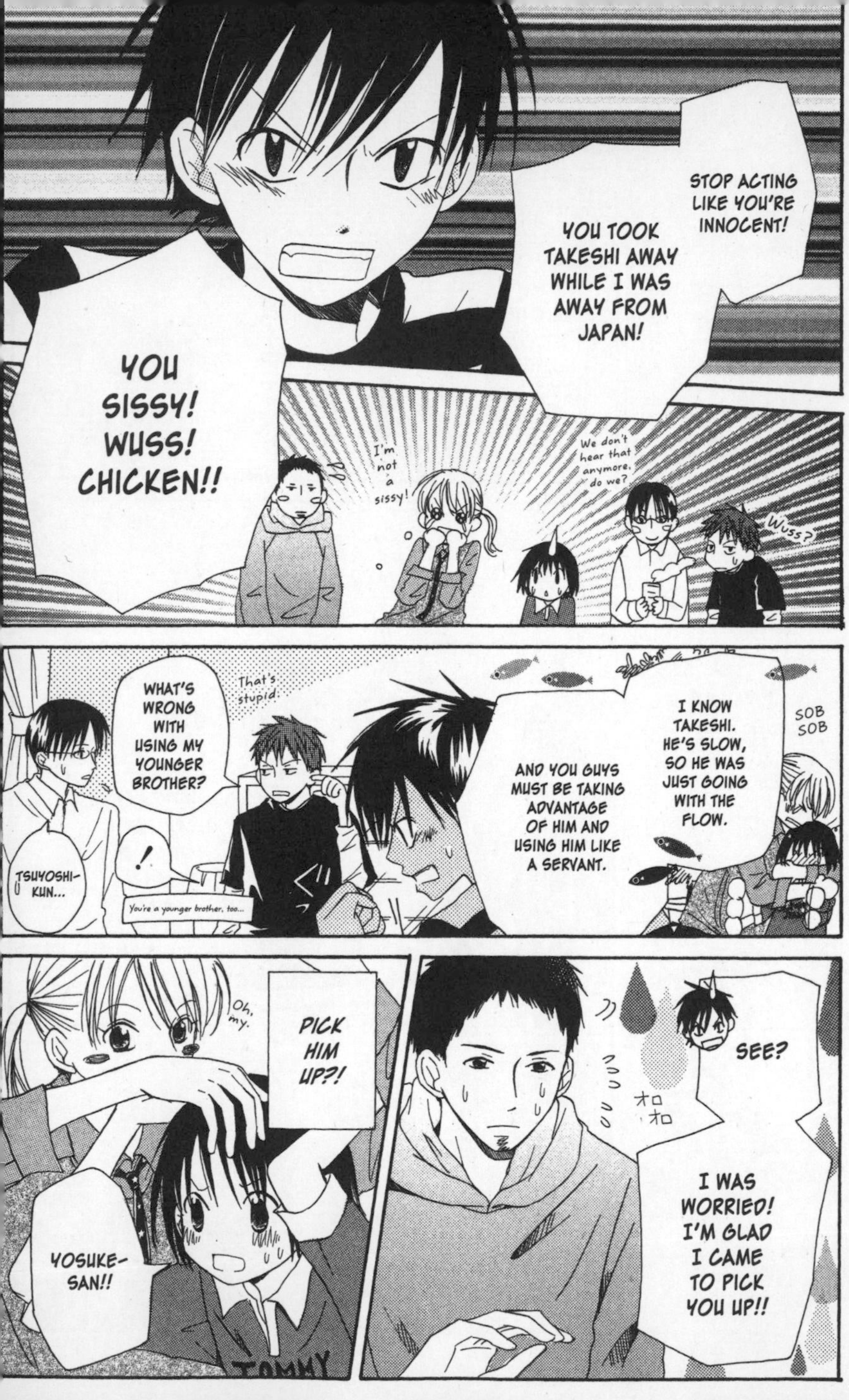
STOP ACTING LIKE YOU'RE INNOCENT!
YOU TOOK TAKESHI AWAY WHILE I WAS AWAY FROM JAPAN!
YOU SISSY! WUSS! CHICKEN!!
Wuss?
We don't hear that anymore, do we?
I'm not a sissy!
SOB SOB
I KNOW TAKESHI. HE'S SLOW, SO HE WAS JUST GOING WITH THE FLOW.
AND YOU GUYS MUST BE TAKING ADVANTAGE OF HIM AND USING HIM LIKE A SERVANT.
That's stupid.
WHAT'S WRONG WITH USING MY YOUNGER BROTHER?
!
You're a younger brother, too...
TSUYOSHI-KUN...
SEE?
I WAS WORRIED! I'M GLAD I CAME TO PICK YOU UP!!
オロオロ
PICK HIM UP?!
Oh, my.
YOSUKE-SAN!!
TOMMY

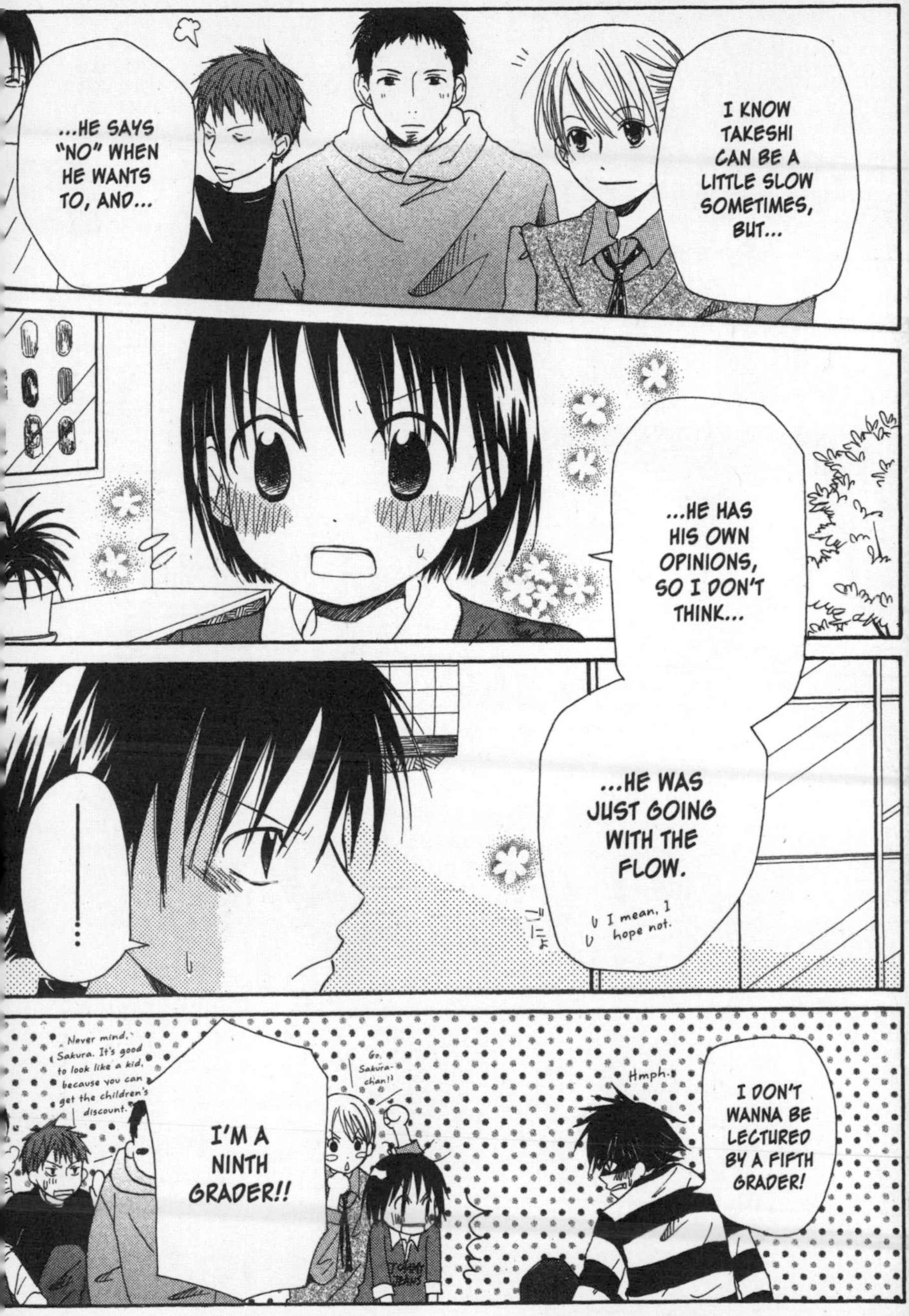

I KNOW TAKESHI CAN BE A LITTLE SLOW SOMETIMES, BUT...
...HE SAYS "NO" WHEN HE WANTS TO, AND...
...HE HAS HIS OWN OPINIONS, SO I DON'T THINK...
...HE WAS JUST GOING WITH THE FLOW.
I mean, I hope not.
......
I DON'T WANNA BE LECTURED BY A FIFTH GRADER!
Hmph.
Go, Sakura-chan!!
I'M A NINTH GRADER!!
Never mind, Sakura. It's good to look like a kid, because you can get the children's discount.

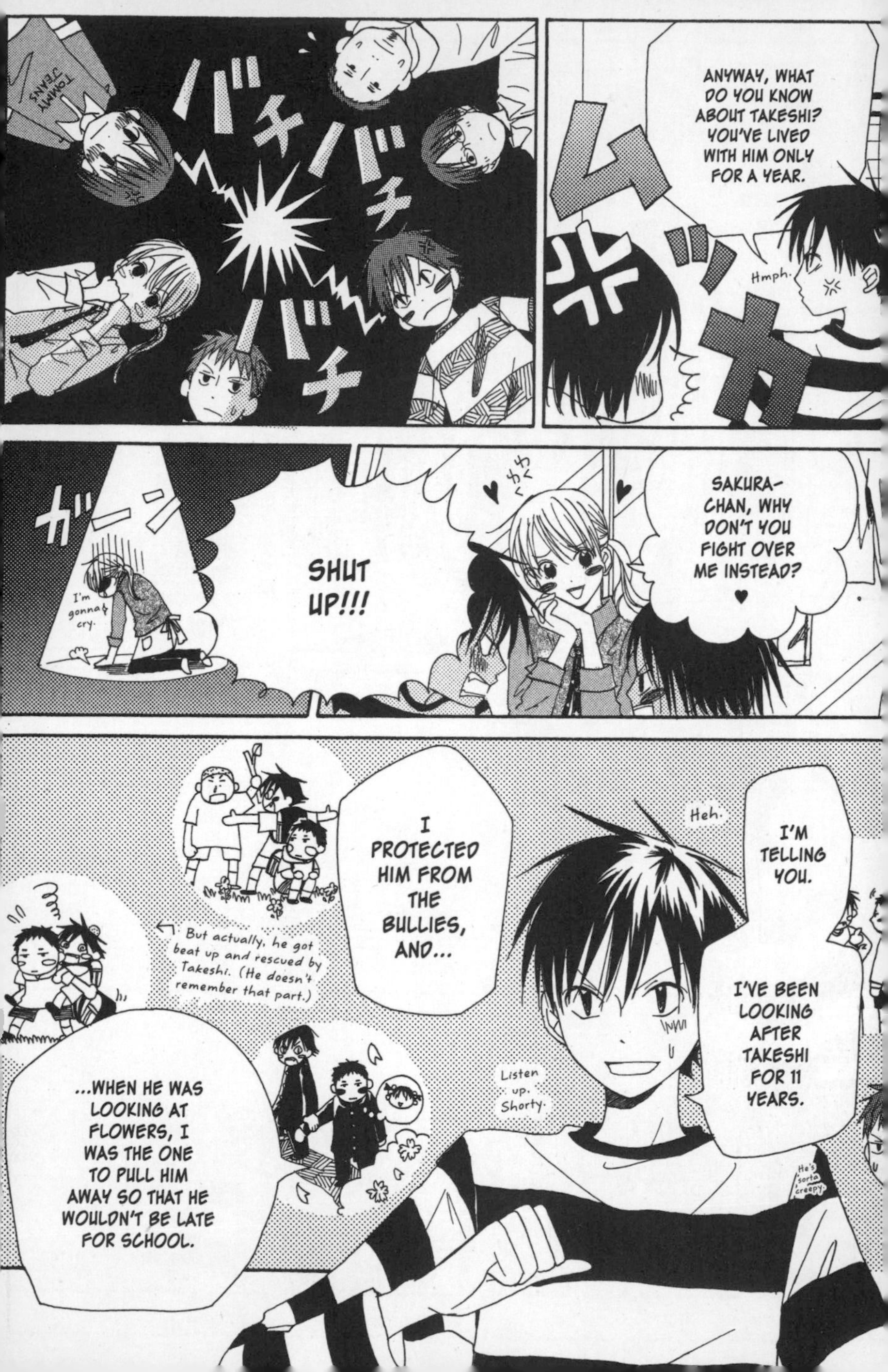
ANYWAY, WHAT DO YOU KNOW ABOUT TAKESHI? YOU'VE LIVED WITH HIM ONLY FOR A YEAR.
Hmph.
ムッカ
バチバチバチ
TOMMY JEANS
SAKURA-CHAN, WHY DON'T YOU FIGHT OVER ME INSTEAD? ♥
わくわく
SHUT UP!!!
ガーン
I'm gonna cry.
Heh.
I'M TELLING YOU.
I'VE BEEN LOOKING AFTER TAKESHI FOR 11 YEARS.
Listen up, Shorty.
He's sorta creepy.
I PROTECTED HIM FROM THE BULLIES, AND...
But actually, he got beat up and rescued by Takeshi. (He doesn't remember that part.)
...WHEN HE WAS LOOKING AT FLOWERS, I WAS THE ONE TO PULL HIM AWAY SO THAT HE WOULDN'T BE LATE FOR SCHOOL.

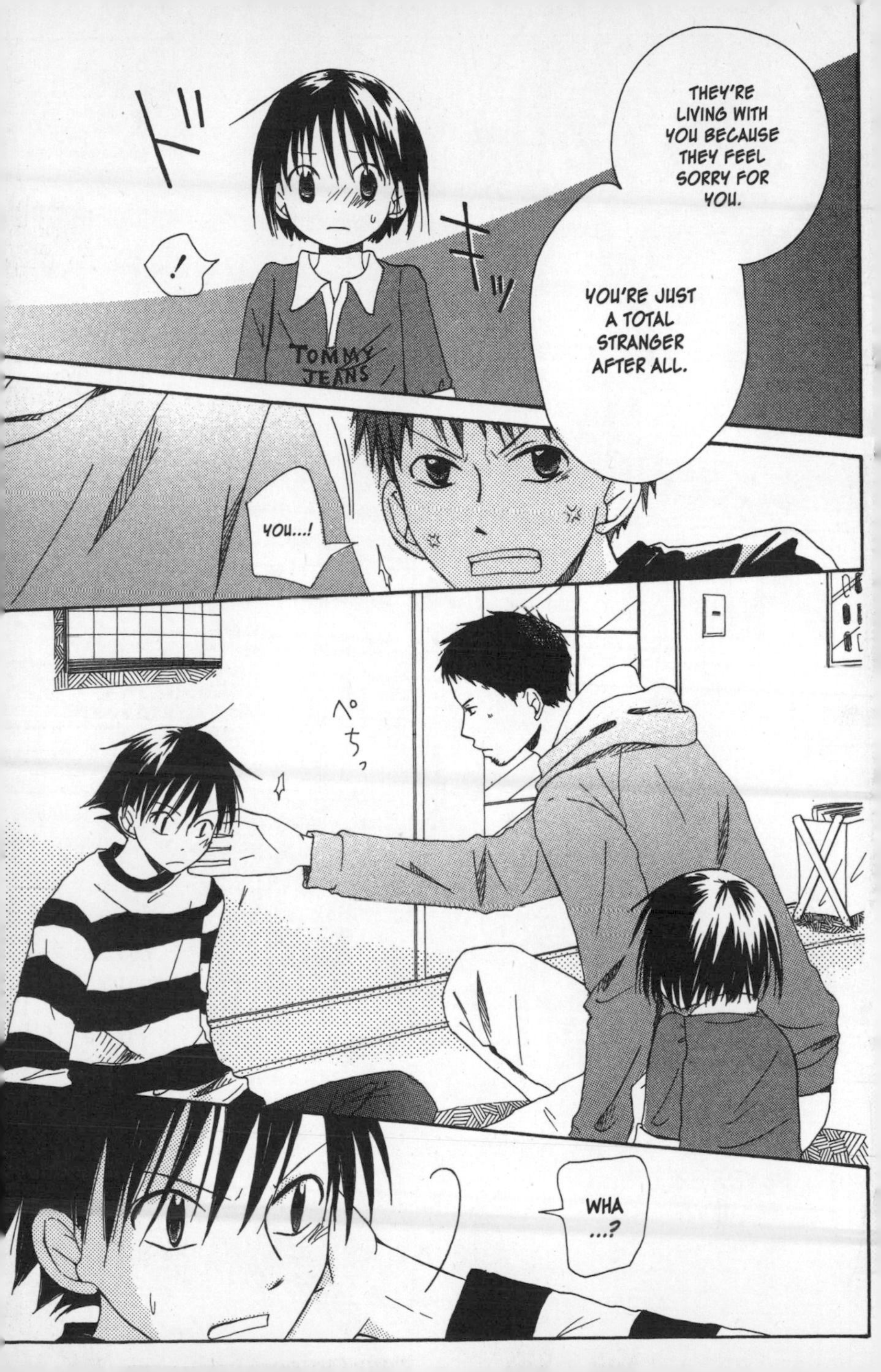
THEY'RE LIVING WITH YOU BECAUSE THEY FEEL SORRY FOR YOU.
YOU'RE JUST A TOTAL STRANGER AFTER ALL.
キッ
ドッ
!
YOU...!
ぺちっ
WHA ...?

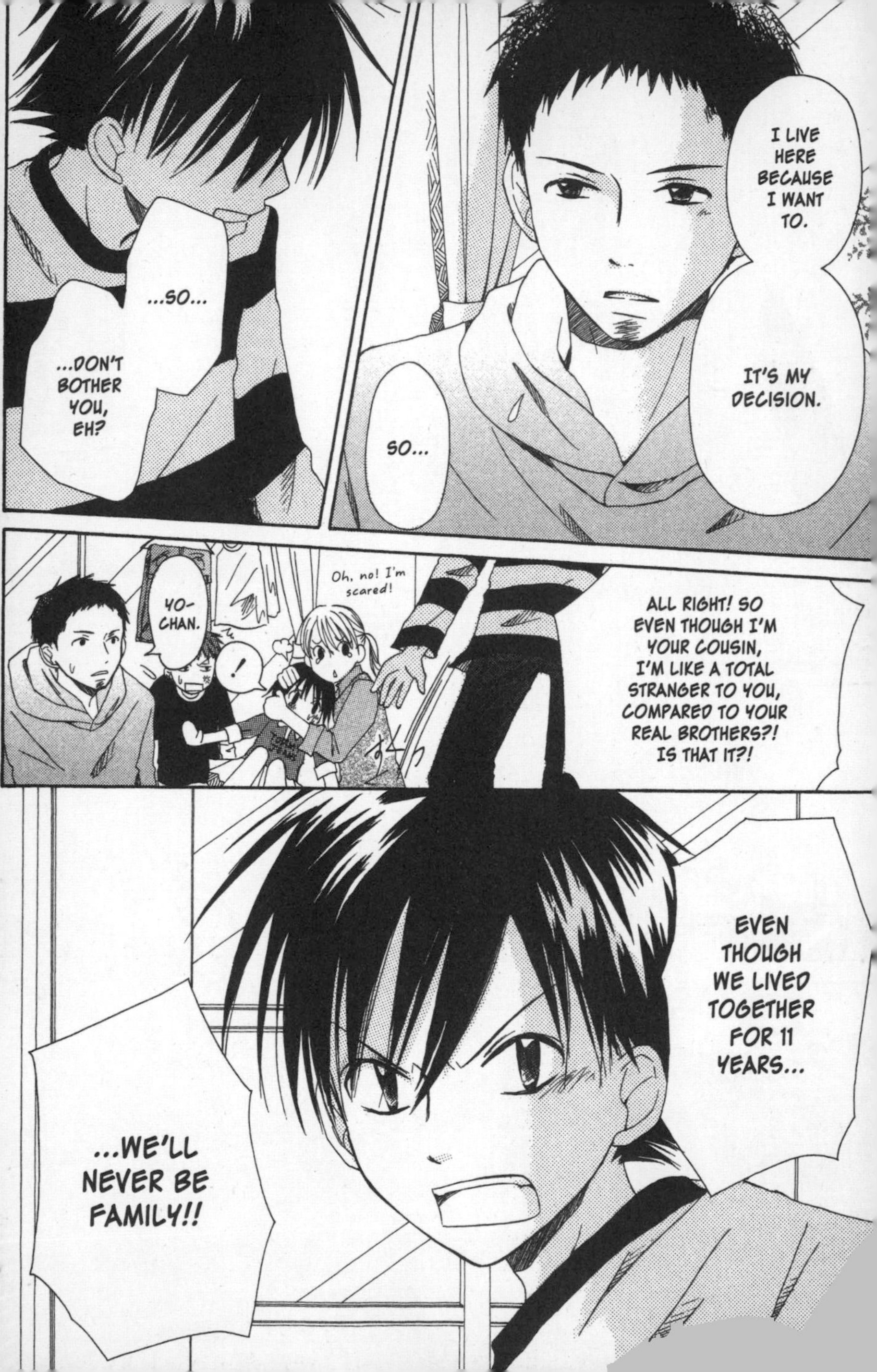
I LIVE HERE BECAUSE I WANT TO.
IT'S MY DECISION.
SO...
...SO...
...DON'T BOTHER YOU, EH?
ALL RIGHT! SO EVEN THOUGH I'M YOUR COUSIN, I'M LIKE A TOTAL STRANGER TO YOU, COMPARED TO YOUR REAL BROTHERS?! IS THAT IT?!
Oh, no! I'm scared!
YO-CHAN.
!
EVEN THOUGH WE LIVED TOGETHER FOR 11 YEARS...
...WE'LL NEVER BE FAMILY!!

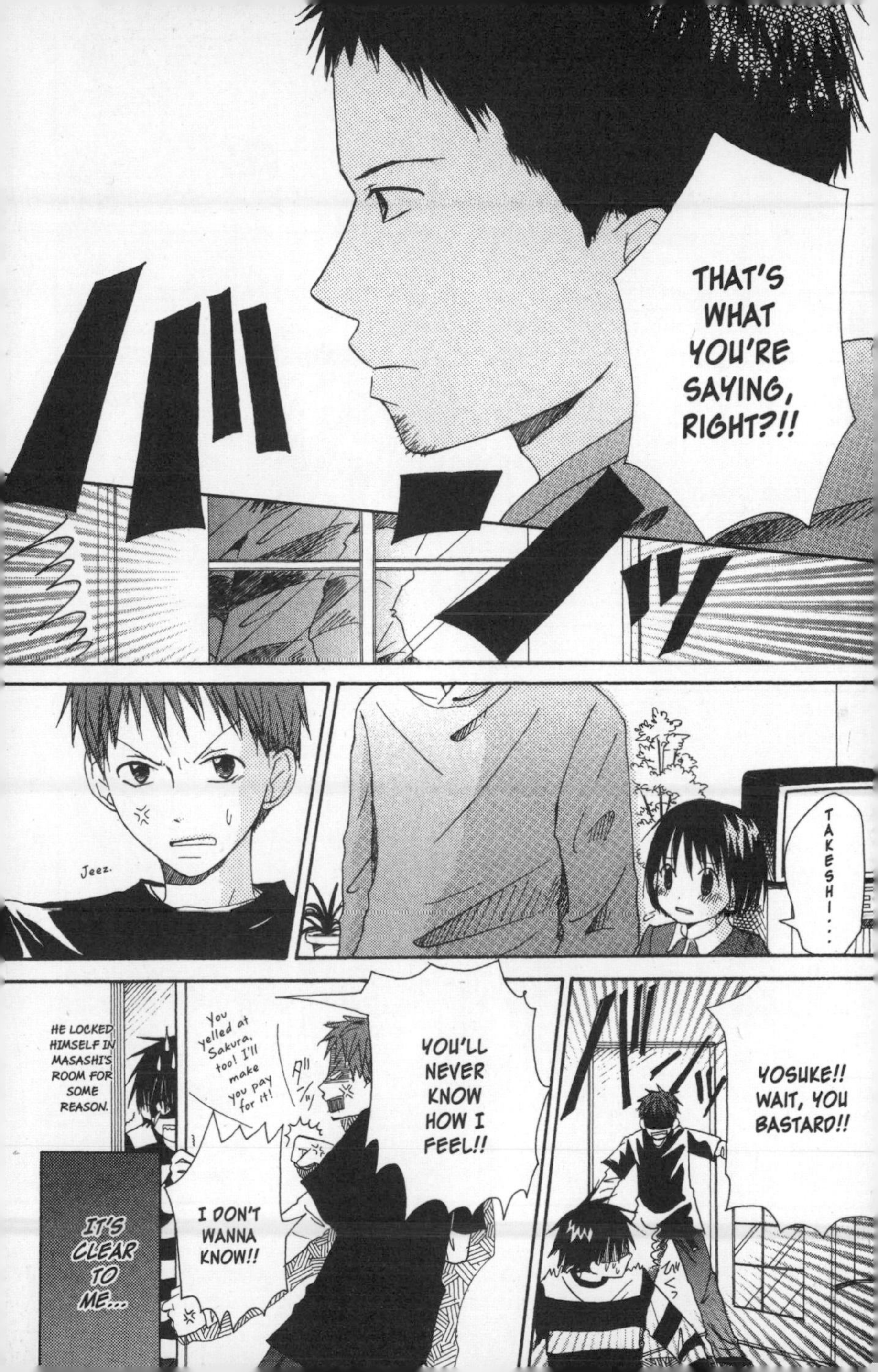
THAT'S WHAT YOU'RE SAYING, RIGHT?!!
TAKESHI...
Jeez.
YOSUKE!! WAIT, YOU BASTARD!!
YOU'LL NEVER KNOW HOW I FEEL!!
You yelled at Sakura, too! I'll make you pay for it!
HE LOCKED HIMSELF IN MASASHI'S ROOM FOR SOME REASON.
I DON'T WANNA KNOW!!
IT'S CLEAR TO ME...

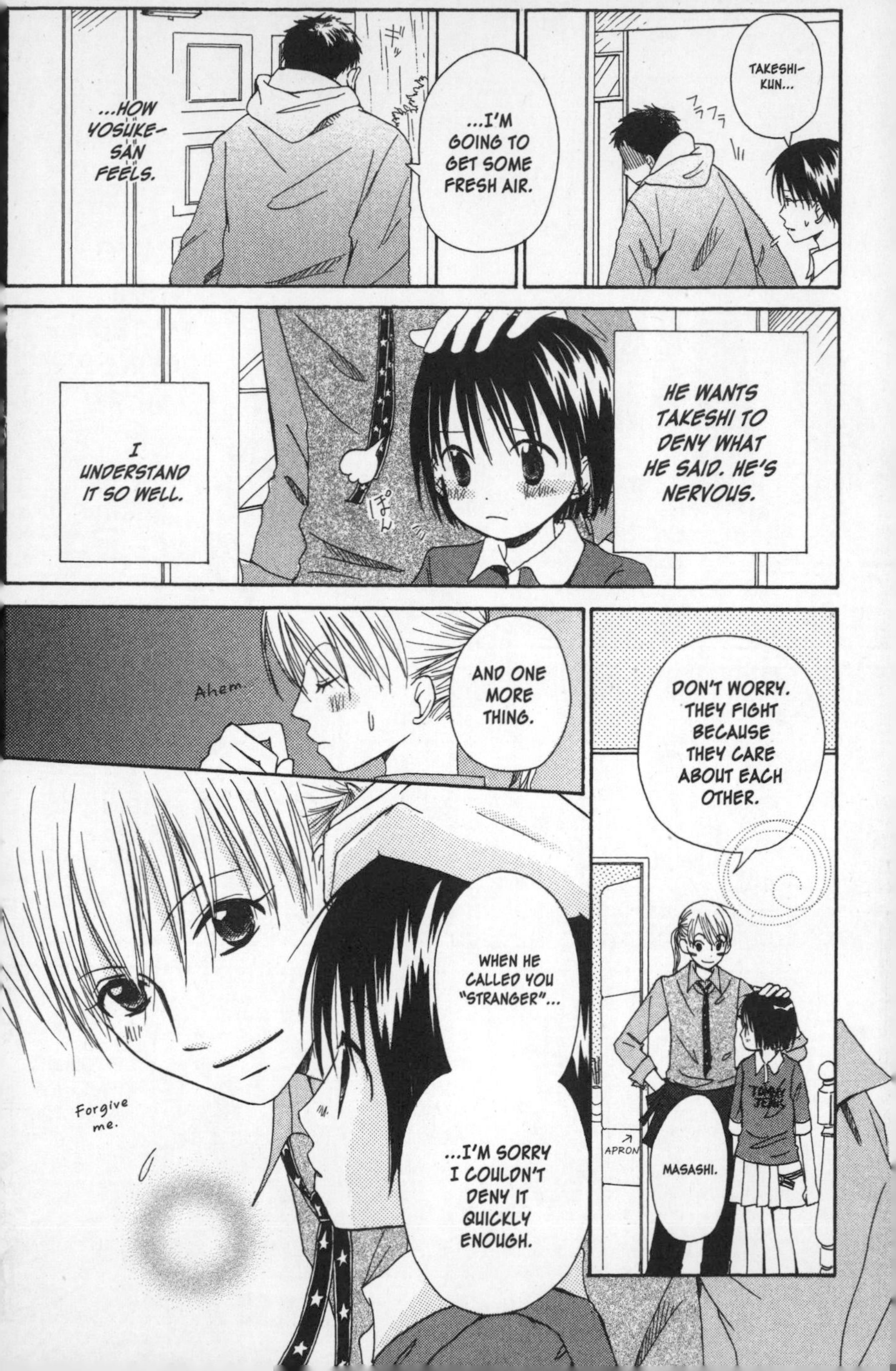
TAKESHI-KUN...
フラフラ
ギッ
...I'M GOING TO GET SOME FRESH AIR.
...HOW YOSUKE-SAN FEELS.
HE WANTS TAKESHI TO DENY WHAT HE SAID. HE'S NERVOUS.
ぽん
I UNDERSTAND IT SO WELL.
DON'T WORRY. THEY FIGHT BECAUSE THEY CARE ABOUT EACH OTHER.
MASASHI.
APRON
AND ONE MORE THING.
Ahem.
WHEN HE CALLED YOU "STRANGER"...
...I'M SORRY I COULDN'T DENY IT QUICKLY ENOUGH.
Forgive me.

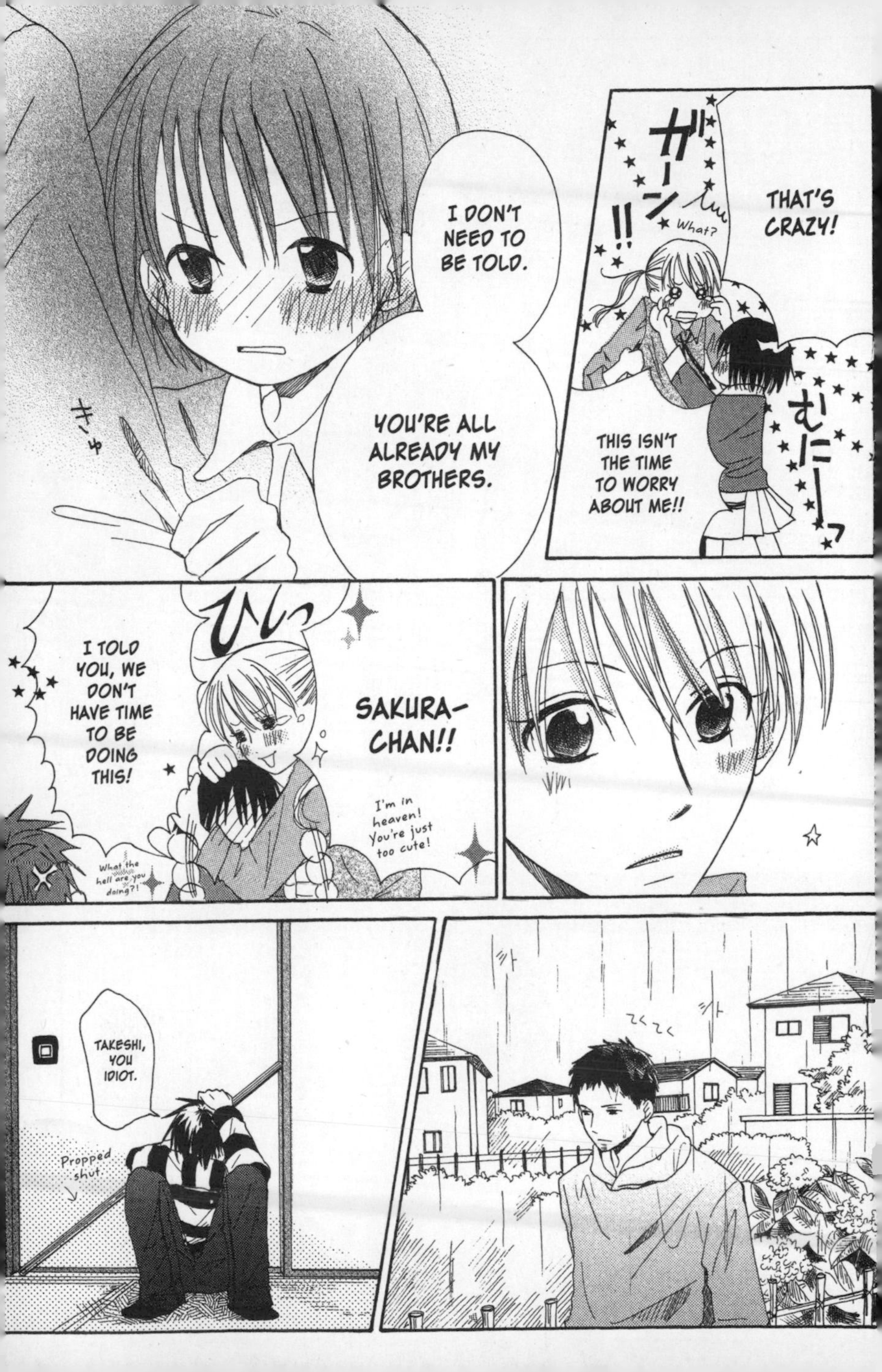
THAT'S CRAZY!
ガーン!!
What?
むにーっ
THIS ISN'T THE TIME TO WORRY ABOUT ME!!
I DON'T NEED TO BE TOLD.
YOU'RE ALL ALREADY MY BROTHERS.
きゅ
SAKURA-CHAN!!
ひしっ
I'm in heaven! You're just too cute!
I TOLD YOU, WE DON'T HAVE TIME TO BE DOING THIS!
What the hell are you doing?!
シト
シト
てくてく
TAKESHI, YOU IDIOT.
Propped shut.

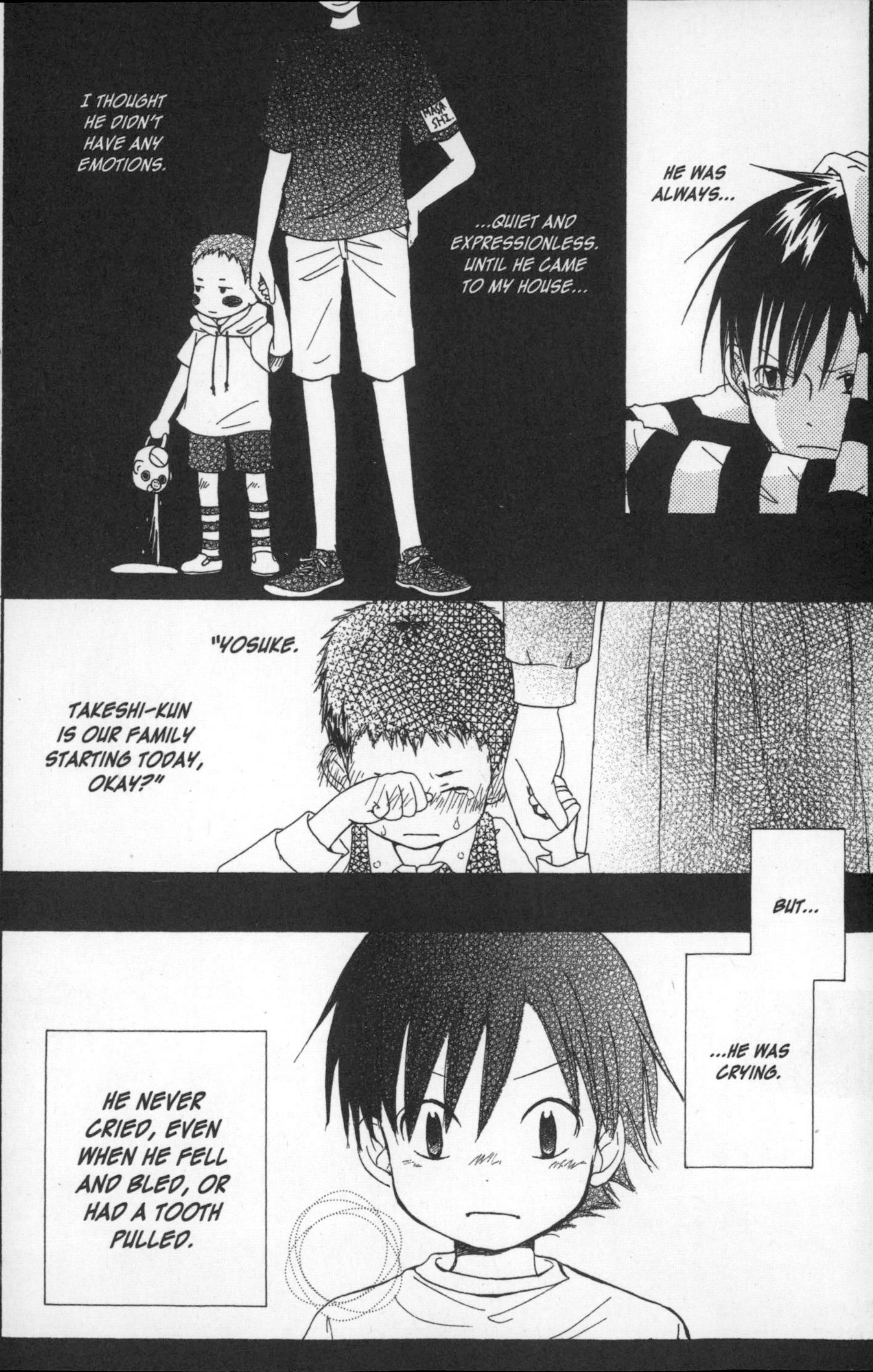
HE WAS ALWAYS...
I THOUGHT HE DIDN'T HAVE ANY EMOTIONS.
...QUIET AND EXPRESSIONLESS. UNTIL HE CAME TO MY HOUSE...
MASA SHI.
"YOSUKE.
TAKESHI-KUN IS OUR FAMILY STARTING TODAY, OKAY?"
BUT...
...HE WAS CRYING.
HE NEVER CRIED, EVEN WHEN HE FELL AND BLED, OR HAD A TOOTH PULLED.

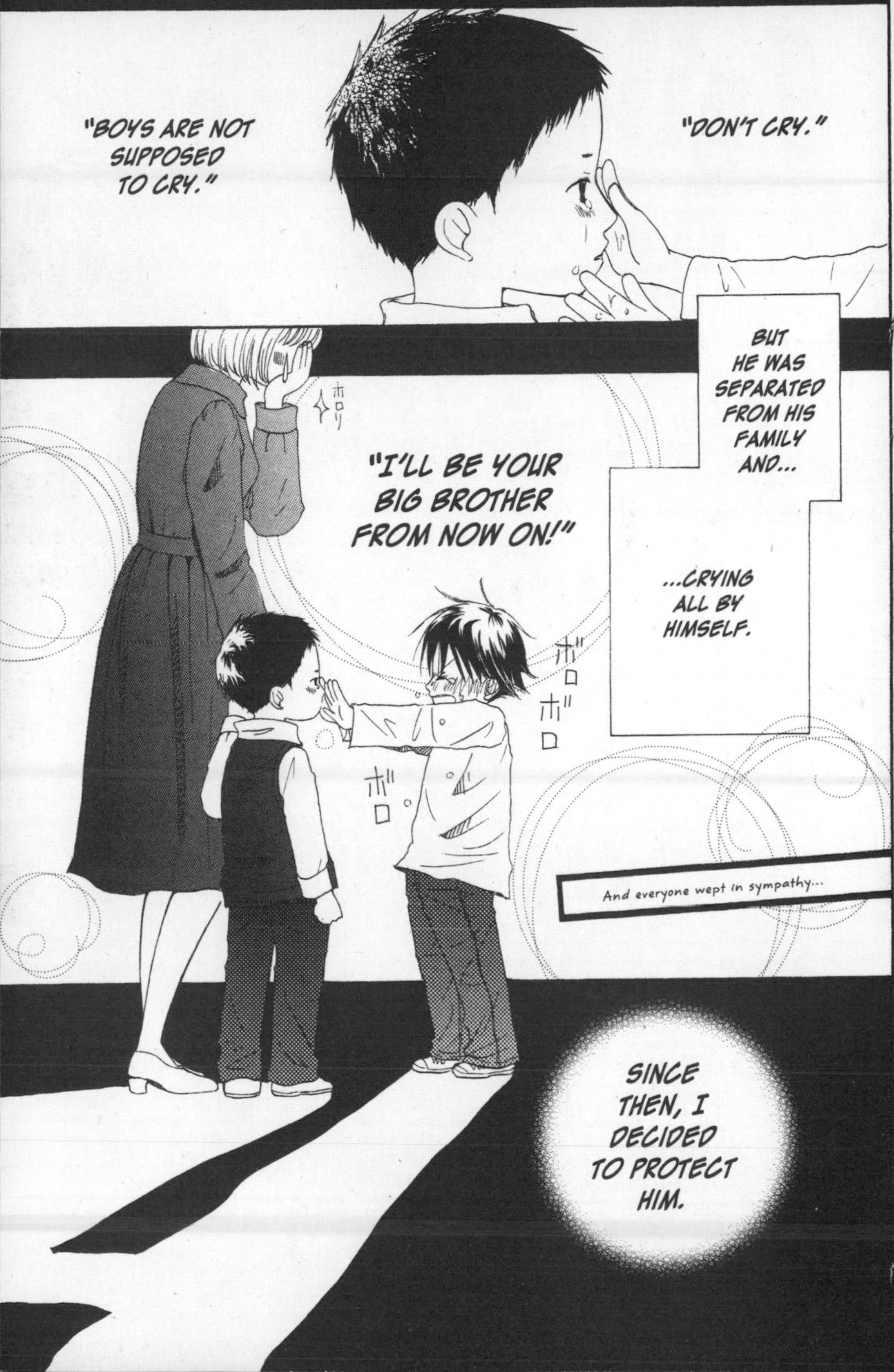
"DON'T CRY."
"BOYS ARE NOT SUPPOSED TO CRY."
BUT HE WAS SEPARATED FROM HIS FAMILY AND...
...CRYING ALL BY HIMSELF.
ボロボロ
"I'LL BE YOUR BIG BROTHER FROM NOW ON!"
ホロリ
ボロ
And everyone wept in sympathy...
SINCE THEN, I DECIDED TO PROTECT HIM.

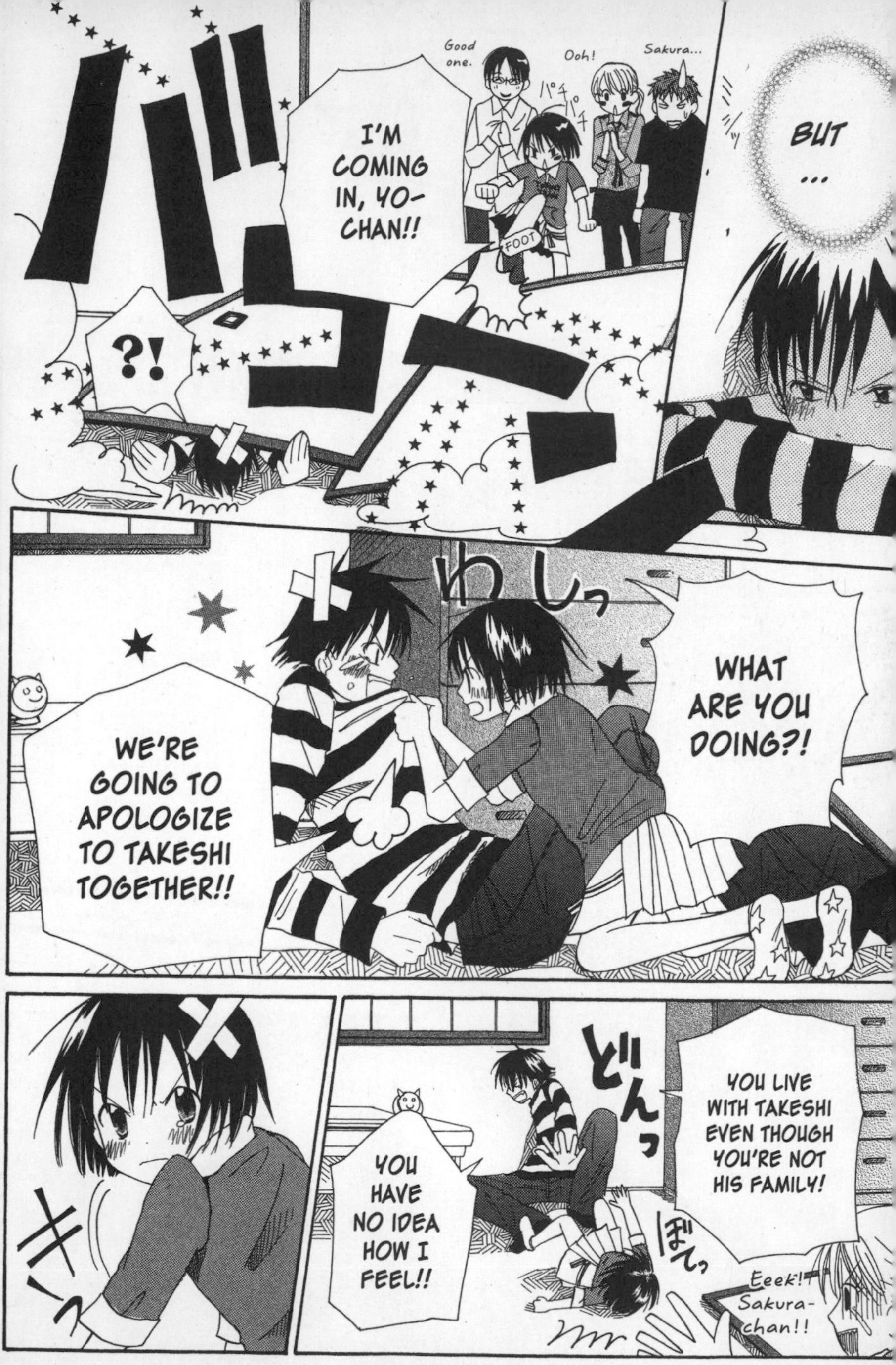
BUT ...
Sakura...
Ooh!
Good one.
パチパチ
I'M COMING IN, YO-CHAN!!
FOOT
バゴーン
?!
WHAT ARE YOU DOING?!
わしっ
WE'RE GOING TO APOLOGIZE TO TAKESHI TOGETHER!!
YOU LIVE WITH TAKESHI EVEN THOUGH YOU'RE NOT HIS FAMILY!
どんっ
YOU HAVE NO IDEA HOW I FEEL!!
ぼてっ
Eeek!! Sakura-chan!!
キッ

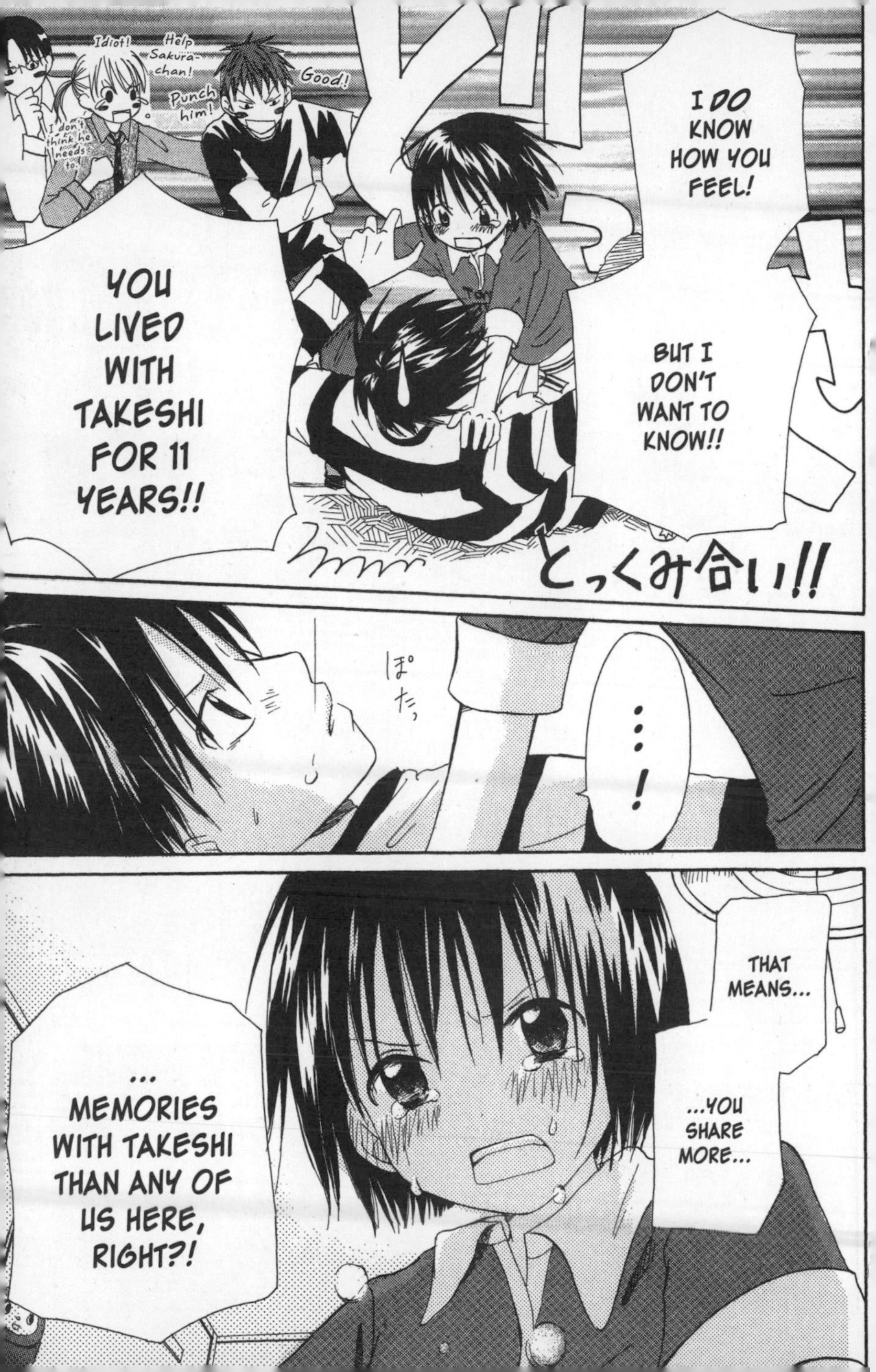
I DO KNOW HOW YOU FEEL!
Good!
Help Sakura-chan!
Punch him!
Idiot!
I don't think he needs to.
BUT I DON'T WANT TO KNOW!!
YOU LIVED WITH TAKESHI FOR 11 YEARS!!
とっくみ合い!!
ぽたっ
...!
THAT MEANS...
...YOU SHARE MORE...
...MEMORIES WITH TAKESHI THAN ANY OF US HERE, RIGHT?!

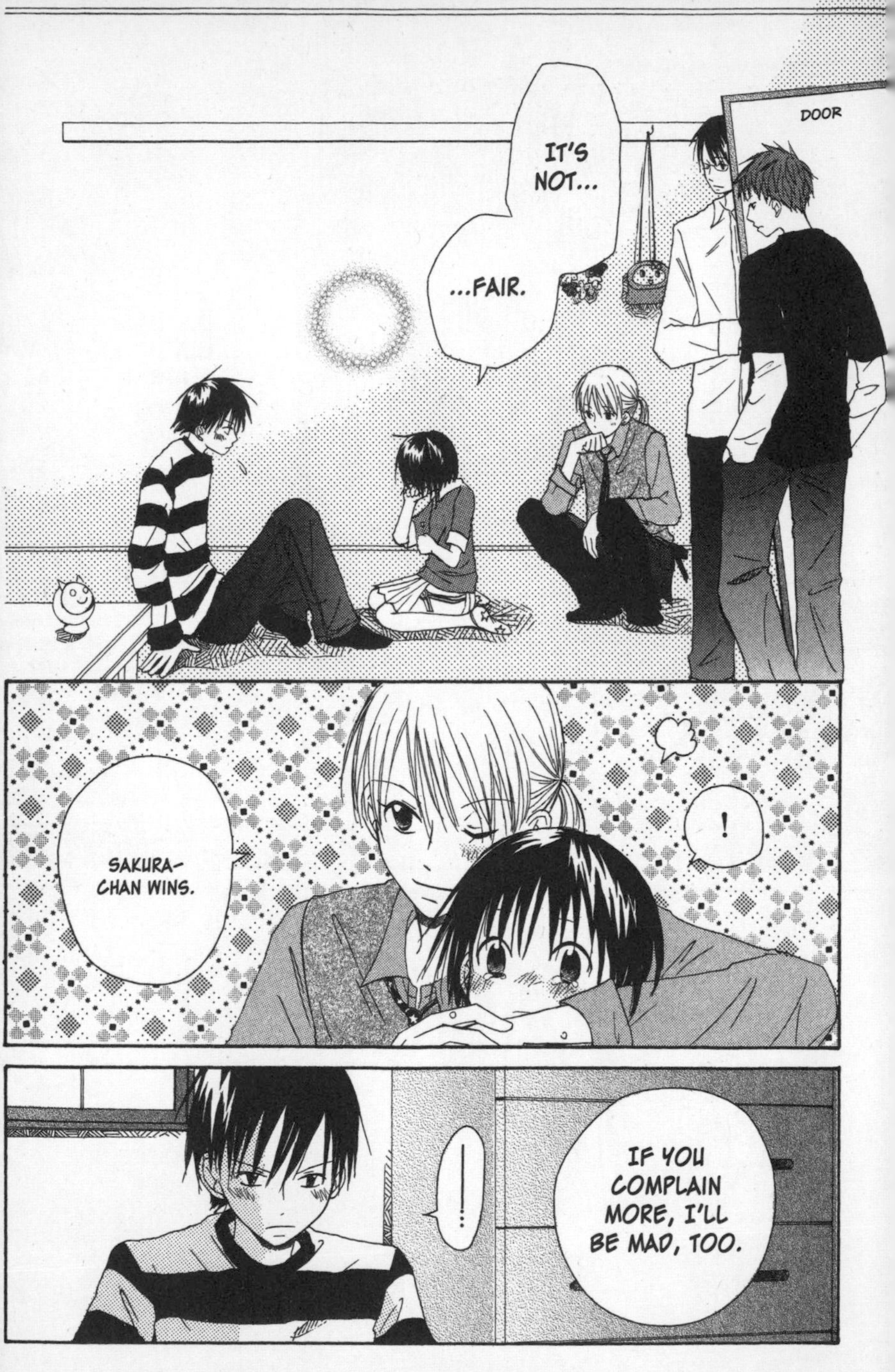
DOOR
IT'S NOT...
...FAIR.
!
SAKURA-CHAN WINS.
IF YOU COMPLAIN MORE, I'LL BE MAD, TOO.
!...

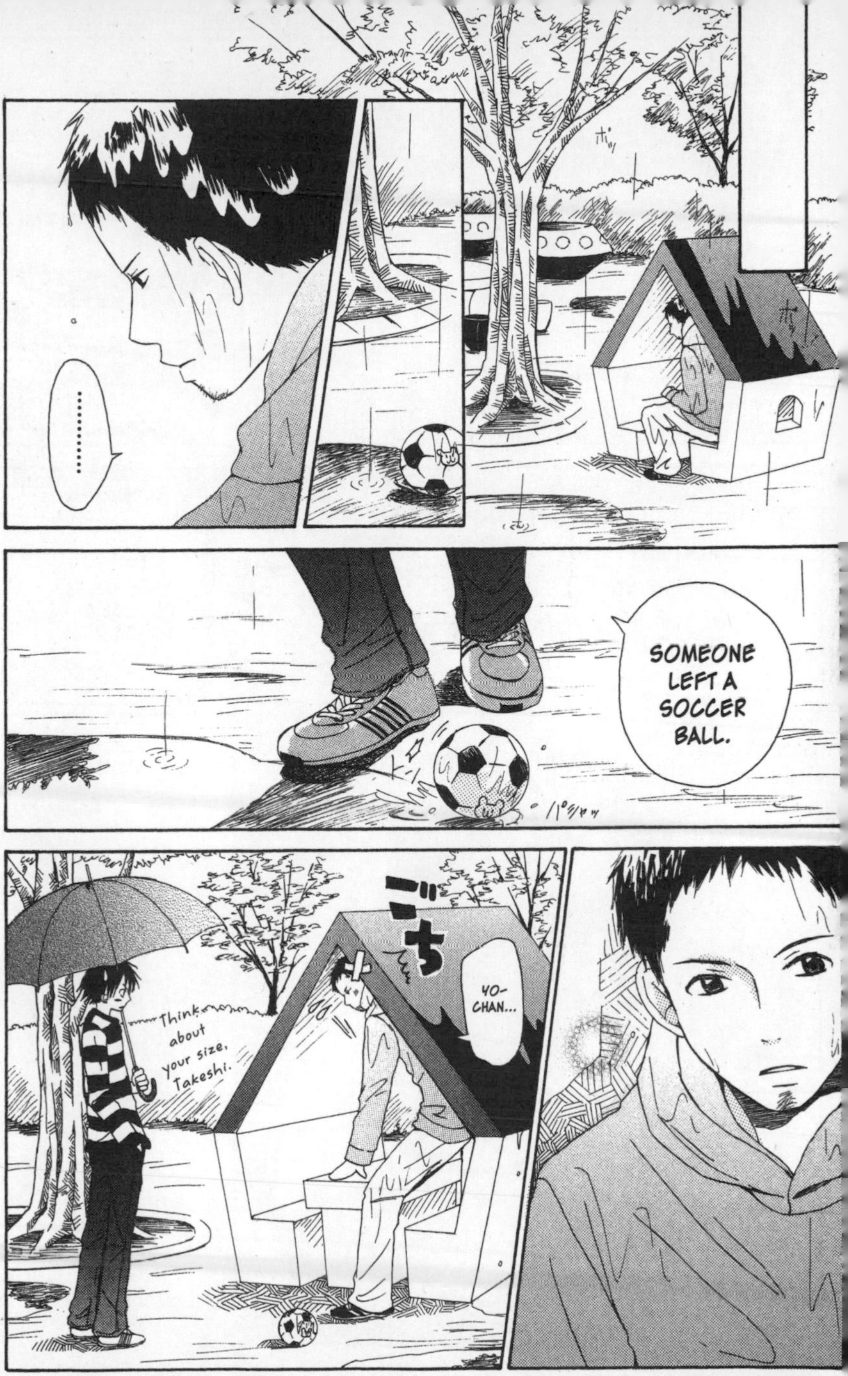

....
SOMEONE LEFT A SOCCER BALL.
YO-CHAN...
Think about your size, Takeshi.

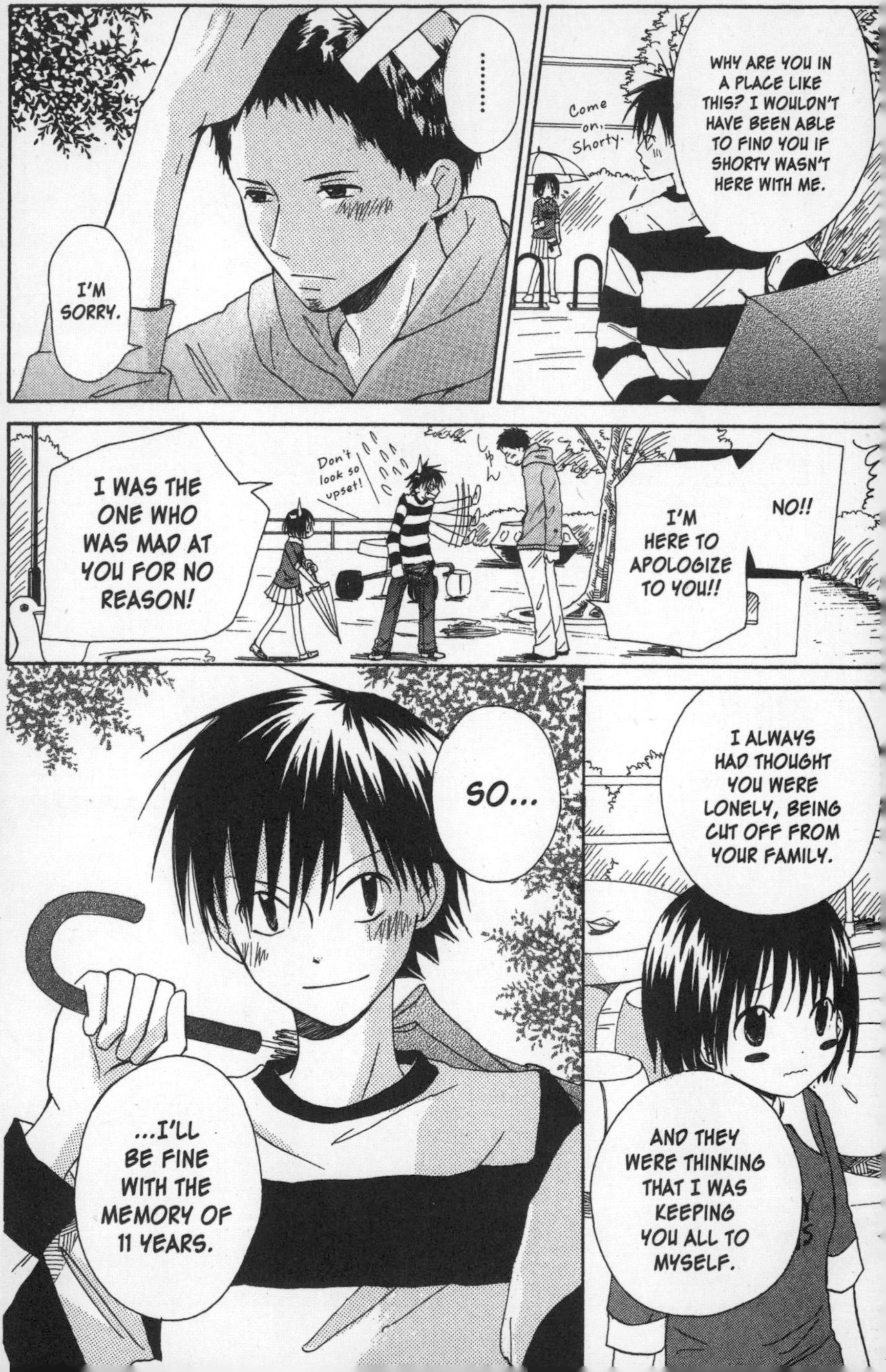
WHY ARE YOU IN A PLACE LIKE THIS? I WOULDN'T HAVE BEEN ABLE TO FIND YOU IF SHORTY WASN'T HERE WITH ME.
Come on, Shorty.
......
I'M SORRY.
NO!!
I'M HERE TO APOLOGIZE TO YOU!!
しゅん
Don't look so upset!
I WAS THE ONE WHO WAS MAD AT YOU FOR NO REASON!
I ALWAYS HAD THOUGHT YOU WERE LONELY, BEING CUT OFF FROM YOUR FAMILY.
AND THEY WERE THINKING THAT I WAS KEEPING YOU ALL TO MYSELF.
SO...
...I'LL BE FINE WITH THE MEMORY OF 11 YEARS.

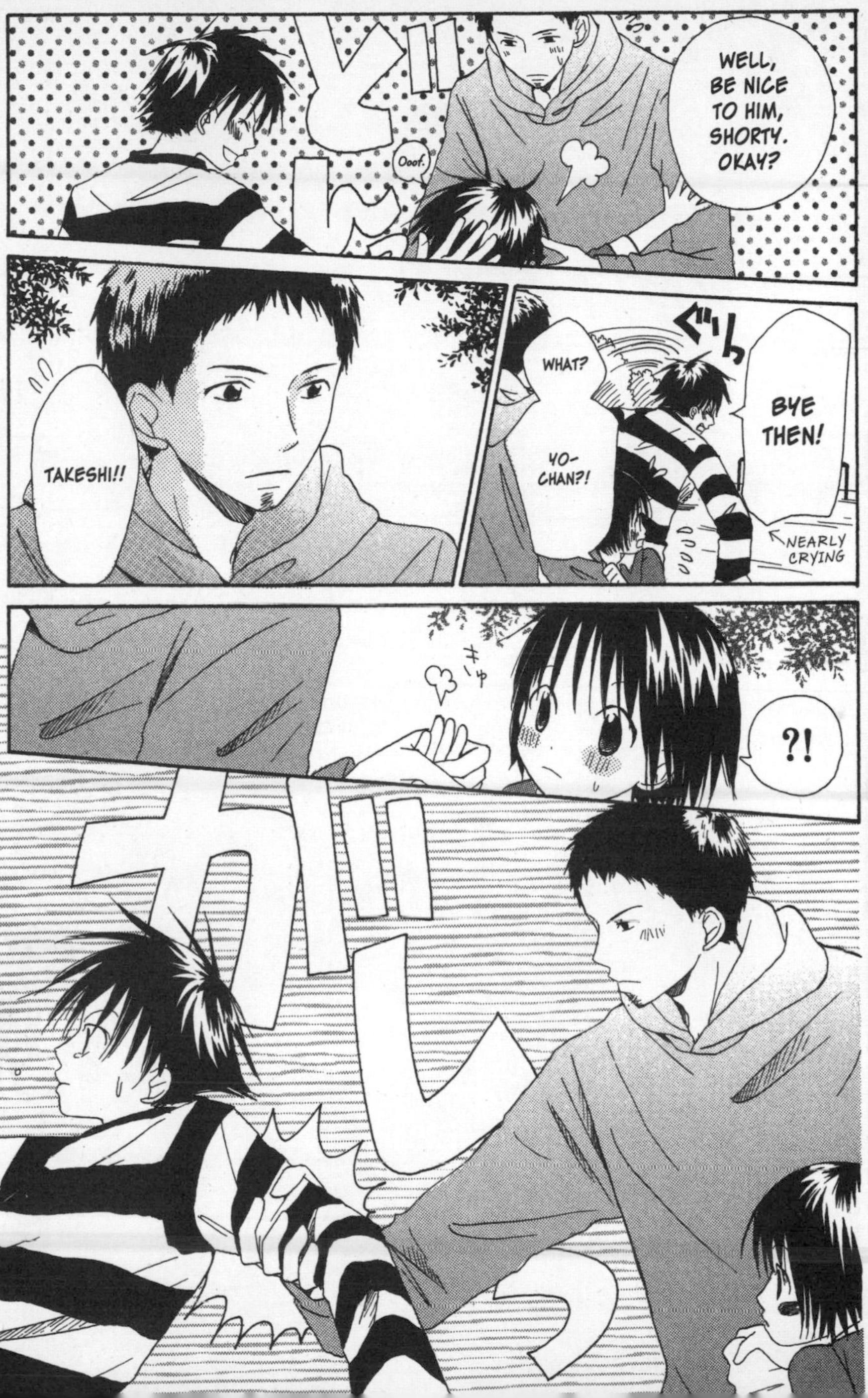
WELL, BE NICE TO HIM, SHORTY. OKAY?
Ooof.
BYE THEN!
WHAT?
NEARLY CRYING
YO-CHAN?!
TAKESHI!!
?!

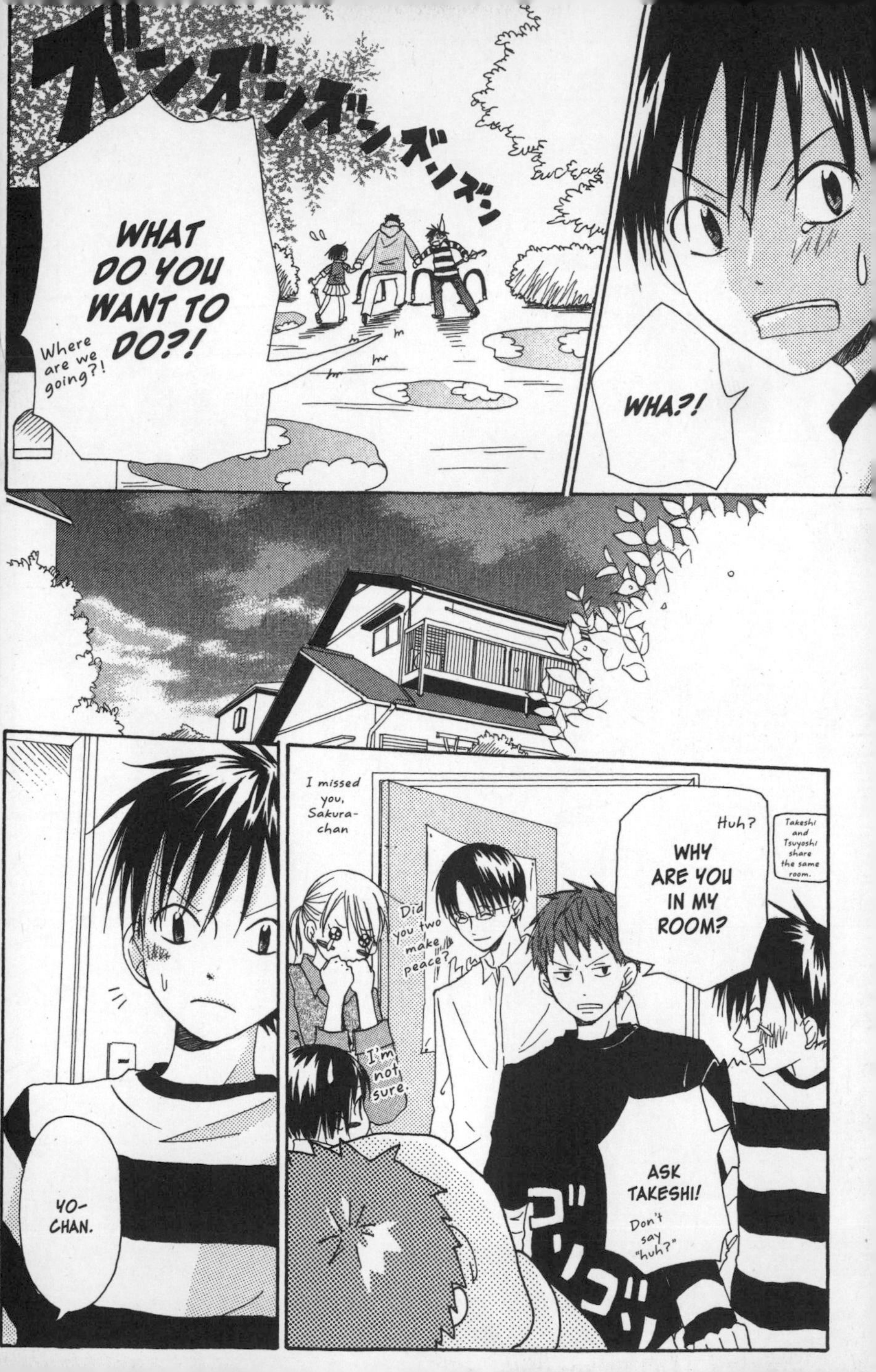
WHA?!
WHAT DO YOU WANT TO DO?!
Where are we going?!
Takeshi and Tsuyoshi share the same room.
Huh?
WHY ARE YOU IN MY ROOM?
I missed you, Sakura-chan
Did you two make peace?
I'm not sure.
ASK TAKESHI!
Don't say "huh?"
YO-CHAN.

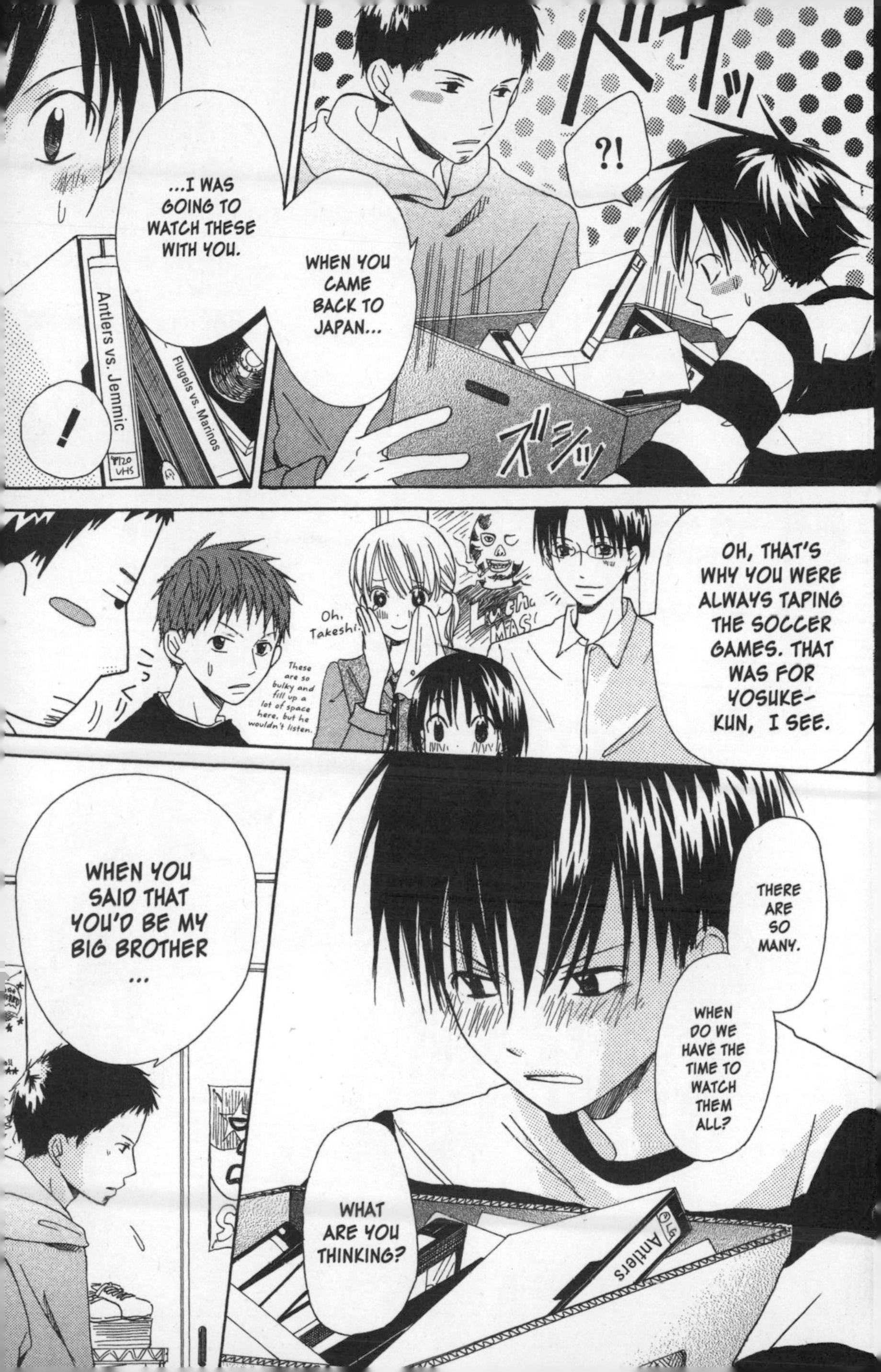
ドサッ
?!
WHEN YOU CAME BACK TO JAPAN...
...I WAS GOING TO WATCH THESE WITH YOU.
Flugels vs. Marinos
Antlers vs. Jemmic
!
ズシッ
OH, THAT'S WHY YOU WERE ALWAYS TAPING THE SOCCER GAMES. THAT WAS FOR YOSUKE-KUN, I SEE.
Oh, Takeshi.
These are so bulky and fill up a lot of space here, but he wouldn't listen.
THERE ARE SO MANY.
WHEN DO WE HAVE THE TIME TO WATCH THEM ALL?
Antlers
WHAT ARE YOU THINKING?
WHEN YOU SAID THAT YOU'D BE MY BIG BROTHER ...

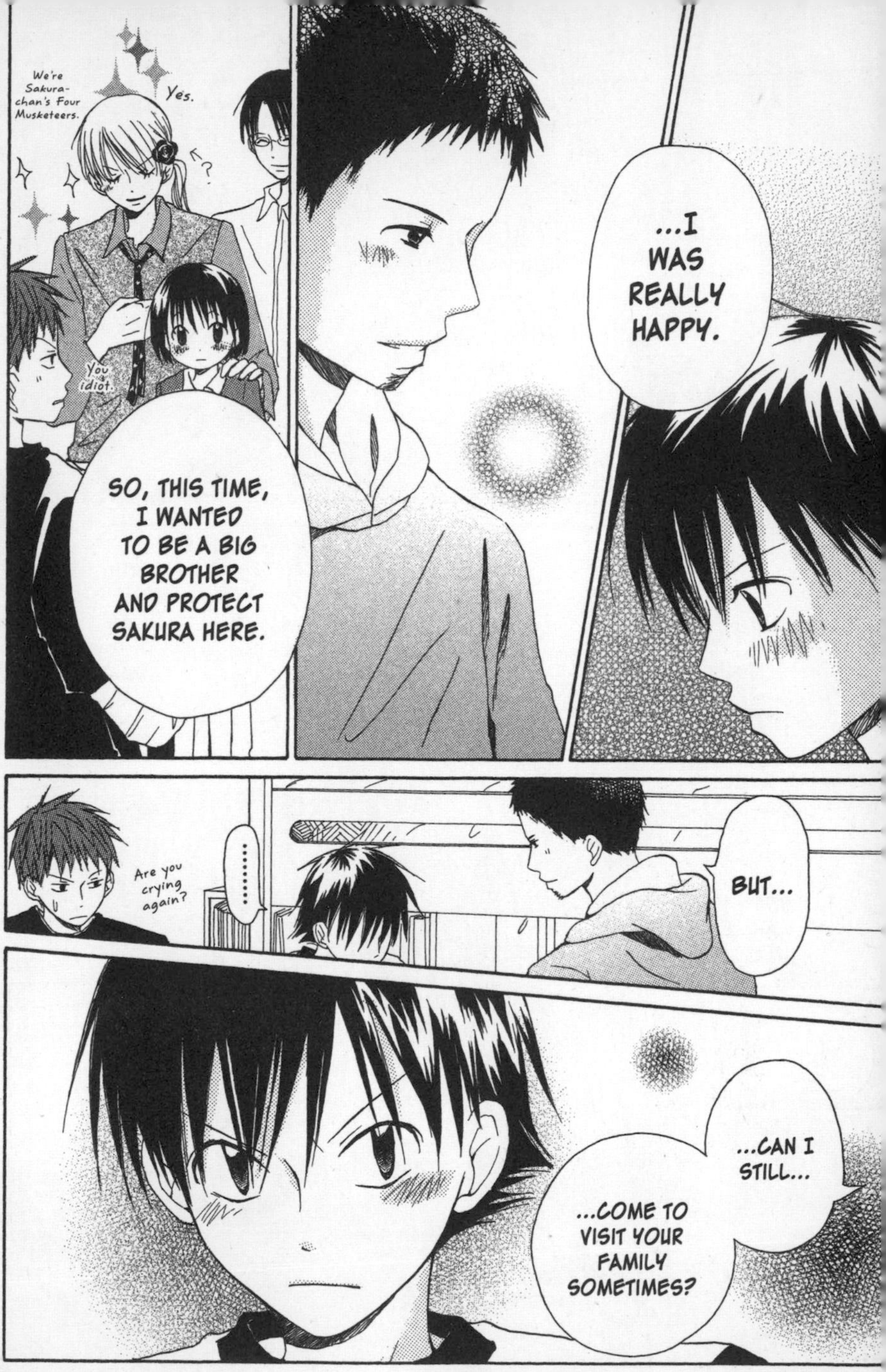
...I WAS REALLY HAPPY.
We're Sakura-chan's Four Musketeers.
Yes.
<?
You idiot.
SO, THIS TIME, I WANTED TO BE A BIG BROTHER AND PROTECT SAKURA HERE.
BUT...
......
Are you crying again?
...CAN I STILL...
...COME TO VISIT YOUR FAMILY SOMETIMES?

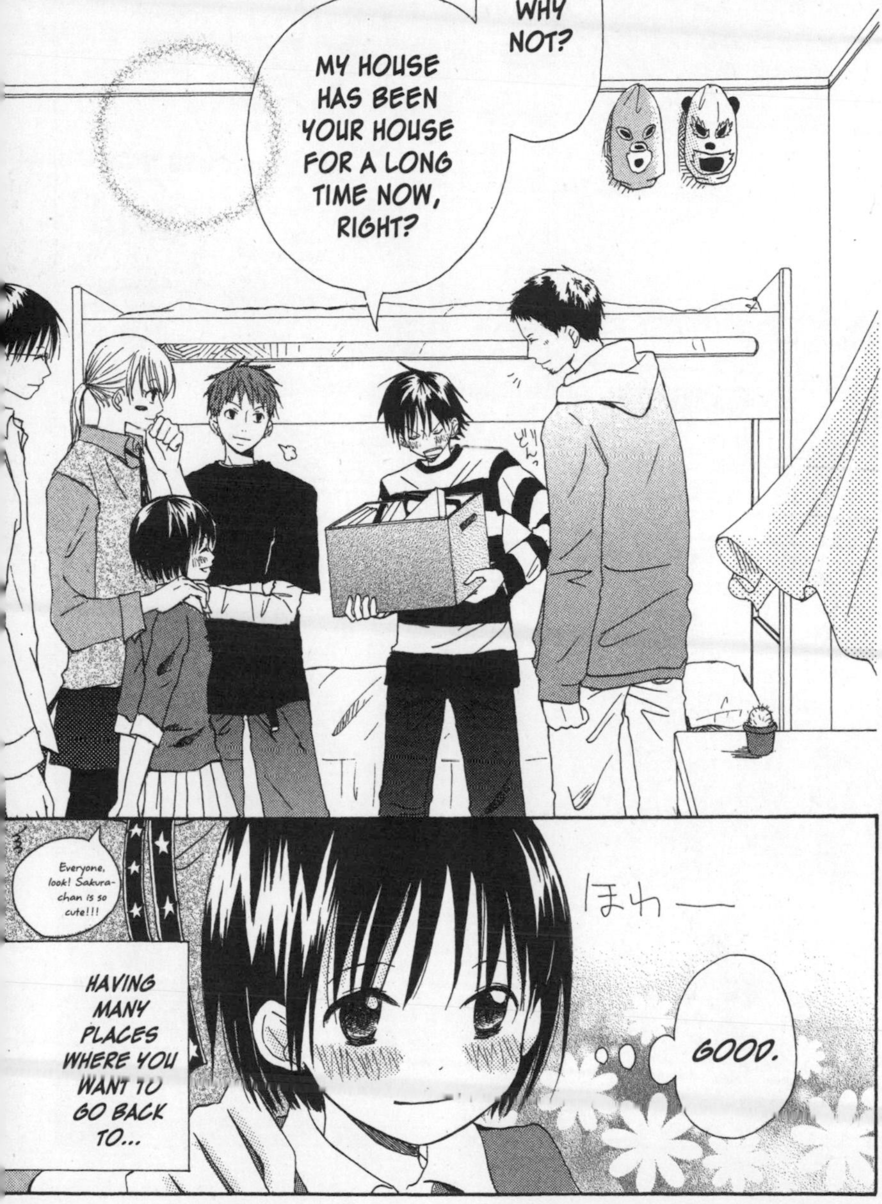
WHY NOT?
MY HOUSE HAS BEEN YOUR HOUSE FOR A LONG TIME NOW, RIGHT?
ほわー
...GOOD.
Everyone, look! Sakura-chan is so cute!!!
HAVING MANY PLACES WHERE YOU WANT TO GO BACK TO...

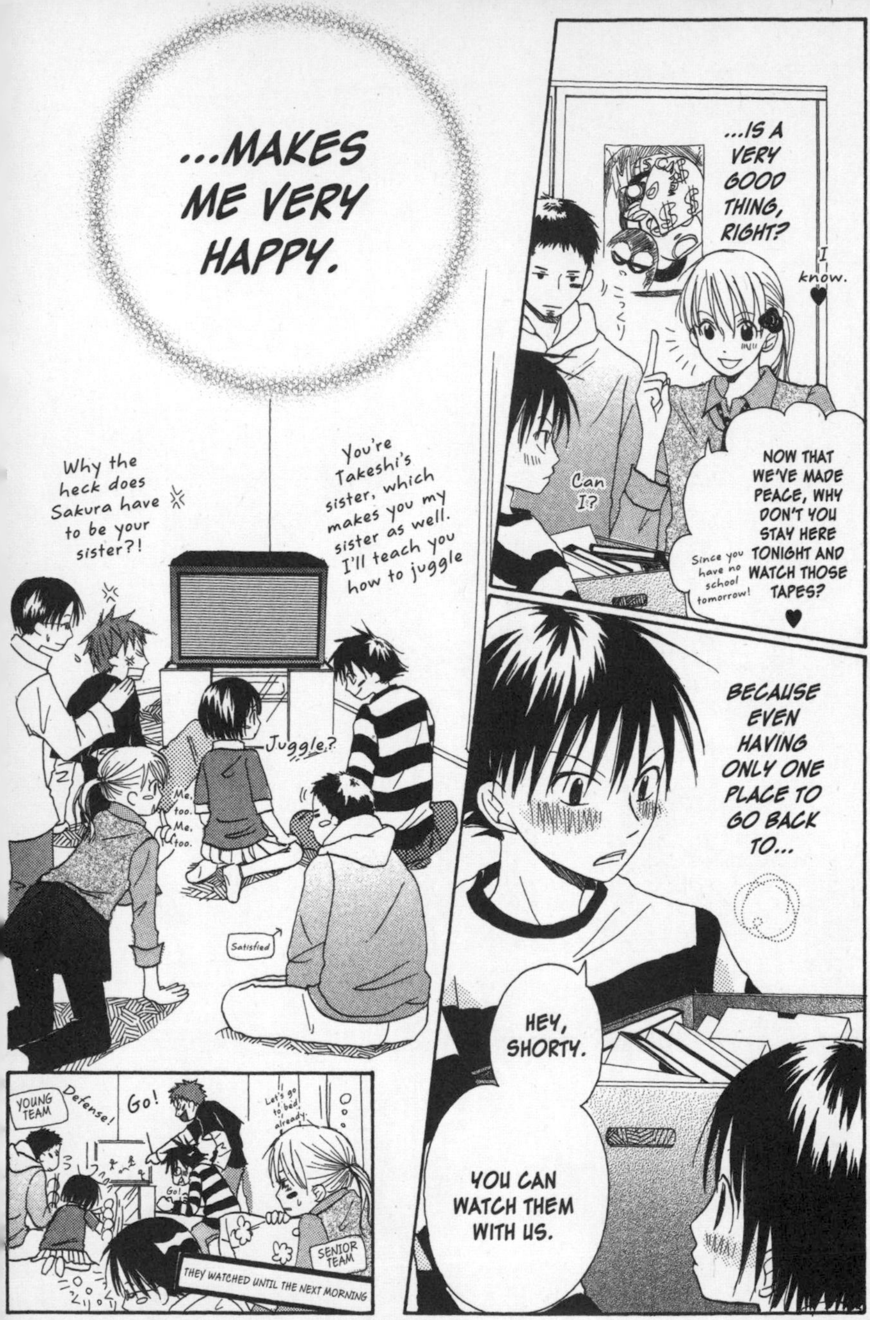
...IS A VERY GOOD THING, RIGHT?
I know.
Can I?
NOW THAT WE'VE MADE PEACE, WHY DON'T YOU STAY HERE TONIGHT AND WATCH THOSE TAPES?
Since you have no school tomorrow!
BECAUSE EVEN HAVING ONLY ONE PLACE TO GO BACK TO...
HEY, SHORTY.
YOU CAN WATCH THEM WITH US.
...MAKES ME VERY HAPPY.
You're Takeshi's sister, which makes you my sister as well. I'll teach you how to juggle
Why the heck does Sakura have to be your sister?!
Juggle?
Me, too. Me, too.
Satisfied
Let's go to bed already.
Go!
Defense!
YOUNG TEAM
Go!
SENIOR TEAM
THEY WATCHED UNTIL THE NEXT MORNING

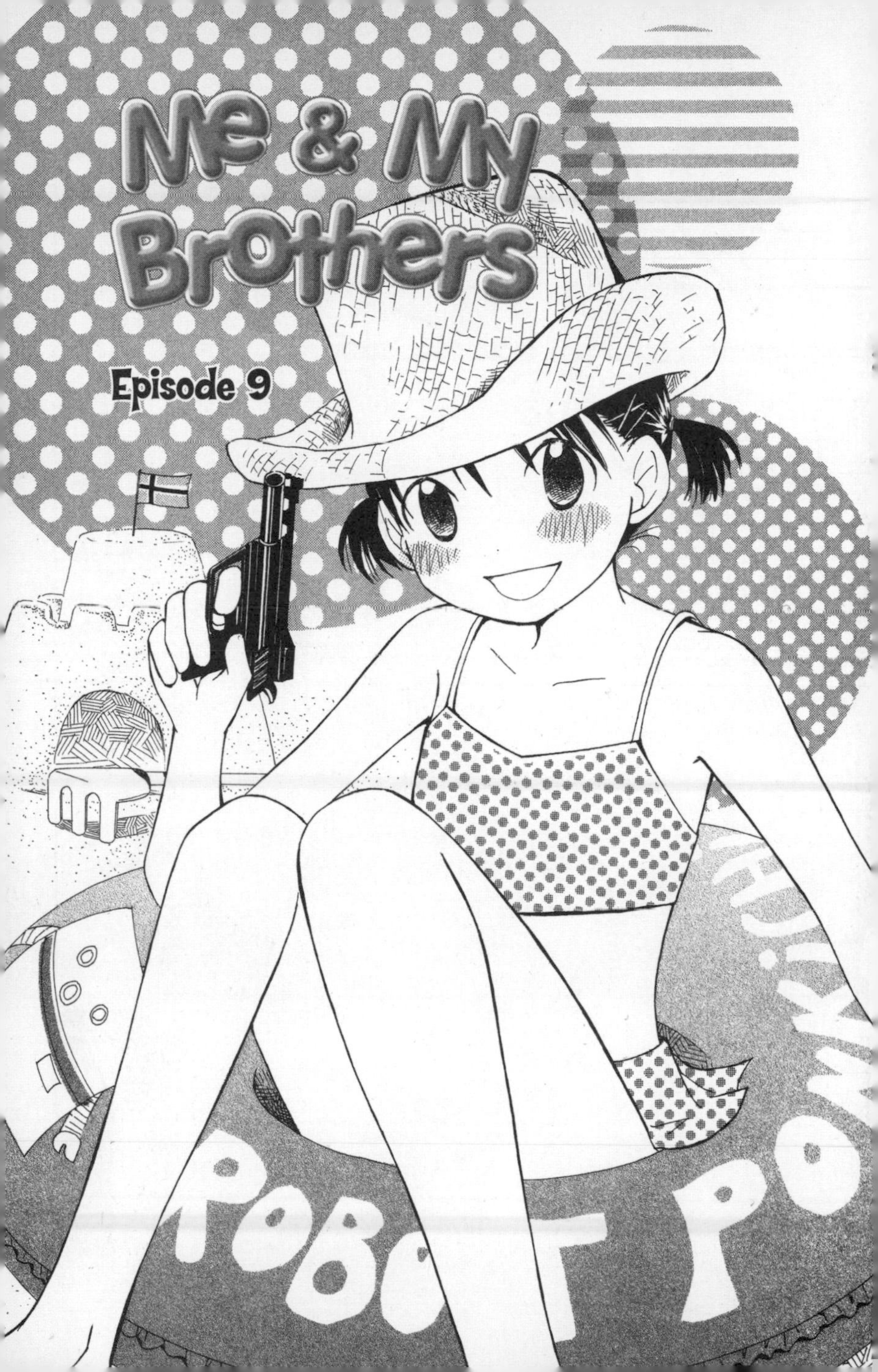
Me & My Brothers
Episode 9
ROBOT POW

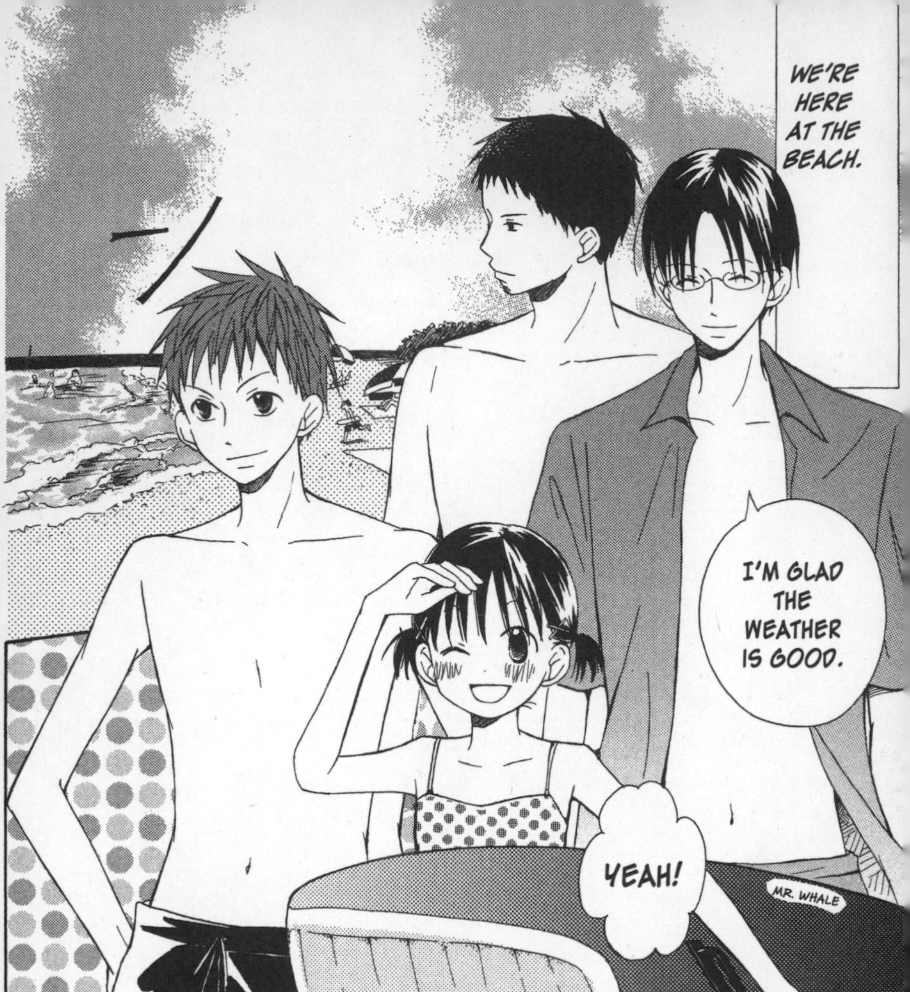
WE'RE HERE AT THE BEACH.
I'M GLAD THE WEATHER IS GOOD.
YEAH!
MR. WHALE

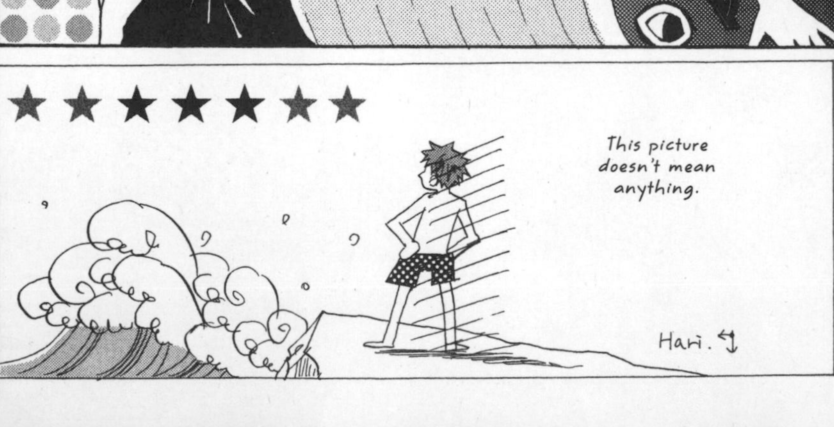
★★★★★★★
This picture doesn't mean anything.
Hari.

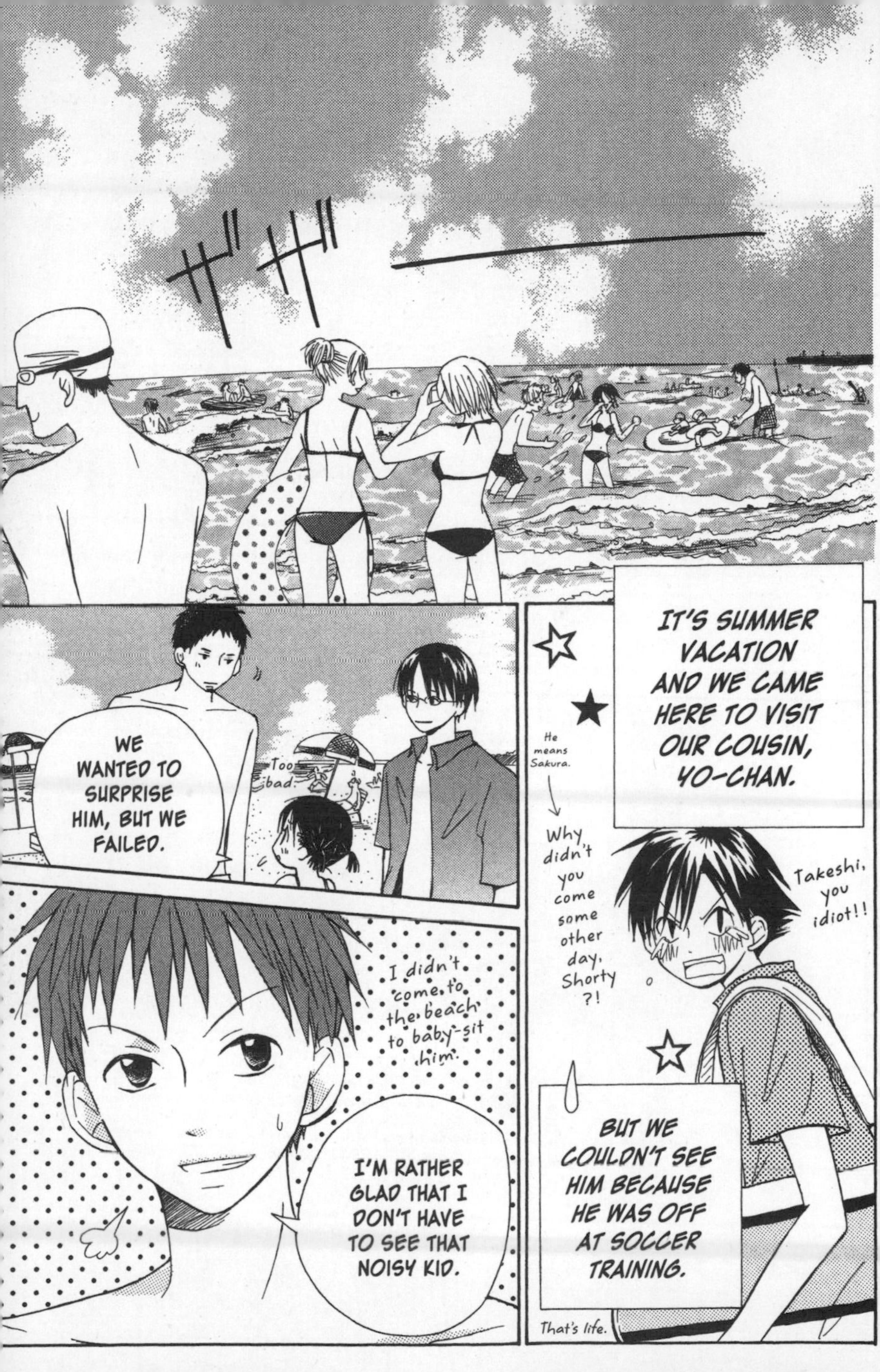
IT'S SUMMER VACATION AND WE CAME HERE TO VISIT OUR COUSIN, YO-CHAN.
Takeshi, you idiot!!
He means Sakura.
Why didn't you come some other day, Shorty?!
BUT WE COULDN'T SEE HIM BECAUSE HE WAS OFF AT SOCCER TRAINING.
That's life.
WE WANTED TO SURPRISE HIM, BUT WE FAILED.
Too bad.
I didn't come to the beach to baby-sit him.
I'M RATHER GLAD THAT I DON'T HAVE TO SEE THAT NOISY KID.

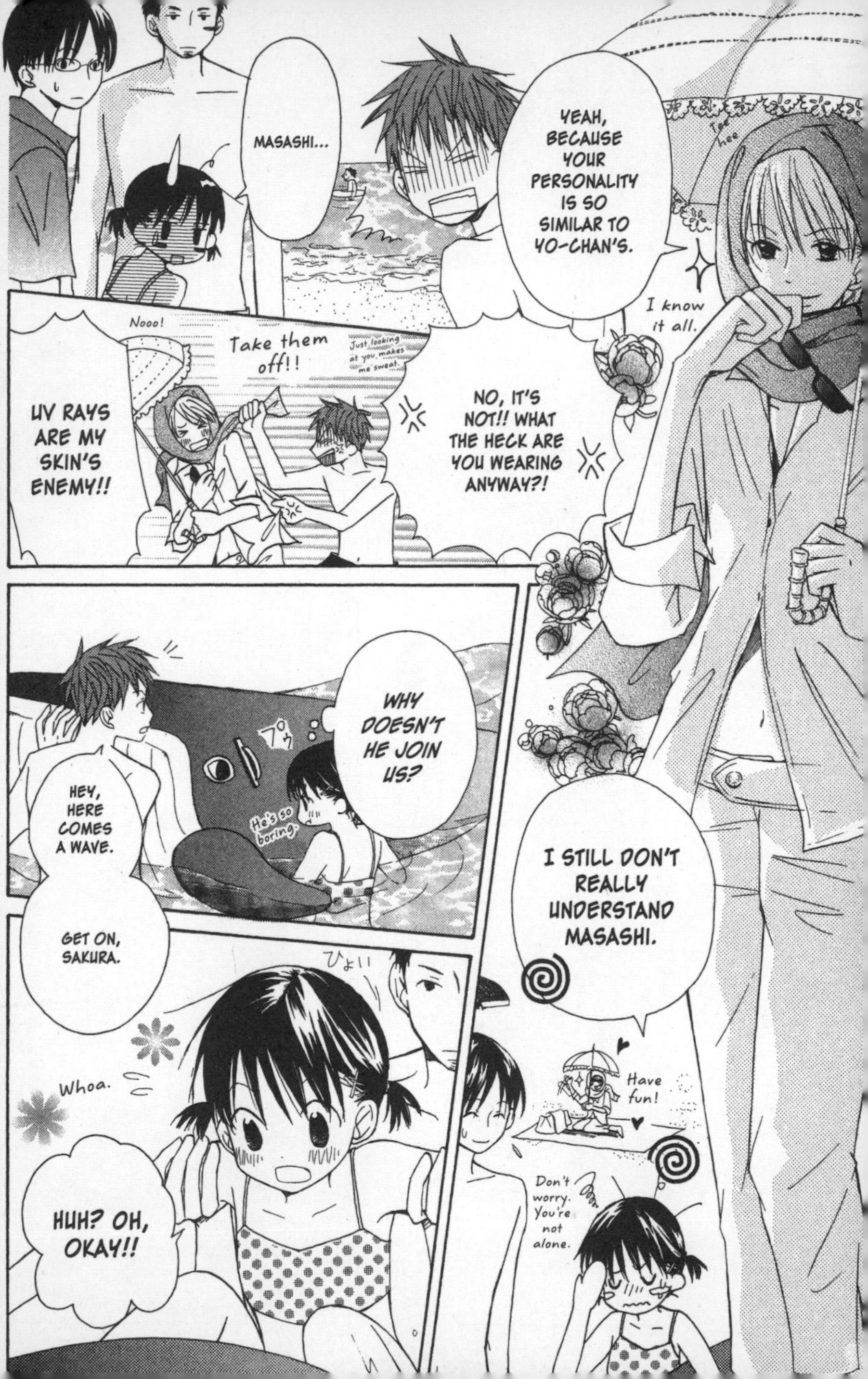
YEAH, BECAUSE YOUR PERSONALITY IS SO SIMILAR TO YO-CHAN'S.
MASASHI...
Tee hee
I know it all.
NO, IT'S NOT!! WHAT THE HECK ARE YOU WEARING ANYWAY?!
Just looking at you makes me sweat.
Take them off!!
Nooo!
UV RAYS ARE MY SKIN'S ENEMY!!
WHY DOESN'T HE JOIN US?
プゥ
He's so boring.
HEY, HERE COMES A WAVE.
I STILL DON'T REALLY UNDERSTAND MASASHI.
Have fun!
Don't worry. You're not alone.
GET ON, SAKURA.
ひょい
Whoa.
HUH? OH, OKAY!!

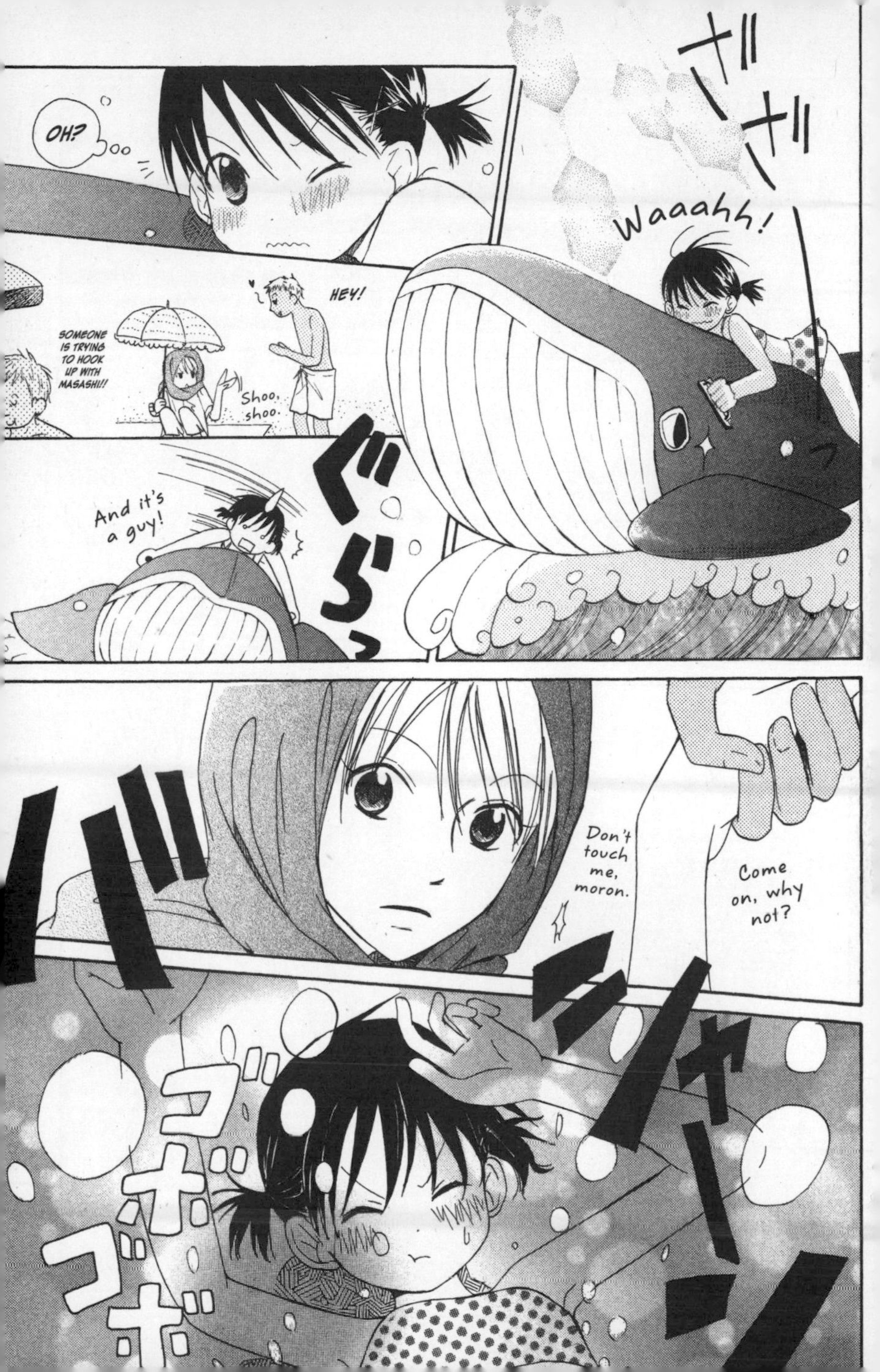
Waaahh!
OH?
HEY!
SOMEONE IS TRYING TO HOOK UP WITH MASASHI!!
Shoo, shoo.
And it's a guy!
Come on, why not?
Don't touch me, moron.

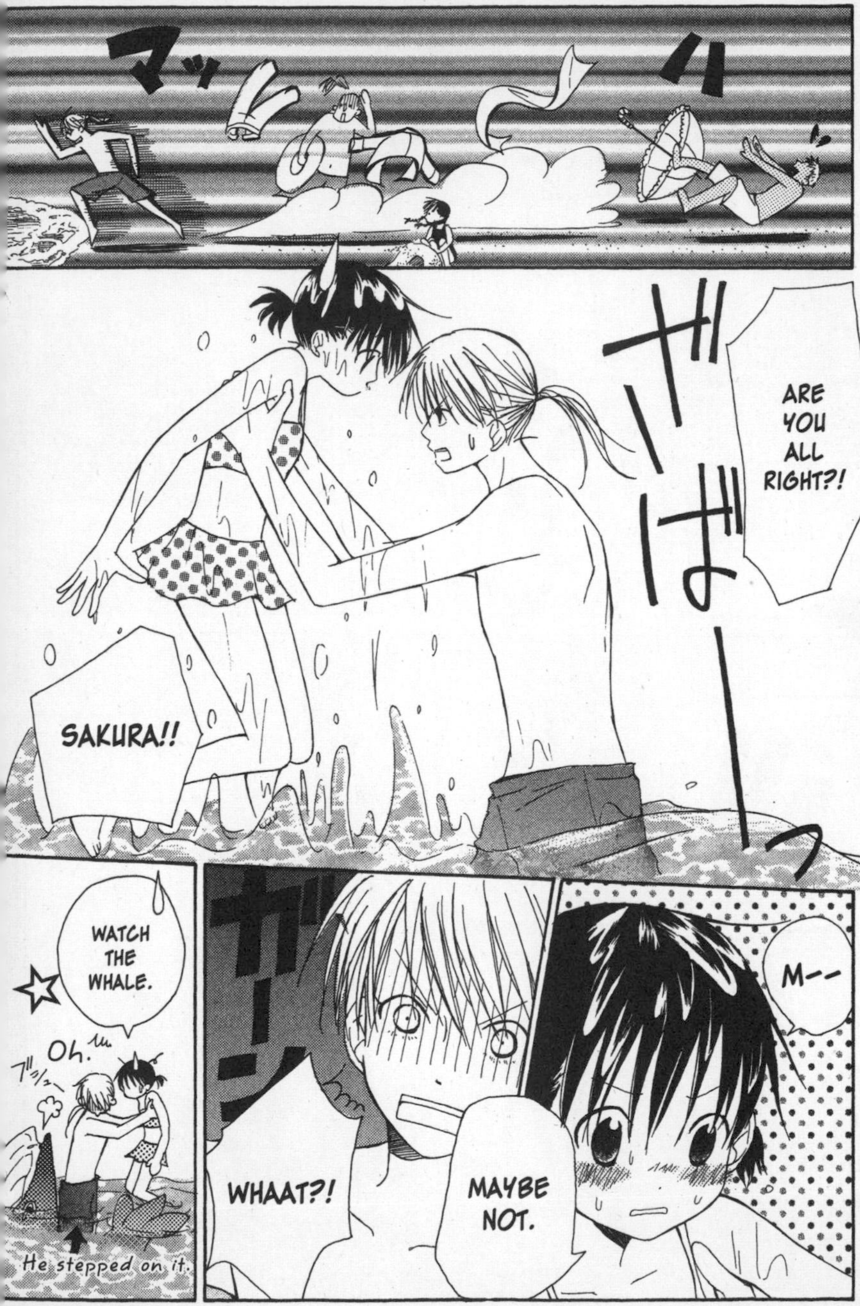
マッハ
ざぼーっ
ARE YOU ALL RIGHT?!
SAKURA!!
M--
MAYBE NOT.
ガーン
WHAAT?!
WATCH THE WHALE.
Oh.
He stepped on it.

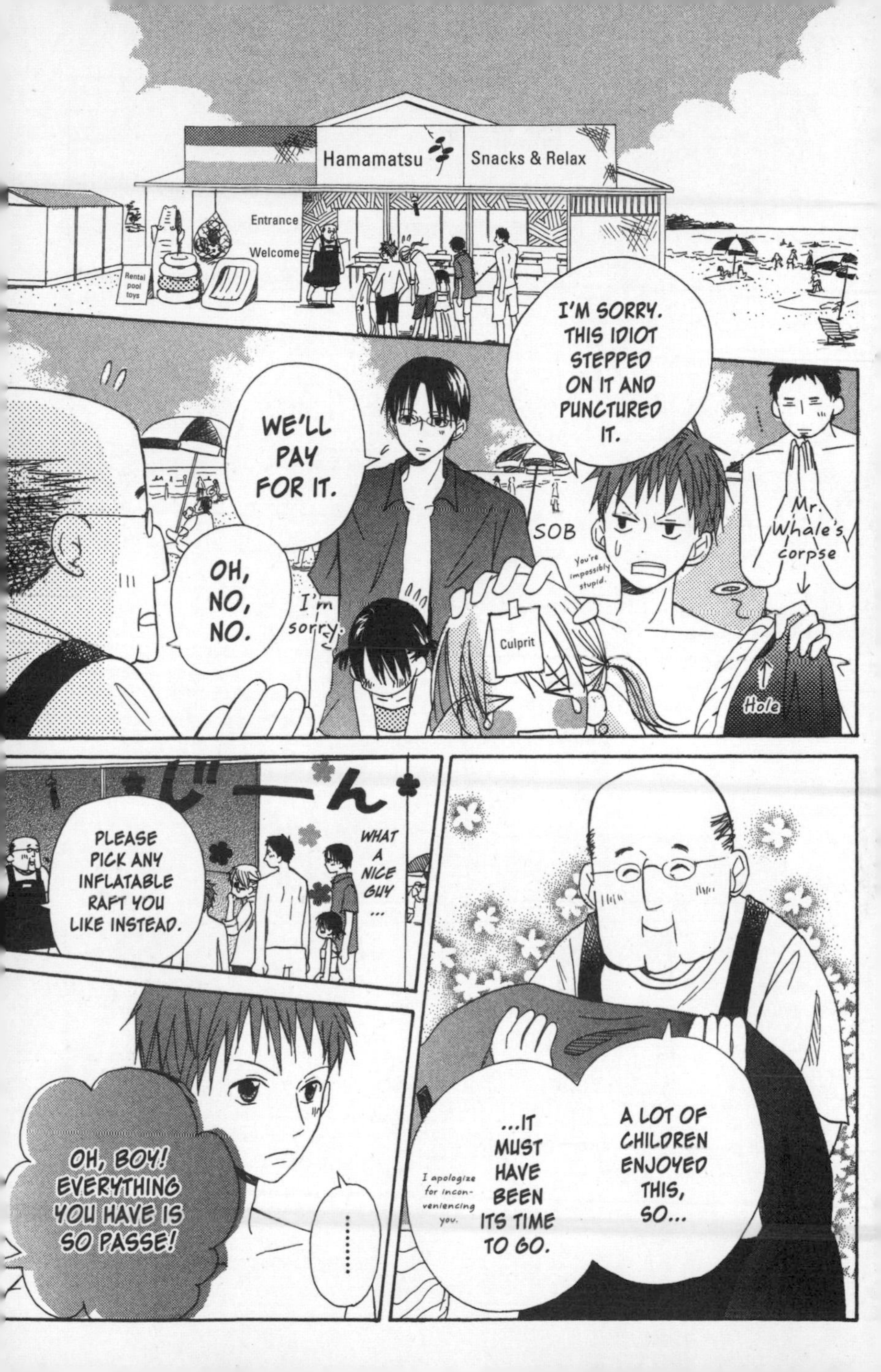
Hamamatsu
Snacks & Relax
Entrance
Welcome
Rental pool toys
I'M SORRY. THIS IDIOT STEPPED ON IT AND PUNCTURED IT.
......
Mr. Whale's corpse
Hole
SOB
You're impossibly stupid.
Culprit
WE'LL PAY FOR IT.
I'm sorry.
OH, NO, NO.
A LOT OF CHILDREN ENJOYED THIS, SO...
...IT MUST HAVE BEEN ITS TIME TO GO.
I apologize for inconveniencing you.
じーん
WHAT A NICE GUY...
PLEASE PICK ANY INFLATABLE RAFT YOU LIKE INSTEAD.
......
OH, BOY! EVERYTHING YOU HAVE IS SO PASSE!

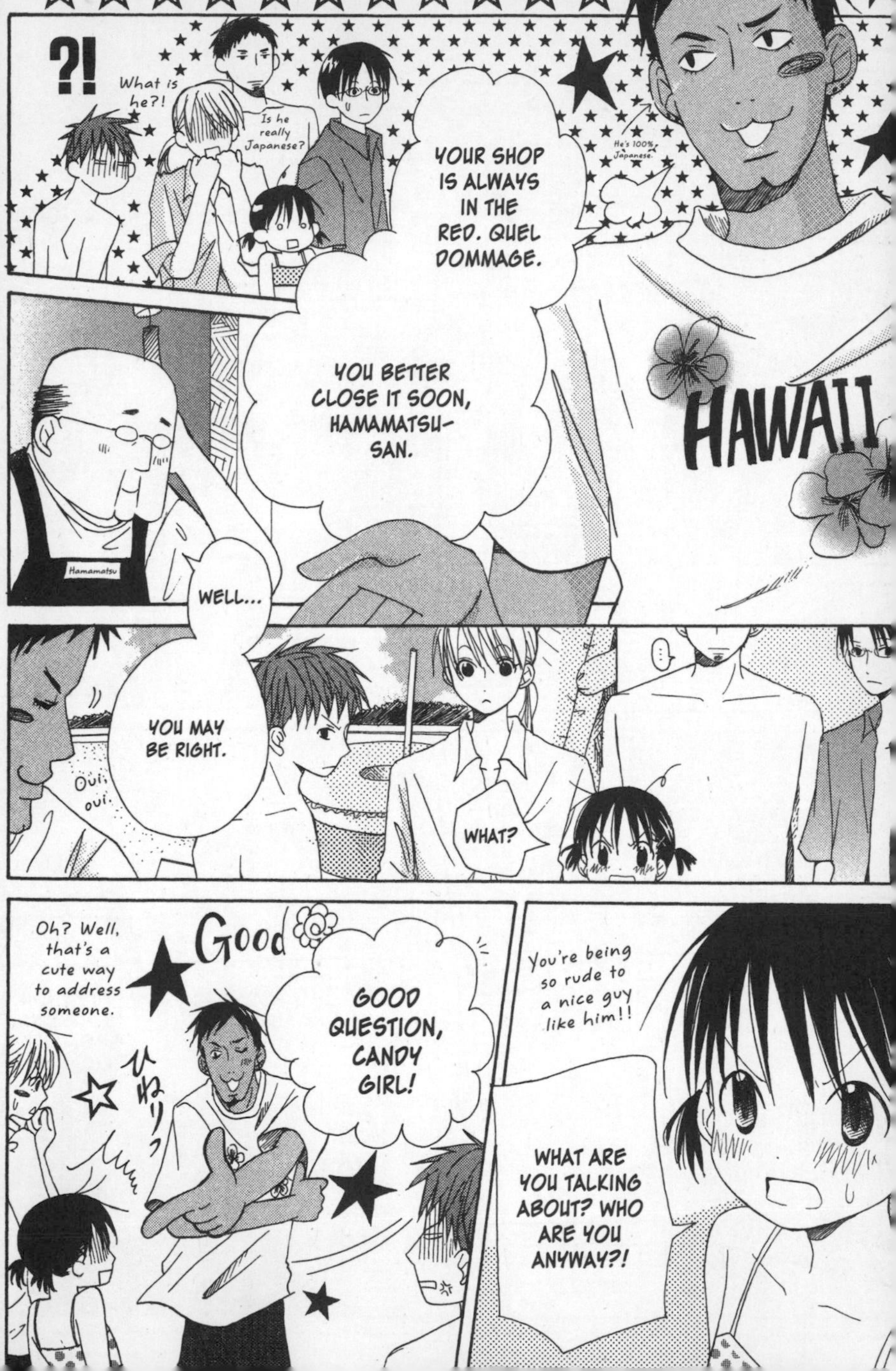
YOUR SHOP IS ALWAYS IN THE RED. QUEL DOMMAGE.
He's 100% Japanese.
?!
What is he?!
Is he really Japanese?
YOU BETTER CLOSE IT SOON, HAMAMATSU-SAN.
Hamamatsu
WELL...
HAWAII
...
WHAT?
YOU MAY BE RIGHT.
Oui, oui.
You're being so rude to a nice guy like him!!
WHAT ARE YOU TALKING ABOUT? WHO ARE YOU ANYWAY?!
GOOD QUESTION, CANDY GIRL!
Good
Oh? Well, that's a cute way to address someone.
ひねりっ

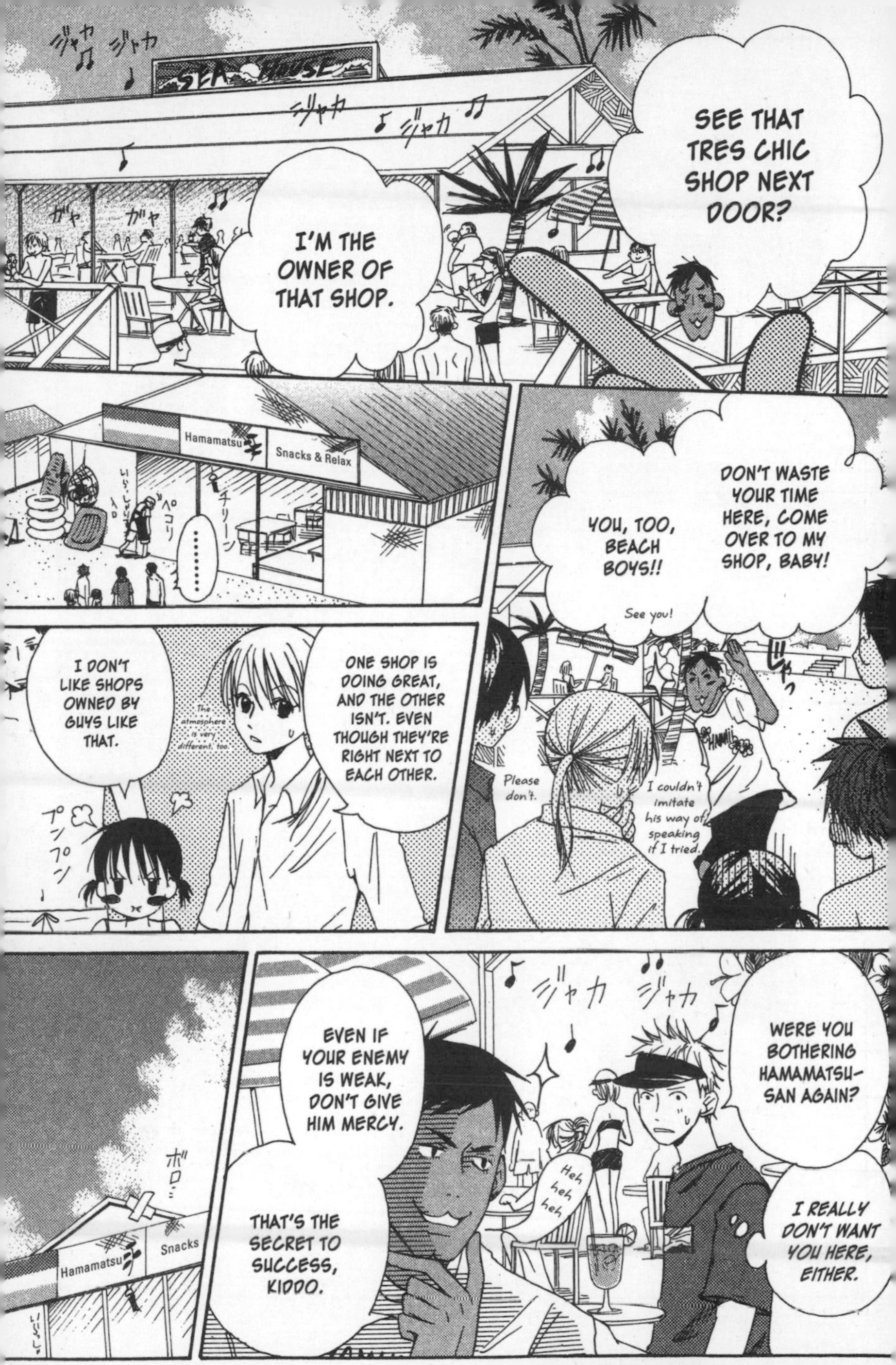
SEA HOUSE
ジャカ ジャカ
ガヤ ガヤ
SEE THAT TRES CHIC SHOP NEXT DOOR?
I'M THE OWNER OF THAT SHOP.
DON'T WASTE YOUR TIME HERE, COME OVER TO MY SHOP, BABY!
YOU, TOO, BEACH BOYS!!
See you!
Hamamatsu
Snacks & Relax
ペコリ
チリーン
....
I couldn't imitate his way of speaking if I tried.
Please don't.
ONE SHOP IS DOING GREAT, AND THE OTHER ISN'T. EVEN THOUGH THEY'RE RIGHT NEXT TO EACH OTHER.
The atmosphere is very different, too.
I DON'T LIKE SHOPS OWNED BY GUYS LIKE THAT.
プンプン
ジャカ ジャカ
WERE YOU BOTHERING HAMAMATSU-SAN AGAIN?
EVEN IF YOUR ENEMY IS WEAK, DON'T GIVE HIM MERCY.
Heh heh heh
I REALLY DON'T WANT YOU HERE, EITHER.
THAT'S THE SECRET TO SUCCESS, KIDDO.
ボロ
Hamamatsu
Snacks

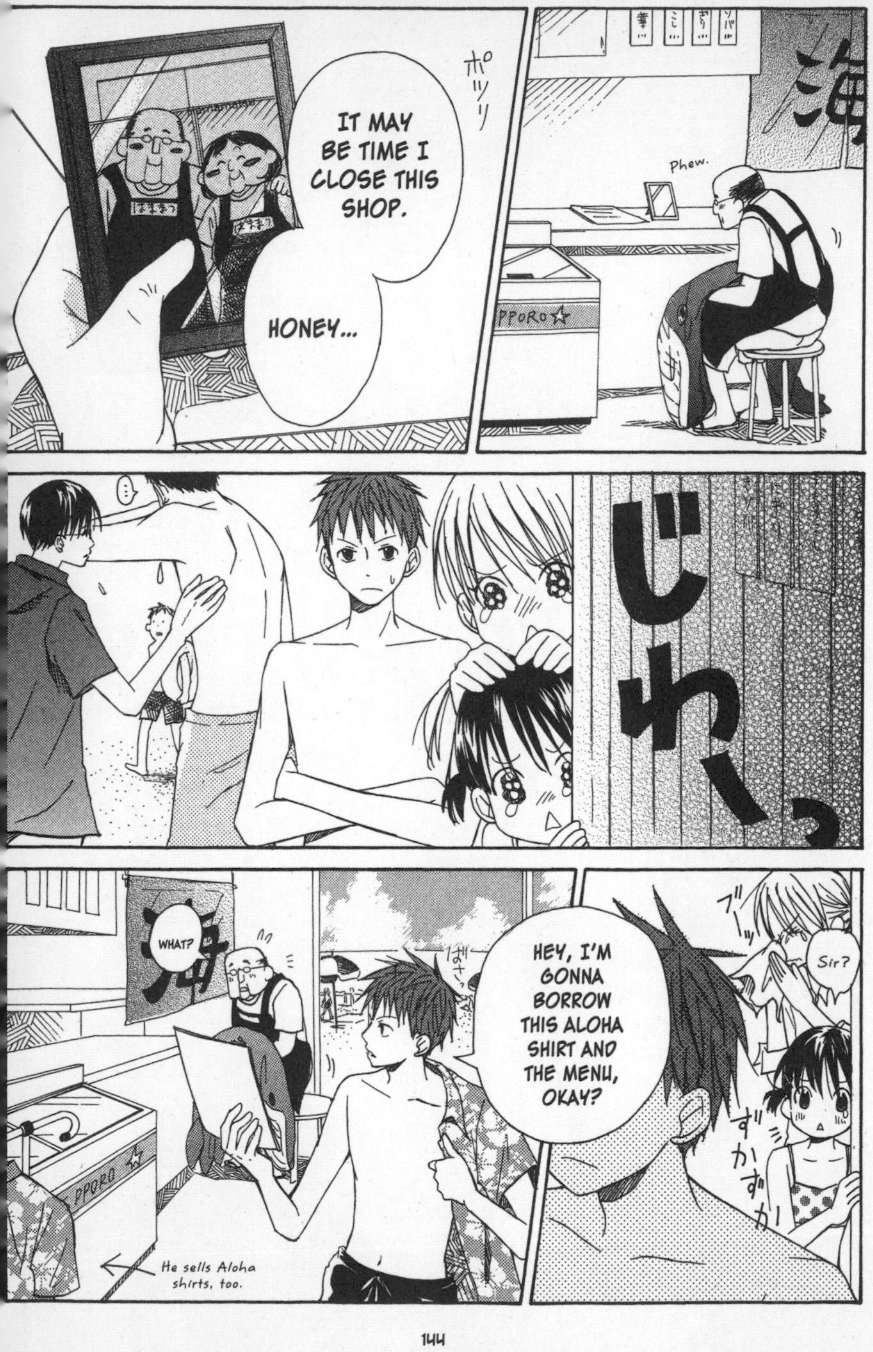
Phew.
ポツリ
IT MAY BE TIME I CLOSE THIS SHOP.
HONEY...
じわっ
...
Sir?
ブーッ
ずかずか
HEY, I'M GONNA BORROW THIS ALOHA SHIRT AND THE MENU, OKAY?
ばさっ
WHAT?
He sells Aloha shirts, too.

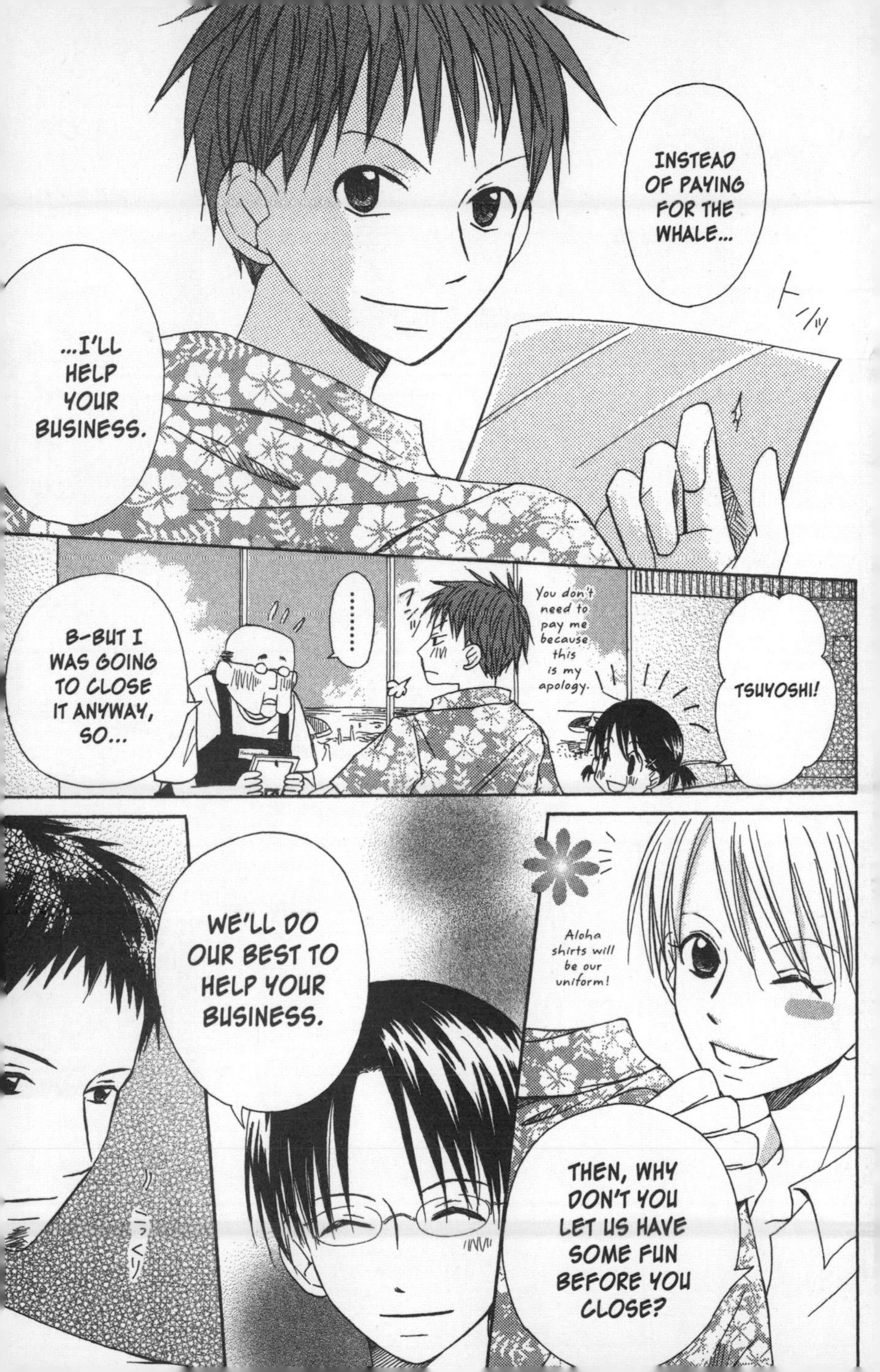
INSTEAD OF PAYING FOR THE WHALE...
...I'LL HELP YOUR BUSINESS.
TSUYOSHI!
You don't need to pay me because this is my apology.
......
B-BUT I WAS GOING TO CLOSE IT ANYWAY, SO...
Aloha shirts will be our uniform!
THEN, WHY DON'T YOU LET US HAVE SOME FUN BEFORE YOU CLOSE?
WE'LL DO OUR BEST TO HELP YOUR BUSINESS.

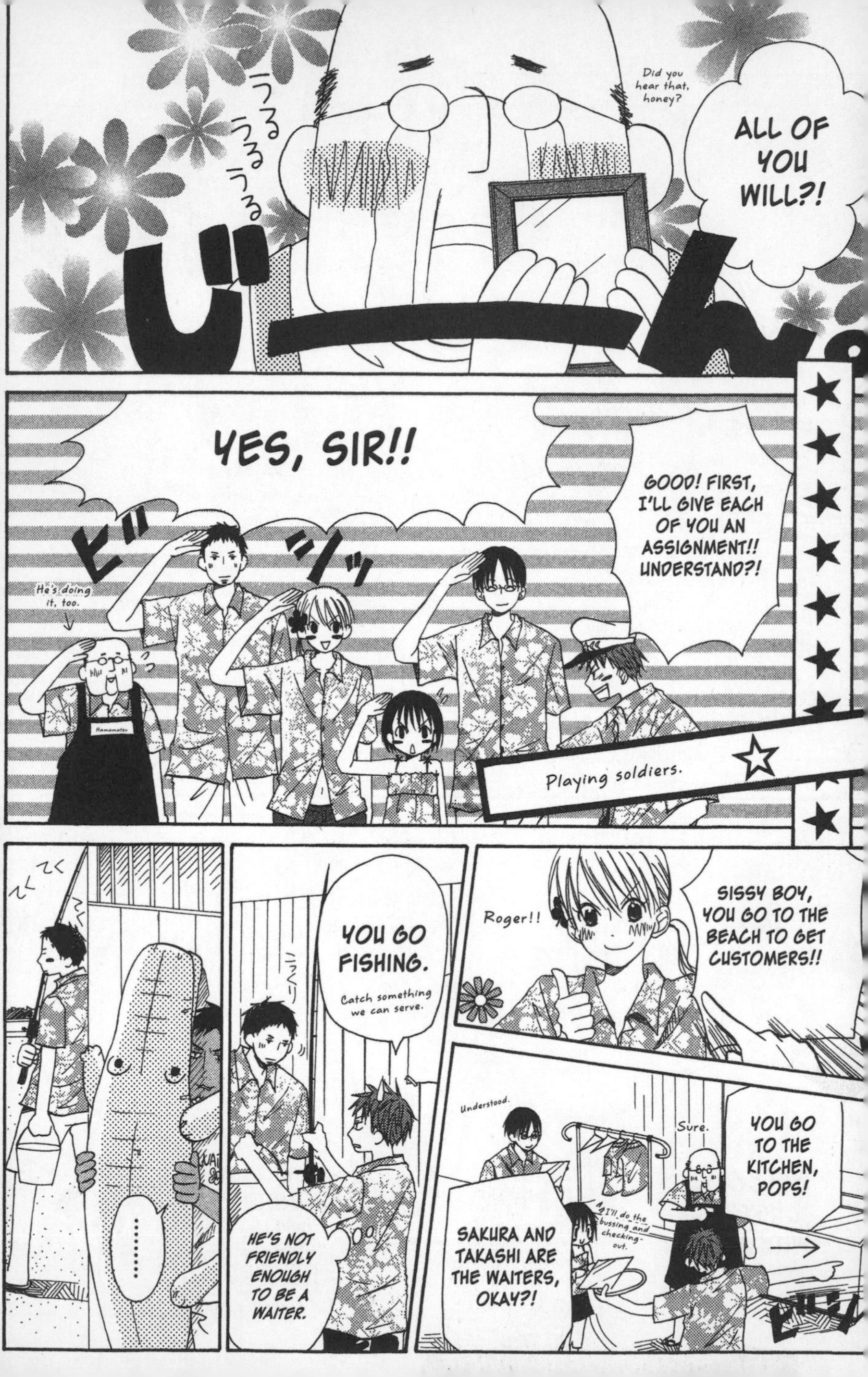
うる
うる
うる
じーん
Did you hear that, honey?
ALL OF YOU WILL?!
YES, SIR!!
GOOD! FIRST, I'LL GIVE EACH OF YOU AN ASSIGNMENT!! UNDERSTAND?!
ビシッ
He's doing it, too.
Hamamatsu
Playing soldiers.
SISSY BOY, YOU GO TO THE BEACH TO GET CUSTOMERS!!
Roger!!
YOU GO TO THE KITCHEN, POPS!
Sure.
Understood.
SAKURA AND TAKASHI ARE THE WAITERS, OKAY?!
I'll do the bussing and checking-out.
YOU GO FISHING.
Catch something we can serve.
こっくり
HE'S NOT FRIENDLY ENOUGH TO BE A WAITER.
てくてく
てく
......

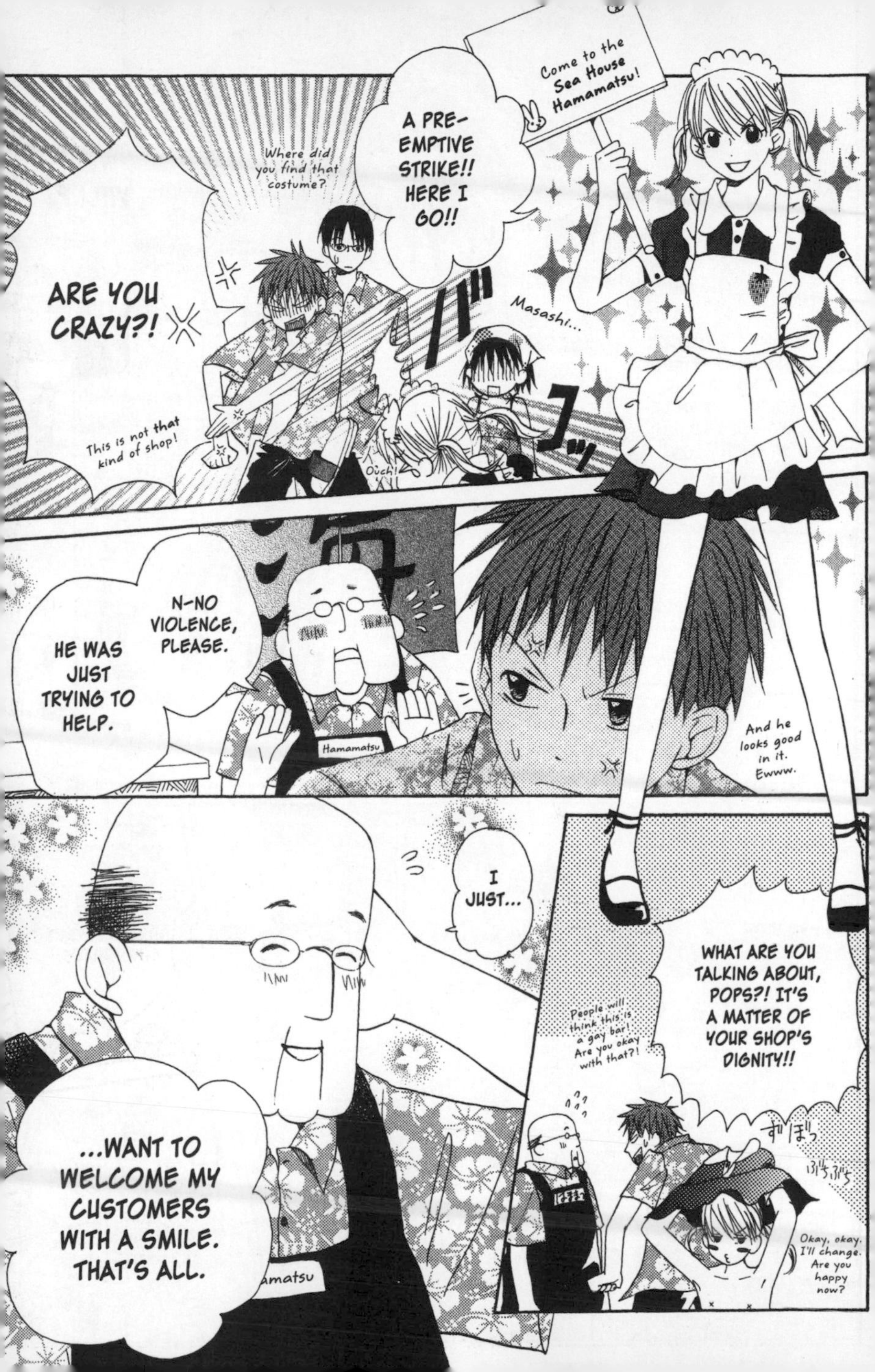
Come to the Sea House Hamamatsu!
A PRE-EMPTIVE STRIKE!! HERE I GO!!
Masashi...
Where did you find that costume?
ARE YOU CRAZY?!
This is not that kind of shop!
Ouch!
And he looks good in it. Ewww.
N-NO VIOLENCE, PLEASE.
HE WAS JUST TRYING TO HELP.
Hamamatsu
WHAT ARE YOU TALKING ABOUT, POPS?! IT'S A MATTER OF YOUR SHOP'S DIGNITY!!
People will think this is a gay bar! Are you okay with that?!
ずぼっ
ぷちぷち
Okay, okay. I'll change. Are you happy now?
I JUST...
...WANT TO WELCOME MY CUSTOMERS WITH A SMILE. THAT'S ALL.

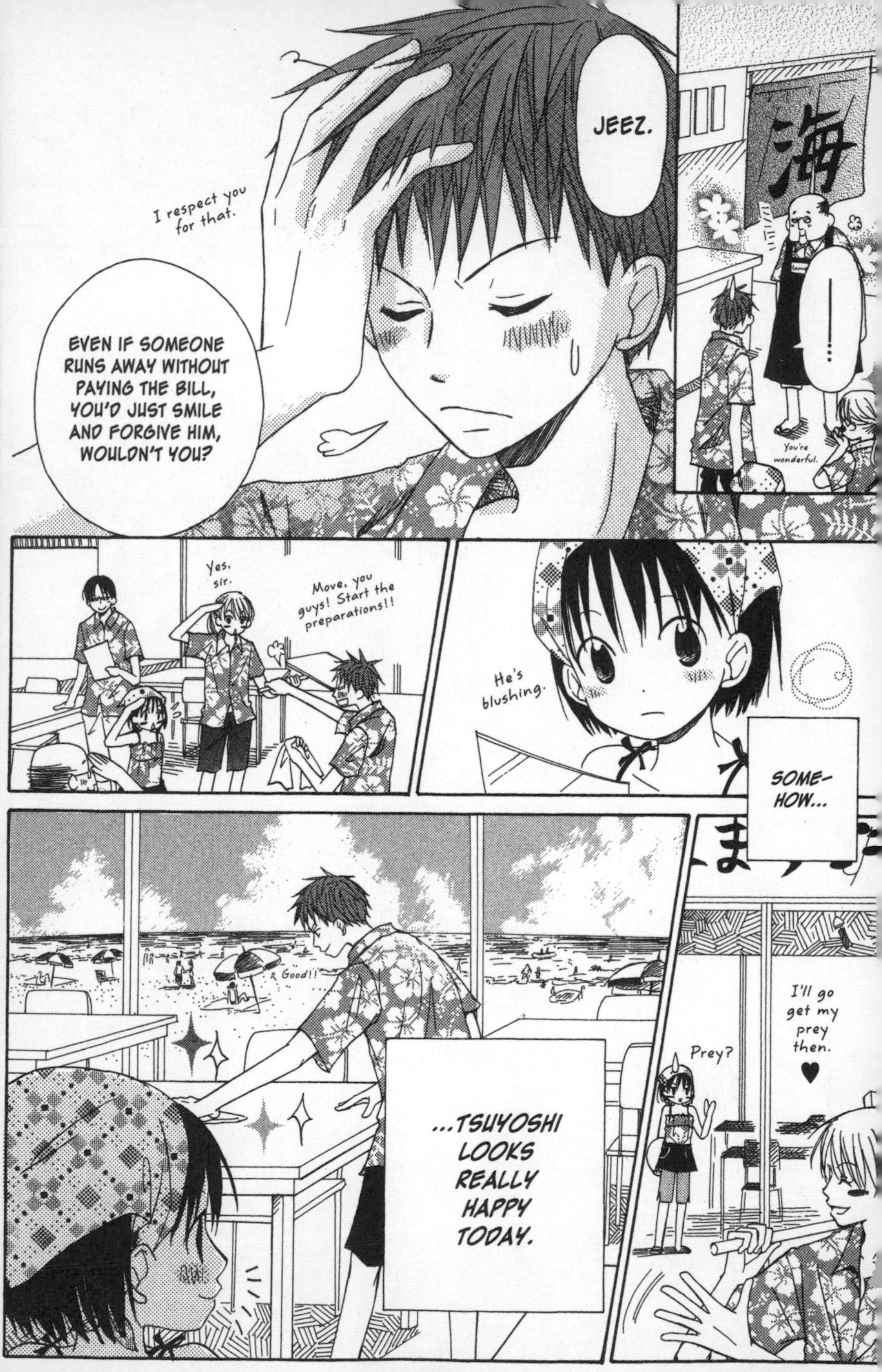
海
...!
You're wonderful.
JEEZ.
I respect you for that.
EVEN IF SOMEONE RUNS AWAY WITHOUT PAYING THE BILL, YOU'D JUST SMILE AND FORGIVE HIM, WOULDN'T YOU?
He's blushing.
SOME-HOW...
Move, you guys! Start the preparations!!
Yes, sir.
I'll go get my prey then. ♥
Prey?
...TSUYOSHI LOOKS REALLY HAPPY TODAY.
Good!!

This corn looks delicious.
They're very fresh.
YOU LIKE DOING THINGS LIKE THIS, DON'T YOU?
Tee hee.
WH-WHY?
TO BE HONEST, I WAS ALWAYS WONDERING WHY YOU WORK SO MANY DIFFERENT PART-TIME JOBS.
You even work every night.
....

☆5☆

It's summer time! The ocean!! A cleft chin! I'm pretty satisfied with the dude with the cleft chin. I think he's handsome. My editor didn't think so, but she said that she wouldn't mind going out with him. That was the best compliment. And the strawberry patterned apron is my favorite.

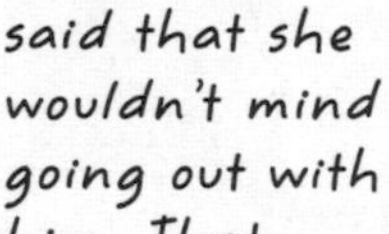

Strawberry.

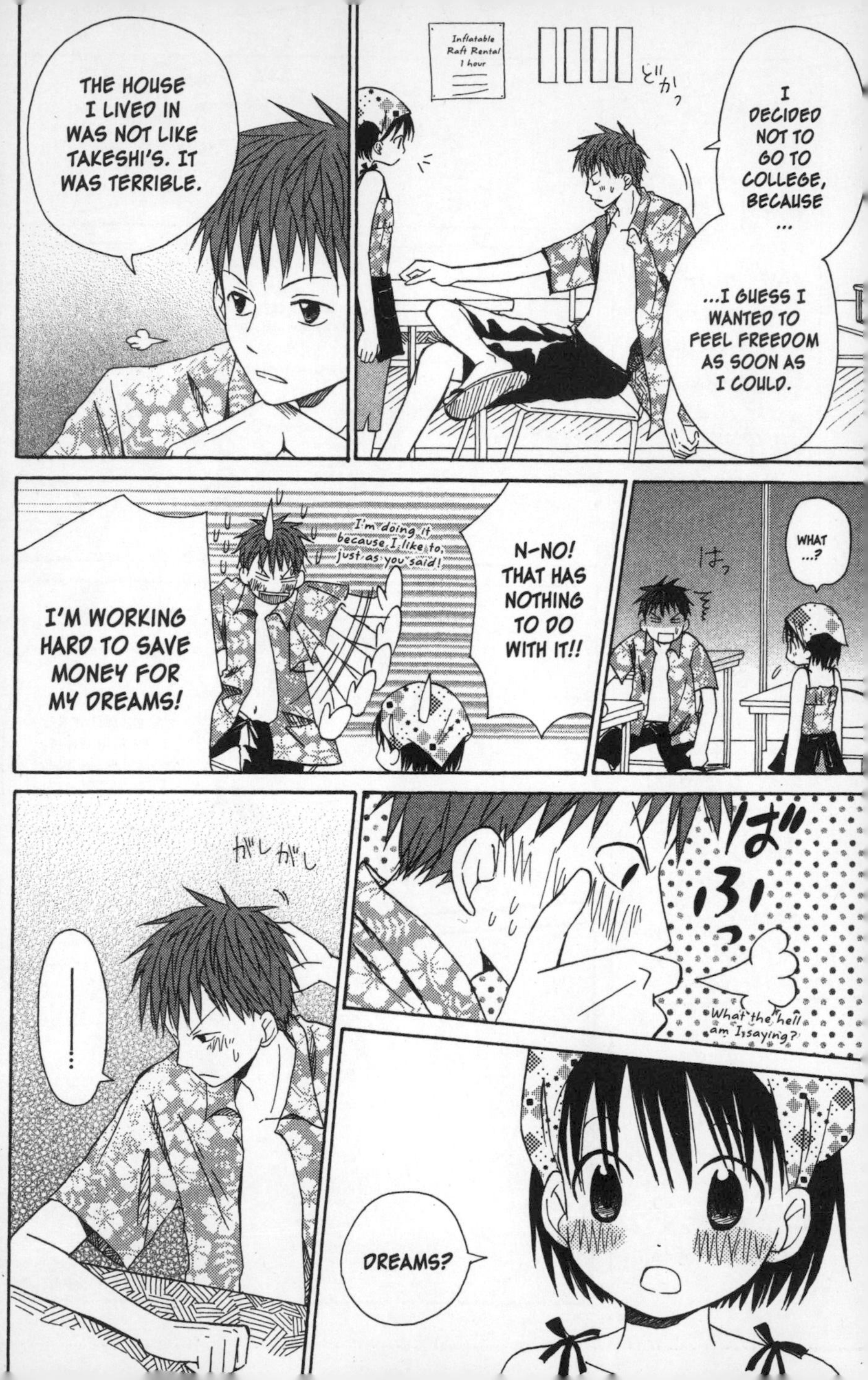
Inflatable Raft Rental 1 hour
どかっ
I DECIDED NOT TO GO TO COLLEGE, BECAUSE ...
...I GUESS I WANTED TO FEEL FREEDOM AS SOON AS I COULD.
THE HOUSE I LIVED IN WAS NOT LIKE TAKESHI'S. IT WAS TERRIBLE.
WHAT ...?
はっ
N-NO! THAT HAS NOTHING TO DO WITH IT!!
I'm doing it because I like to, just as you said!
I'M WORKING HARD TO SAVE MONEY FOR MY DREAMS!
ばふっ
What the hell am I saying?
DREAMS?
がしがし
......

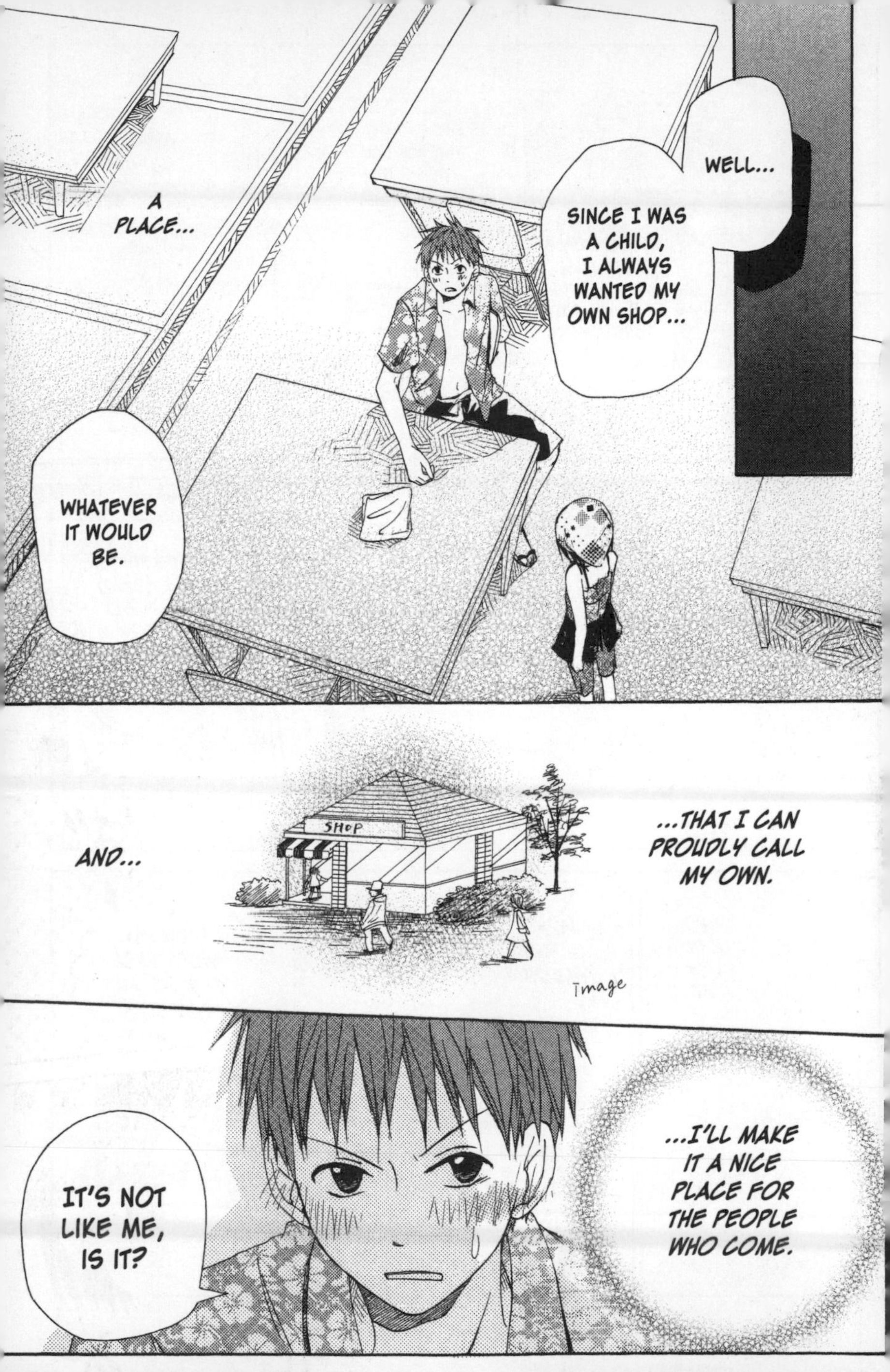
WELL...
SINCE I WAS A CHILD, I ALWAYS WANTED MY OWN SHOP...
A PLACE...
WHATEVER IT WOULD BE.
...THAT I CAN PROUDLY CALL MY OWN.
SHOP
AND...
Image
...I'LL MAKE IT A NICE PLACE FOR THE PEOPLE WHO COME.
IT'S NOT LIKE ME, IS IT?

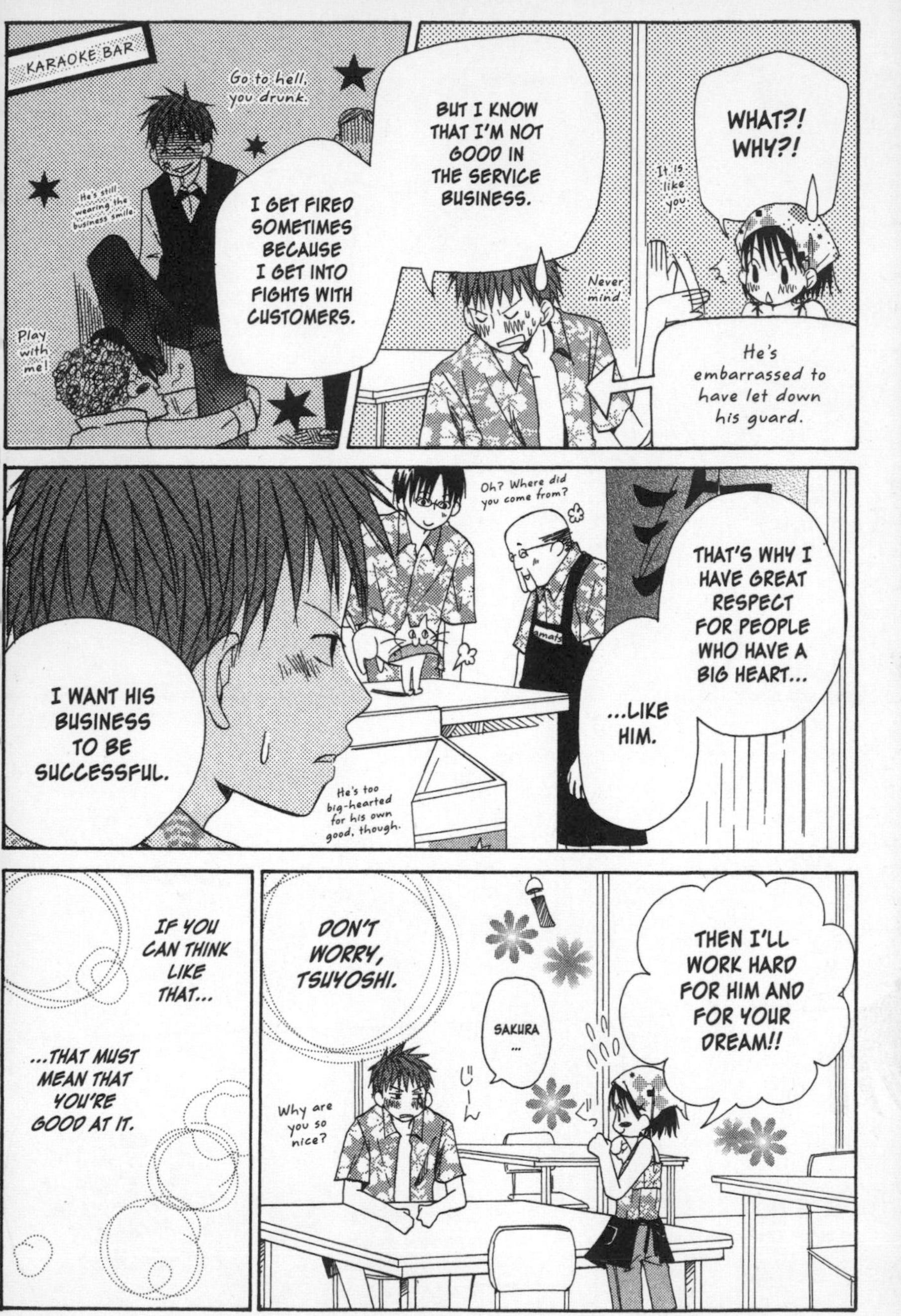
WHAT?! WHY?!
It is like you.
Never mind.
He's embarrassed to have let down his guard.
BUT I KNOW THAT I'M NOT GOOD IN THE SERVICE BUSINESS.
I GET FIRED SOMETIMES BECAUSE I GET INTO FIGHTS WITH CUSTOMERS.
KARAOKE BAR
Go to hell, you drunk.
He's still wearing the business smile
Play with me!
THAT'S WHY I HAVE GREAT RESPECT FOR PEOPLE WHO HAVE A BIG HEART...
...LIKE HIM.
Oh? Where did you come from?
He's too big-hearted for his own good, though.
I WANT HIS BUSINESS TO BE SUCCESSFUL.
THEN I'LL WORK HARD FOR HIM AND FOR YOUR DREAM!!
ぐっ
SAKURA...
じーん
DON'T WORRY, TSUYOSHI.
Why are you so nice?
IF YOU CAN THINK LIKE THAT...
...THAT MUST MEAN THAT YOU'RE GOOD AT IT.

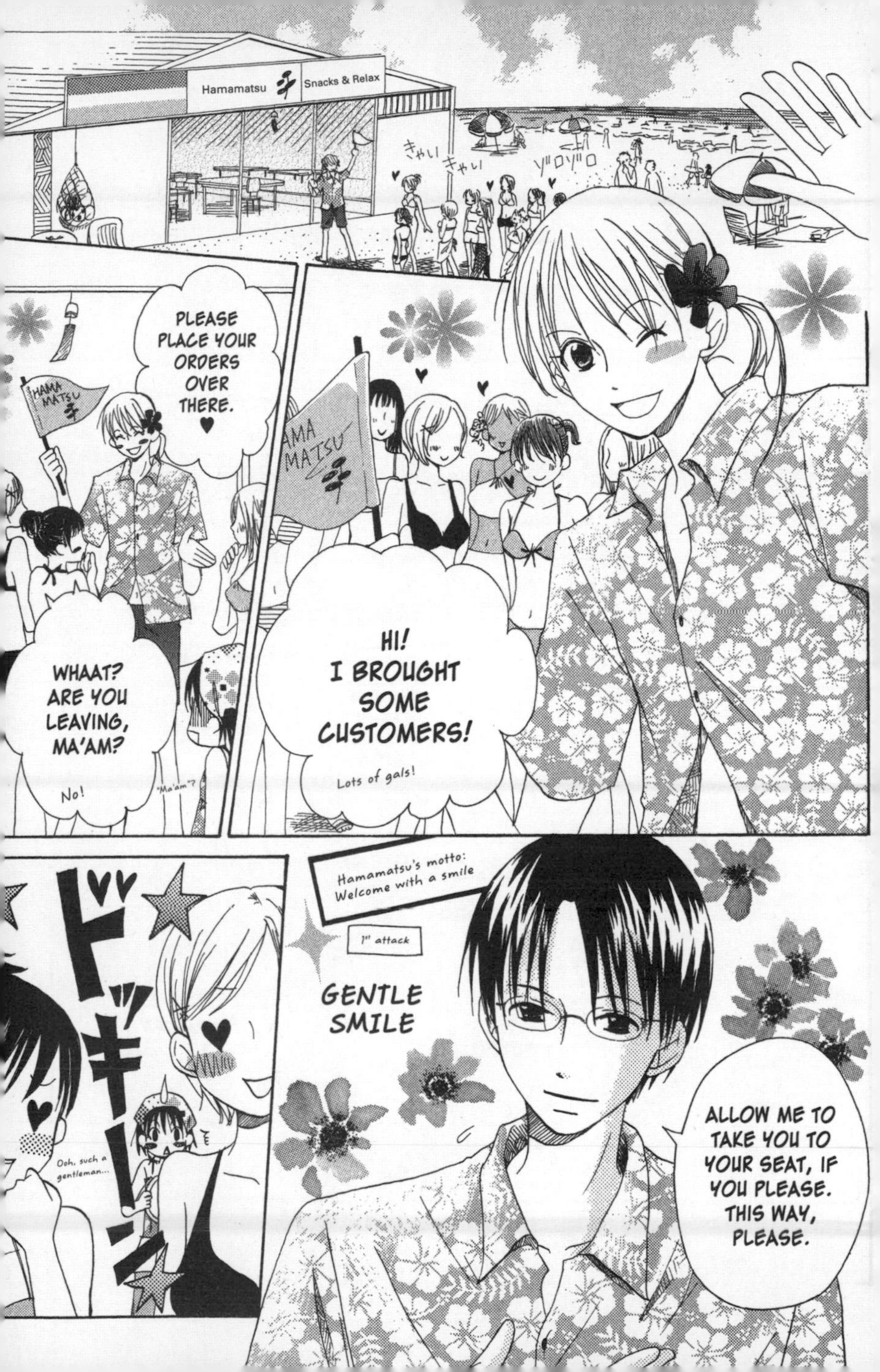

Hamamatsu
Snacks & Relax
きゃい きゃい
ゾロゾロ
HI! I BROUGHT SOME CUSTOMERS!
Lots of gals!
HAMA MATSU
HAMA MATSU
PLEASE PLACE YOUR ORDERS OVER THERE. ♥
WHAAT? ARE YOU LEAVING, MA'AM?
No!
"Ma'am"?
Hamamatsu's motto: Welcome with a smile
1st attack
GENTLE SMILE
ALLOW ME TO TAKE YOU TO YOUR SEAT, IF YOU PLEASE. THIS WAY, PLEASE.
ドッキーン
Ooh, such a gentleman...

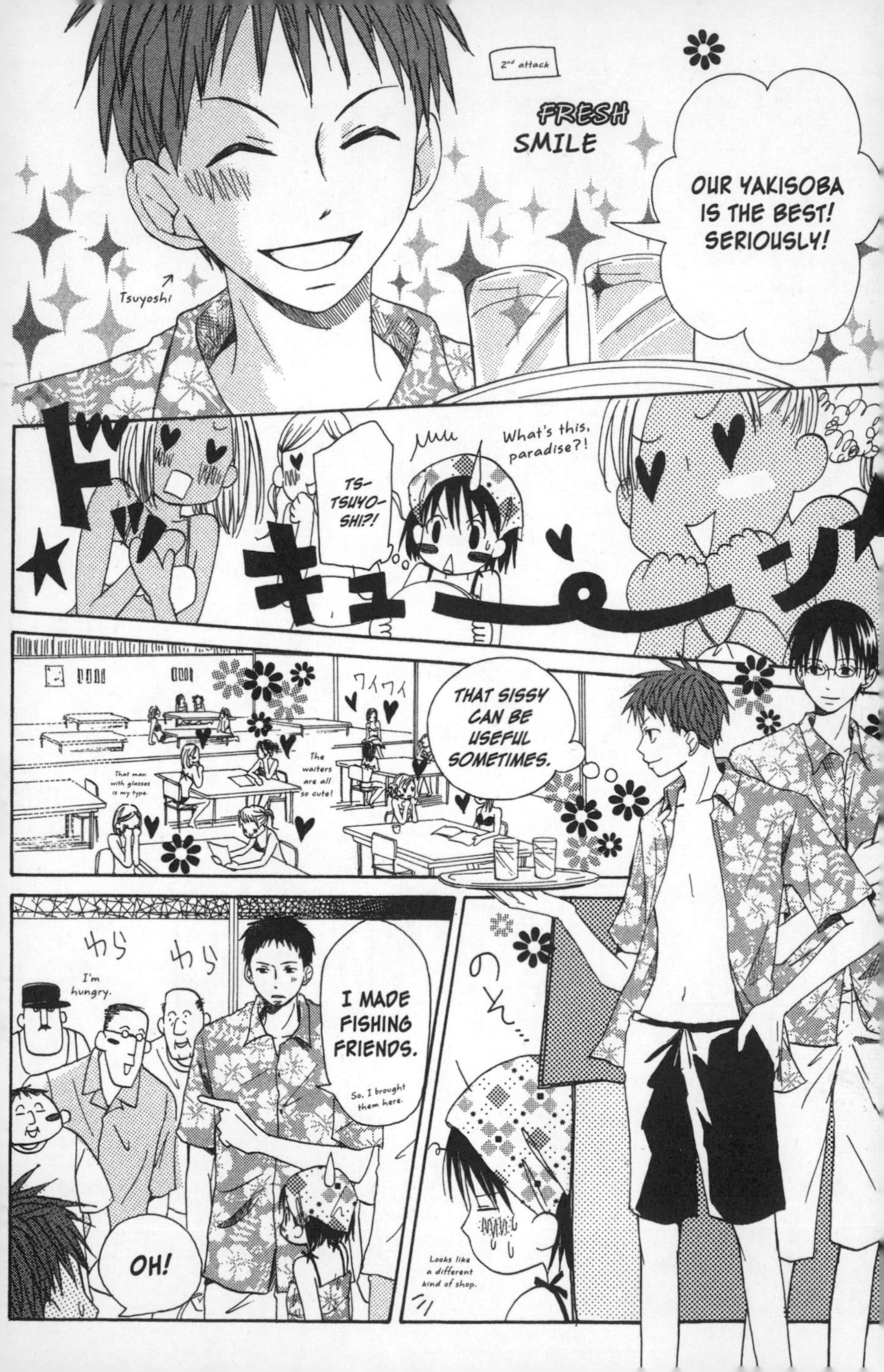
OUR YAKISOBA IS THE BEST! SERIOUSLY!
2nd attack
FRESH SMILE
Tsuyoshi
What's this, paradise?!
TS-TSUYO-SHI?!
ドッキューン
THAT SISSY CAN BE USEFUL SOMETIMES.
ワイワイ
The waiters are all so cute!
That man with glasses is my type.
のそ…
Looks like a different kind of shop.
I MADE FISHING FRIENDS.
So, I brought them here.
わら わら
I'm hungry.
OH!

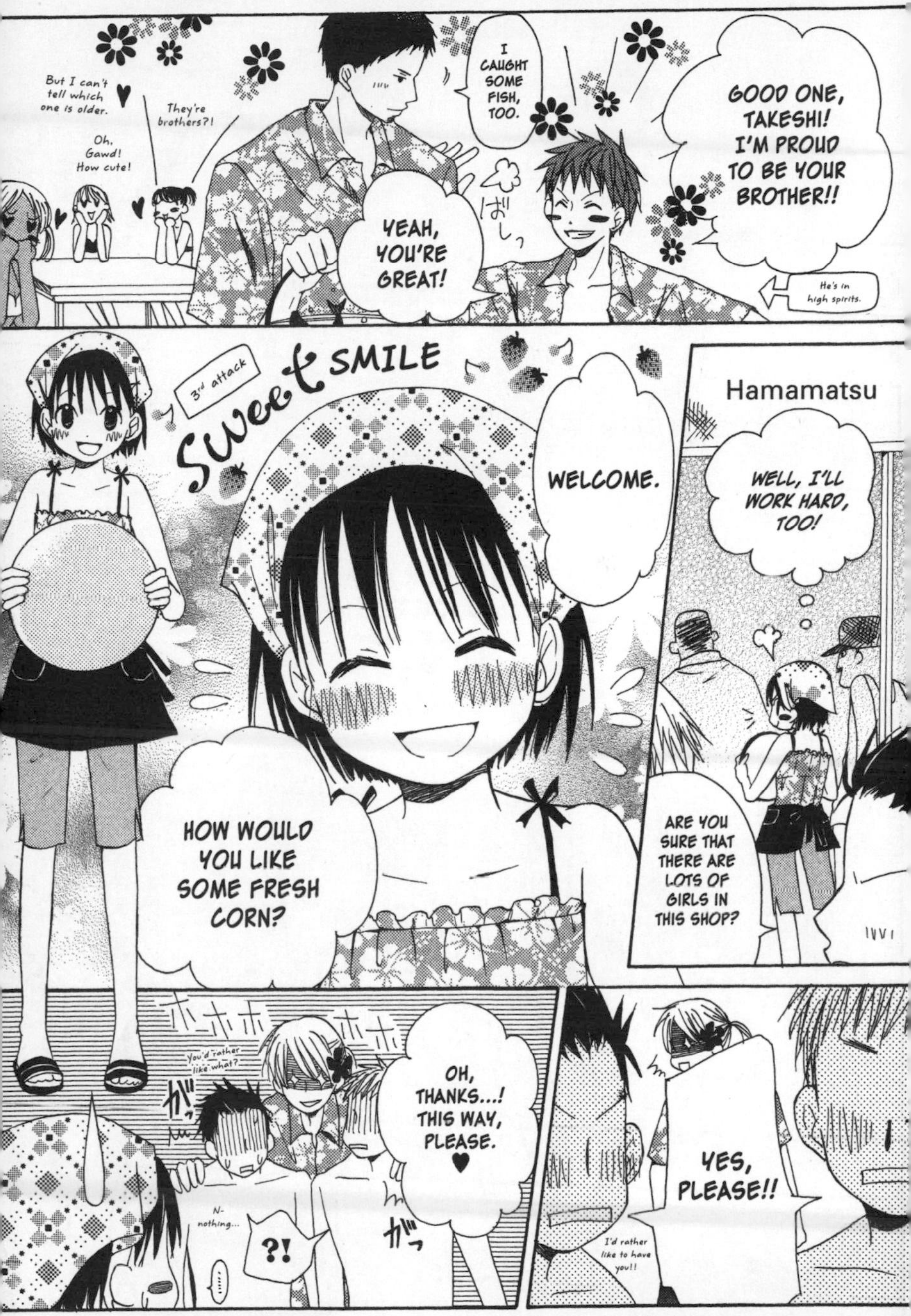

GOOD ONE, TAKESHI! I'M PROUD TO BE YOUR BROTHER!!
I CAUGHT SOME FISH, TOO.
He's in high spirits.
ぱしっ
YEAH, YOU'RE GREAT!
They're brothers?!
Oh, Gawd! How cute!
But I can't tell which one is older.
Hamamatsu
WELL, I'LL WORK HARD, TOO!
ARE YOU SURE THAT THERE ARE LOTS OF GIRLS IN THIS SHOP?
WELCOME.
Sweet SMILE
3rd attack
HOW WOULD YOU LIKE SOME FRESH CORN?
YES, PLEASE!!
I'd rather like to have you!!
OH, THANKS...! THIS WAY, PLEASE. ♥
ホホホ ホホ
You'd rather like what?
ガッ
N- nothing...
?!
ガッ

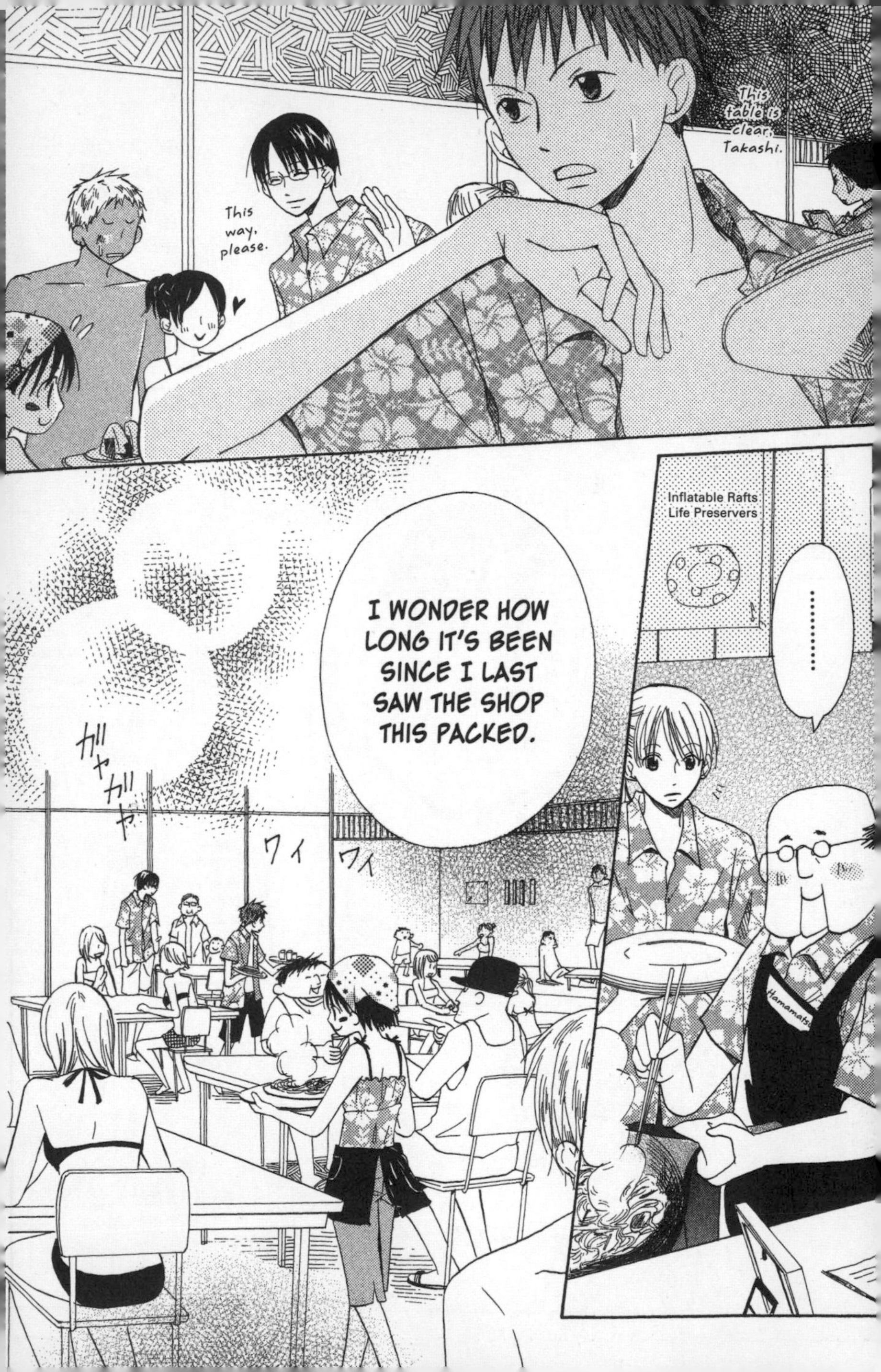
This table is clear, Takashi.
This way, please.
Inflatable Rafts
Life Preservers
....
I WONDER HOW LONG IT'S BEEN SINCE I LAST SAW THE SHOP THIS PACKED.
ガヤガヤ
ワイワイ

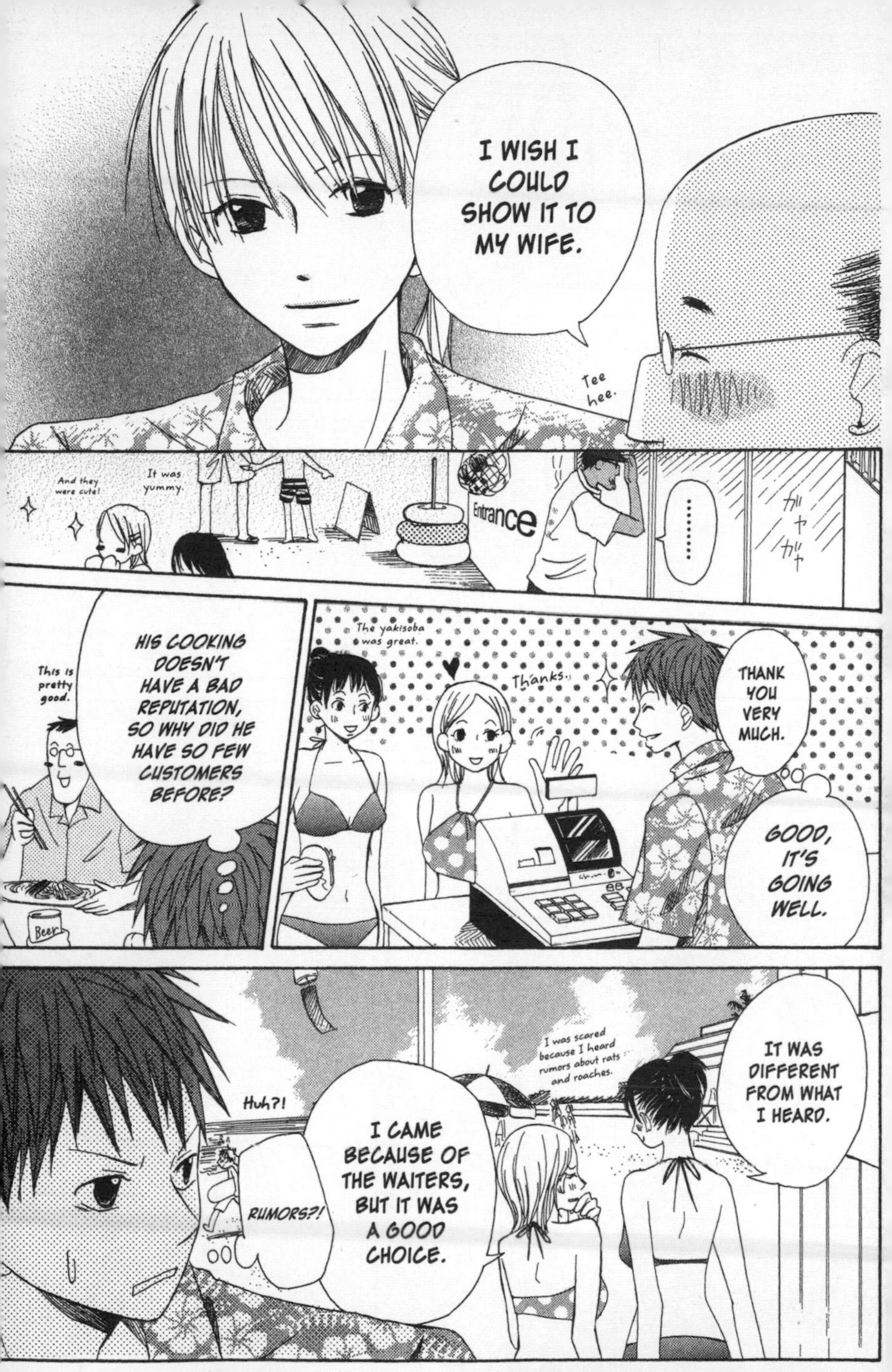
I WISH I COULD SHOW IT TO MY WIFE.
Tee hee.
ガヤガヤ
......
Entrance
It was yummy.
And they were cute!
THANK YOU VERY MUCH.
GOOD, IT'S GOING WELL.
Thanks.
The yakisoba was great.
HIS COOKING DOESN'T HAVE A BAD REPUTATION, SO WHY DID HE HAVE SO FEW CUSTOMERS BEFORE?
This is pretty good.
Beer
IT WAS DIFFERENT FROM WHAT I HEARD.
I was scared because I heard rumors about rats and roaches.
I CAME BECAUSE OF THE WAITERS, BUT IT WAS A GOOD CHOICE.
Huh?!
RUMORS?!

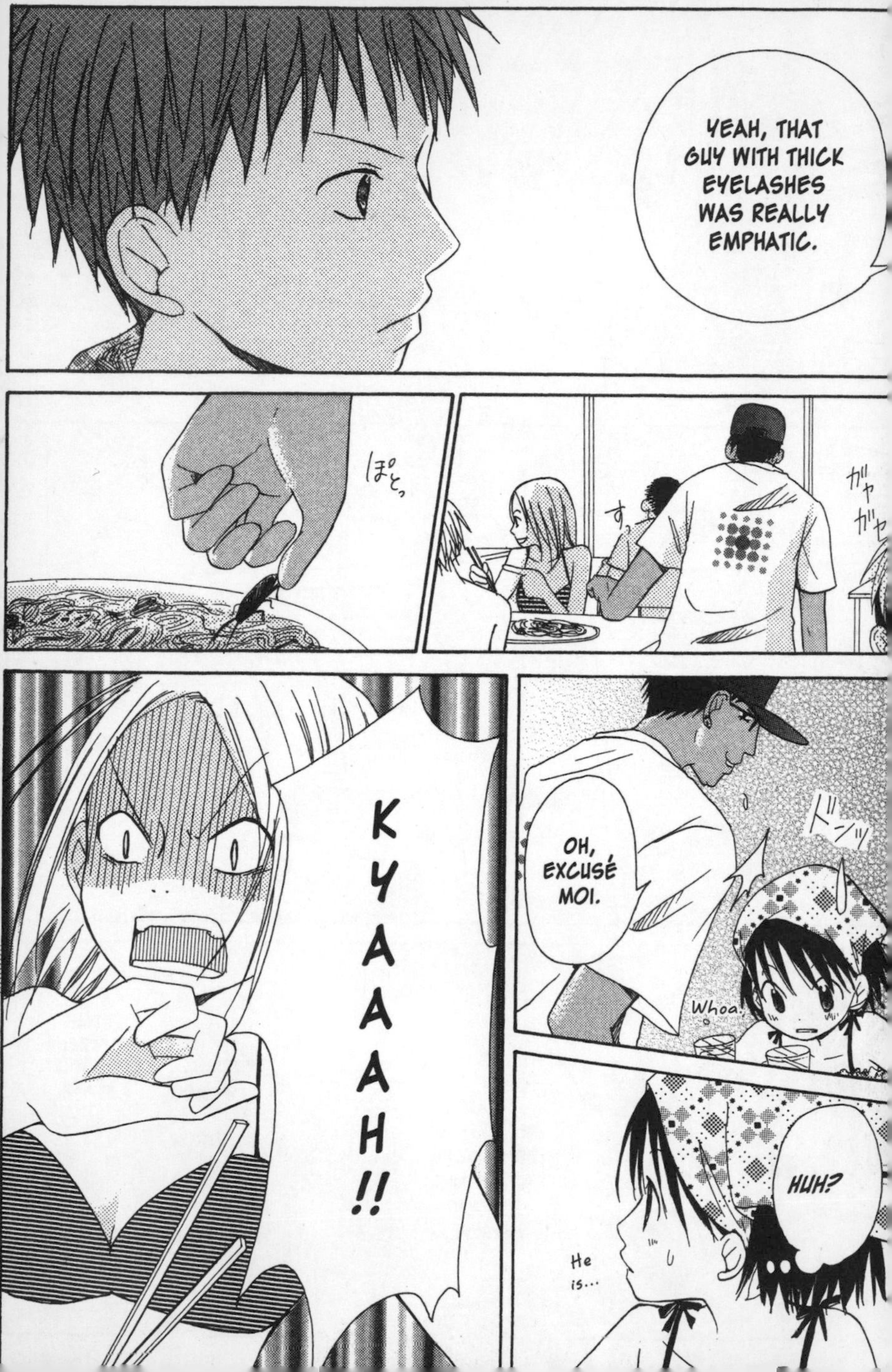
YEAH, THAT GUY WITH THICK EYELASHES WAS REALLY EMPHATIC.
ガヤガヤ
す
ぽとっ
OH, EXCUSÉ MOI.
ドンッ
Whoa.
HUH?
He is...
KYAAAH!!

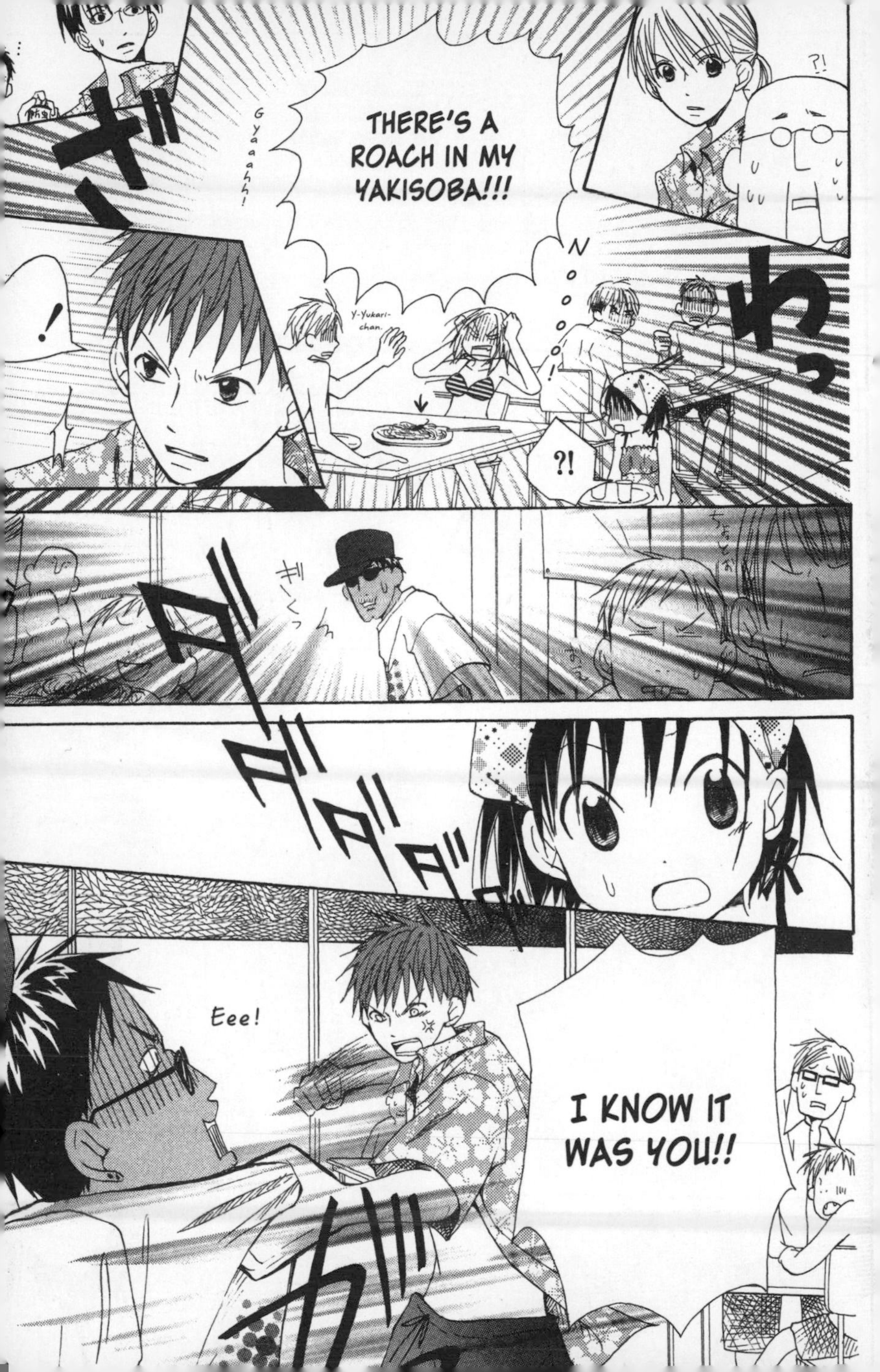

?!
...
Gyaaahh!
THERE'S A ROACH IN MY YAKISOBA!!!
Noooo!
Y-Yukari-chan.
?!
!
I KNOW IT WAS YOU!!
Eee!

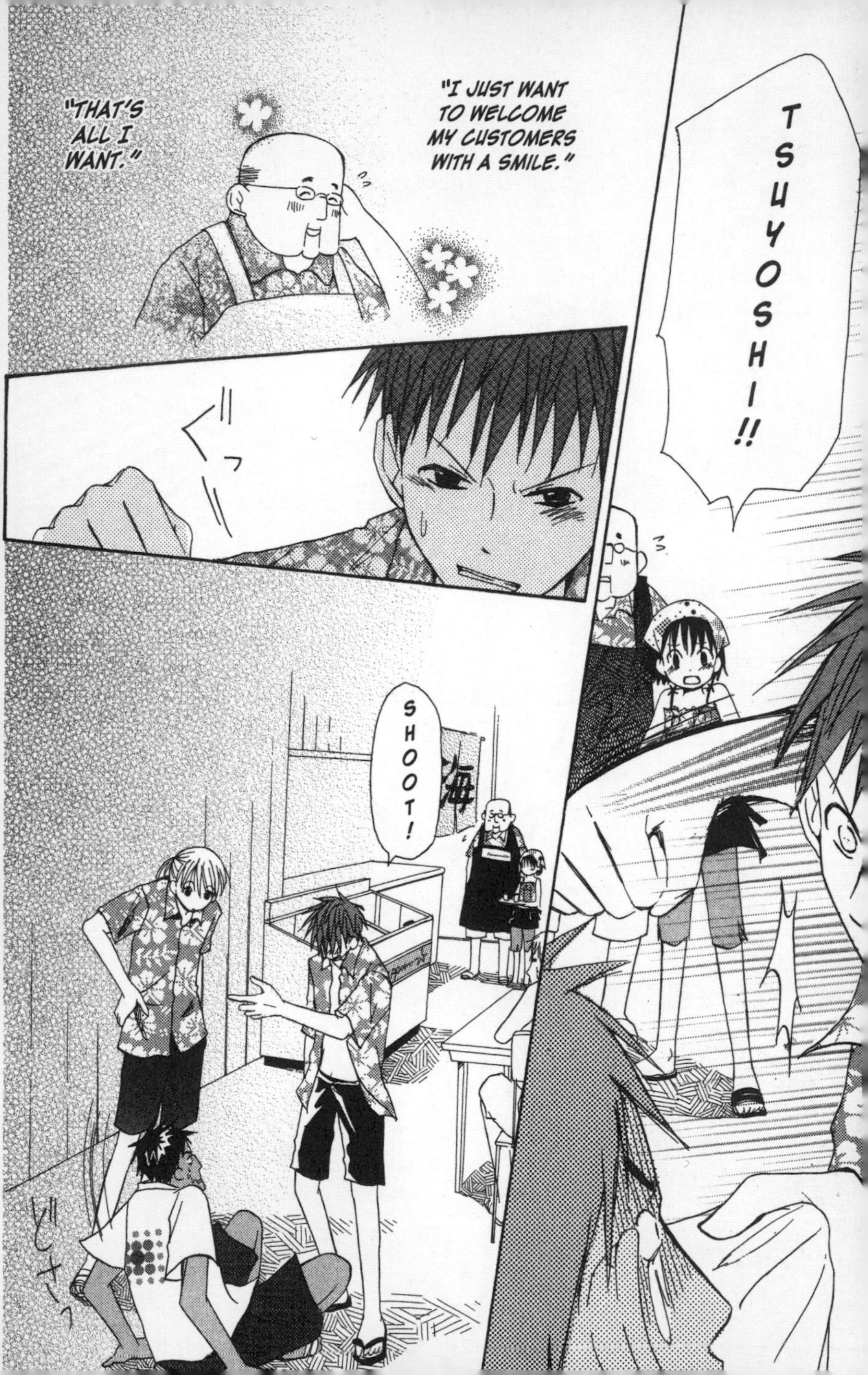
TSUYOSHI!!
"I JUST WANT TO WELCOME MY CUSTOMERS WITH A SMILE."
"THAT'S ALL I WANT."
SHOOT!

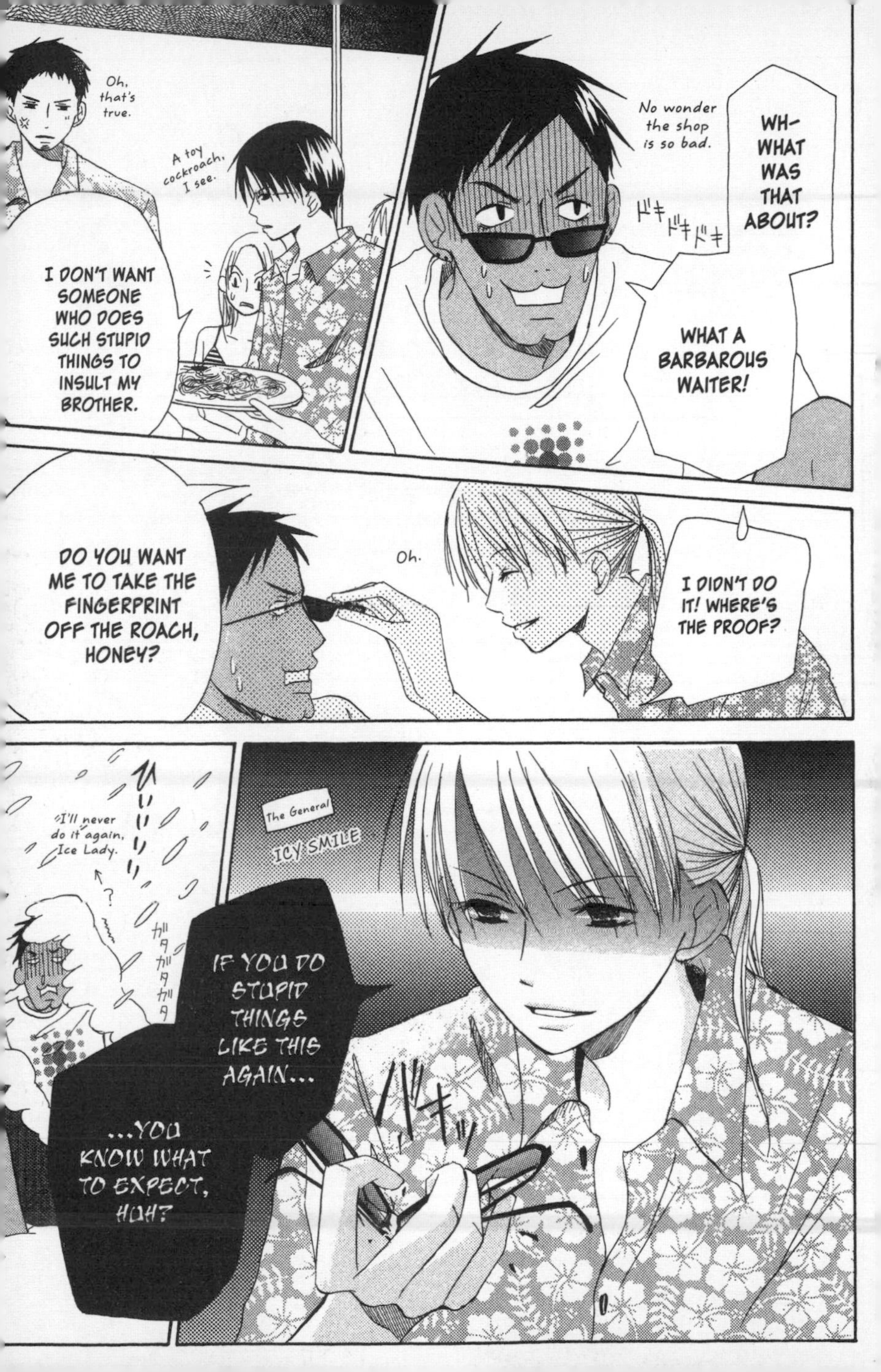
No wonder the shop is so bad.
WH-WHAT WAS THAT ABOUT?
ドキドキドキ
WHAT A BARBAROUS WAITER!
Oh, that's true.
A toy cockroach, I see.
I DON'T WANT SOMEONE WHO DOES SUCH STUPID THINGS TO INSULT MY BROTHER.
I DIDN'T DO IT! WHERE'S THE PROOF?
Oh.
DO YOU WANT ME TO TAKE THE FINGERPRINT OFF THE ROACH, HONEY?
The General
ICY SMILE
IF YOU DO STUPID THINGS LIKE THIS AGAIN...
...YOU KNOW WHAT TO EXPECT, HUH?
バキッ
ひぃぃぃぃ
I'll never do it again, Ice Lady.
ガタガタガタ

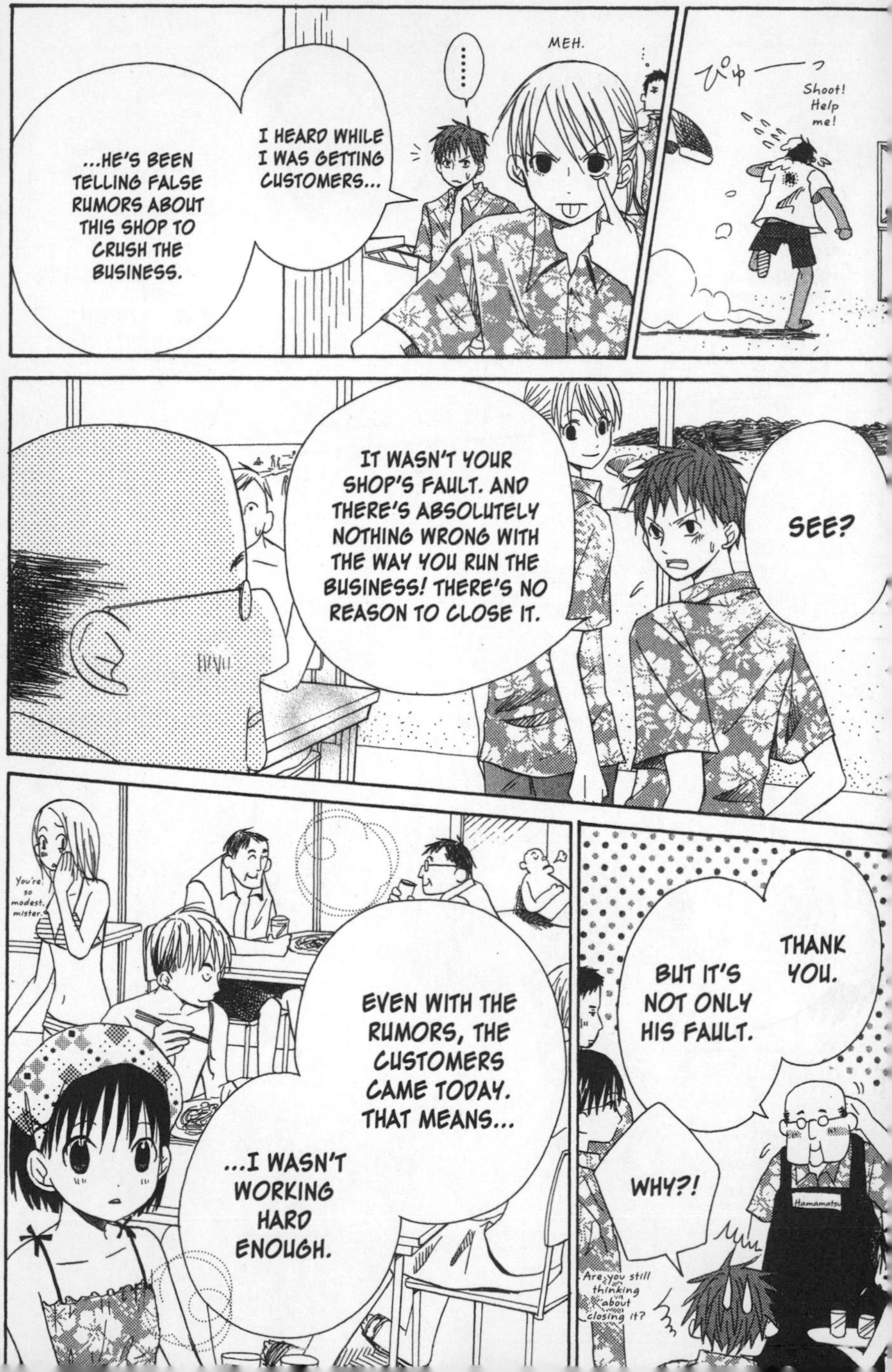
ぴゅーっ
Shoot! Help me!
MEH.
......
I HEARD WHILE I WAS GETTING CUSTOMERS...
...HE'S BEEN TELLING FALSE RUMORS ABOUT THIS SHOP TO CRUSH THE BUSINESS.
SEE?
IT WASN'T YOUR SHOP'S FAULT. AND THERE'S ABSOLUTELY NOTHING WRONG WITH THE WAY YOU RUN THE BUSINESS! THERE'S NO REASON TO CLOSE IT.
THANK YOU.
BUT IT'S NOT ONLY HIS FAULT.
Hamamatsu
WHY?!
Are you still thinking about closing it?
You're so modest, mister.
EVEN WITH THE RUMORS, THE CUSTOMERS CAME TODAY. THAT MEANS...
...I WASN'T WORKING HARD ENOUGH.

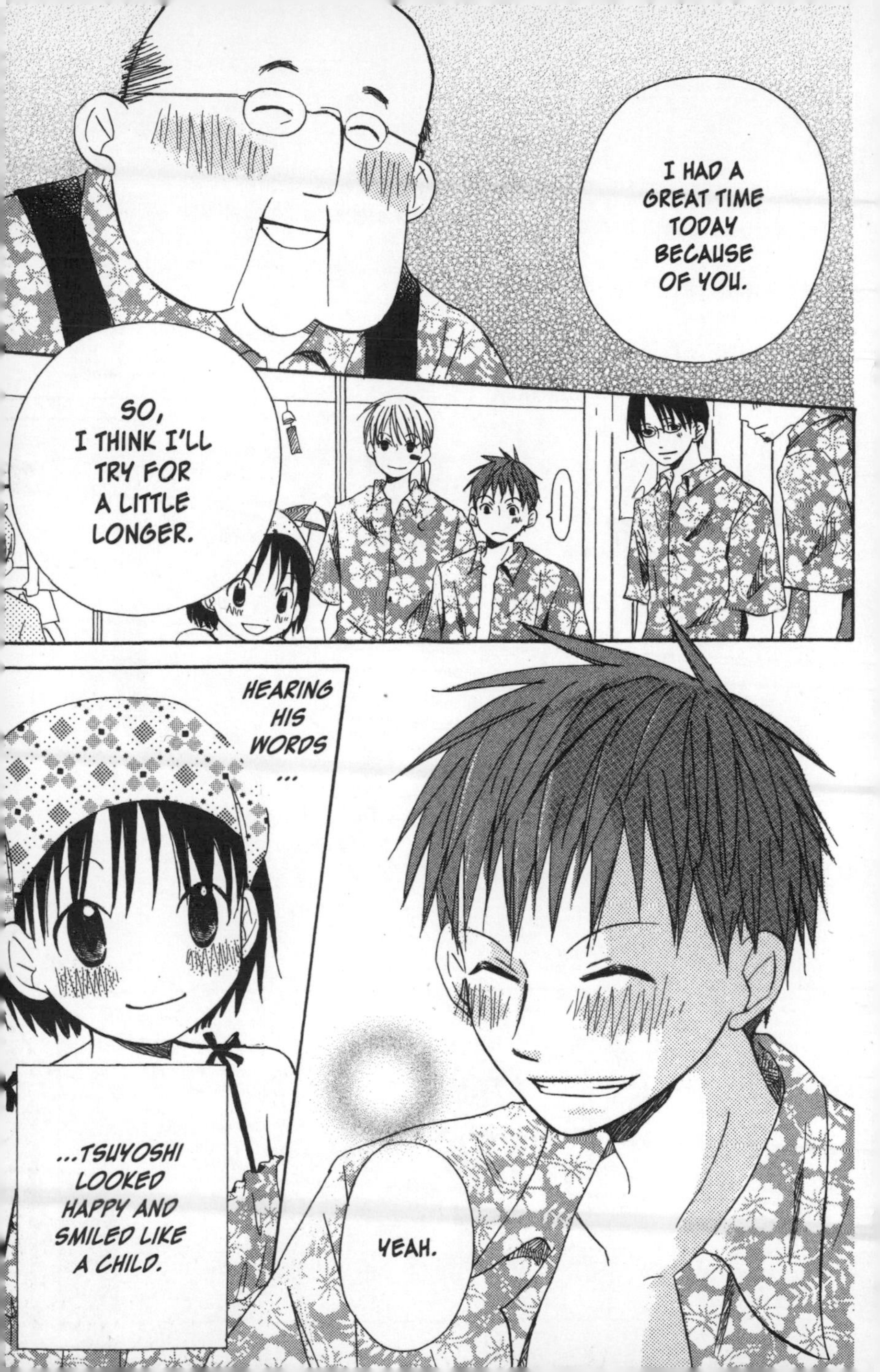
I HAD A GREAT TIME TODAY BECAUSE OF YOU.
SO, I THINK I'LL TRY FOR A LITTLE LONGER.
YEAH.
HEARING HIS WORDS ...
...TSUYOSHI LOOKED HAPPY AND SMILED LIKE A CHILD.

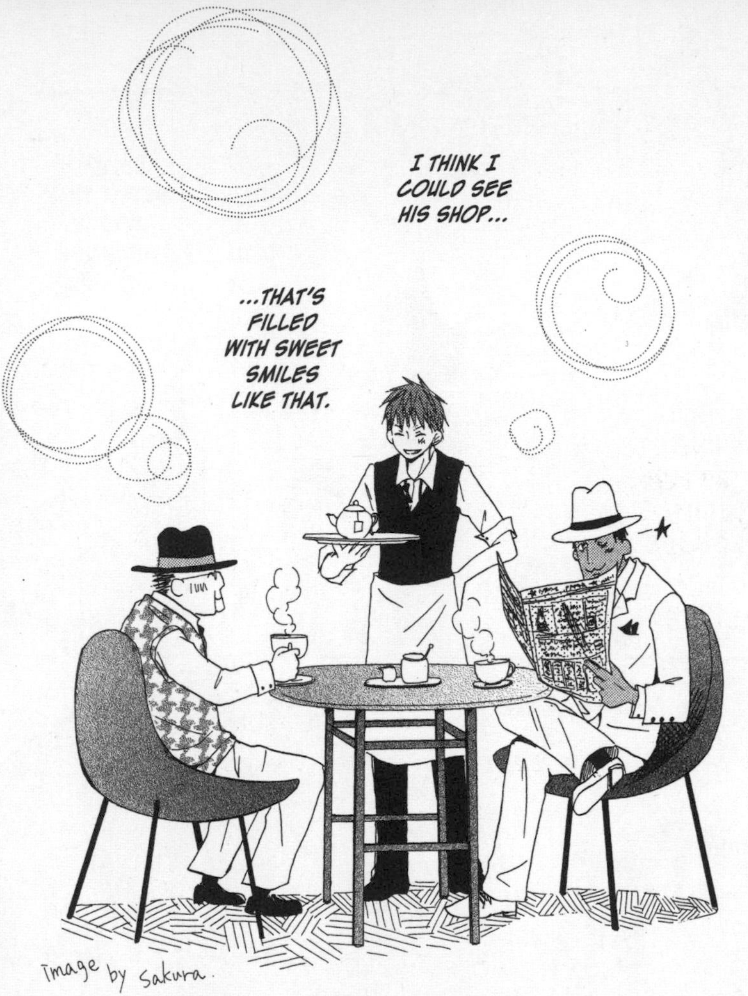
I THINK I COULD SEE HIS SHOP...
...THAT'S FILLED WITH SWEET SMILES LIKE THAT.
Image by Sakura

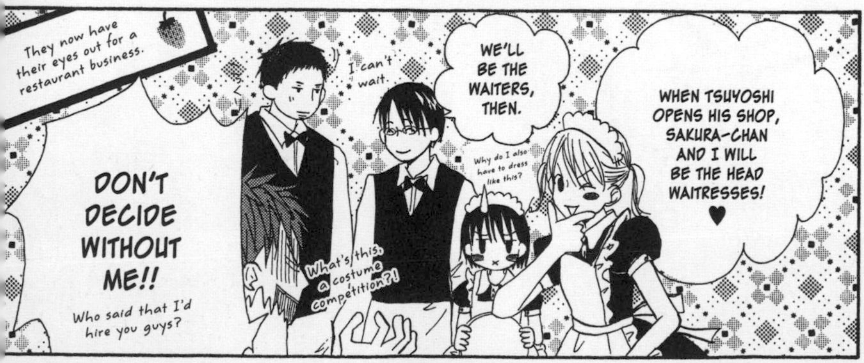
WHEN TSUYOSHI OPENS HIS SHOP, SAKURA-CHAN AND I WILL BE THE HEAD WAITRESSES! ♥
WE'LL BE THE WAITERS, THEN.
I can't wait.
Why do I also have to dress like this?
What's this, a costume competition?!
DON'T DECIDE WITHOUT ME!!
Who said that I'd hire you guys?
They now have their eyes out for a restaurant business.

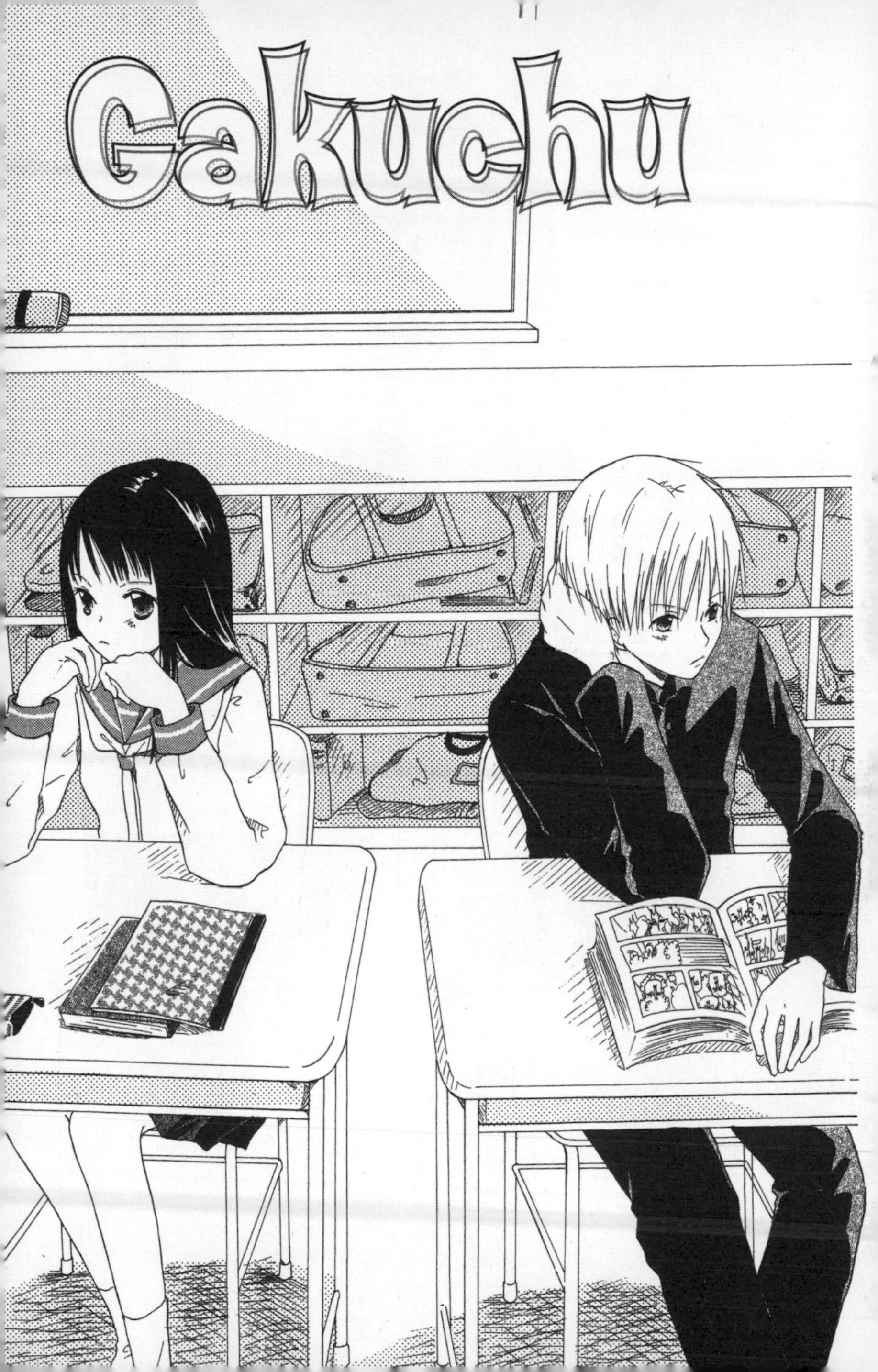
Gakuchu

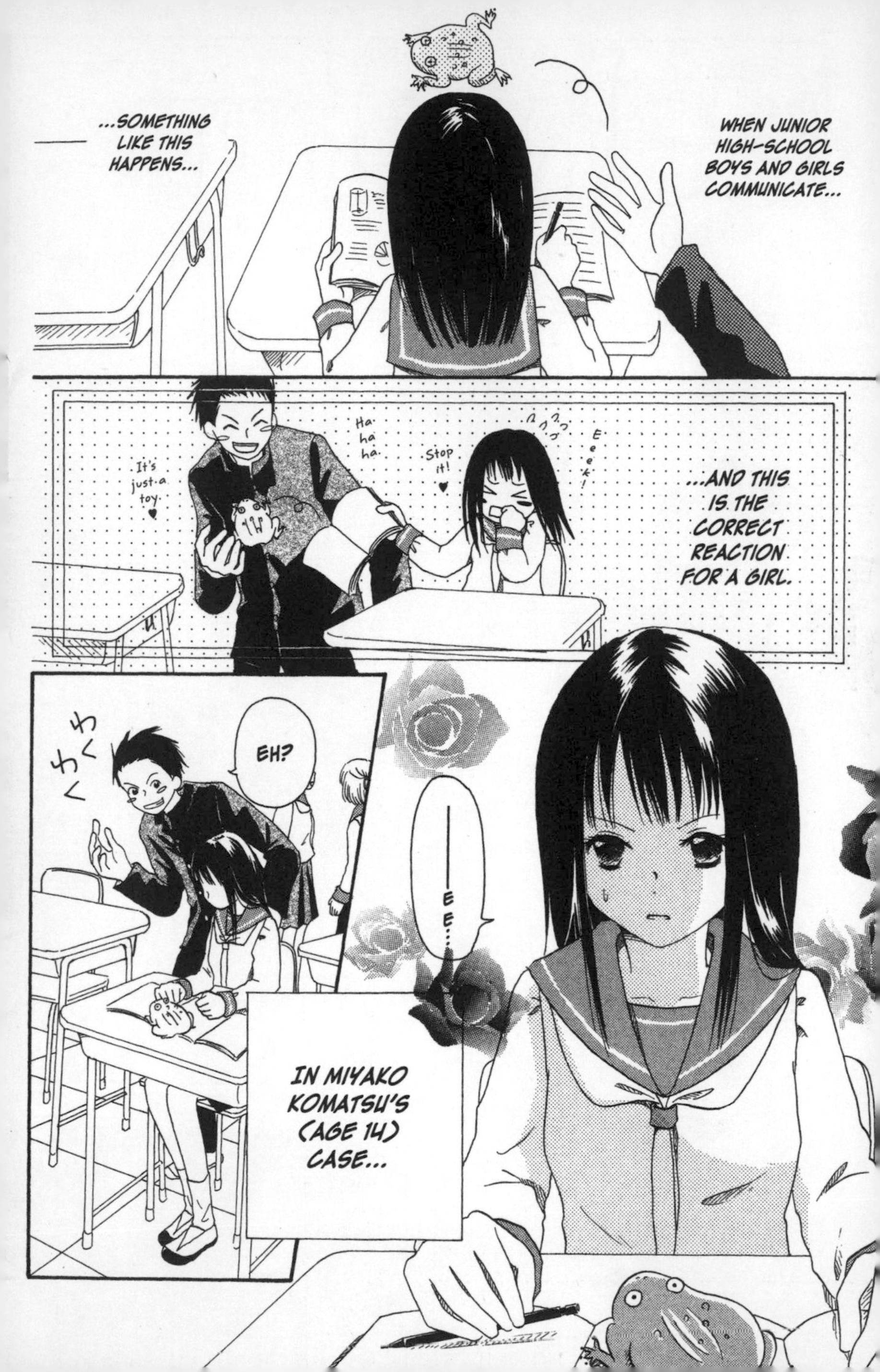
WHEN JUNIOR HIGH-SCHOOL BOYS AND GIRLS COMMUNICATE...
...SOMETHING LIKE THIS HAPPENS...
...AND THIS IS THE CORRECT REACTION FOR A GIRL.
Eeeek!
Stop it!
Ha ha ha.
It's just a toy.
IN MIYAKO KOMATSU'S (AGE 14) CASE...
EH?
わくわく
E E...

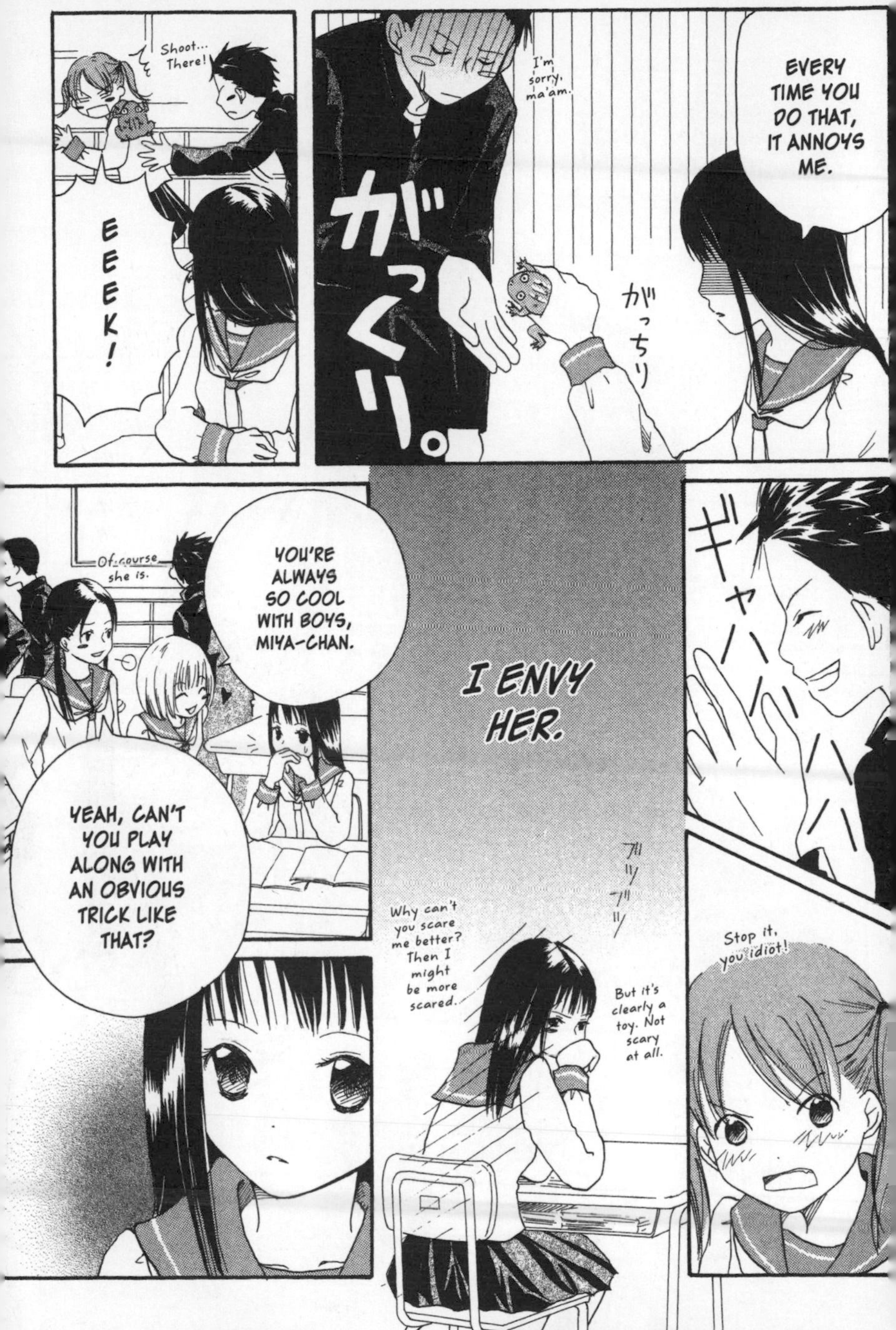
EVERY TIME YOU DO THAT, IT ANNOYS ME.
がっちり
I'm sorry, ma'am.
がっくり。
Shoot... There!
EEEEK!
ギャハハハ
Stop it, you idiot!
I ENVY HER.
ブツブツ
But it's clearly a toy. Not scary at all.
Why can't you scare me better? Then I might be more scared...
YOU'RE ALWAYS SO COOL WITH BOYS, MIYA-CHAN.
Of course she is.
YEAH, CAN'T YOU PLAY ALONG WITH AN OBVIOUS TRICK LIKE THAT?

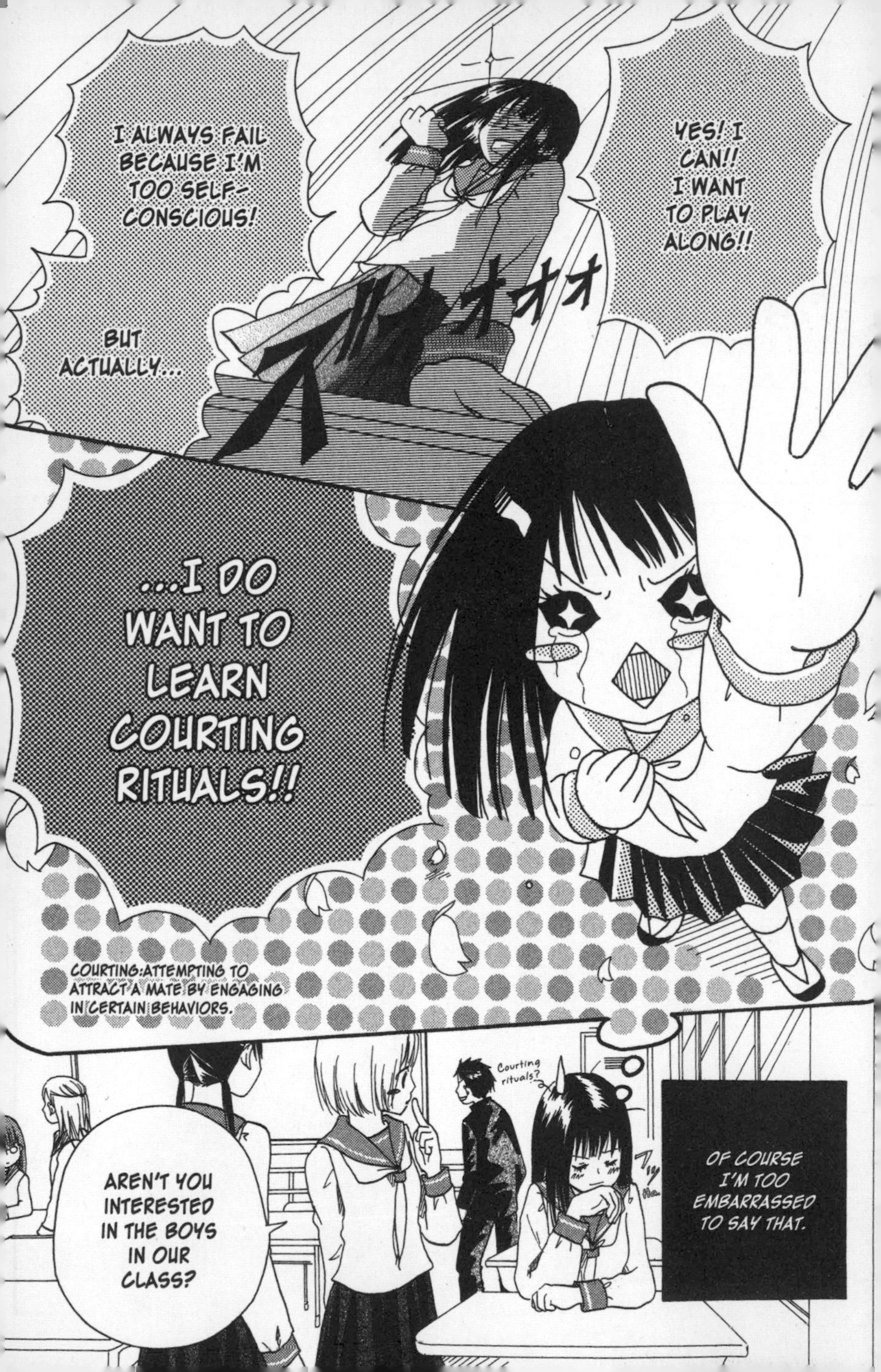
YES! I CAN!! I WANT TO PLAY ALONG!!
I ALWAYS FAIL BECAUSE I'M TOO SELF-CONSCIOUS!
BUT ACTUALLY...
...I DO WANT TO LEARN COURTING RITUALS!!
COURTING:ATTEMPTING TO ATTRACT A MATE BY ENGAGING IN CERTAIN BEHAVIORS.
Courting rituals?
OF COURSE I'M TOO EMBARRASSED TO SAY THAT.
AREN'T YOU INTERESTED IN THE BOYS IN OUR CLASS?

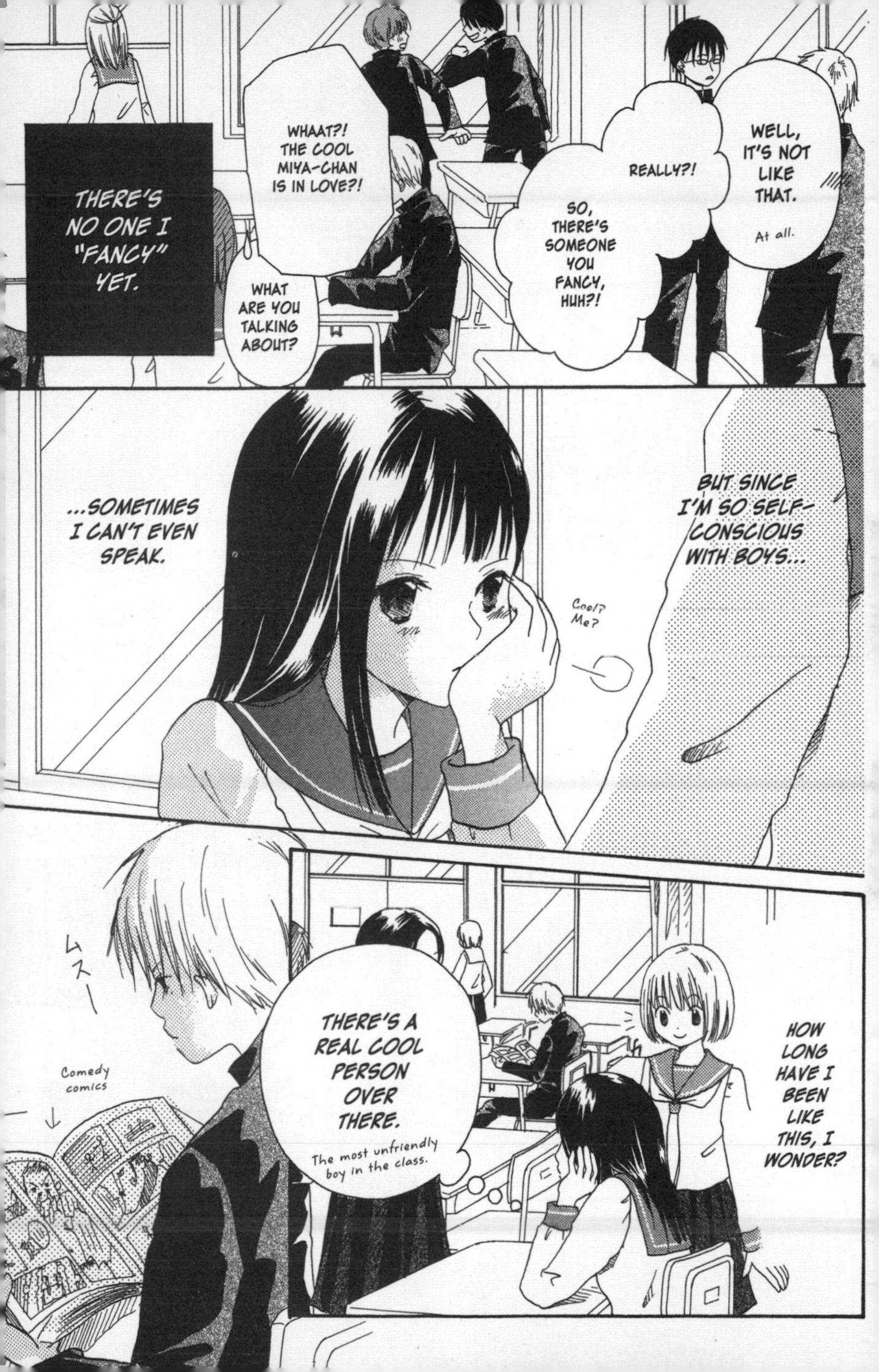
WELL, IT'S NOT LIKE THAT.
At all.
REALLY?!
SO, THERE'S SOMEONE YOU FANCY, HUH?!
WHAAT?! THE COOL MIYA-CHAN IS IN LOVE?!
WHAT ARE YOU TALKING ABOUT?
THERE'S NO ONE I "FANCY" YET.
BUT SINCE I'M SO SELF-CONSCIOUS WITH BOYS...
Cool? Me?
...SOMETIMES I CAN'T EVEN SPEAK.
HOW LONG HAVE I BEEN LIKE THIS, I WONDER?
THERE'S A REAL COOL PERSON OVER THERE.
The most unfriendly boy in the class.
ムスー
Comedy comics

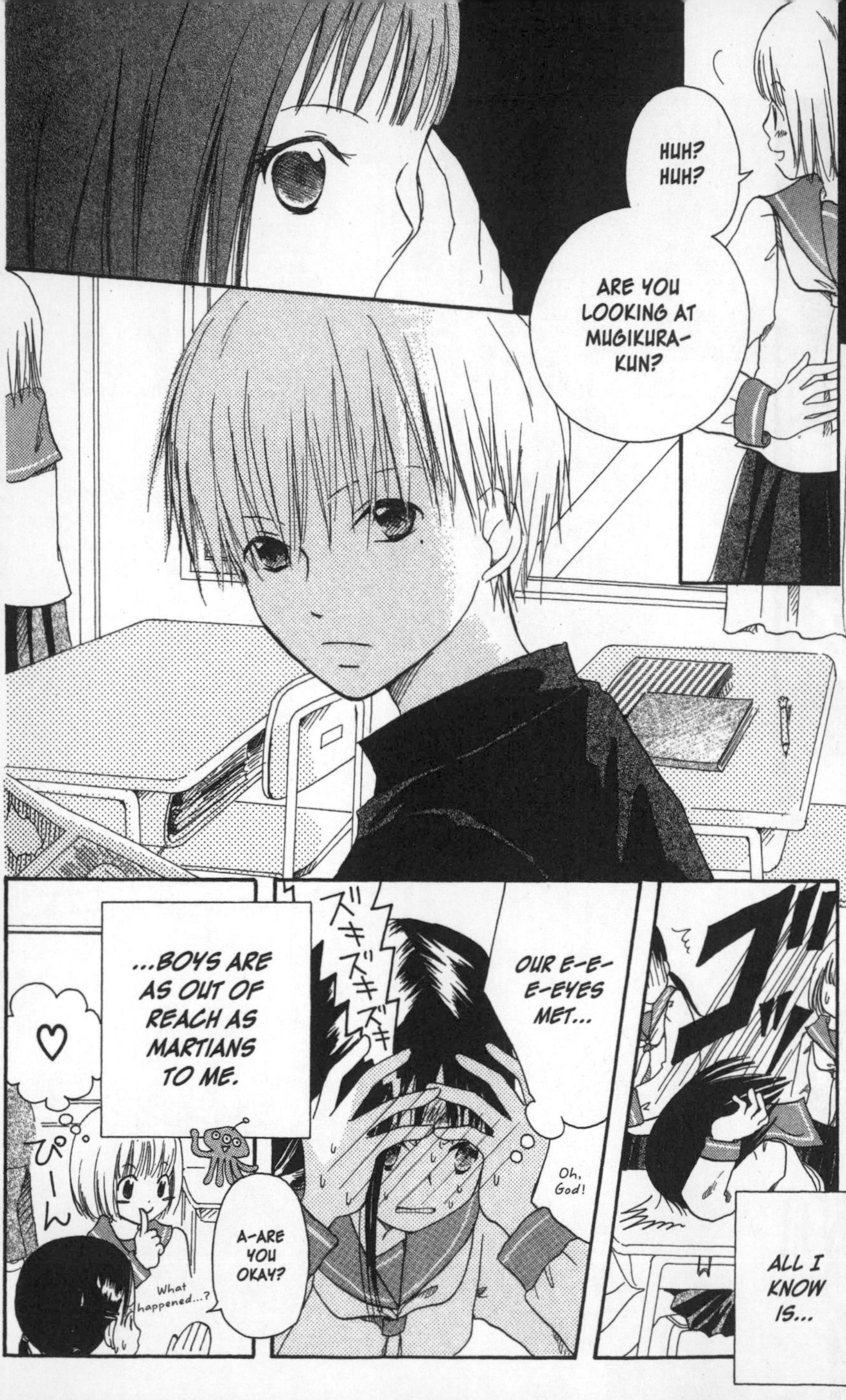
HUH? HUH?
ARE YOU LOOKING AT MUGIKURA-KUN?
ALL I KNOW IS...
ズキズキズキ
OUR E-E-E-EYES MET...
Oh, God!
A-ARE YOU OKAY?
...BOYS ARE AS OUT OF REACH AS MARTIANS TO ME.
♡
ぴーん
What happened...?

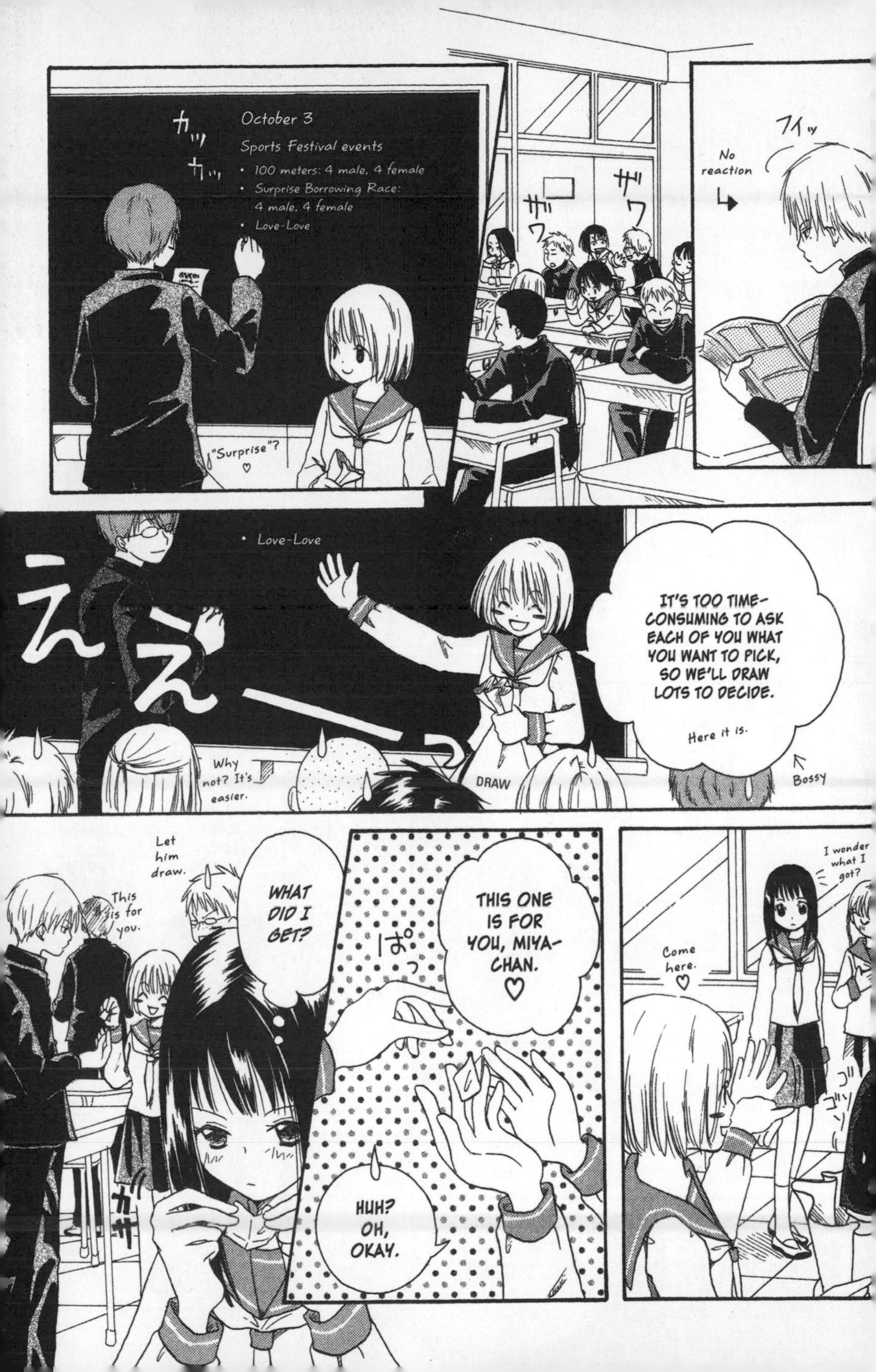
フイッ
No reaction
ザワ
ザワ
カッ
カッ
October 3
Sports Festival events
• 100 meters: 4 male, 4 female
• Surprise Borrowing Race: 4 male, 4 female
• Love-Love
"Surprise"? ♡
IT'S TOO TIME-CONSUMING TO ASK EACH OF YOU WHAT YOU WANT TO PICK, SO WE'LL DRAW LOTS TO DECIDE.
Here it is.
Bossy
DRAW
Why not? It's easier.
ええー
• Love-Love
I wonder what I got?
Come here. ♡
ゴソ
ゴソ
THIS ONE IS FOR YOU, MIYA-CHAN. ♡
ぱっ
HUH? OH, OKAY.
WHAT DID I GET?
Let him draw.
This is for you.
ガサ

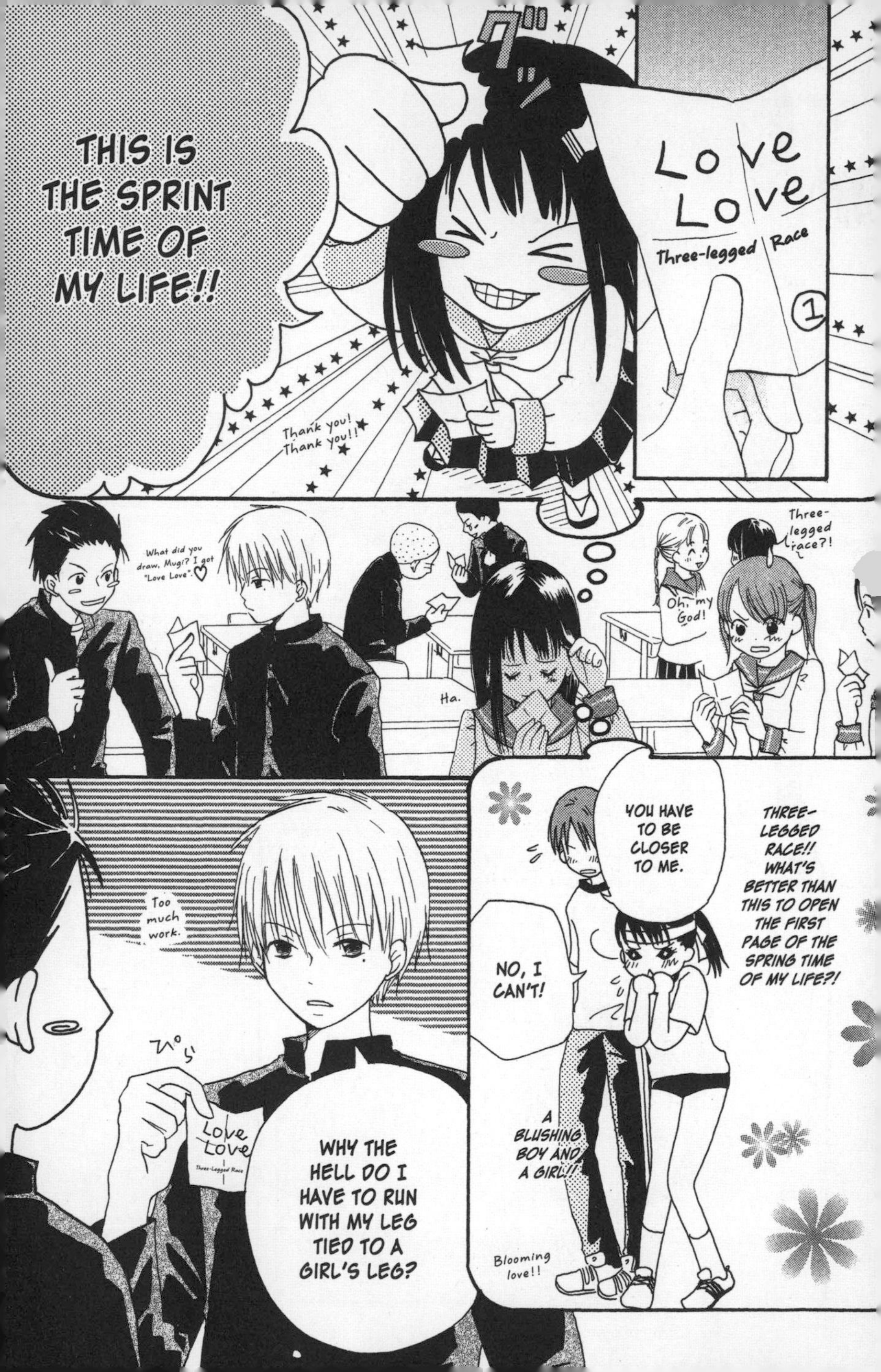
Love Love
Three-legged Race
1
Thank you! Thank you!!
THIS IS THE SPRINT TIME OF MY LIFE!!
Three-legged race?!
Oh, my God!
Ha.
What did you draw, Mugi? I got "Love Love".♡
THREE-LEGGED RACE!! WHAT'S BETTER THAN THIS TO OPEN THE FIRST PAGE OF THE SPRING TIME OF MY LIFE?!
YOU HAVE TO BE CLOSER TO ME.
NO, I CAN'T!
A BLUSHING BOY AND A GIRL!!
Blooming love!!
Too much work.
ぴら
Love Love
Three-Legged Race
WHY THE HELL DO I HAVE TO RUN WITH MY LEG TIED TO A GIRL'S LEG?

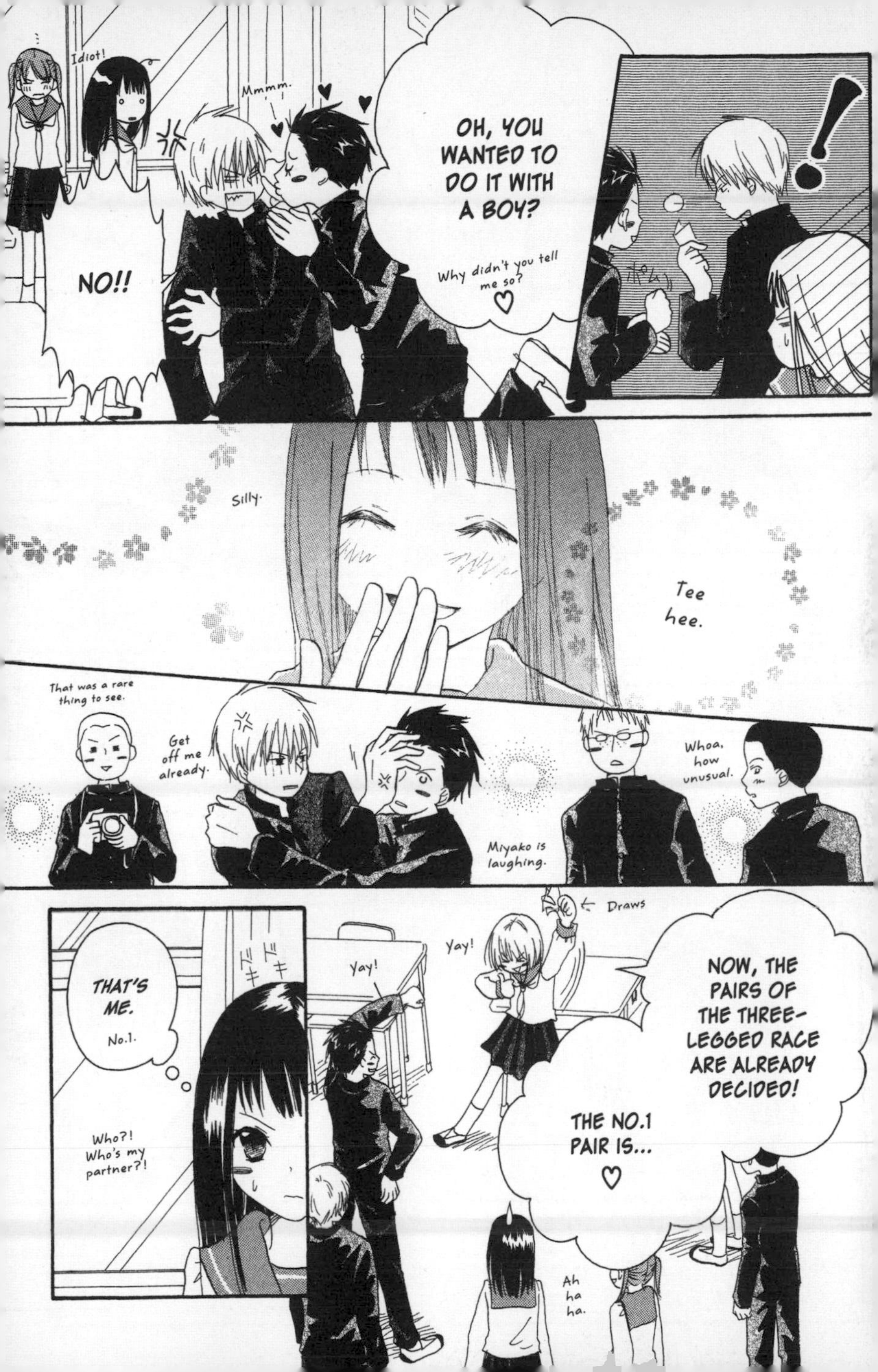
!
ポム
OH, YOU WANTED TO DO IT WITH A BOY?
Why didn't you tell me so? ♡
Mmmm.
NO!!
Idiot!
Tee hee.
Silly.
Whoa, how unusual.
Miyako is laughing.
Get off me already.
That was a rare thing to see.
NOW, THE PAIRS OF THE THREE-LEGGED RACE ARE ALREADY DECIDED!
THE NO.1 PAIR IS... ♡
← Draws
Yay!
Yay!
Ah ha ha.
ドキドキ
THAT'S ME.
No.1.
Who?! Who's my partner?!

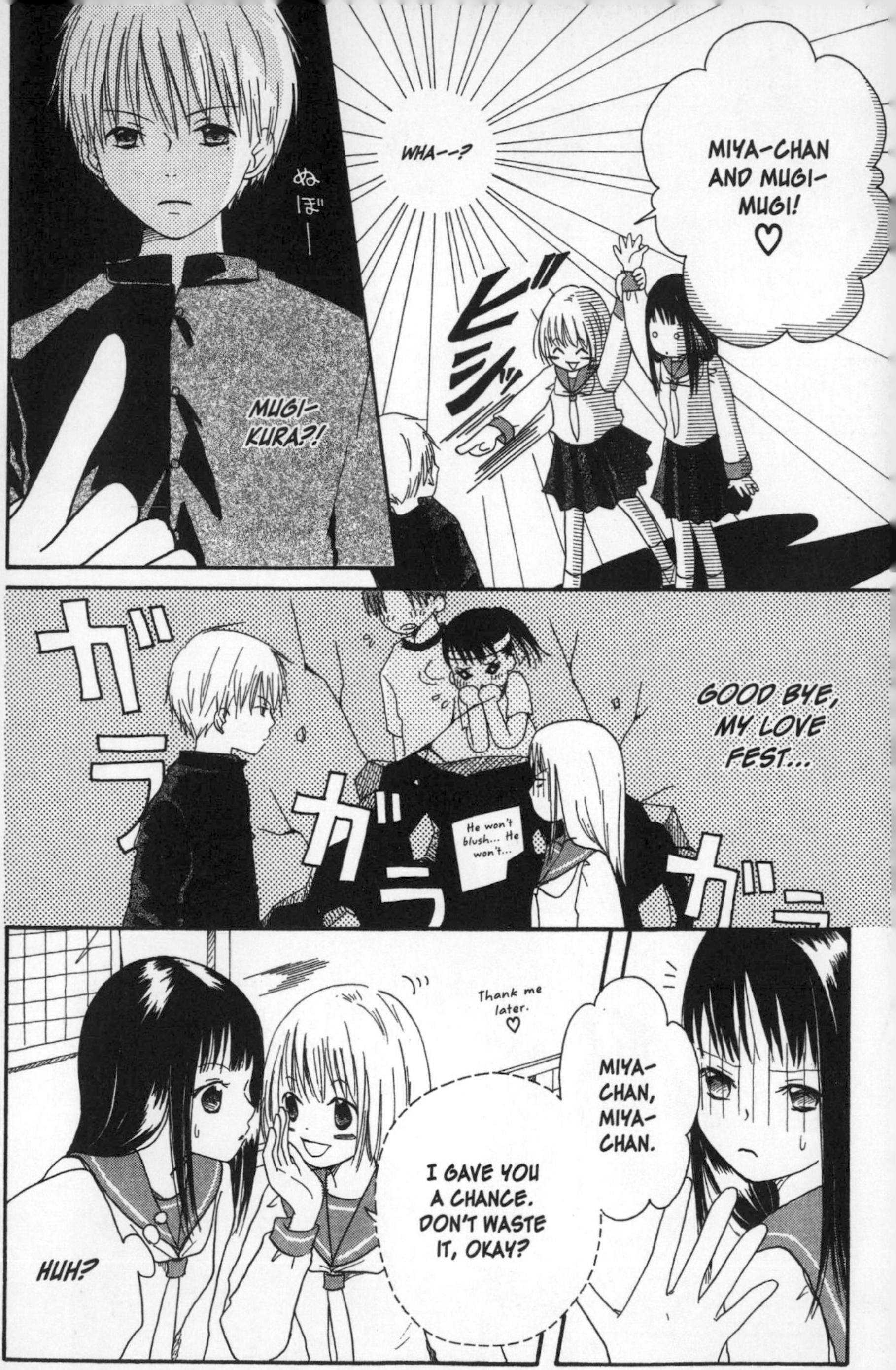
MIYA-CHAN AND MUGI-MUGI! ♡
WHA--?
ビシッ
ぬぼー
MUGI-KURA?!
GOOD BYE, MY LOVE FEST...
ガラ
ガラ
He won't blush... He won't...
ガラ
MIYA-CHAN, MIYA-CHAN.
Thank me later. ♡
I GAVE YOU A CHANCE. DON'T WASTE IT, OKAY?
HUH?

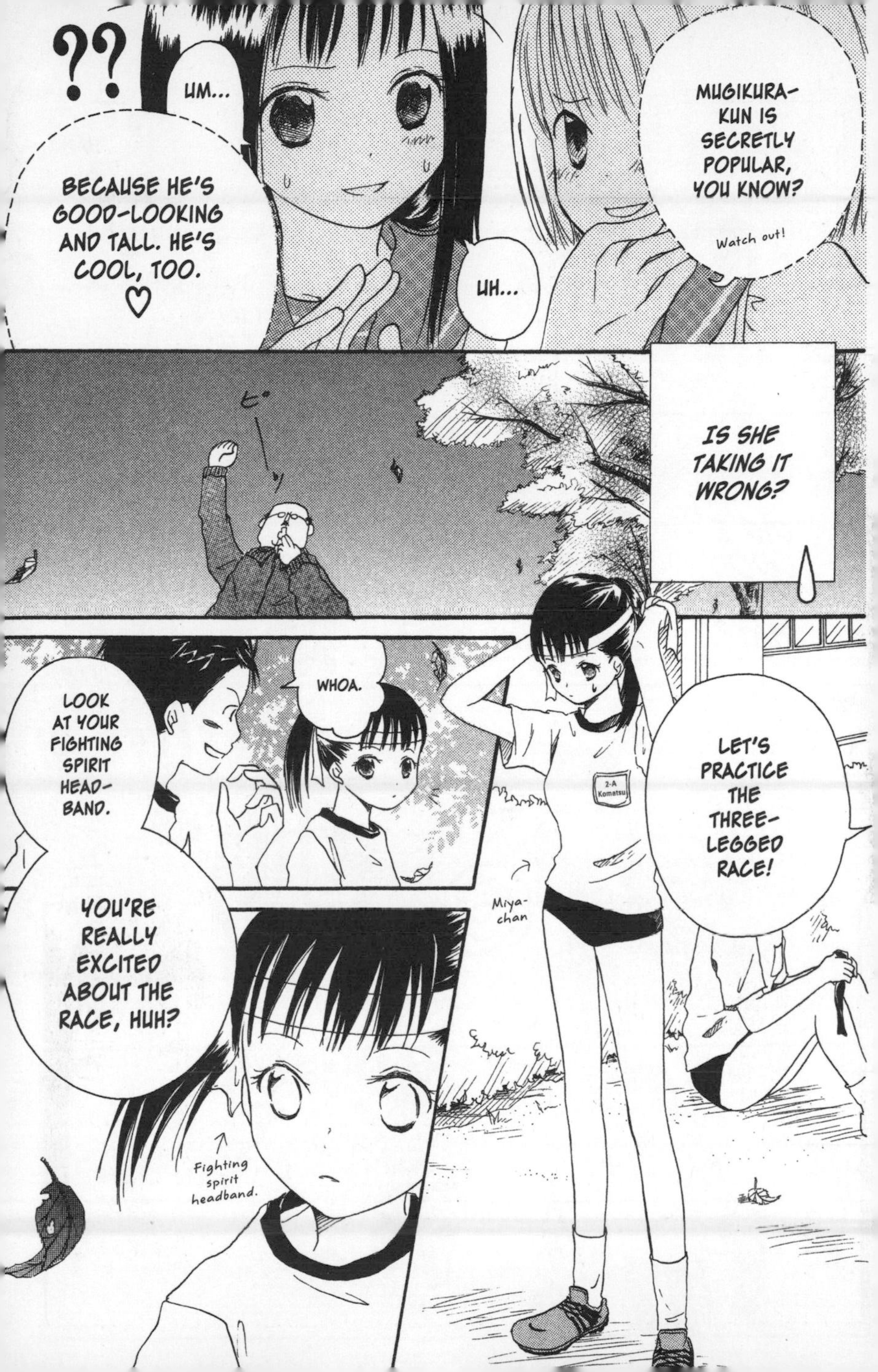
MUGIKURA-KUN IS SECRETLY POPULAR, YOU KNOW?
Watch out!
??
UM...
BECAUSE HE'S GOOD-LOOKING AND TALL. HE'S COOL, TOO. ♡
UH...
IS SHE TAKING IT WRONG?
ピーッ
LET'S PRACTICE THE THREE-LEGGED RACE!
2-A Komatsu
Miya-chan
WHOA.
LOOK AT YOUR FIGHTING SPIRIT HEADBAND.
YOU'RE REALLY EXCITED ABOUT THE RACE, HUH?
Fighting spirit headband.

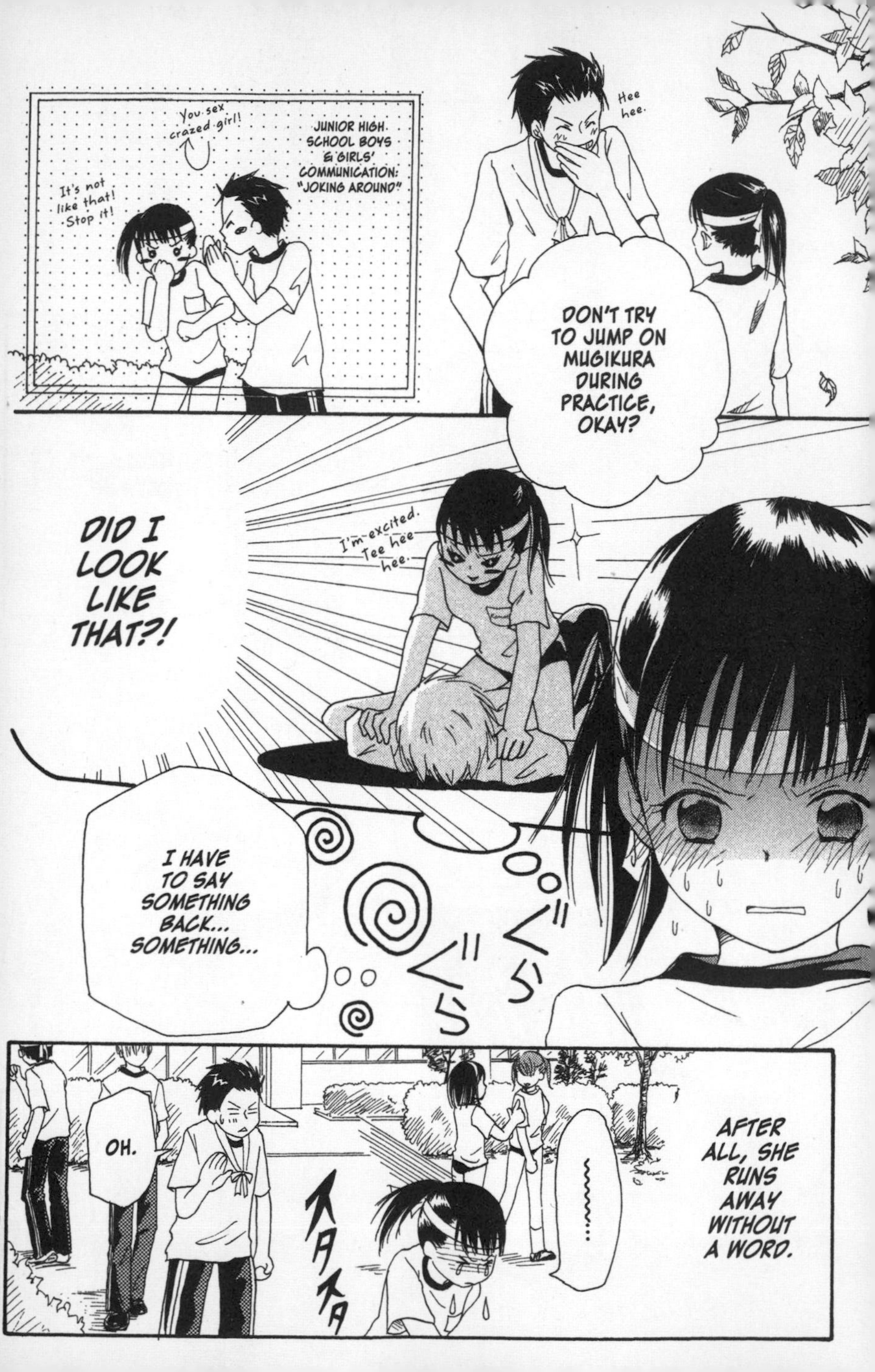
Hee hee.
DON'T TRY TO JUMP ON MUGIKURA DURING PRACTICE, OKAY?
JUNIOR HIGH SCHOOL BOYS & GIRLS' COMMUNICATION: "JOKING AROUND"
You sex crazed girl!
It's not like that! Stop it!
I'm excited. Tee hee hee.
DID I LOOK LIKE THAT?!
I HAVE TO SAY SOMETHING BACK... SOMETHING...
ぐら ぐら
AFTER ALL, SHE RUNS AWAY WITHOUT A WORD.
......
タタタ
OH.

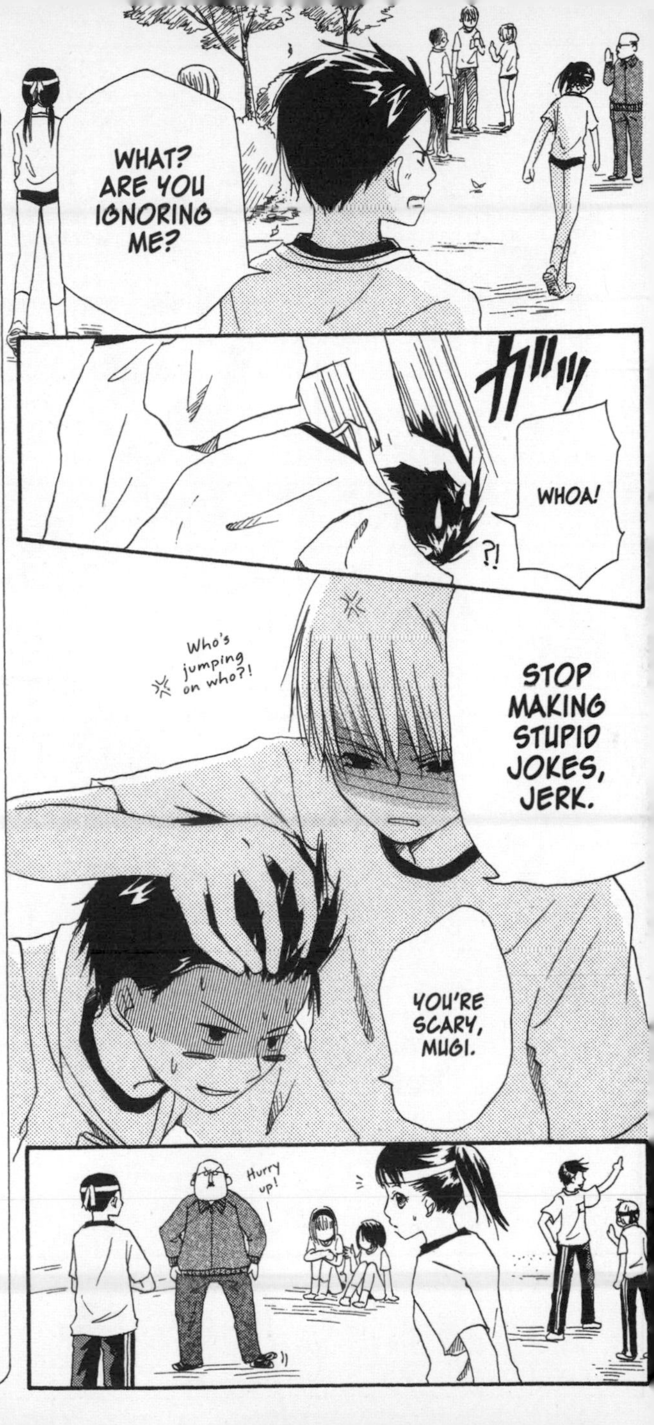
WHAT? ARE YOU IGNORING ME?
ガッ
WHOA!
?!
STOP MAKING STUPID JOKES, JERK.
Who's jumping on who?!
YOU'RE SCARY, MUGI.
Hurry up!

☆ 6 ☆

"Gakuchu." I kind of like it. I'm secretly hoping to continue the story. It's not that I have an idea though.

♥ ♥ ♥

I did my best, thinking, "since I'm a shojo manga artist, I want to write a love comedy!", but this is the level I'm at. It's not even love yet, and I regret it...or not. I wrote a bonus manga of "Gakuchu," even though no one asked me to, and it doesn't show any love, either. Why can't I...? Well, good bye, then!

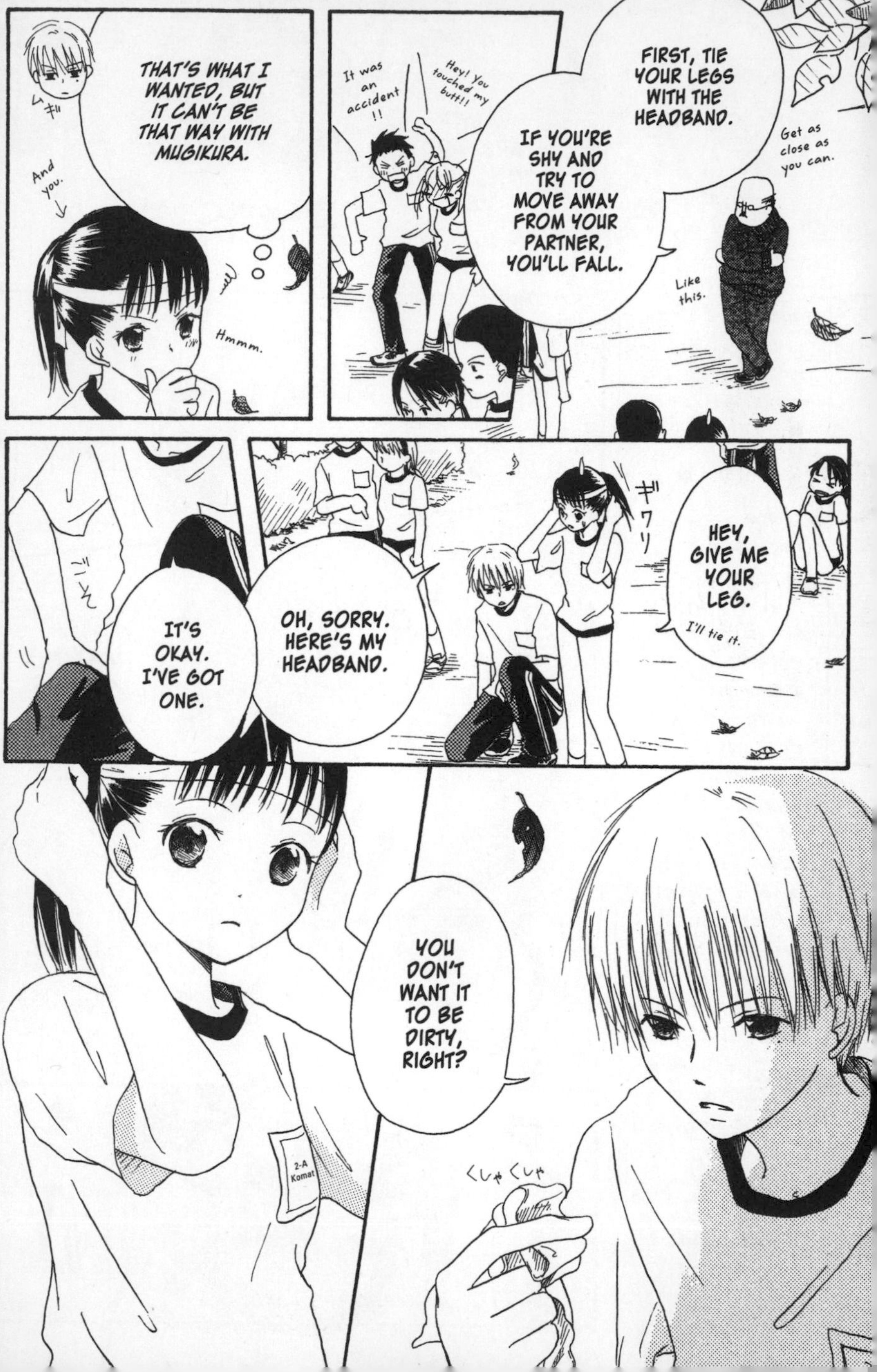
FIRST, TIE YOUR LEGS WITH THE HEADBAND.
IF YOU'RE SHY AND TRY TO MOVE AWAY FROM YOUR PARTNER, YOU'LL FALL.
Get as close as you can.
Like this.
Hey! You touched my butt!!
It was an accident!!
THAT'S WHAT I WANTED, BUT IT CAN'T BE THAT WAY WITH MUGIKURA.
And you.
Hmmm.
HEY, GIVE ME YOUR LEG.
I'll tie it.
OH, SORRY. HERE'S MY HEADBAND.
IT'S OKAY. I'VE GOT ONE.
YOU DON'T WANT IT TO BE DIRTY, RIGHT?
くしゃくしゃ
2-A
Komat

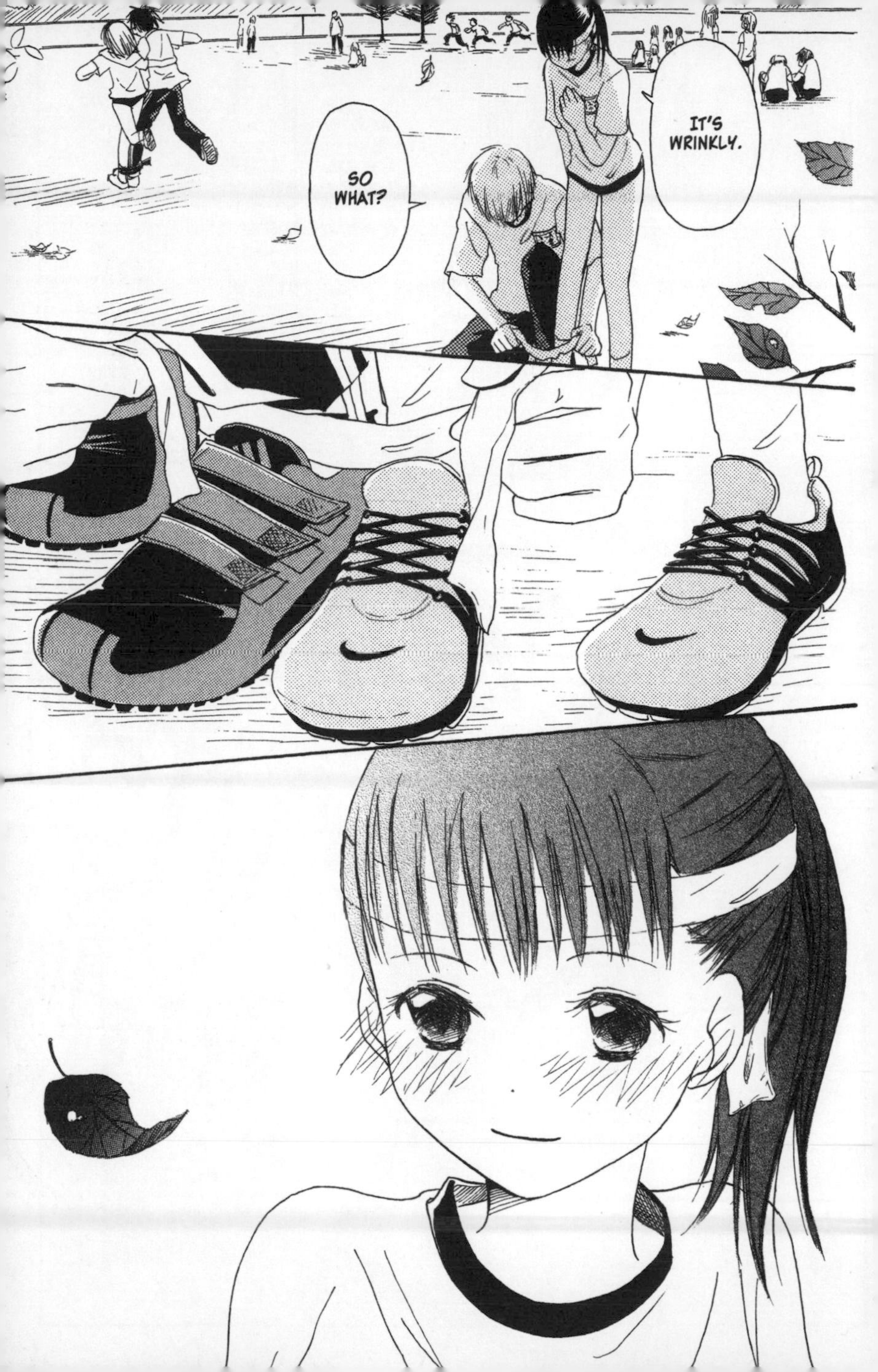
IT'S WRINKLY.
SO WHAT?

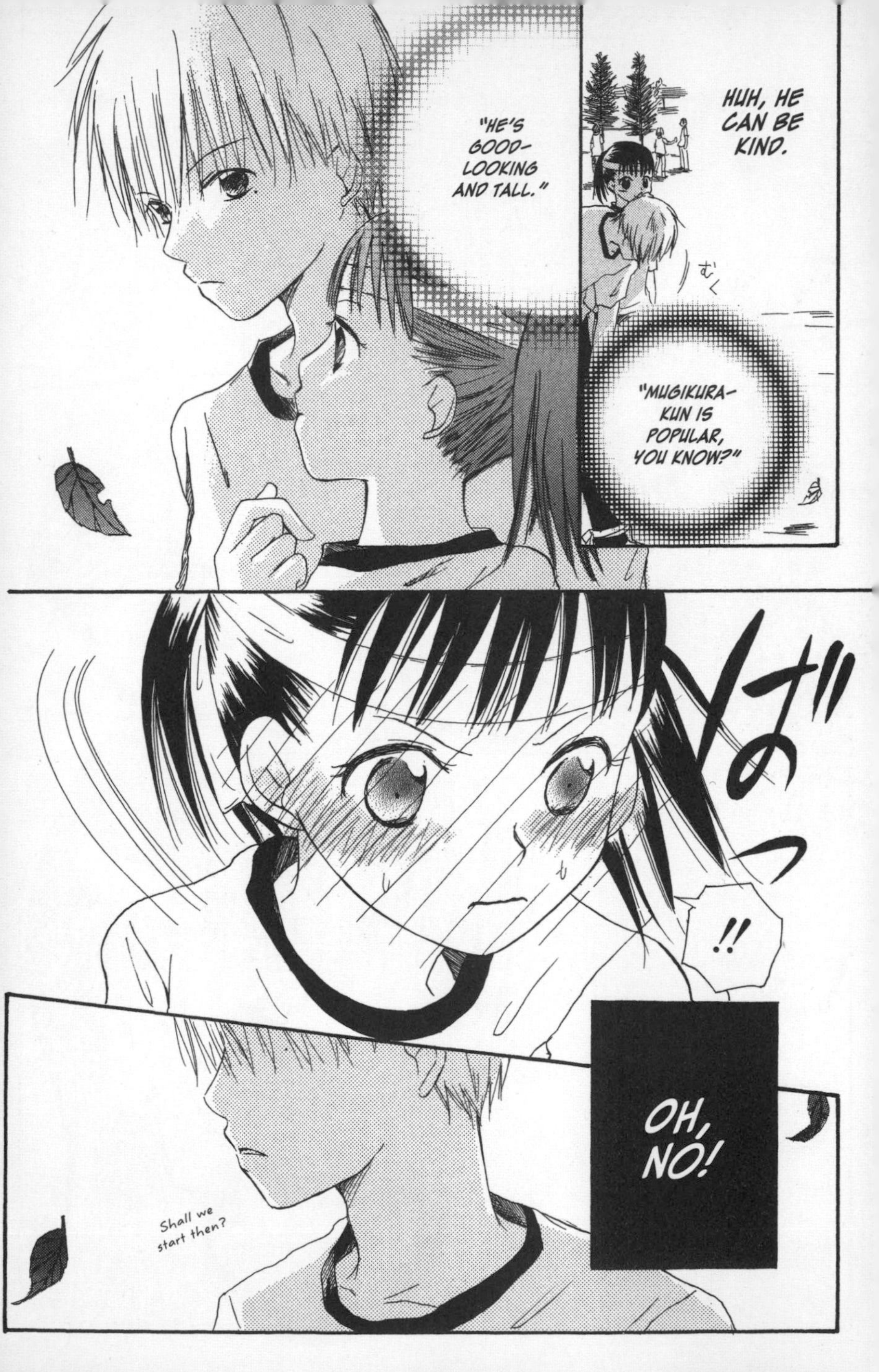
HUH, HE CAN BE KIND.
むく
"MUGIKURA-KUN IS POPULAR, YOU KNOW?"
"HE'S GOOD-LOOKING AND TALL."
ぼっ
!!
OH, NO!
Shall we start then?

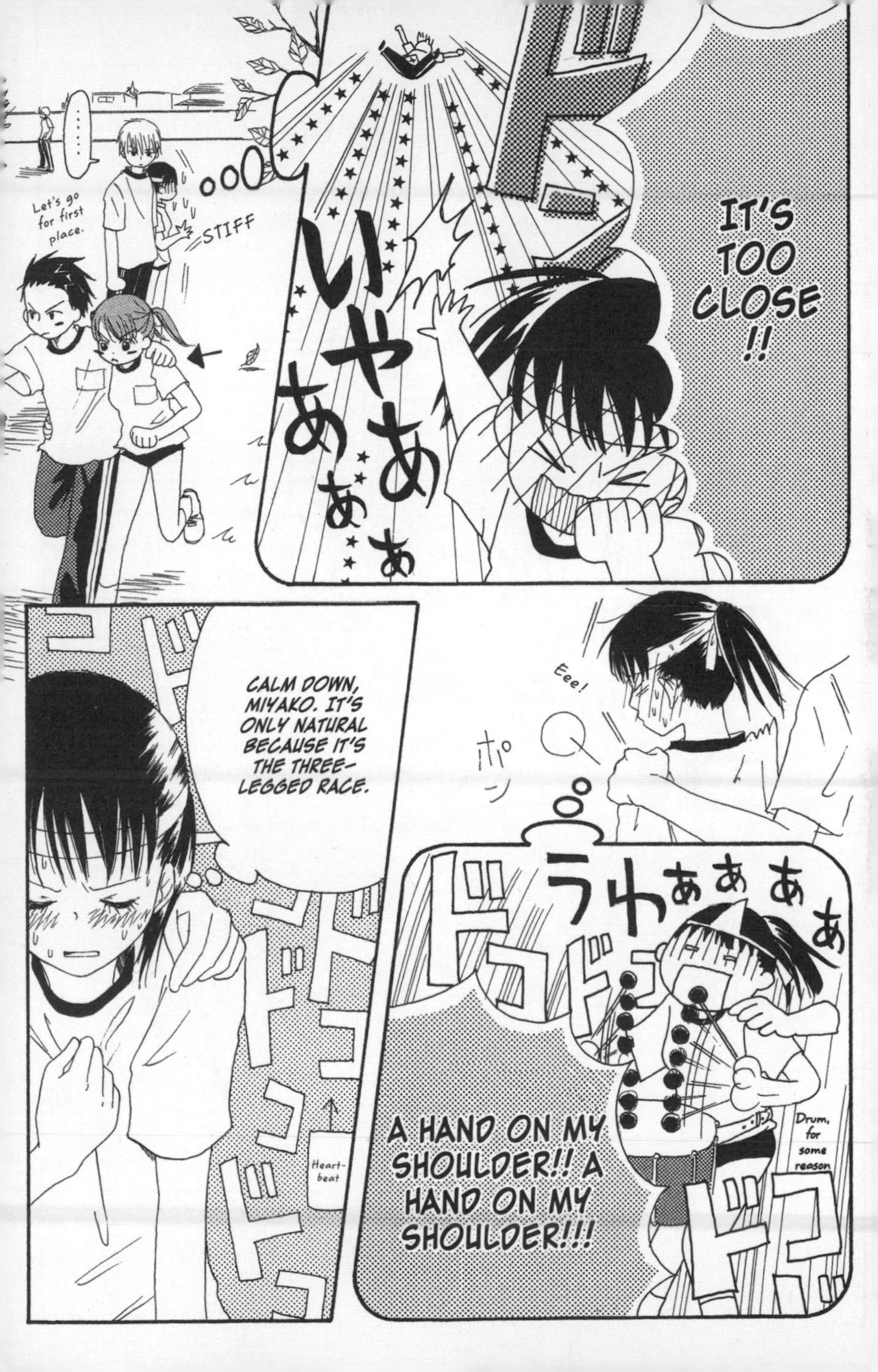

IT'S TOO CLOSE!!
いやあぁぁ
......
STIFF
Let's go for first place.
Eee!
ポン
うやぁぁぁぁ
A HAND ON MY SHOULDER!! A HAND ON MY SHOULDER!!!
Drum, for some reason
CALM DOWN, MIYAKO. IT'S ONLY NATURAL BECAUSE IT'S THE THREE-LEGGED RACE.
Heart-beat

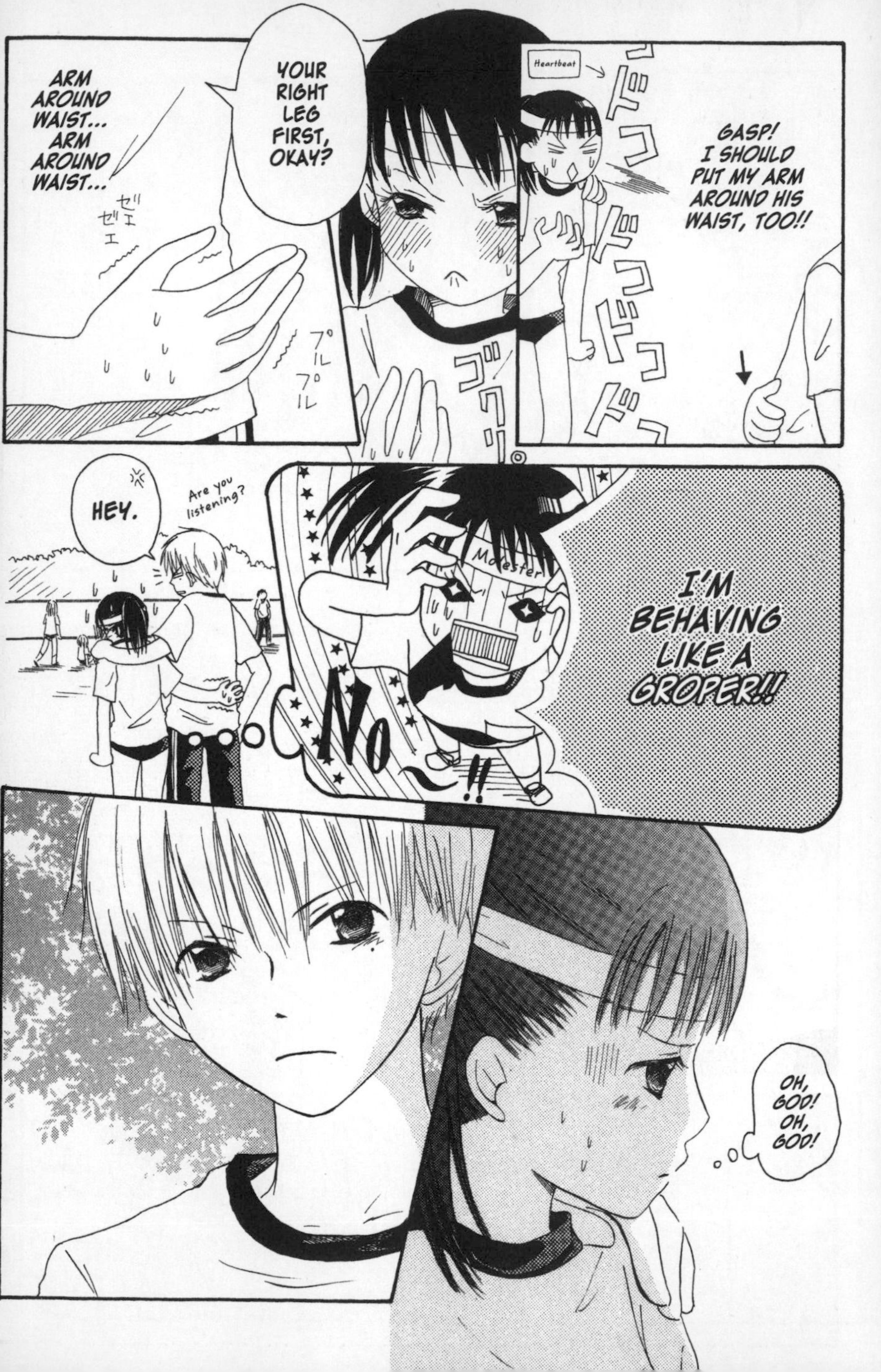
Heartbeat
GASP! I SHOULD PUT MY ARM AROUND HIS WAIST, TOO!!
ゴクッ
YOUR RIGHT LEG FIRST, OKAY?
ARM AROUND WAIST... ARM AROUND WAIST...
ゼェ ゼェ
プル プル
Molester
I'M BEHAVING LIKE A GROPER!!
No~!!
HEY.
Are you listening?
OH, GOD! OH, GOD!

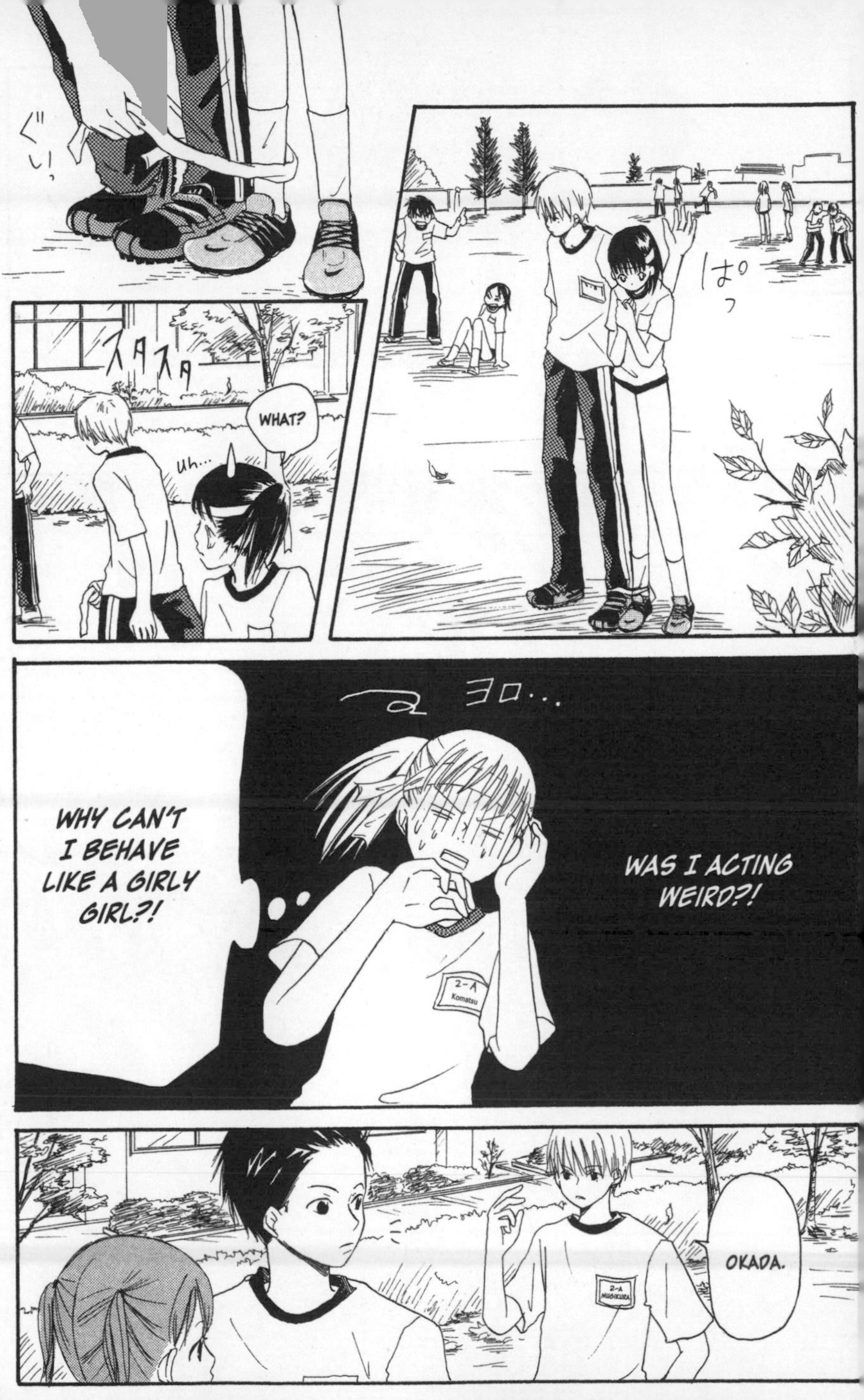
ぱっ
ぐい
WHAT?
スタスタ
Uh...
ヨロ…
WAS I ACTING WEIRD?!
WHY CAN'T I BEHAVE LIKE A GIRLY GIRL?!
2-A
Komatsu
OKADA.
2-A
MUGIKURA

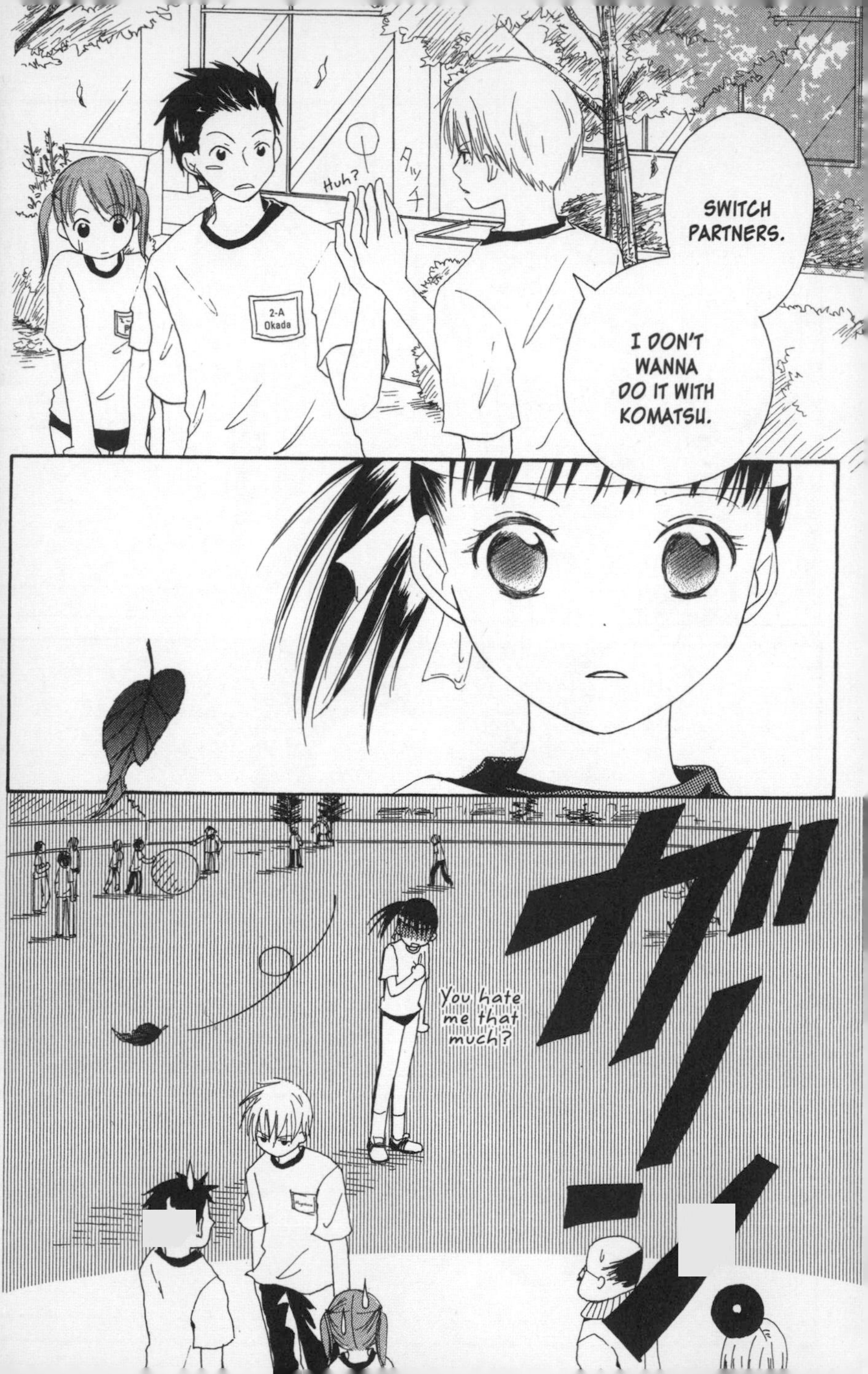
SWITCH PARTNERS.
I DON'T WANNA DO IT WITH KOMATSU.
Huh?
2-A Okada
You hate me that much?

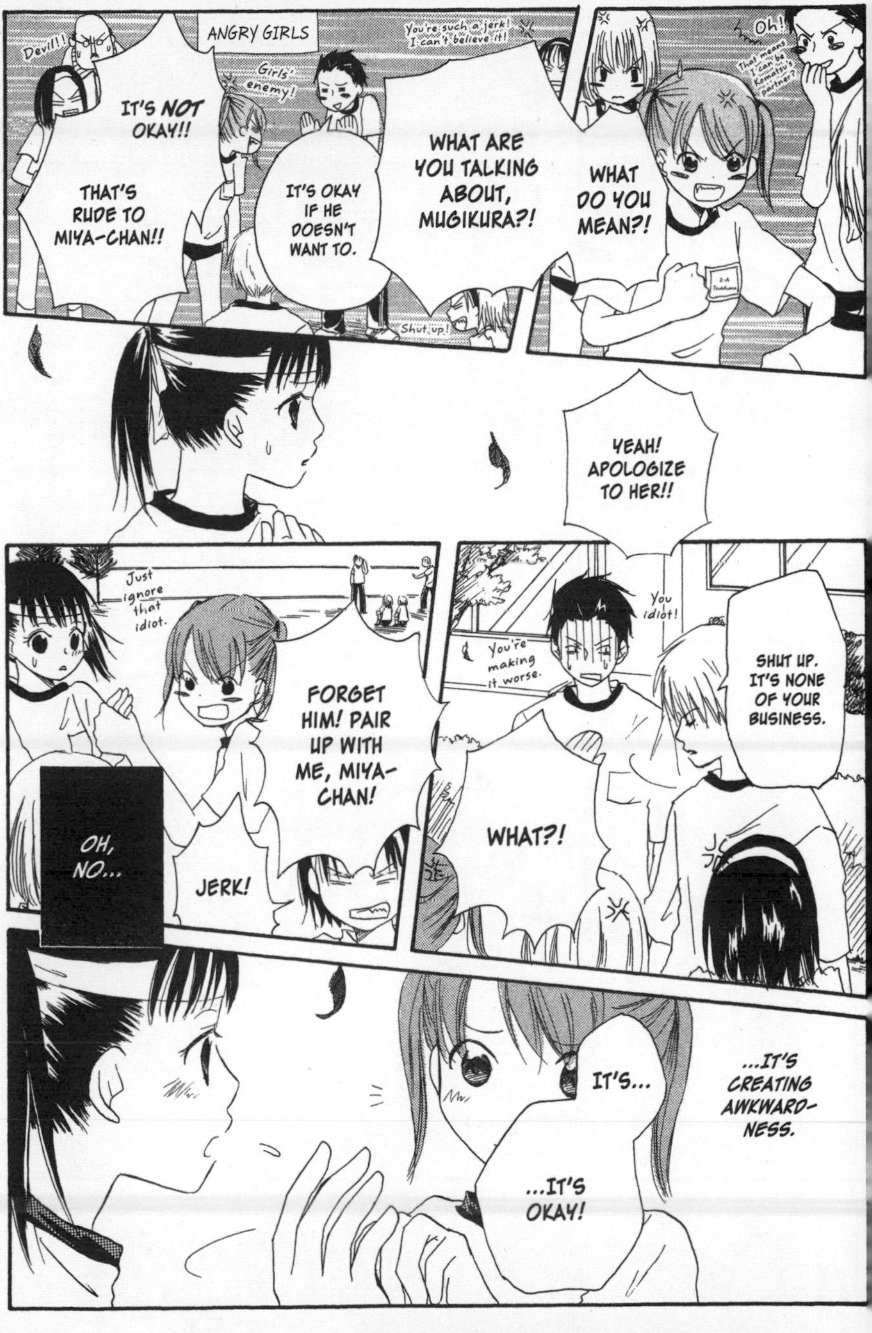
WHAT DO YOU MEAN?!
Oh!
That means I can be Komatsu's partner?
WHAT ARE YOU TALKING ABOUT, MUGIKURA?!
You're such a jerk! I can't believe it!
ANGRY GIRLS
Girls' enemy!
IT'S OKAY IF HE DOESN'T WANT TO.
Devil!!
IT'S NOT OKAY!!
THAT'S RUDE TO MIYA-CHAN!!
Shut up!
YEAH! APOLOGIZE TO HER!!
You idiot!
SHUT UP. IT'S NONE OF YOUR BUSINESS.
You're making it worse.
WHAT?!
FORGET HIM! PAIR UP WITH ME, MIYA-CHAN!
Just ignore that idiot.
JERK!
OH, NO...
...IT'S CREATING AWKWARDNESS.
IT'S...
...IT'S OKAY!

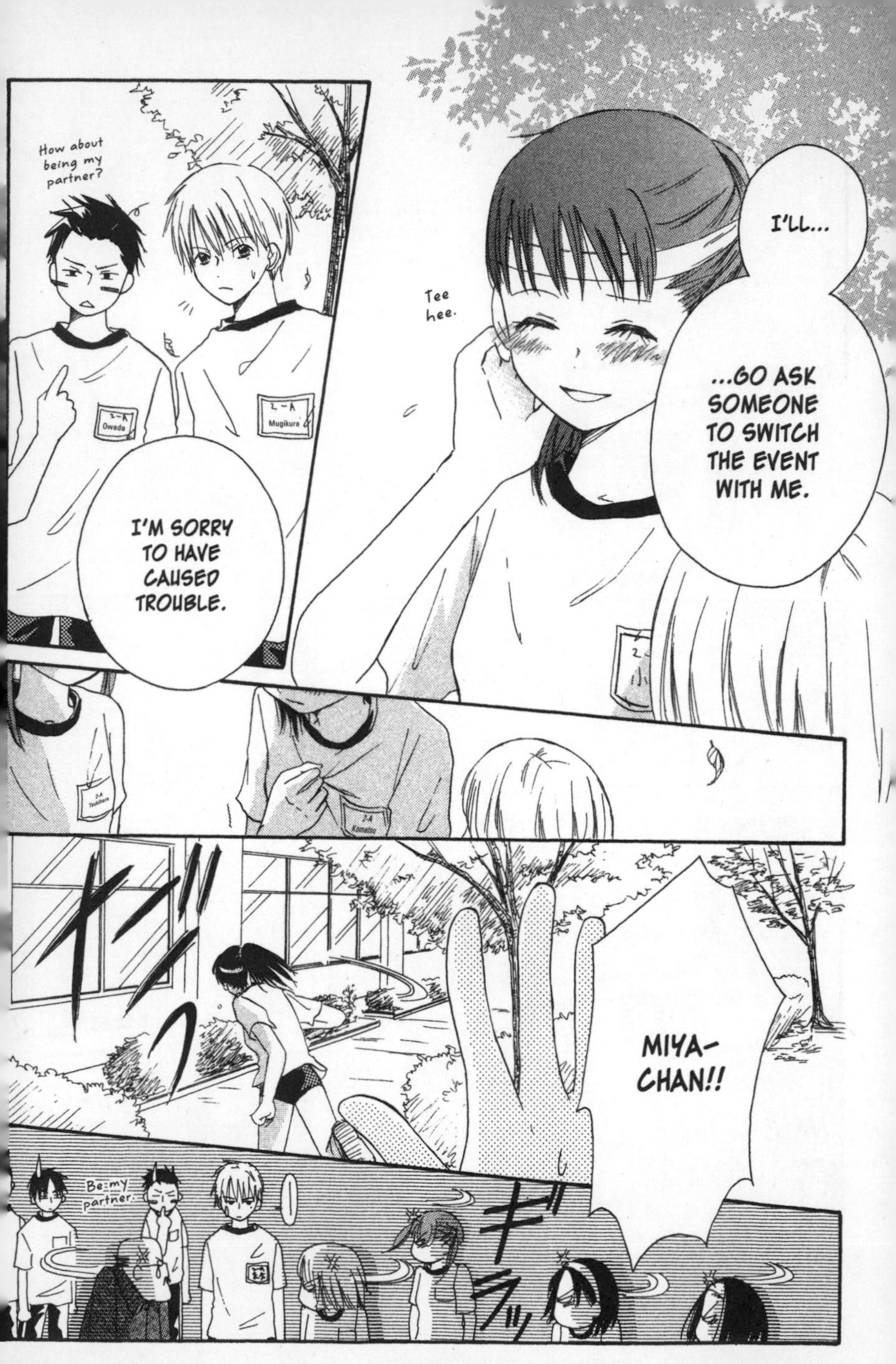
I'LL...
...GO ASK SOMEONE TO SWITCH THE EVENT WITH ME.
Tee hee.
How about being my partner?
2-A Owada
2-A Mugikura
I'M SORRY TO HAVE CAUSED TROUBLE.
MIYA-CHAN!!
Be my partner.

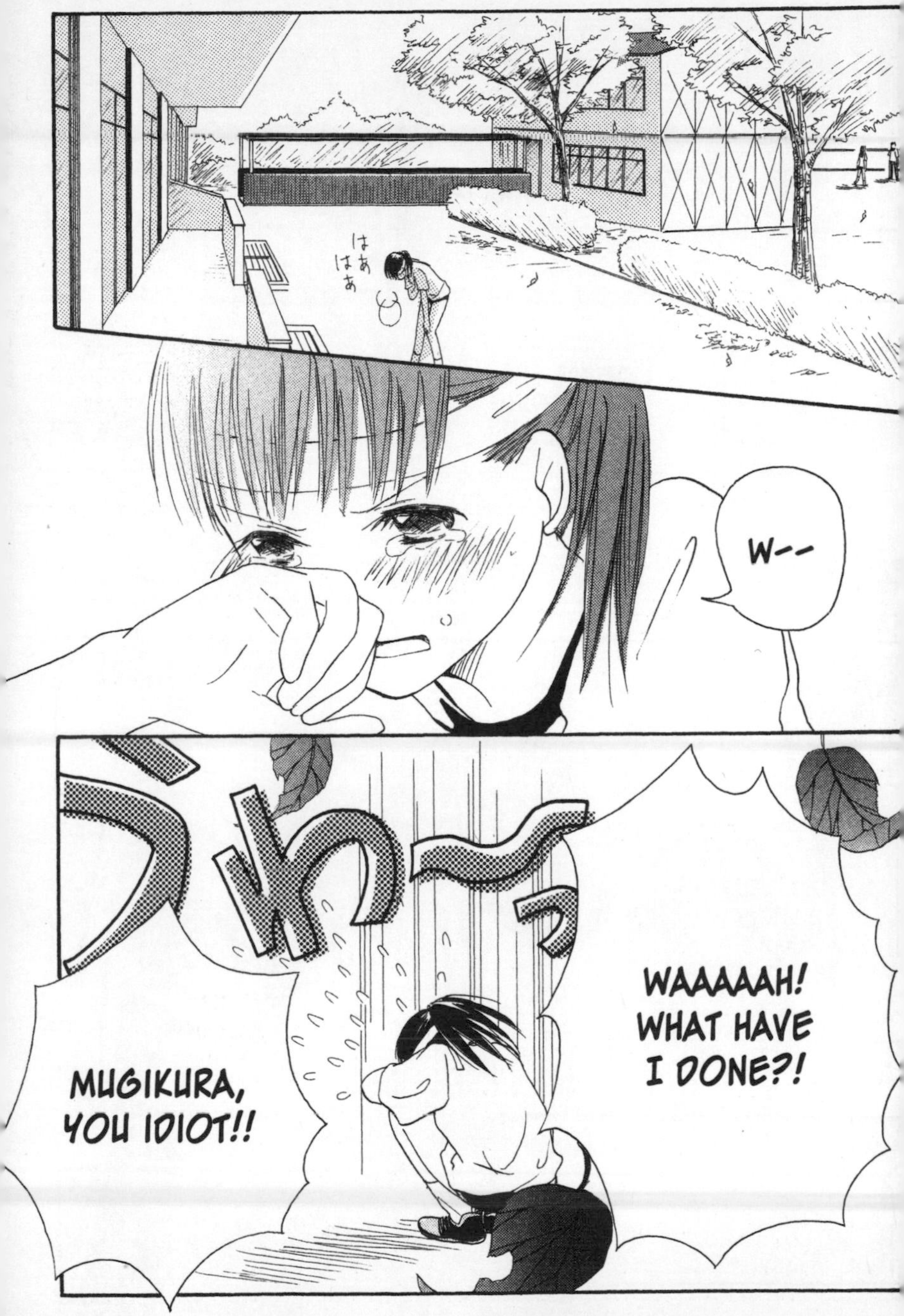
はあ
はあ
W--
WAAAAAH! WHAT HAVE I DONE?!
うわ〜っ
MUGIKURA, YOU IDIOT!!

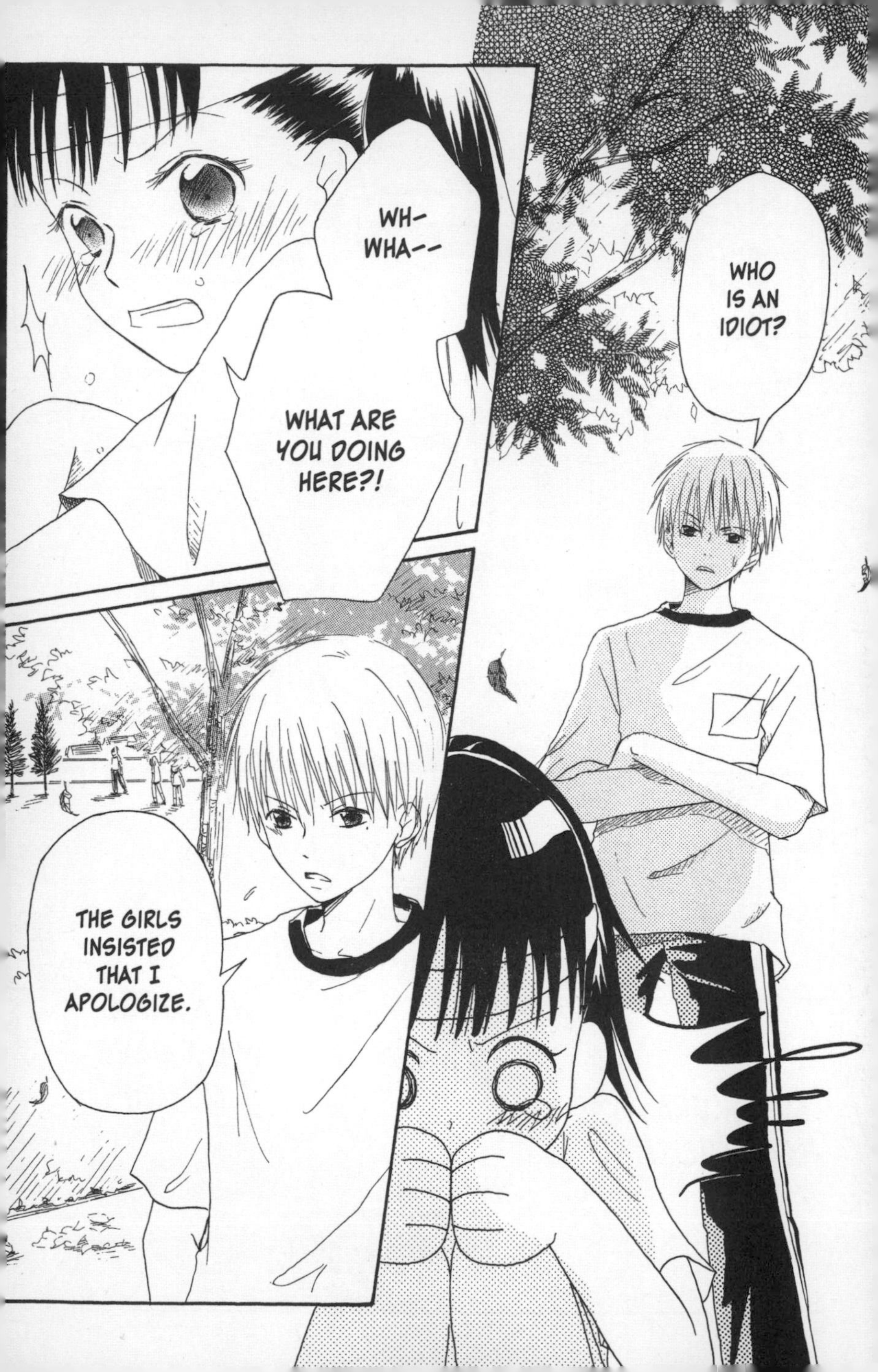
WHO IS AN IDIOT?
WH- WHA--
WHAT ARE YOU DOING HERE?!
THE GIRLS INSISTED THAT I APOLOGIZE.

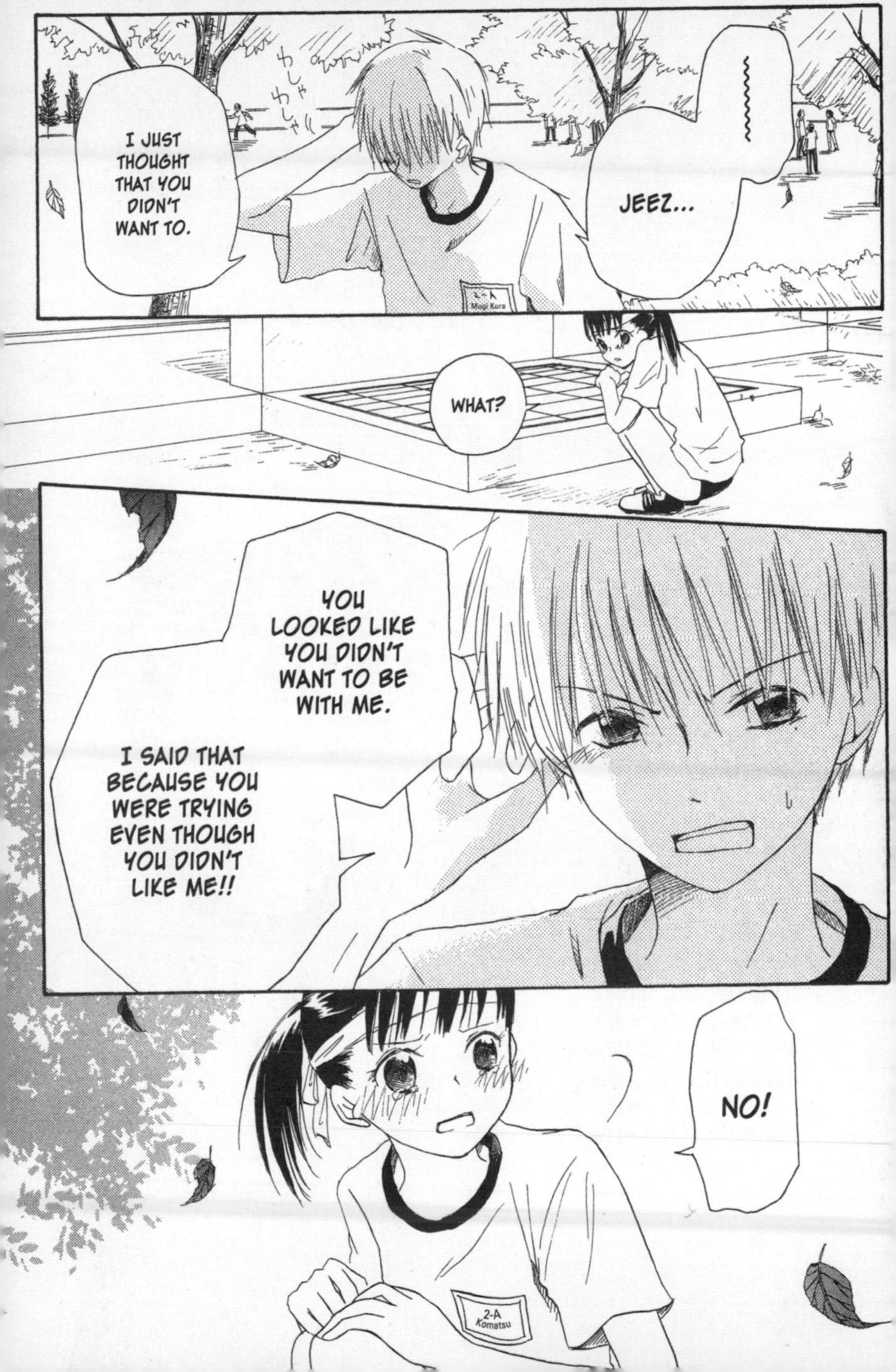
JEEZ...
I JUST THOUGHT THAT YOU DIDN'T WANT TO.
WHAT?
YOU LOOKED LIKE YOU DIDN'T WANT TO BE WITH ME.
I SAID THAT BECAUSE YOU WERE TRYING EVEN THOUGH YOU DIDN'T LIKE ME!!
NO!
2-A Komatsu

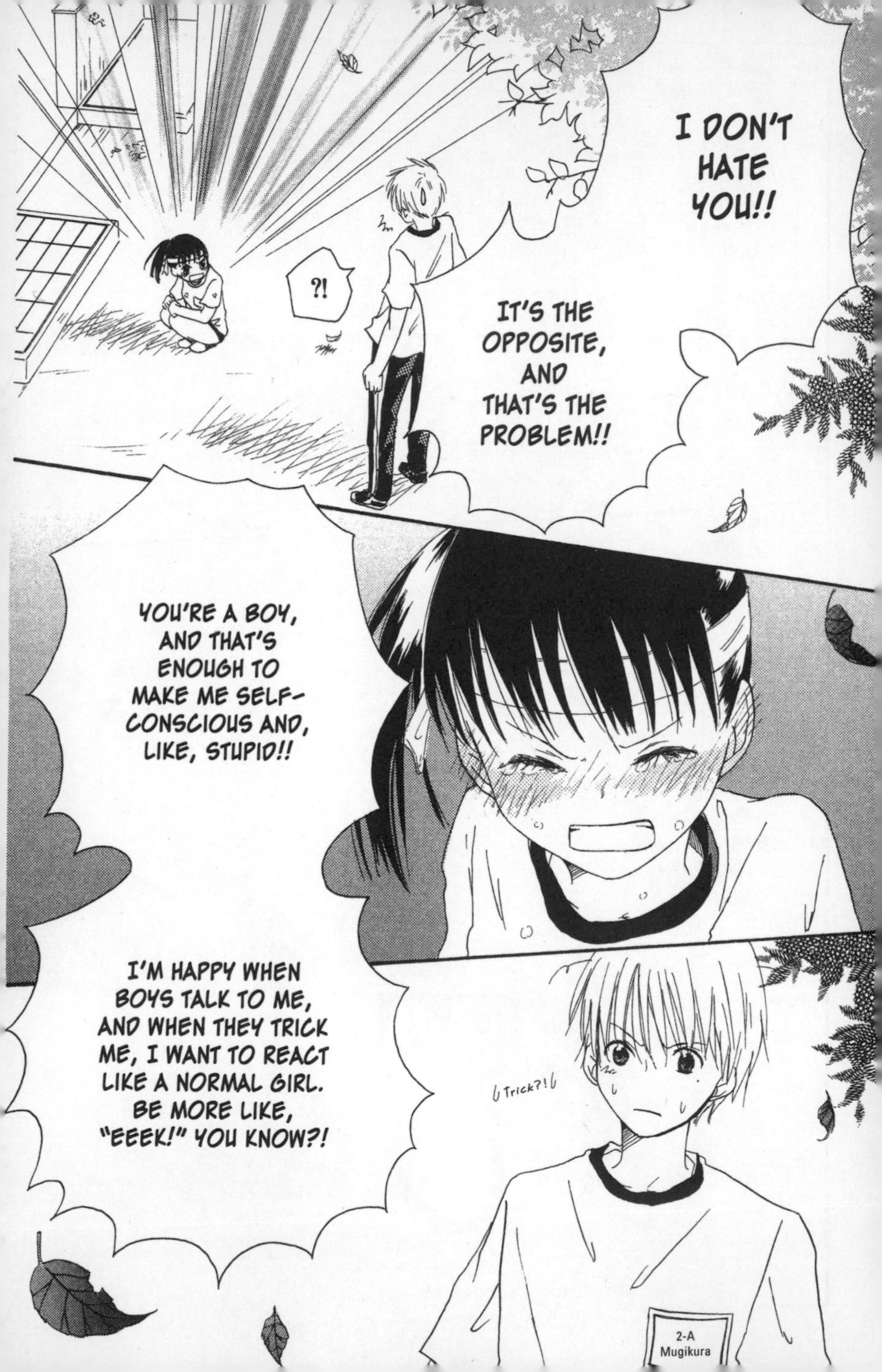
I DON'T HATE YOU!!
IT'S THE OPPOSITE, AND THAT'S THE PROBLEM!!
?!
YOU'RE A BOY, AND THAT'S ENOUGH TO MAKE ME SELF-CONSCIOUS AND, LIKE, STUPID!!
I'M HAPPY WHEN BOYS TALK TO ME, AND WHEN THEY TRICK ME, I WANT TO REACT LIKE A NORMAL GIRL. BE MORE LIKE, "EEEK!" YOU KNOW?!
Trick?!
2-A Mugikura

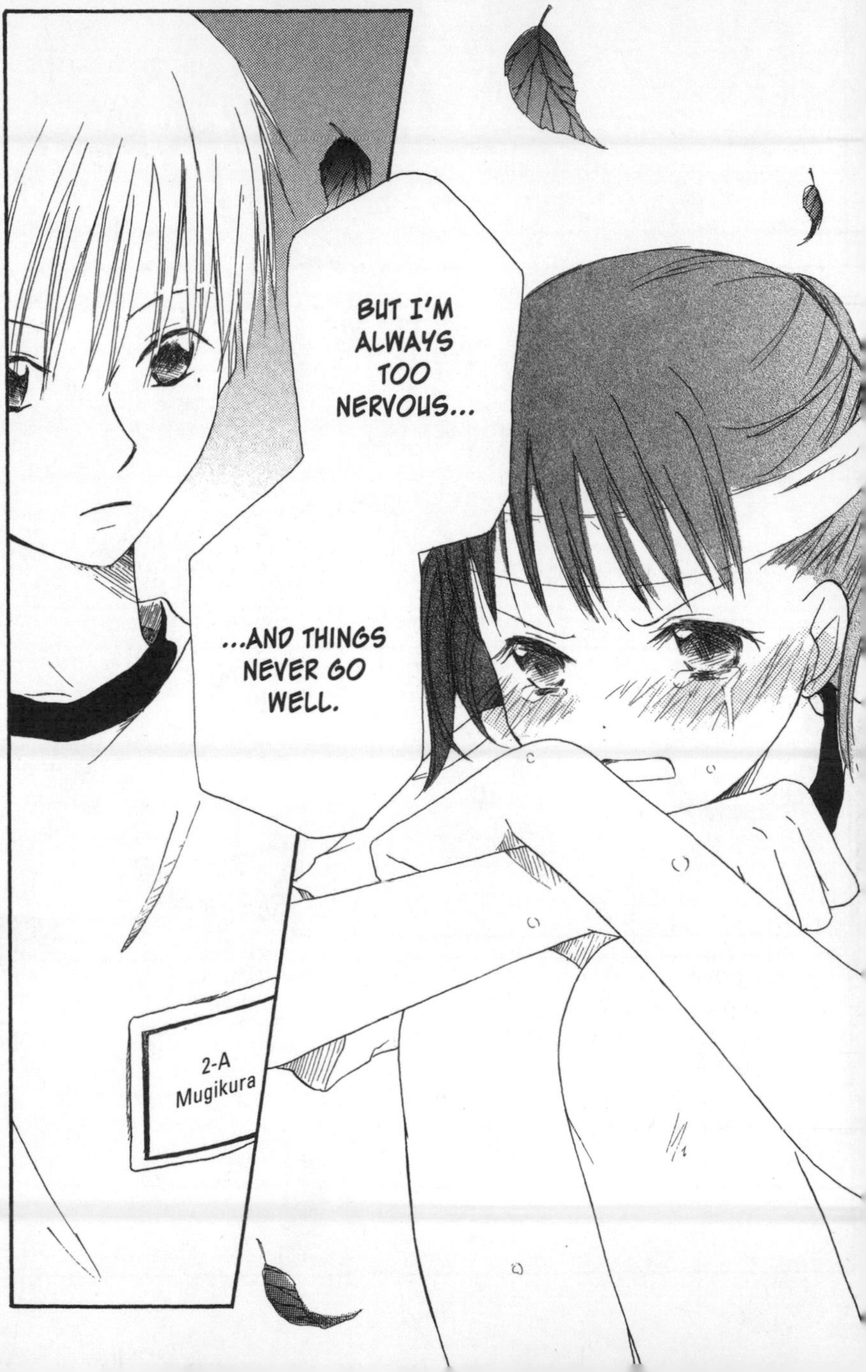
BUT I'M ALWAYS TOO NERVOUS...
...AND THINGS NEVER GO WELL.
2-A Mugikura

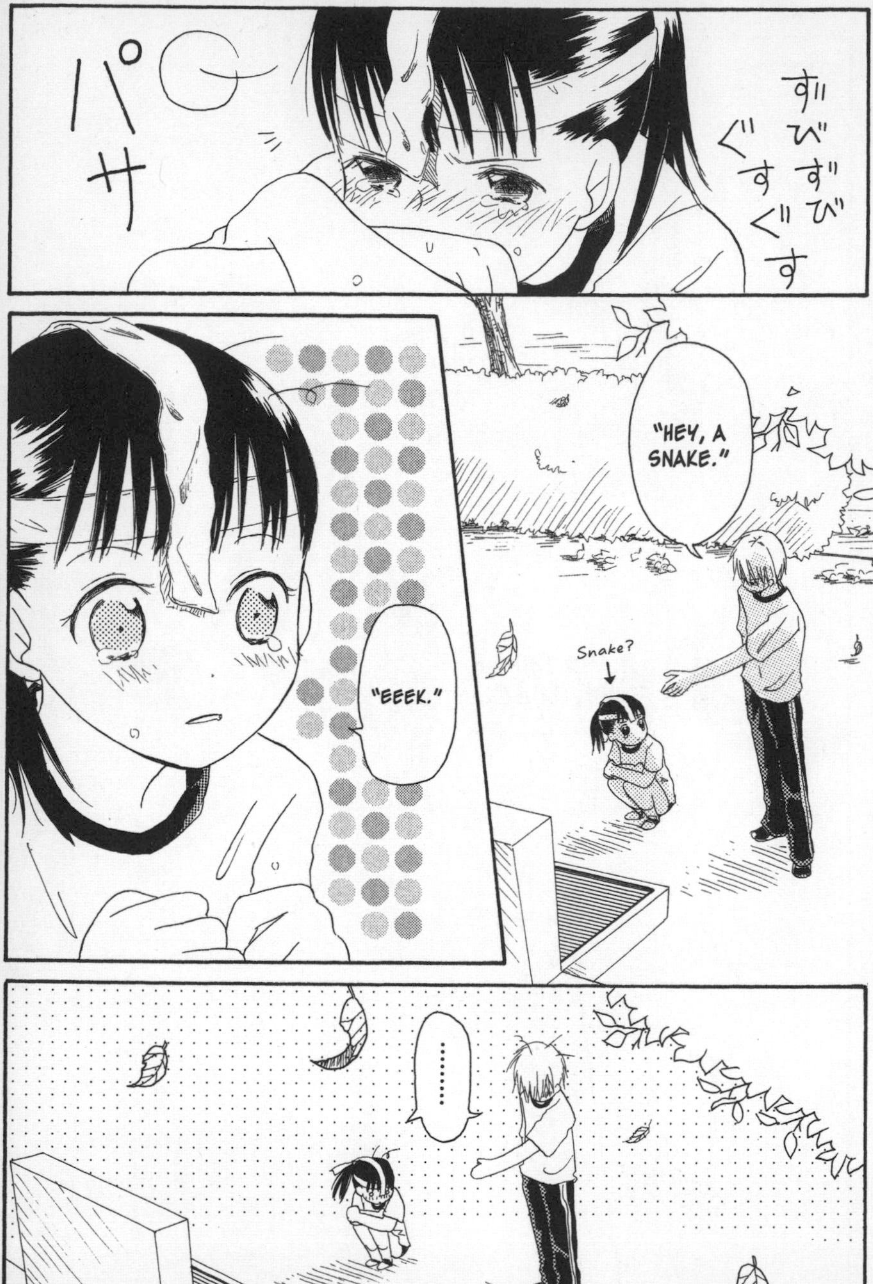
ずびずび ぐすぐす
パサ
"HEY, A SNAKE."
Snake?
"EEEK."
....

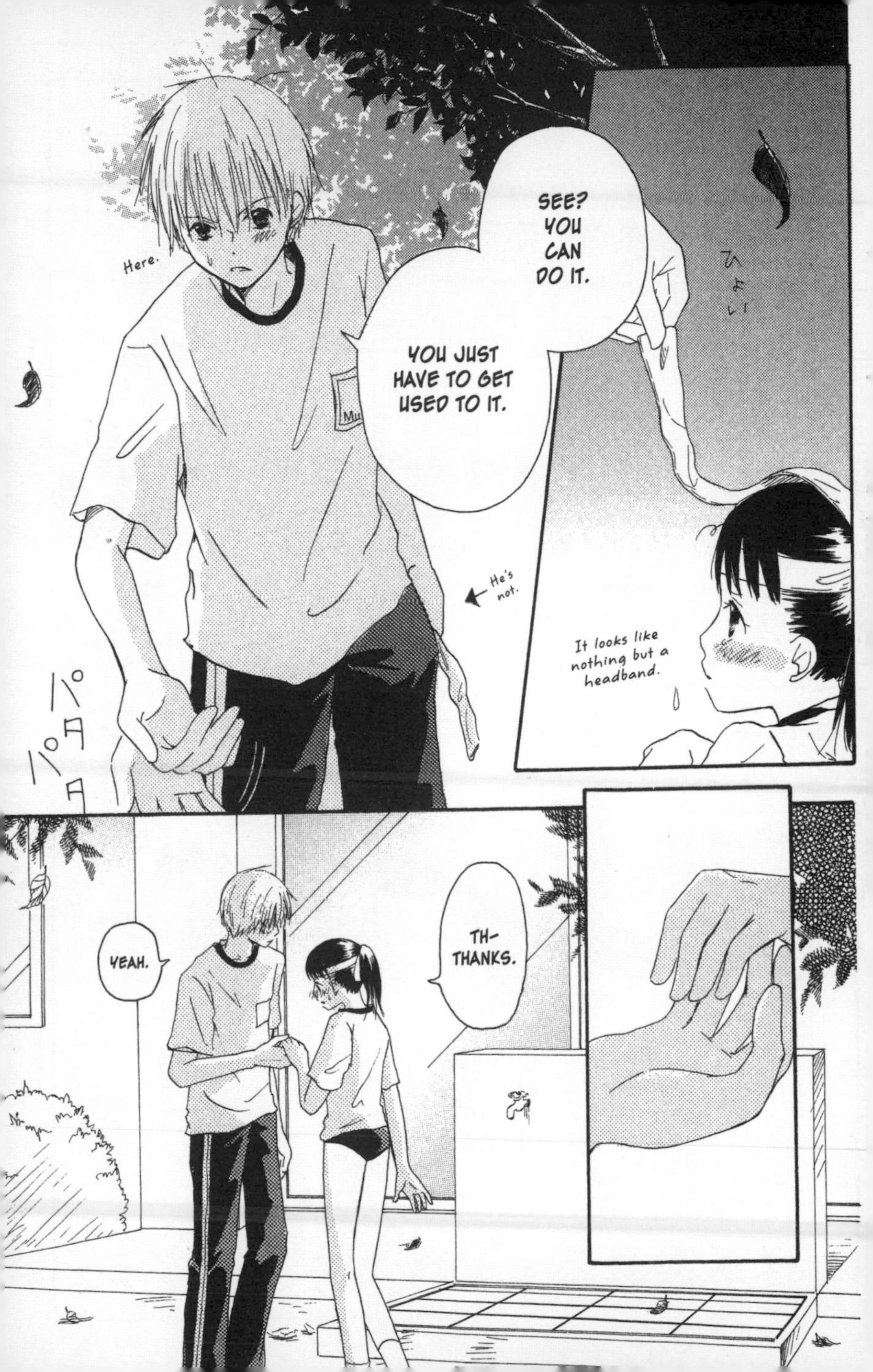
ひょい
It looks like nothing but a headband.
SEE? YOU CAN DO IT.
YOU JUST HAVE TO GET USED TO IT.
Here.
He's not.
パタパタ
TH- THANKS.
YEAH.

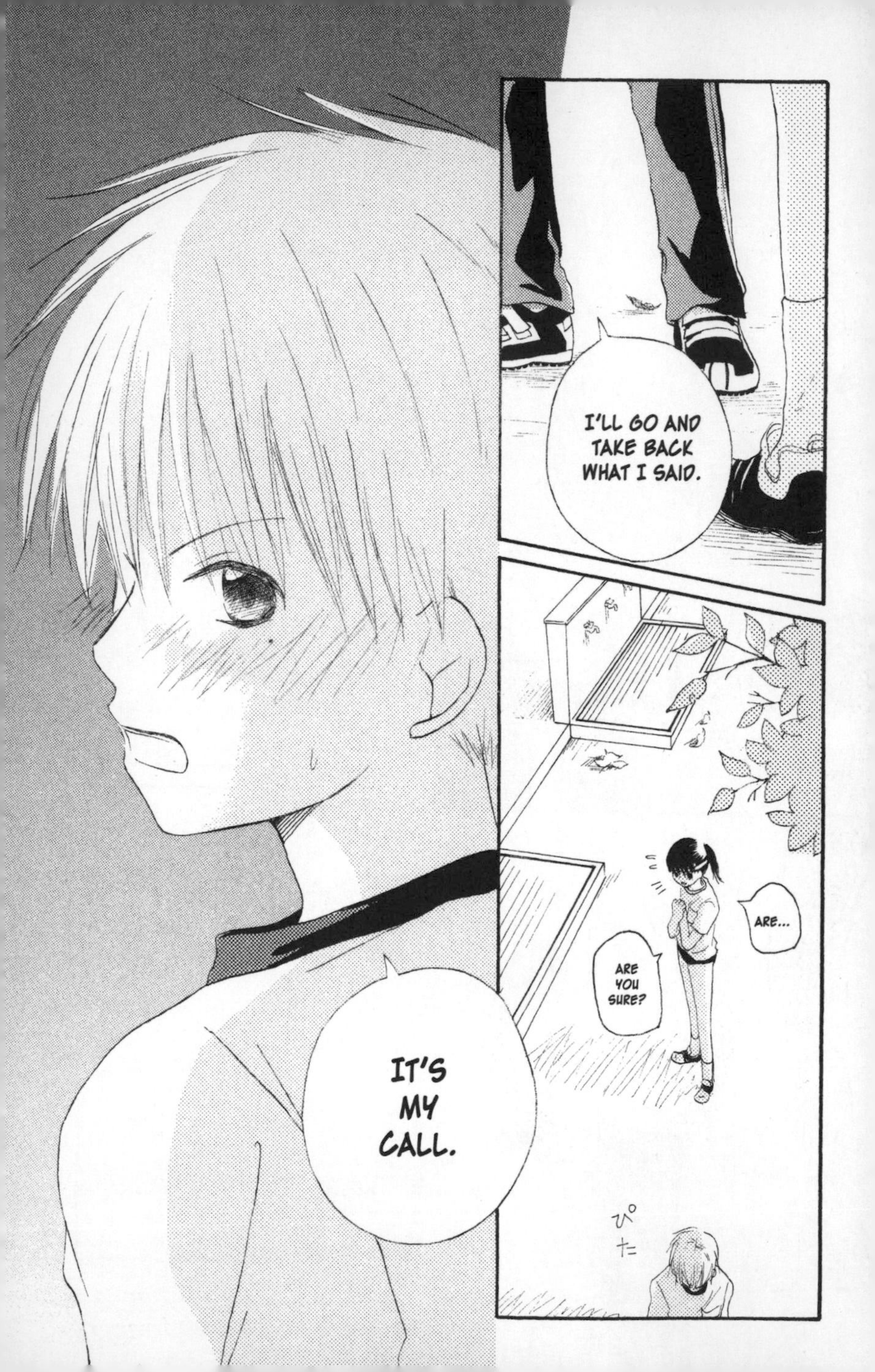
I'LL GO AND TAKE BACK WHAT I SAID.
ARE...
ARE YOU SURE?
ぴた
IT'S MY CALL.

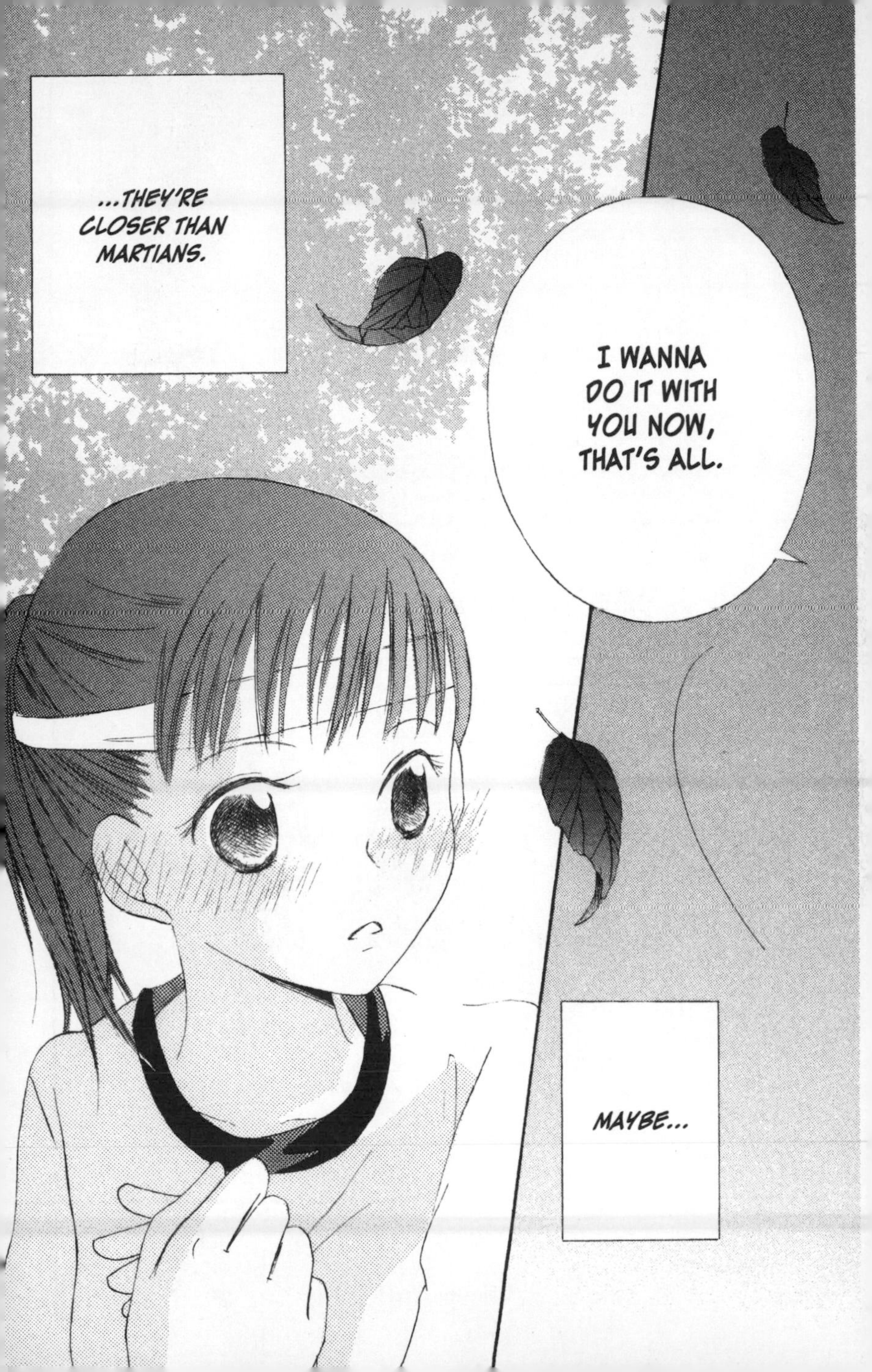
...THEY'RE CLOSER THAN MARTIANS.
I WANNA DO IT WITH YOU NOW, THAT'S ALL.
MAYBE...

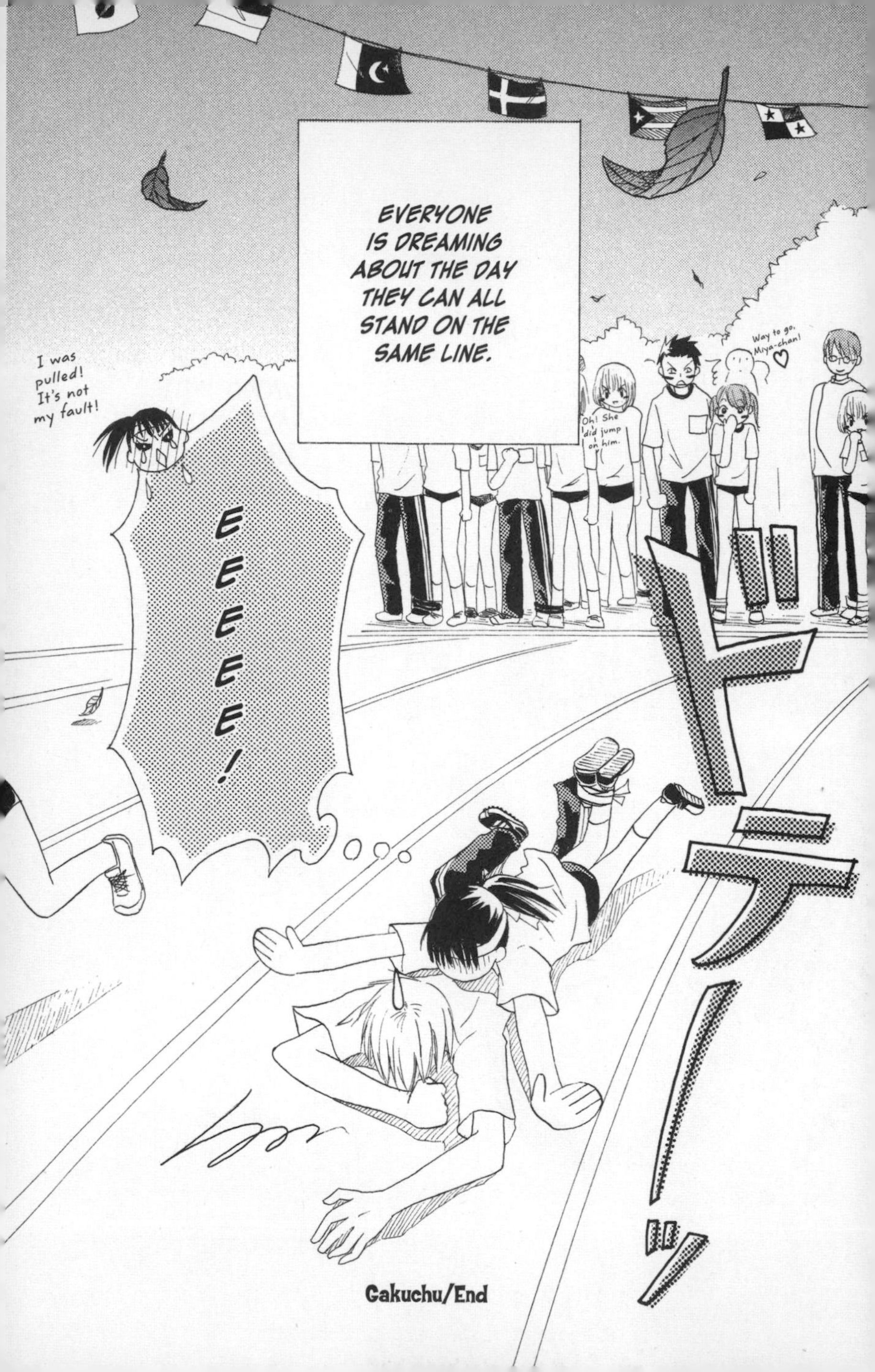
EVERYONE IS DREAMING ABOUT THE DAY THEY CAN ALL STAND ON THE SAME LINE.
Way to go, Miya-chan! ♡
Oh! She did jump on him.
ドテーッ
I was pulled! It's not my fault!
EEEEE!
Gakuchu/End

Bonus Page

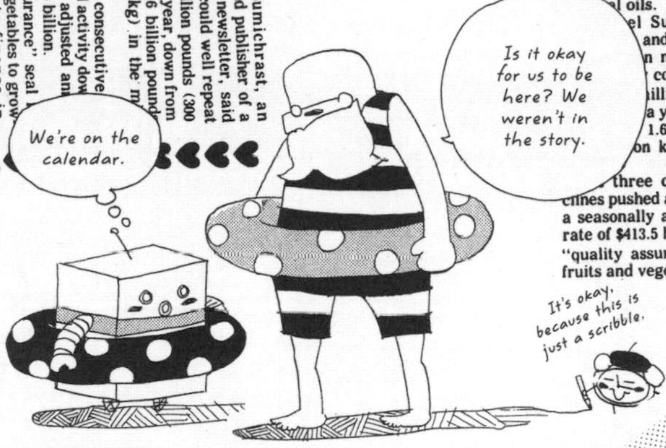

Is it okay for us to be here? We weren't in the story.
We're on the calendar.
It's okay, because this is just a scribble.

I was going to make a bonus manga about "Tsuyoshi and Takeshi's First..." series (?), but I gave it up because I couldn't come up with a good story. So I made a Gakuchu bonus manga instead.
I like drawing junior high school students.

If you'd like to send me comments about my book, here's the address:

TOKYOPOP
5600 Wilshire Blvd. Suite 2000
Los Angeles, CA 90036
Attn: Hyun Joo Kim

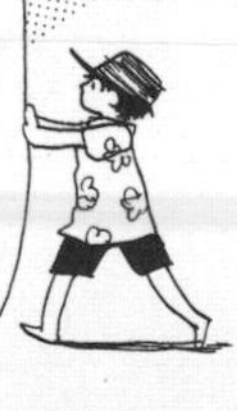

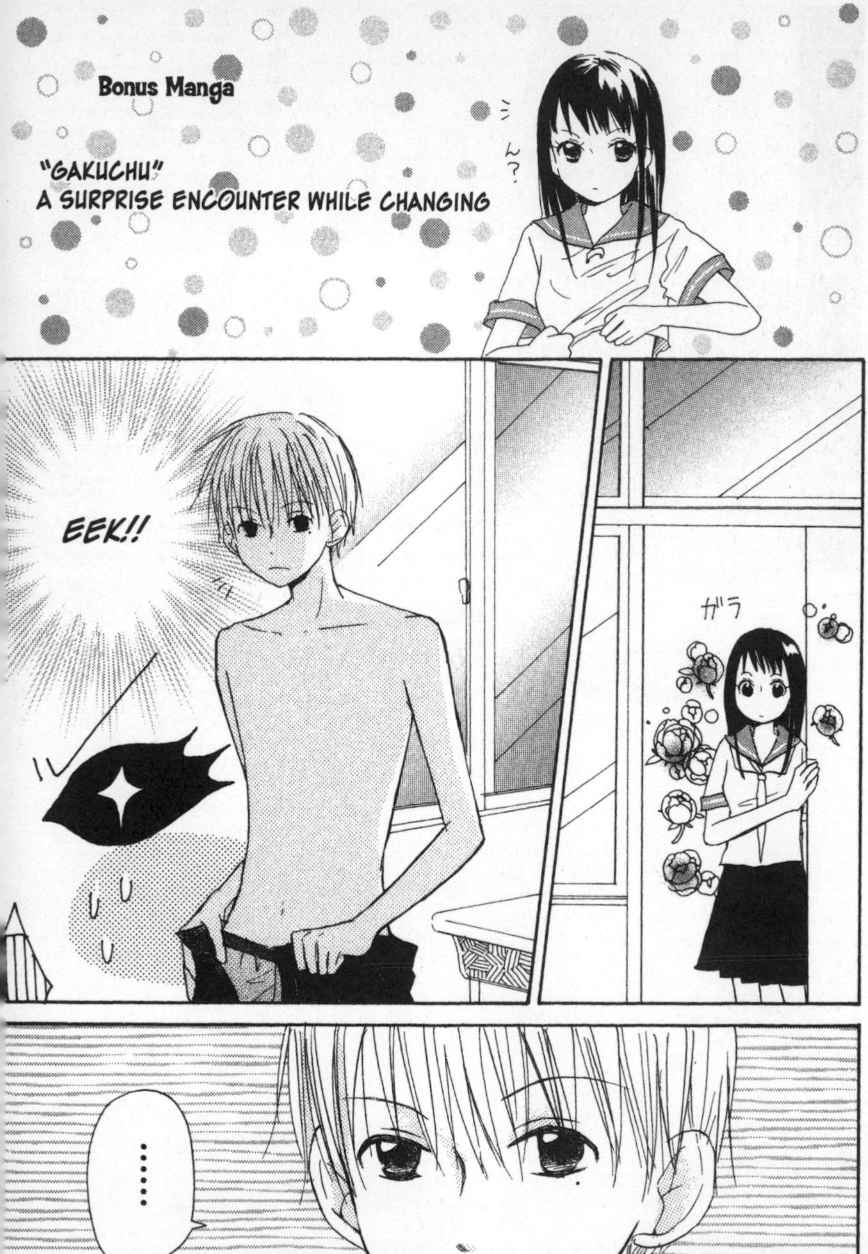
Bonus Manga
"GAKUCHU"
A SURPRISE ENCOUNTER WHILE CHANGING
ん?
ガラ
EEK!!
......

↳ He's thinking about nothing.

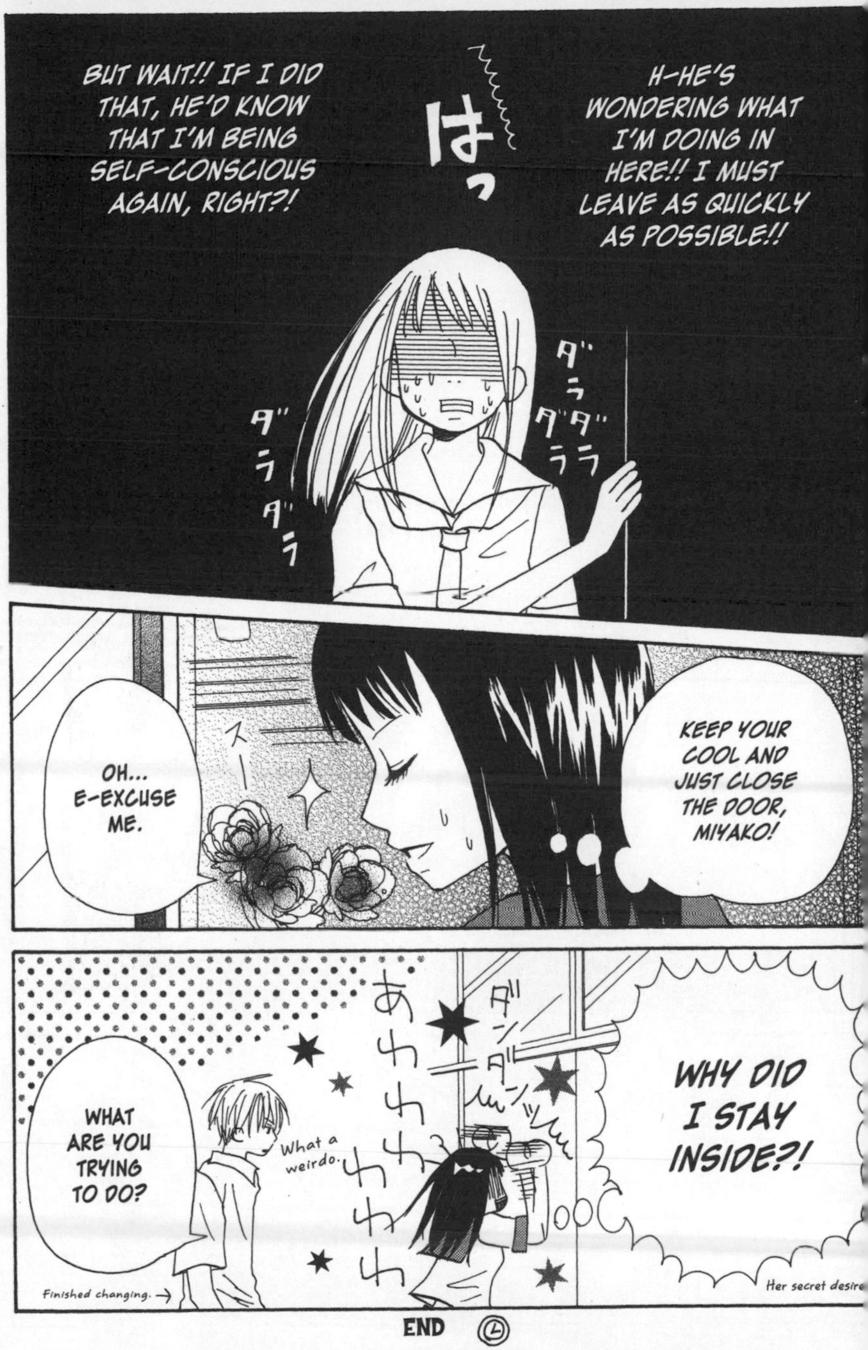
H-HE'S WONDERING WHAT I'M DOING IN HERE!! I MUST LEAVE AS QUICKLY AS POSSIBLE!!
はっ
BUT WAIT!! IF I DID THAT, HE'D KNOW THAT I'M BEING SELF-CONSCIOUS AGAIN, RIGHT?!
ダラダラ
ダラダラ
KEEP YOUR COOL AND JUST CLOSE THE DOOR, MIYAKO!
スー
OH... E-EXCUSE ME.
WHY DID I STAY INSIDE?!
Her secret desire
ダンッ
あわわわわわ
What a weirdo.
WHAT ARE YOU TRYING TO DO?
Finished changing.

END

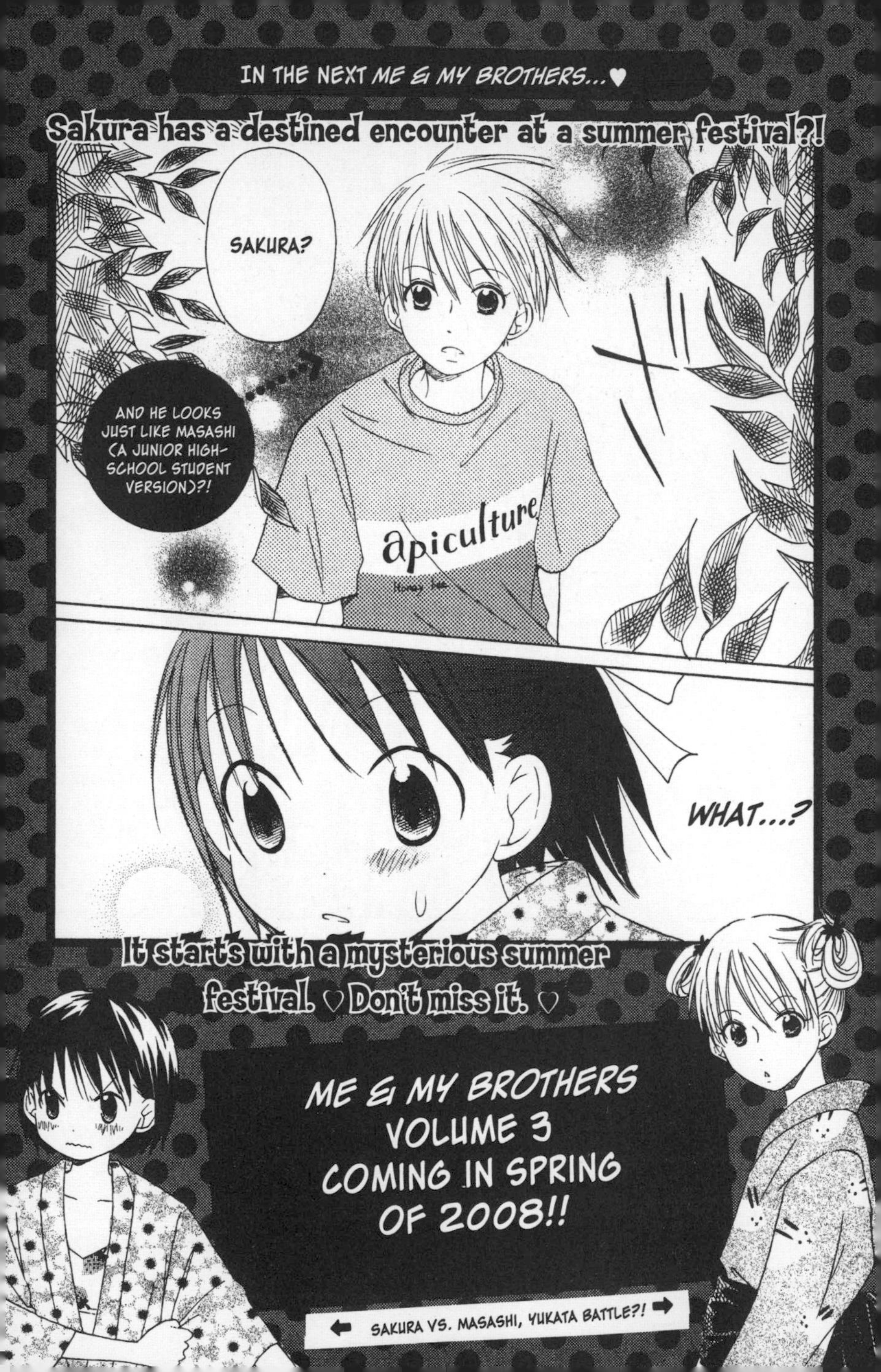
IN THE NEXT ME & MY BROTHERS...♥
Sakura has a destined encounter at a summer festival?!
SAKURA?
AND HE LOOKS JUST LIKE MASASHI (A JUNIOR HIGH-SCHOOL STUDENT VERSION)?!
apiculture
WHAT...?
It starts with a mysterious summer festival. ♡ Don't miss it. ♡
ME & MY BROTHERS VOLUME 3 COMING IN SPRING OF 2008!!
SAKURA VS. MASASHI, YUKATA BATTLE?!

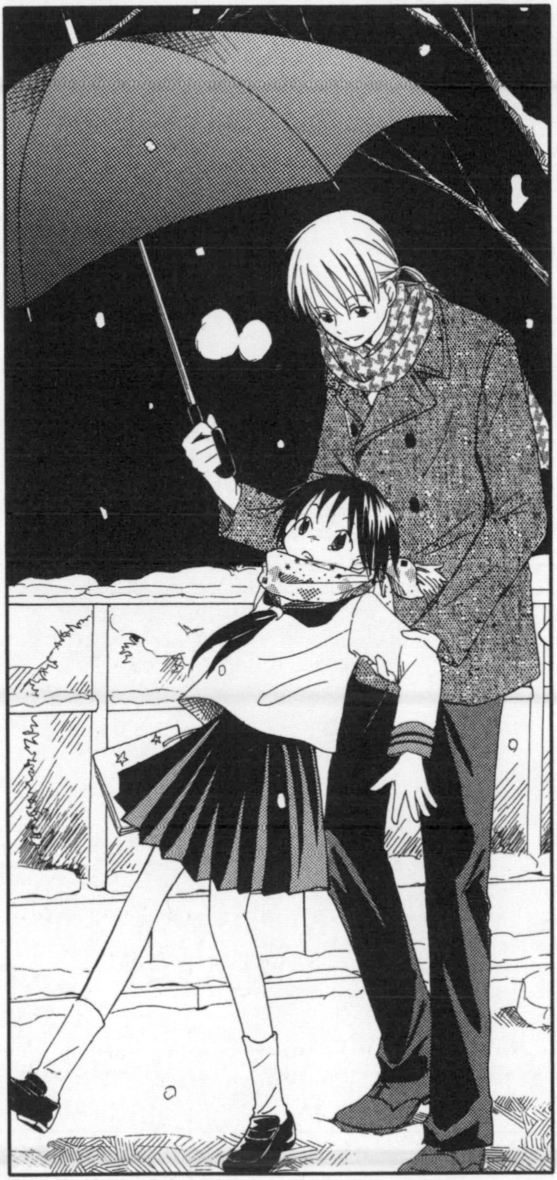

Fruits Basket

By Natsuki Takaya

Volume 18

The next volume of the bestselling series is here!

Everyone knows Isuzu is in the hospital...or is she? While everyone is searching for her, Isuzu is hatching a scheme that may allow her to break the curse!

The #1 selling shojo manga in America!

ROMANCE

T TEEN AGE 13+

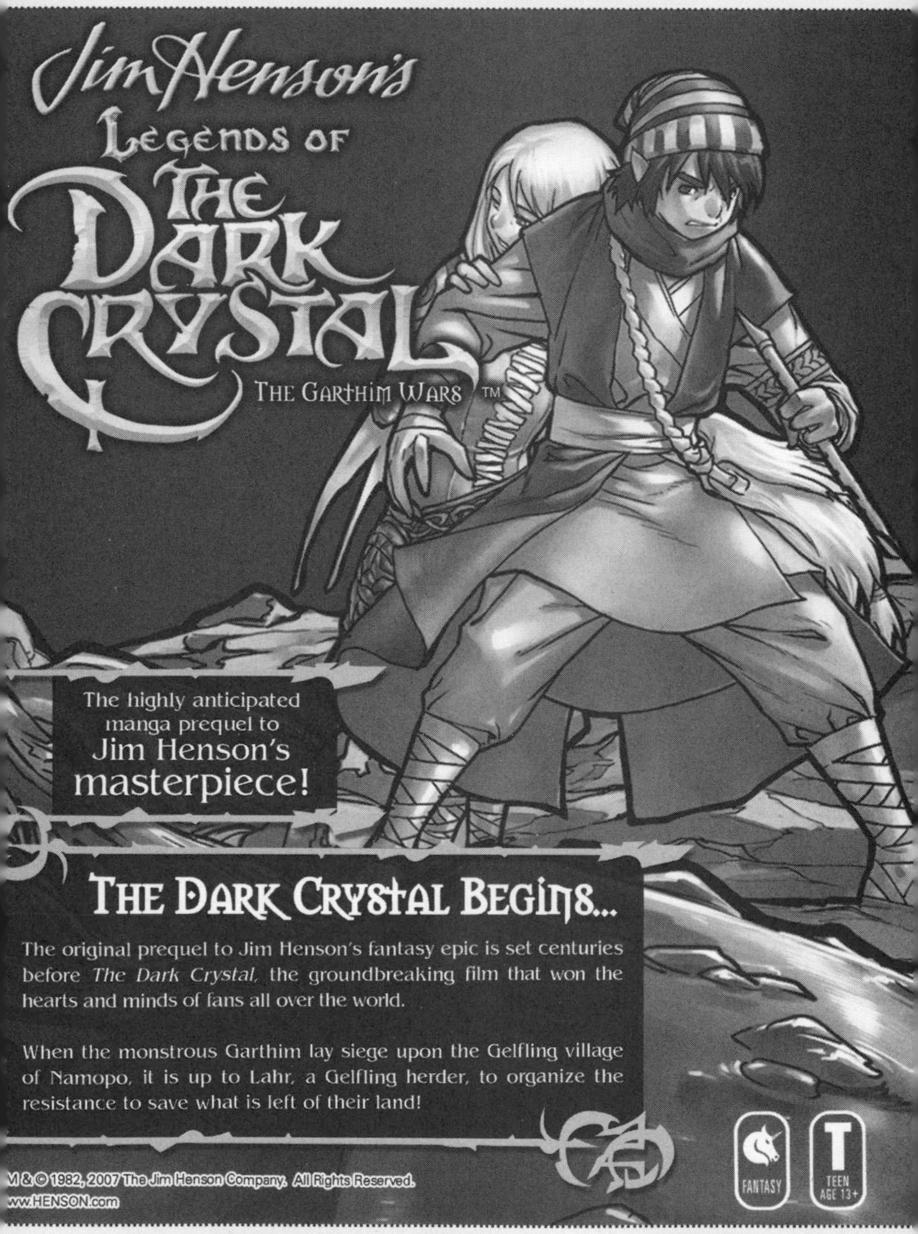
Jim Henson's
Legends of
The Dark Crystal
The Garthim Wars ™
The highly anticipated manga prequel to Jim Henson's masterpiece!
The Dark Crystal Begins...
The original prequel to Jim Henson's fantasy epic is set centuries before The Dark Crystal, the groundbreaking film that won the hearts and minds of fans all over the world.
When the monstrous Garthim lay siege upon the Gelfling village of Namopo, it is up to Lahr, a Gelfling herder, to organize the resistance to save what is left of their land!
M & © 1982, 2007 The Jim Henson Company. All Rights Reserved.
ww.HENSON.com
FANTASY
T
TEEN AGE 13+

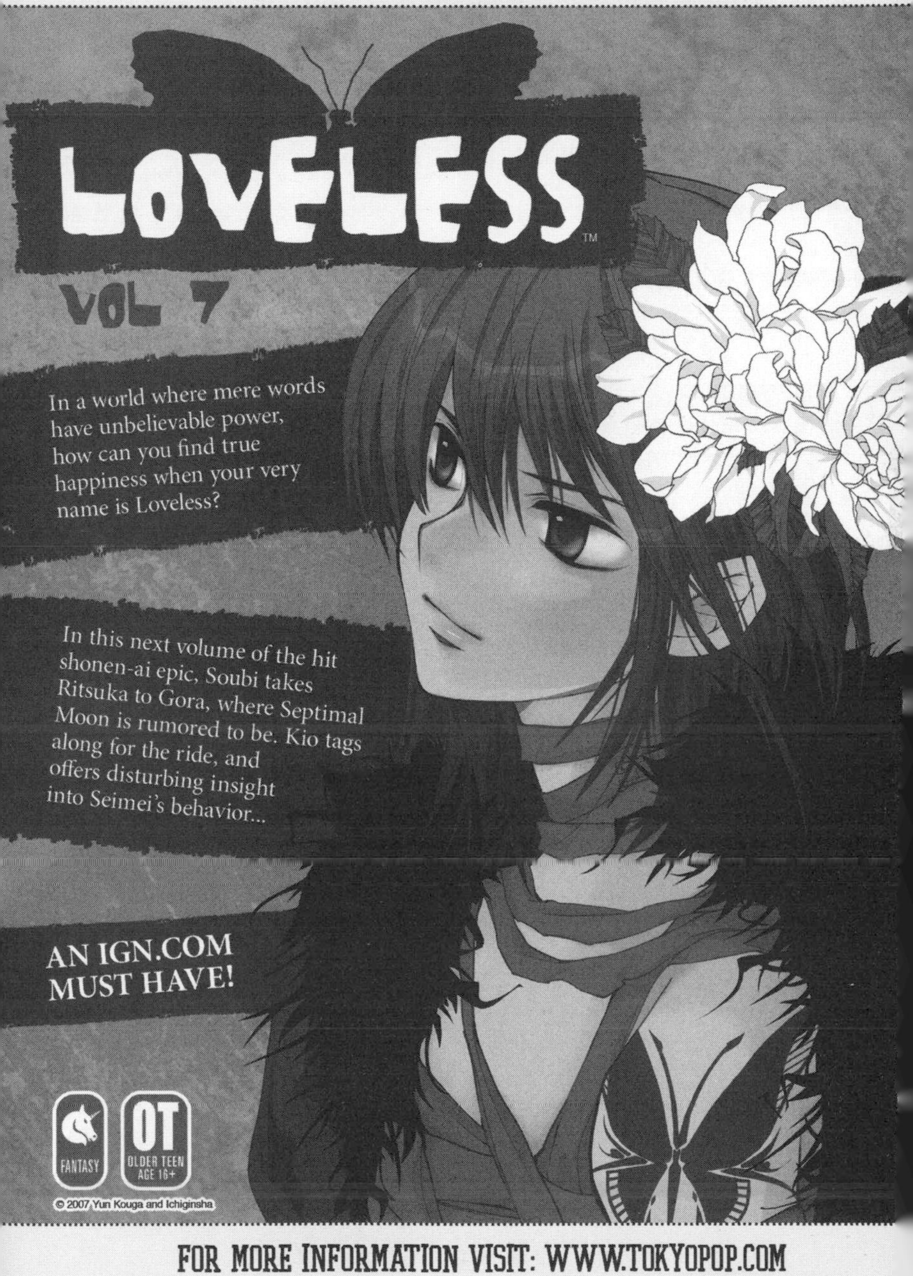
LOVELESS™
VOL 7
In a world where mere words have unbelievable power, how can you find true happiness when your very name is Loveless?
In this next volume of the hit shonen-ai epic, Soubi takes Ritsuka to Gora, where Septimal Moon is rumored to be. Kio tags along for the ride, and offers disturbing insight into Seimei's behavior...
AN IGN.COM MUST HAVE!
FANTASY
OT
OLDER TEEN AGE 16+
© 2007 Yun Kouga and Ichiginsha

VOLUME 2: SILENT NOISE

TRINITY BLOOD™
RAGE AGAINST THE MOONS

THE TRINITY BLOOD FRANCHISE RAGES ON!

Nothing is quite as it seems...

A mysterious weapon called Silent Noise destroys
Barcelona and threatens Rome... Abel Nightroad
battles personal demons... And the Duchess of Milan is in
more danger than she knows... The next volume of the
thrilling Pop Fiction series rages with sound and fury!

"INSTANTLY GRIPPING."
—NEWTYPE USA

POP
FICTION

STOP!

This is the back of the book. You wouldn't want to spoil a great ending!

This book is printed "manga-style," in the authentic Japanese right-to-left ormat. Since none of the artwork has been flipped or altered, readers et to experience the story just as the creator intended. You've been sking for it, so TOKYOPOP® delivered: authentic, hot-off-the-press, nd far more fun!

DIRECTIONS

1
2
3
4
5
6
7
8
9
10

If this is your first time reading manga-style, here's a quick guide to help you understand how it works.

It's easy... just start in the top right panel and follow the numbers. Have fun, and look for more 100% authentic manga from TOKYOPOP®!

THE MANGA REVOLUTION · LEADING · 漫画革命